CHING LING FOO

CHING LING FOO

America's First Chinese Superstar

Samuel D. Porteous

DROWSY EMPEROR PRESS

Published by
Drowsy Emperor Press
Unit 507, 5/Floor
Chinachem Golden Plaza
77 Mody Road
Tsim Sha Tsui East, Kowloon, Hong Kong

Copyright © 2020 by Samuel D. Porteous

All rights reserved. No part of this book may be reproduced or transmitted in any form or by in any means, electronic or mechanical, including photocopying, recording, or by any information storage and retrieval system, without the written permission of the Publisher, except where permitted by law.

Manufactured in the United States of America,
or in the United Kingdom when distributed elsewhere.

Porteous, Samuel D.
Ching Ling Foo:
America's First Chinese Superstar
ISBN: 978-1-951943-20-2
ebook ISBN: 978-1-951943-21-9
LCCN: 2020909447

Cover design by: Samuel Porteous (Scobie)
Copyediting by: Kevin Anderson & Associates
Interior design: Medlar Publishing Solutions Pvt Ltd., India

All images and illustrations in *Ching Ling Foo: America's First Chinese Superstar* unless otherwise indicated are copyright Drowsy Emperor Ltd. and not to be reproduced without written permission.

www.ChingLingFooBio.com

ACKNOWLEDGEMENTS

This book would not have been possible without the support and contributions of my wife and partner, Zhang Guo Li (张国丽), who for over five years has worked with me at Drowsy Emperor and on our wider "China in the Western Imagination" project, of which this Ching Ling Foo biography is but one part. Thanks, too, are owed to Dai Ming Jian (戴明鑑), John McBride, Gordon LaFortune, and Jim Hildebrandt—essential initial supporters of this work.

Scholarly support was provided by Jim Steinmeyer whose advice and insight as I brought the various elements of this book together proved invaluable. Harvard University's Houghton Library, the Shanghai Public Library system and its unmatched collections, Magic Circle Librarian Bill Goodwin, James Hagy, the China Documentary Research Center, and the Conjuring Arts Research Center stand as notable examples of all the other numerous individuals, private collections, museums, and educational and professional institutions, in China, the U.S. and elsewhere who so selflessly and often so cheerfully assisted me in the years-long search for one more piece of information on a fascinating and not-to-be-forgotten turn-of-the-century Chinese conjurer.

A NOTE ON NAMES

Ching Ling Foo (金陵福) was the stage name used by Zhu Liankui (朱連魁), also known as Chee Ling Qua. In referring to this visionary performer and polymath, this biography, which is primarily focused on his public life as seen in the West, will to avoid confusion use the name "Ching Ling Foo"—and just "Foo", in most instances, as was the practice of most Western media at the time. In doing so, we note the stage name Ching Ling Foo was adopted by the magician at least a decade before his first triumphal tour of America in 1898. It should also be noted that "Ching," not "Foo," would have been the performer's surname in proper Chinese usage.

For clarity's sake, the book will in most cases also use the current Romanized spelling of Chinese personal and place names, where possible. For example, the name "Beijing" will be used instead of the older spelling "Peking," and "Tianjin" will be used instead of Tien-Tsin.

Finally, given its negative connotations, the word "Chinaman," which was a term commonly used during Foo's career, will be replaced (except where explicitly important to the context) with "Chinese" or "Chinese man," depending on the usage.

Jean-Baptiste Perroneau, "*Magicien Chinois*," 1738–1745.
Metropolitan Museum of Art, New York, NY.

"Magic is the only honest profession. A magician promises to deceive you and he does".
(American magician Karl Germain, 1878–1959)

"All history becomes subjective; in other words, there is properly no history, only biography."
(Ralph Waldo Emerson, 1803–1882)

TABLE OF CONTENTS

Foreword by Jim Steinmeyer   xi
Preface   xv
Introduction   xvii

CHAPTER ONE
Ching Ling Foo, The Early Years—Man and Mythology   1

CHAPTER TWO
The 1898 Omaha World's Fair—First Step
towards Unprecedented Fame and Fortune   13

CHAPTER THREE
After Omaha—Hopkins Helps Foo's Troupe Find a Larger Stage   35

CHAPTER FOUR
The Sensational Deportation Trial of Ching Ling Foo   47

CHAPTER FIVE
May 1899–January 1900—Post-Deportation Trial; Peak Foo:
Acme of Fame and Fortune   59

CHAPTER SIX
January 1900 to April 1900—Peak Foo Crests—Things Come Apart   127

CHAPTER SEVEN
As Chung Ling Soo Emerges and the Boxers Upend Tianjin,
Foo Returns to China   145

CHAPTER EIGHT
Soo's Fame Grows as Foo Back on his Feet in Shanghai
Prepares for his Next Tour   169

CHAPTER NINE
Foo vs. Soo The 1905 World Championship of Chinese Magic   181

CHAPTER TEN
1906–1911, The Interim Years: A Prolonged Victory Lap for Soo
and a Golden Era for Foo Imitators in America and Elsewhere — 215

CHAPTER ELEVEN
October–November 1911—Foo Produces China's First
Documentary, *Wuchang Uprising*; Plays Significant Role in Collapse
of the Qing Dynasty and Emergence of the Chinese Republic — 243

CHAPTER TWELVE
November 1912—"He's Back!" Foo Returns to America
to Triumph at Hammerstein's — 249

CHAPTER THIRTEEN
Foo the "Wildcatter" Takes on the United Booking Office (UBO)
Monopoly and Headlines the Legendary Ziegfeld Follies — 281

CHAPTER FOURTEEN
May 1913—Post-Follies, Foo Continues Wild Success, Overcomes
More UBO Shenanigans, Disrupts Vaudeville's 'Small Time'/'Big Time'
Continuum — 311

CHAPTER FIFTEEN
October 1913—Foo Tours with Legendary Diva and "Dictator
of Fashion" Lillian Russell's "All Star Feature Festival" — 337

CHAPTER SIXTEEN
November 1913–January 1914—Another Tour, Another Diva;
Foo Tours with Avant-Garde Entertainer Gertrude Hoffman,
"The Woman Who Dares" — 351

CHAPTER SEVENTEEN
January 1914–October 1914—More Contractual Troubles and Difficult
Bookings Force Foo to Europe, and Unknowingly, Straight into
World War I — 371

CHAPTER EIGHTEEN
November 1914–March 1915—New York to California; Foo Returns
for a Triumphant American Farewell — 391

CHAPTER NINETEEN
1916—Foo Eases into Semi-Retirement in Shanghai — 417

CHAPTER TWENTY
1917–1922—Soo Makes an Anti-Climatic WWI Era Visit to Shanghai;
Soo, Then Foo, Pass Away — 421

Epilogue: The Rich Legacy of the Original Chinese Conjurer — 437

APPENDIX A
Illustrations — *441*

APPENDIX B
End Notes — *451*

FOREWORD

by Jim Steinmeyer

Once upon a time, a long time ago, a mysterious land—a land of mysterious traditions and concealed arts—decided to introduce itself to the rest of the world.

It did this not with a statesman or craftsman or poet, but by sending its greatest wizard to demonstrate what he could do—to impress and charm and inspire awe about the mysterious land. It was actually a diplomacy of magic.

There's no question that he was a great wizard. The rest of the world quickly proclaimed him so. He changed the way other wizards thought, and what they considered possible and impossible. He inspired imitations and began contentious arguments about his miracles—and, of course, intrigued everyone about the mysterious land that could have produced such a man.

He was also wise enough to realize that every culture had its wizards and had developed its own sort of magic. As he made magic, he also watched, learned, and was inspired. And so, he returned to his own mysterious land a far greater wizard than he'd been before.

The moral of the story is that a great wizard learns his craft and then makes magic. But a *truly* great wizard understands that "magic" is always in the perception of his audience. And so—with new audiences, new opportunities, and new ideas of what is impossible—a truly great wizard never stops learning.

Actually, there were many morals to this story, and you're now holding them in your hand in Samuel Porteous's remarkable book, *Ching Ling Foo, America's First Chinese Superstar*.

The story is not a legend. It's history. The land was China. The wizard was Ching Ling Foo, and the long-ago era was the time of vaudeville, when a wizard and his troupe could travel on trains to America's largest cities and establish his preeminence in popular showplaces. In fact, Ching Ling Foo, the charismatic Asian magician, transfixed American audiences and established a taste for Asian culture and Asian skills. He was a superstar. And he was, as Porteous makes clear in this fascinating new biography, a truly great and truly versatile wizard.

As a writer on the history of magic and magicians, I've been dealing with the aftermath of Ching Ling Foo—which corresponded to the Golden Age of Magic in the West—and the powerful influence of this master. He befriended the great American magicians of the era, who quickly recognized him as a colleague. These included Harry Kellar, Harry Houdini, and David Abbott. In my book, *The Glorious Deception*, I told the story of an inventive American magician, William Robinson, who was gripped with simultaneous envy and admiration when he encountered Ching Ling Foo. Ambitiously, Robinson changed the course of his career. Working in disguise, he outraced Ching Ling Foo to Europe, becoming Chung Ling Soo (a name intended to deliberately generate confusion). Robinson erased his previous identity and achieved fame as the world's greatest "Chinese" magician, a favorite with British audiences between 1900 and 1918. He even challenged the real Ching Ling Foo to a duel of magic, in a bold attempt to establish which one of them was the real Chinese wizard. This affront may have served as Ching Ling Foo's most powerful lesson about western culture.

In the West, we've been fascinated with what Ching Ling Foo had left behind. In this book, the author effectively explains the origins of this wizard, and how his return to China inspired important new achievements.

It's a story that, quite simply, could not have been told in the days of Ching Ling Foo's success. His career was so intermingled with the secrecy of magic, the stereotypes of Asian culture, and the exaggerations of vaudeville publicists that it seemed inevitable that this wizard would be shrouded in layers of mystery. So, it's remarkable that Porteous has determinately decided to link the stories—the East and the West—at a time when we are able to appreciate the efforts to link divergent cultures. Here is the truth of Ching Ling Foo, and the honor which has been long overdue a master magician and unexpected diplomat in the world of show business. It is, as any great wizard can tell you, a story about what we think is impossible.

Jim Steinmeyer, described by the New York Times as the "celebrated invisible man—inventor, designer, and creative brain behind many of the great stage magicians of the last quarter-century", is also one of the field's preeminent historians and author of best-selling books about magic and magic history, including Hiding the Elephant, The Glorious Deception, *and* The Last Greatest Magician in the World.

PREFACE

Why did you write "Ching Ling Foo: America's First Chinese Superstar?" That's a question I get a lot. Here's my three-pronged answer. First, because as a story teller, artist, and illustrator the romance of Foo's tale with its almost unbelievable scale, breadth and color captured my imagination. I came to Foo via the curious tale of Chung Ling Soo a.k.a. William Robinson, the American who stole Foo's act, and I never looked back. Quite simply, the Original Chinese Conjurer's life with its combination of peak era stage magic, the irrepressible global village that was vaudeville, and international intrigue is one fascinating, beautiful, almost unbelievable yarn. Second, as an optimist who believes in the net good in humanity, despite all indications to the contrary, this story of cultural exchange, people to people diplomacy, and good natured barrier transcendence ultimately warmed my heart. Third, because, as a former risk analyst, I recognized Foo and his troupe's multi-faceted history still speaks to and informs us on the modern roots of the ongoing uneasy push/pull relationship between China and the West, particularly America; a dynamic that, given the multiple existential crises the planet now faces, will likely have the definitive impact on whether human civilization, as we know it, makes it into the 22nd century.

INTRODUCTION

"I can recall to this day the tremendous fanfare that accompanied the arrival of Ching Ling Foo, the great Chinese magician, to this country; and how we hustled down to the theatre as fast as we could to get close to the footlights to see every single thing that was going on. And how Ching Ling Foo, this dignified and very tall Chinese, in his magnificently embroidered robes, suddenly turned a somersault, and came up with a large bowl of live goldfish in his outstretched hand, and a kindly and amused smile on his face, which made me feel good all over. In fact, it still makes me feel good."
(Dwight Taylor, noted American playwright, screenwriter, and child of vaudeville veterans[1])

Ching Ling Foo's story is a magical one that, with its focus on the interaction of Chinese and Western cultures, geopolitical tensions, international intrigue, nativism, the importance of celebrity and disruptive technological developments seemingly has much resonance for our current era.

Even a partial list of the Original Chinese Conjurer's accomplishments still dazzle.

- One of the highest paid and most popular performers in American vaudeville, twice breaking box office records from 1898–1900 and again from 1912–1915,
- Inspired a mania for Chinese magic, a seemingly endless list of copycats, and one real genius: William Robinson, a.k.a. Chung Ling Soo, the doomed rival with whom Foo would become paired for eternity.
- Subject of a historic, precedent-setting deportation trial, closely followed across the U.S.
- Maker, in 1899, of the first sound recordings of Chinese music and singing.
- Instigator of the infamous 1905 London "World Championship of Chinese Magic." This much-hyped "War of the Wizards" would pit Foo against archrival Chung Ling Soo, the stage name of American performer William Robinson—the man who had appropriated both Foo's act and his identity. The contest and its denouement would result in an enduring mystery when, at the last minute, the sphinxlike Foo walked away from his own challenge. (This biography will provide, for the first time, a plausible and research-based solution to this otherwise puzzling outcome.)
- Maker, in 1911, of *Wuchang Uprising*, considered by many to be China's first documentary. This daring and innovative war documentary, which played to rapt audiences in theaters across China, would play a significant role in rallying opposition to the Qing Dynasty and the founding of the Chinese Republic.
- From 1912–1915, during vaudeville's last gasp as America's premier form of entertainment, would break, along with daughter (and bilingual ragtime singing sensation) Chee Toy, records for salary and box offices, and break more barriers by headlining the legendary Ziegfeld Follies and then touring

with Lillian Russell and Gertrude Hoffman—the Oprah/Gwyneth Paltrow and Lady Gaga of their day.
- In the 1930s, more than a decade after his death, his impact on the evolution of the film industry would be acknowledged when the man who would become known as the father of film special effects—and an inspiration for George Lucas's *Star Wars*—would identify Foo as the man who mentored him in the field of optical illusion.

Beyond all this—and there is more—perhaps the genial and charismatic Chinese conjurer's greatest legacy was in the area of person-to-person diplomacy. In the era of the uniquely discriminatory Chinese Exclusion Act, over a period of almost 20 years, Ching Ling Foo and his talented family, through the joyful and dignified presentation of their sheer talent and shared humanity managed to introduce to an American public awash in very hostile representations of the Chinese involving opium, deceit, vice, and 'otherness' what was aptly termed a very "different picture."

CHAPTER ONE

CHING LING FOO, THE EARLY YEARS—MAN AND MYTHOLOGY

As with most legendary magicians, the various stories regarding Ching Ling Foo's early years, presented to his adoring audiences, reflect a healthy mix of fact and fiction often geared more towards promotional effect than accurate biography.

The more 'reliable' accounts of Foo's early life before he achieved fame include unfiltered recollections of Foo regarding his past, Chinese scholarly notes, what emerged regarding Foo's life during his sensational 1899 deportation trial, and a version of Foo's early life based on private discussions with Foo recounted by his great friend Harry Kellar, the "Dean of American Magicians."

What Has Been Said

Foo was born on March 11th, 1854 into a relatively comfortable family of merchants based in and around the bustling international port of Tianjin, at a time when that increasingly cosmopolitan city had not yet been laid low by the Boxer Rebellion. It seems clear that Foo's family was comparatively well off, and likely numbered among the Chinese upper-middle class of the time. This supposition is supported by reports that in later years, when not on stage, Foo wore clothing embossed with the image of a three-clawed dragon, a sign of the Chinese middle class.[2] Four-clawed dragons were the province of the nobility, while clothing decorated with a five-clawed dragon motif could only be worn by members of the Chinese royal family—distinctions often gleefully ignored by Foo's many future Western imitators.

The first significant event in young Foo's life of which we have knowledge is the death of the nascent necromancer's father when Foo was just nine years old. As a young boy, Foo saw much of China and even travelled widely abroad. His interest in conjuring and legerdemain was reportedly first inspired by his observation of street magicians and the more lucrative tricks and ruses used by the professional card players and gamblers that would have been abundant in any 19th-century Chinese port city the size of Tianjin.

According to accounts credited to Kellar and a direct account by Foo, a childhood illness that left Foo bedridden for some time around the age of ten accelerated his interest in, and development of, his legerdemain and palming skills. In 1913, the conjurer, looking back on his life, proudly recounted how he had used this youthful illness to perfect his skills. During this period, Foo discovered, working to counteract the boredom that came with being bedridden, "that the hands could be used in many mysterious ways." He began to mimic the moves of the magicians and gamblers he had earlier espied. "One day my mother brought me a couple of dried dates, a favorite dish with my countrymen. I played with these until I had evolved a scheme whereby I could make them disappear even while they were in my own hands. I was entranced. I began to practice upon larger things.[3]"

Another widely confirmed and important element of Foo's childhood, extant in both Chinese and Western records, is that at some point in his childhood, Foo developed a stutter or speech impediment. It is not clear if this manifested itself before or after his father passed away. However, it was pronounced enough that Foo was given the nickname "Zhu the Stutterer," and this impediment was noted in both Chinese and English accounts of his early life.[4]

In fact, the young Foo's will to overcome the challenge presented by his speech impediment may have had a decisive influence on his passion for magic, a skill which enabled him to communicate with and impress people in a manner that did not rely on speech. His stutter, to a certain extent, explained his development of a performance style, consistent before Western, Chinese, or mixed audiences, which involved working in relative silence on stage and engaging the audience only rarely, while a humorous assistant or announcer handled most of the verbal communications with the crowd.

As show business—and magic in particular—was not seen in China as a completely respectable profession, Foo's family reportedly did what it could to redirect his interest back towards the family's successful mercantile roots. Young Foo, while still fascinated by magic and legerdemain, reportedly took a position with a commercial entity, in concession to his family's demands, whose business included the manufacture of Diabolo spinning tops—popular at the time—whose internal mechanisms could be manipulated to make the devices perform startling feats, including some that seemed to defy the laws of gravity. As a result, Foo, given his inherent skills and interest in showmanship, soon became expert in the use of Diabolos. These devices, not surprisingly, would figure in his troupe's performances in later years.

Despite Foo's family's best efforts and his success in the business world, Foo's attraction to the world of magic as he grew into adulthood not only endured; it became stronger. According to the Kellar account, around the age of 15, Foo stopped living with his grandmother and joined a Tianjin society of Chinese magicians, with whom he studied magic for five years. In this telling, after his training, Foo then focused entirely on magic, touring the Chinese provinces and perfecting his art. He then journeyed to Beijing and sought to make his name among the great magicians of the capital. Not long after his arrival, the superior conjuring skills he demonstrated in his performances soon made him a favorite magician of the Beijing public.

Continuing with Foo's preferred narrative of his early life, word of the Chinese conjurer's skills soon reached a son of China's Prince Ching, who, after attending a performance by Foo, arranged for the conjurer to perform at the palace, which led to Foo earning the accolade "court conjurer to the Empress of China." Foo carried this title—which provided great honor but not a lot of money—for a few years, then returned to his village, married, reportedly established a "juggling arts" or magic school in Tianjin, and toured China's major cities with great success, leveraging the credibility of having performed for the Chinese court.[5] During these tours—which included China's rich, trade-dependent southern coastal cities—the amiable Foo successfully entertained before Western, Chinese and mixed audiences.

This experience would serve as a springboard to Foo being selected for his life-changing opportunity at the 1898 Omaha Exposition, also commonly referred to as the 1898 World's Fair.

Foo's preferred narrative of his early life, as recounted by Kellar,[6] in many parts jibes with a brief account of his life that emerged from a Tianjin-based Chinese author. However, in the Chinese writer's version of Foo's early years, young Foo's focus on magic as a primary career was a more gradual phenomenon.

In the account set out in the Chinese journal *Acrobatic History*, Foo, in his early adulthood, balanced his passion for magic with work at a family-connected business where he counterbalanced the awkwardness created by his speech impediment with his personal charm, and rapidly developing skills as a conjurer. The young Foo's innate likeability, along with his magic skills, contributed greatly to his success with his trading firm, which enabled Foo at a relatively young age to travel throughout China and even overseas. As Foo's fame as a magician and related opportunities grew, Foo began to focus more and more on his career as an entertainer.

A significant development in this period was a performance Foo reportedly gave on a foreign ship in Tianjin's harbor as early as 1874, when Foo was just 20 years old. He gave subsequent similar shipboard performances before foreign audiences in Shanghai and other parts of Southern China in the era of "gunboat diplomacy," when foreign warships intent on maintaining the privileges awarded them by China's foreign concessions filled Chinese harbors. This chronology would also fit with Kellar's claims that he first met Foo in Shanghai sometime in the late 1870s, when Kellar performed in the city as part of the Royal Illusionists Troupe that included an ill-fated Hungarian, Ling Look, masquerading as a fire-eating, red hot sword-swallowing Chinese magician.[7]

Not long after this initial encounter with Kellar, Foo would put together a troupe with which he would tour. During an interview in London in 1905, Foo spoke directly—in "broken," but not "pidgin," English—about his past to an English reporter. In this accounting, Foo claimed to have toured India with his troupe in 1878 when he was just 24 years old, as well as the Straits Settlements, which would, of course, have included Singapore and the Philippines, where he was a huge success.[8]

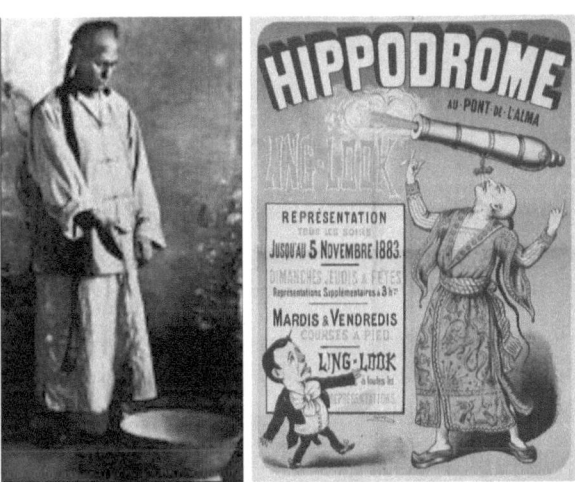

To the left is an early undated photo from the pre-Omaha part of Ching Ling Foo's career, displaying the Chinese conjurer with one of his bowls from his signature production illusion. To the right is a French poster promoting a performance of an early contemporary of Foo, who Houdini claimed was the Hungarian conjurer David Gueter. "Ling Look" toured briefly with Kellar. One of his signature effects was swallowing a sword blade, which had been partially rammed down a musket, then firing the musket, thus driving the sword completely down his throat.

This concludes what has been most credibly *said* about Foo, both by himself and others. We now move on to what we *know*.

What We Know

This mix of the magic and the mercantile in Foo's life would continue through 1880, when, as a 26-year-old he joined the venerable Wah Yuen Lung trading firm, which had offices throughout China and in San Francisco. This is one of the first pieces of information regarding Foo's early life that is solidly documented. Evidence for Foo's engagement by the trading firm was introduced by Foo's legal counsel and accepted by the court during Foo's 1899 deportation trial in Chicago.[9] It also appears Foo spent significant time in San Francisco between 1880 and 1885, as the judge in the deportation case ruled Foo's 14-year-old son was born in that city in 1885 and thus a U.S. citizen.

Foo Troupe Had Long Successful History in Asia Prior to US Triumph

We also know with certainty that, contrary to what has been written by some, Foo was performing as a professional magician and using the carefully selected stage name Ching Ling Foo (金陵福), with its attractive connotations (in Chinese) of gold and happiness, for almost a decade prior to his arrival in Omaha in 1898.

By 1890, according to the North China *Herald*—the principal English-language publication of old Shanghai—the "Ching Ling Foo Troupe" was already well-established, and indeed "famous," among Chinese and foreign audiences alike in the wealthy, foreigner-infused Asian ports of Hong Kong, Shanghai, and Singapore. Indeed, as Foo's fame in the West grew, many established Western magicians beyond just Kellar claimed to have encountered Foo during their own earlier tours of Asia in the 1880s and 1890s. Among these was Bert Powell, who—during Foo's first tour of the U.S. which lasted from 1898 until

1900—noted encountering Foo and his prowess at producing things from under his colorful shawl in Singapore, during a tour of Asia Powell had undertaken years earlier.[10]

As regards the nature of a Foo troupe performance, an examination of an 1890 engagement at the Shanghai Philharmonic Hall indicates that almost a decade before their triumph at the Omaha World's Fair, the Foo troupe had established the core elements of their act that would persist in their performances over the next 25 years.

Even in 1890, it was all there. Foo's mastery of traditional Chinese magic—impressive production tricks including making a great bowl of water, lighted lanterns, and other fanciful objects appear seemingly from nowhere—were already an established part of the act. In addition, Foo would delight the audience with his fire-eating skills and his trained swallows, which seemingly died, resurrected and flew at his command. Backing Foo up were his supporting cast of contortionists, plate spinners, and acrobats juggling great heavy vases. Even Foo's alleged childhood passion, the Diabolo spinning top—which went through several cycles of popularity in the West and Asia in the 1800s—made an appearance in these early performances, refuting "the laws of gravitation" as Foo would coax the top to "ascend a piece of string."[11]

It is important to note that the very variety-act structure of the Foo troupe's performance was ideal for a stage magician. It allowed Foo to divert attention to the troupe's other acts, as Foo, unnoticed, would leave the stage periodically to prepare for new feats of magic backstage and the other performers took the spotlight.

An Entertainment Institution in Asia for Both Western and Chinese Audiences

Throughout the 1890s, within Asian entertainment circles, the Foo troupe's fame increased as they earned the reputation of transcending the traditional—and for the Asian market, sometimes wearily familiar—Chinese magician/juggler variety show. They did so by introducing new acts and illusions and instilling in even well-known acts novel elements and exciting flourishes that rendered even jaded local and foreign audiences highly appreciative.[12]

It was during this period that the increasingly renowned Foo troupe reached the apex of the Asian theatrical market when it appeared to widespread acclaim, within a matter of months, in Hong Kong under the patronage of the British governor, and in Singapore under the patronage of the deputy governor of that territory.

Presciently, Western reviewers at the time noted that if the Foo troupe really wanted to take the next step and capture foreign audiences in Europe and/or North America, the troupe would need to modify their custom of operating solely in the Mandarin Chinese dialect. The fact that their act was presented in Mandarin was a clear indicator the troupe originated from northern China. One of Foo's early nicknames, "The Wizard of the North," also gave a nod to his Tianjin origins.

These same reviewers also helpfully suggested that if the highly popular Foo troupe was indeed interested in conquering new territories and taking on Europe or the U.S., it could perhaps also add a musical element to the show and get a "European manager"[13]—all wise suggestions that Foo would ultimately follow.

Typical of the warm critical recognition the Foo troupe received during its pre-Omaha World's Fair Asian successes was an August 1897 review of the troupe's performance at the Shanghai Lyceum, a foreign-owned venue with about 700 seats patronized by both foreign and Chinese theatregoers. In the laudatory assessment, Foo the conjurer is described as, once more, transforming even "somewhat stale" tricks into something new with his artistry and ability to build an illusion.

In this context, the impressed reviewer notes that when Foo does a traditional "production" trick, it is not with eggs or other small articles that can be easily manipulated. No, when Foo conjures an object out of thin air—typically while stylishly chanting odd magic phrases to the accompaniment of eerie music—that object is a large one.

In fact, in Foo's signature act, it was a very large crystal bowl containing multiple gallons of water, several merrily swimming goldfish and sometimes a few ruffled and quacking low-comedy ducks. All this produced, in a flash from underneath, nothing more than a colorful and elaborately embroidered four-foot-by-four-foot cloth, which, seconds earlier, had lain flat on the stage, which had previously been checked by the audience to confirm there were no trap doors.

At this relatively early stage in Foo's career, reviewers assessing reasons for Foo's success in an Asian market crowded with similarly equipped performers rightly focused on the Chinese magician's artistry, ability to engage an audience, and stylish presentation skills. Later on, these same skills would play a major role in the Foo troupe's capacity to overcome the ocean of copycats their success in the U.S. would generate.

To the left, an interior sketch of the "Old" Shanghai Lyceum, a regular venue for the Foo troupe. The Lyceum was an anchor of Shanghai's entertainment scene from 1873–1926, and often hosted the most famous acts coming through Shanghai.
To the right is a photo of what the Shanghai Lyceum looks like now.

FOO'S SIGNATURE BOWL PRODUCTION TRICK

It is important to dwell on Foo's production tricks and how he did them, as they served for decades as the signature element of his performance.
Here's how Foo typically performed his legendary bowl trick.

Before the illusion began, the audience would be invited on stage to check the floor for trap doors or other devices. Once this was done, a large Chinese-style rug would be dragged out onto the stage by supporting members of the troupe, unfolded, and placed on the floor. Foo would then walk on stage wearing his trademark robe, a somewhat somber, long, dark blue traditional *changshan*, with a pillbox hat and a small, colorfully embroidered shawl about four feet by four feet draped over his left shoulder.

Having obtained the crowd's attention, Foo would then slowly roll up his sleeves, draw the shawl from his shoulder, and rapidly display it from all angles to the audience to establish there was nothing under, or attached to, the fabric. Foo, starting softly and building in volume, would then begin to chant the required incantation, all while artfully transfixing the audience with his varying expressions and deep, soulful eyes. Then, in a flash, the shawl would be dramatically cast down flat upon the rug that was previously placed on the stage floor. Foo and his assistant would then race forward, each taking one end of the shawl in their hands, and in a lightning stroke, fling the shawl up to reveal a large crystal bowl brim-full of water, stocked with very live goldfish, bobbing apples, and in many instances, a few quacking ducks.

As the excited ducks now waddling across the stage were gathered up by assistants, the audience would be informed that the bowl now before them contained three buckets of water and weighed over 95 pounds. This would be demonstrated by Foo methodically dipping large pails into the crystal bowl and emptying them out into other pails carried off stage by his assistants. A charismatic and smiling Foo would then bathe in the applause of a startled audience.

While in this instance it was ducks, an audience never knew just what Foo was going to produce from under his magic shawl. Over the years, crowds saw bowls of water, children (sometimes two), plates of food, and even a scale model of a Chinese temple with lighted windows and a candle on top. Critics agreed that while you might never know what Foo was going to do during one of his shows, it was usually something that exceeded all expectations.[14,15]

The Foo Troupe Was Always More Than Just Foo

Another key element of the evolving Foo troupe, even in its early days, was Foo's strong supporting cast. The Foo troupe was never just a conjuring show. It was very much like the modern Cirque de Soleil, which itself borrows heavily from traditional Chinese circuses—a variety show, with Foo the conjurer very much at its center, but featuring talented supporting acts throughout the performance.

A late 1897 performance of the Foo troupe exemplified this quality. In reviewing the show, a writer, after discussing Foo's conjuring, singled out three supporting acts worthy of particular praise.

First was the "grotesque in the extreme" and "very cleverly done" double-headed boy trick, performed by a young Foo troupe contortionist. In this illusion, described as "an entire novelty and a very ingenious," a contortionist with a very lifelike copy of his head stealthily attached to the underside of his posterior and concealed under a short robe, would flip over on his hands, a movement that would simultaneously shroud his actual head and reveal the copy. The young contortionist would then proceed to walk about the stage on his hands—now covered with gloves resembling shoes—while impressively using his legs as arms and his feet as hands to perform such feats as drinking tea, washing his face and sitting down on a chair to "roars of laughter." The second act that caught his eye was a strongman juggler capable of tossing 20-kilogram Chinese porcelain vases to great heights in the air and then catching them, still spinning, on his forehead or knuckles—all while telling jokes or singing comic snippets of popular Western songs. The third supporting act he felt worthy of note was a "curious acrobatic feat" which later would become known as a 'strong hair' act. In these acts, acrobats swung across the stage while hanging by the hair of their queues, which was attached to ropes anchored to the stage's ceiling—"and curious-looking objects they were."[16]

Clearly, Foo was not afraid to share the stage with talented supporting players whose popularity sometimes rivalled his own.

Even at the height of their fame in Asia, however, more than one observer noted that the Foo troupe, while very well received and successful in that continent would, "on the principle prophets are not honored in their own country," no doubt go over even more spectacularly in Europe or North America, where their offerings, given the relative novelty of all things Asian in those more Western climes and a lack of first-hand familiarity with Chinese magicians, acrobats, contortionists, and the like, would exert an even stronger air of exoticism and lure of the East.[17]

CHAPTER TWO

THE 1898 OMAHA WORLD'S FAIR—FIRST STEP TOWARDS UNPRECEDENTED FAME AND FORTUNE

Such an opportunity began to materialize in 1897 when plans for the upcoming Omaha Trans-Mississippi International Exhibition (the Omaha World's Fair) began to take form.

The late 19th century was the golden age of world's fairs and exhibitions. Since the tremendously successful London Crystal Palace exhibition of 1851, cities and countries around the world vied to host these promotional (and thus far, economically stimulating) extravaganzas that celebrated and promoted new technologies, manufacturers, and the international exchanges rapidly characterizing global commerce and politics—all while educating and entertaining the host population. According to Mark Kishlansky, the prime motive behind Britain's seminal "Great Exhibition" was for the empire to make "clear to the world its role as industrial leader."[18]

Among the most successful world expositions, after the inaugural London event, were those hosted by Philadelphia in 1876, Paris in 1889 and Chicago in 1893.

The Omaha World's Fair was ceremonially opened by President McKinley's press of a button transmitting an electrical impulse from the White House in Washington, D.C. to Omaha, which lit the thousands of lights embedded in the exhibition's center: the neoclassical buildings surrounding an artificial quarter-mile lagoon.

In 1898, it was plucky and ambitious "Gateway to the West" Omaha's turn. Between June 1st and October 31st of 1898, over 2.6 million people would come to Omaha, a city barely 44 years old to experience an exposition focused on celebrating and promoting the development of the American West and the United States' emerging role as a global power. Financially supported by Washington and regional business leaders eager to reverse the momentum of several recent economic downturns, the 184-acre exhibition grounds radiated out from a newly constructed artificial quarter-mile lagoon. At the exhibition's center, surrounding the lagoon, was a "New White City" of fantastic electrically-lit neo-classical buildings serving as exhibition halls that rivaled in grandeur what had been created for the famed Chicago Exhibition of 1893.

As with the very successful 1893 Chicago World's Fair, the Chinese Manchu government did not officially participate in the Omaha Fair. However, American-based Chinese businessmen jockeyed for the opportunity to put together a Chinese exhibit, meant, as the other countries' exhibits were, to introduce their nation and its culture and products—all the while, ideally, turning a tidy profit.[19]

The men who made it happen: Treasury Secretary Lyman Gage and an 1888 newspaper illustration of Chicago Chinese-American businessman Hip Lung.

In 1897, the two groups of Chinese businessmen competing to obtain the right to finance and manage Omaha's Chinese Pavilion even travelled to Washington to personally lobby then Treasury Secretary, Lyman J. Gage, who was responsible for the decision. Both groups were backed by rival major U.S. railway lines interested in the business that came with shipping the people and materials required for the building of a major Chinese exhibition across the country.[20]

Ultimately, the Mee Lee Wah Village Company consortium, fronted by major Chicago Chinese-American businessman Hip Lung, received the Chinese Village concession.

The Mee Lee Wah company's design for the exposition's Chinese Village set out to recreate on a miniature scale life in a Chinese city. The Chinese Village envisaged would involve almost 250 Chinese participants and included a Chinese tea house, A Chinese "Joss House" (temple), a Chinese bazaar, a Chinese restaurant, gardens, and a Chinese theater featuring continuous performances. Interspersed among the major buildings would be an ethnographic display, typical of world's fairs of the era displaying 'ordinary' Chinese people going about their days. The Chinese organizers' goal was to recreate a Chinese city in miniature, representing all classes of Chinese life and illustrating their customs, amusements, goods, and religions.

To find the population to both build and populate their Chinese city in miniature, and do so within budget, Mee Lee Wah Company representatives headed to China in search of staff who could both erect and man the various elements of the village and the performers who would keep the Chinese Theater's continuous performances going.

In bringing so many Chinese from China into the U.S. for the purposes of the Omaha fair, the Chinese-American organizers had to navigate the 1882 China Exclusion Act. Since the act excluded all Chinese except a very narrow class of merchants and select others from entering the U.S., a special act of Congress had to be enacted to enable the production of special certificates for the hundreds of Chinese who would be required for the construction and operation of the planned exhibits. The required special act was passed with the support of U.S. Treasury Secretary Lyman J. Gage on June 20th, 1897.[21]

Omaha's "Chinese Village" Emerges

On May 6th, 1898, the first Chinese arrived at the newly built Omaha railway station. Under the careful gaze of a U.S. government Chinese inspector, over 200 Chinese were transported via rail from San Francisco in a special train of seven passenger railway cars and two freight cars. The Chinese brought with them 1,000 sacks of rice, smoked fish and other materials to help ease their stay in far-off Omaha. The newly arrived group included translators, actresses, teachers, merchants, and the Chinese painters, decorators, and carpenters who would design and erect the Chinese village. The train was greeted by a huge crowd that reportedly included almost all the local Chinese and those from neighboring states. Upon arrival, the inspector who had been escorting the Chinese across the country handed off his supervisory authority to Omaha customs officials, who would later distribute to the Chinese arrivals the certificates which authorized their presence in the U.S.[22]

Crowds in and around the entrance to the China Pavilion of the 1898 Omaha World's Fair. The Chinese "city" graced by American and Chinese flags was entered through a gate in the large building across from the Pabst Pavilion in the top photo. It was one of the most popular attractions at the Fair. One of the main reasons for this popularity was the performances of the Ching Ling Foo troupe.

The arrival in Omaha of the first Chinese working at the exposition was cause for excitement. The Chinese Village was one of the most anticipated elements of the planned midway, and the people of Omaha were eager to see what the Chinese builders would create.

The construction of the various structures took the assembled Chinese a little over a month, and the Chinese Village was officially opened on June 12th. Contemporary reports somewhat optimistically described the structures as "exact reproductions of those used in the city of Pekin."[23] Imported bamboo was a major building material, and the Chinese artisans reportedly did an excellent job, given the circumstances, in recreating the architecture and the "odd, fantastic design" elements of their homeland for the Omaha crowd.[24]

By early June, the miniature Chinese city was peopled with almost 250 Chinese men, women, and children "representing all classes of Chinese life", illustrating "their customs, amusements, industries, and religious ceremonies."[25] Wire service pieces published across the U.S. promoted the educational and entertainment value of the Chinese Village in the ethnocentric language of the time. "The Chinese Village, with its picturesque moon-eyed Celestials, its quaint nooks and corners, its wealth of curios, its corps of skilled artisans who will display their art in painting, carving in wood and ivory, and embroidery—native theatre with their queer, unintelligible interpretation of the drama, their religious exercises and the worship of the great dragon, their wonderful uneatable meals, with chop-sticks, a rug and stool as unmanageable accessories: All this will prove an attractive novelty to the thousands who study the doings of this strange, soft-voiced, and ever-entertaining people."[26]

Reviews of the Chinese Village, which was located on the West Midway (the enormous grounds contained both an East and a West Midway) found the Chinese exhibition had lived up to its hype. The Chinese café and numerous tea houses, with their "queer but

Tickets to the Omaha Exhibition's Chinese Village and Chinese Theater.

nonetheless pleasing decorations" and the Chinese bazaar, "a costly collection of exquisite Chinese wares—wonderful curios gathered from all parts of the celestial empire" proved great successes.

The Chinese theater also proved a hit with the crowds. The Chinese opera, and the theatrical performers engaged for the Omaha exhibition received high praise. "The performances in the theater are continuous and large crowds always go away singing the praises of the fine array of talent engaged."[27]

"THE YELLOW DANGER"

At about the same time the Chinese Pavilion opened in Omaha, in July of 1898, M.P. Shiel published *The Yellow Danger*, a book cobbled together from a fictional magazine serial he wrote to feed into the public's strong interest in the ongoing crisis that China was facing in the 1880s. China's territory at the time was slowly being divided up among aggressive, expansionist European powers, as well as Japan and Russia. The enormously successful book featured what would become a popular fictional 'invasion narrative', wherein the West, in response to this aggression, faces a threat from an invading China. The book's villain, Dr. Yen How, was supposedly inspired by Dr. Sun Yat-Sen, who first gained fame in Western eyes when he was kidnapped and imprisoned in the Chinese Embassy in London for attempting to overthrow the Qing Dynasty. Sales of *The Yellow Danger* would surge again in 1900, when the Boxer Rebellion seemed to confirm the book's theme of Chinese hostility towards the West.

Shiel's Asian villain, Dr. Yen How, also served as an inspiration to author Sax Rohmer for his more famous Asian villain, Fu Manchu. Elements of the iconic Western concept of the Chinese magician created by Ching Ling Foo and his many imitators were also supposed to have influenced Rohmer, who earlier in his life had worked both as an aspiring vaudeville writer and journalist and was very familiar with the stage milieu of the time and its various acts.

THE 1898 OMAHA WORLD'S FAIR **19**

Interestingly, Shiel considered the magazine serial and the resultant book to be "hackwork" written rapidly for profit and to take advantage of popular sentiment. Regardless, it remained his most popular book; it was republished several times and was of a piece with the popular Yellow Peril narrative of the time, which was personified in Hermann Knackfuss's notorious 1895 lithograph (commissioned by Kaiser Wilhelm), *Peoples of Europe, Guard Your Dearest Goods*; it later became famous as *The Yellow Peril*.

"PEOPLE OF EUROPE GUARD YOUR MOST PRECIOUS POSSESSIONS" ALSO KNOWN AS "THE YELLOW PERIL"
Herman Knackfuss (1895)

Premised on the Asian reaction to European imperialism, M.P. Shiel's novel *The Yellow Danger* was published and met with tremendous success in 1898.

Just three years earlier, in the service of European imperialism in China, Hermann Knackfuss produced the notorious lithograph "*Peoples of Europe, Guard Your Dearest Goods*", also known as "*The Yellow Peril*"—designed and commissioned by Germany's Kaiser Wilhelm, complete with a menacing, glowing Buddha riding a dragon, to warn of the Asian threat.

'LAWLESSNESS' AND TECHNOLOGICAL DISRUPTION AT THE OMAHA EXPOSITION: LIQUOR ON SUNDAYS AND THE UNLICENSED USE OF NEW PORTABLE CAMERAS

Not a month into the exhibition, the Chinese Village, along with the Bohemian or German Village and the Pabst and Schlitz Pavilions, would be admonished for selling beer on Sunday.[28] Nearly all the beer concessions are said to have ignored the ban on the Sunday sale of beer. The preferred modus operandi for the scofflaws was to serve the beer in cups and saucers as "cold tea."

Fair organizers also had to deal with policing a new technology, personal 'portable' Kodaks and other brands of box camera. To protect the business of professional photographers who had paid for the right to produce photographs, a fee and tag system was established by the Fair for personal cameras. Attendees were reportedly happy to pay the required one-dollar fee to take their cameras on to the fairgrounds. Fair guards were instructed to seize untagged cameras, resulting in some comical misunderstandings when the 'boxes' they wished to seize turned out to be something else.

In one account, one of the Fair guards, spotting a man carrying a suspicious-looking black box without a tag, set out after him. Once the guard had caught up to him, he loudly insisted the man would need a permit "to use that thing." "Don't need a permit," replied the man. By this time, a crowd had gathered to witness the altercation. The guard then repeated himself: "I don't want to make you any trouble, but ..." The man persisted. "I don't intend to buy a permit and you can't make me." Straightening himself up, the guard stated, "Now look here mister." The man seemed pleased by the crowd that had gathered and rose to the occasion. He looked the guard in the eye and said, "I don't need any permit, and I'm going to use it right now. Just watch me!" The man winked at the crowd, took a quick seat, popped open the box, and extracted ... a sandwich. The crowd roared and the now-sheepish guard returned to post.

Foo Family Hit of the Fair

First and foremost, among the Chinese theatrical talent attracting the crowds amidst the sprawling and highly competitive Midway was the Ching Ling Foo troupe, which was appearing as part of the continuous entertainment to be provided in the Chinese Theater. The Chinese magician's colorful troupe for the Omaha engagement was comprised of the core elements that he had already worked with on stage for

MIDWAY AMUSEMENTS.
Trans-Mississippi and International Exposition, Omaha.
These attractions on the Midway are worth seeing and are recommended by this paper's Omaha representative.

CHINESE VILLAGE AND THEATRE
The most instructive entertainment on the Midway. Do not fail to see the Ching Ling Foo troupe of acrobats, jugglers and magicians.

The core of the Foo troupe as they would have appeared during the Omaha World's Fair: Ching Ling Foo, his wife Hai Quai and their two children, Foo Quai the boy acrobat/contortionist, and Chee Tai, the bilingual singing tot.

over a decade. The Omaha team included Foo as the master Chinese conjurer; Foo's "small-footed" wife Hai Quai; Chee Tai (later Chee Toy), their adorable toddler daughter, who Foo often produced out of thin air; a "slack wire" performer, Foo Quai; Foo's son, Harry Foo; Foo's humorous assistant, a juggler of heavy vases; a horizontal bar performer; and an acrobat/contortionist.

The Foo troupe's American fame came quickly. A guide to the Midway published by the Nebraska *State Journal* and authored by their Omaha correspondent singled out the Chinese Village and the Foo troupe in particular as "the most instructive entertainment on the Midway." The guide to the Fair the paper published daily stated boldly, "Do not fail to see the Ching Ling Foo troupe of acrobats, jugglers, and magicians!"[29] This guide, with its recommendation for the Chinese

Village and the Foo troupe, would appear in this key Nebraska publication throughout the duration of the exposition.

Accounts vary as to how Ching Ling Foo and his troupe came to participate in the China Village of the Omaha Fair. There is some question as to whether Foo was already in San Francisco at the time he and his troupe were engaged for the Omaha Exhibition, or whether he was engaged by a general agent for the Fair while in Peking (Beijing) for what would turn out to be a bargain sum of $600 for the length of the Fair.[30] Certainly, in some accounts given by Foo or his representatives, the story is told that Foo was already in San Francisco when the Chinese performers were heading there. This rendition may or may not have something to do with U.S. immigration laws at the time, since, if one examines what was argued by Foo's counsel in his deportation case, they had to say Foo was in San Francisco before he came to Omaha if his status as a "duly authorized merchant of the United States" was still to be valid. If Foo had returned to China without notifying U.S. authorities, he would have lost this status. However, we can see from records of his performances in Asia that even by late 1897 Foo was not in the U.S. So it is very likely he was, in fact, hired in China and came over for the show after, at some earlier point, having left America without notifying the appropriate immigration authorities.[31]

The fact that the Chinese theater did so well on the Midway was no small feat. The competition for visitors' attention and coin was intense. There were thrilling water-chute rides, demonstrations of the new technological wonder "Dr. Roentgen's X-Rays" that were even riskier to one's health, and giant swings. Other Midway attractions included "Hagenback's Trained Wild Animal Show", situated right across from the Chinese Village. Also nearby was "The Cyclorama", which recreated the legendary Civil War battle between the only two ironclad ships of the time, the *Merrimack* and the *Monitor*. "Chiquita, the Living Doll", an exhibition built around a young Cuban

The competition: "Roentgen Wonderful Ray of Light" and the pavilion devoted to "Chiquita the Living Doll." (Courtesy Trans-Mississippi and International Exposition Digital Archive, University of Nebraska-Lincoln)

lady presented as "a Veritable Cuban Fairy" at "twenty-six inches" tall, also proved an enormous hit.[32]

For those fairgoers who dared, there was even a visit to "Heaven and Hell" on offer. This exhibit featured a saloon where, escorted by "monks," visitors could drink beverages from hollowed-out human skulls, served on tables made from coffins while attended to by waitresses dressed in "widow's weeds." On the menu was Schlitz beer, lemonade, soda and sandwiches "a la Diabolo," or brimstone wafers. The exhibit would later reopen with the less controversial name "Darkness and Dawn."

Unfortunately, this auspicious start for the Foo troupe would turn to tragedy less than two months into the exposition, when it was reported that a boy working with the troupe—identified as one of Foo's sons, but not Foo Quai—was struck down by fever. The young performer's funeral was attended by all the Chinese in the village and the local Chinese population. Some local media made specific note of the lack of any particular Chinese ceremonies of a public nature other than the wearing of "white badges of mourning", and were particularly struck by the fact that "a number" of the local Chinese attending the funeral "were accompanied by white wives."[33] Papers reported that Foo and the other members of the troupe, despite their heartbreak, continued to perform, and as they did, the acclaim accorded them continued to grow.[34,35]

As a consequence, in a pattern that would be repeated across the American cities Foo would later perform in, he and his family's popularity and charm led to a steady stream of social courtesies, invitations for meals, and other get-togethers tendered by "the society people" of the host city. During their time in Omaha, several receptions were given for "Mr. and Mrs. Ching Ling Foo" in their honor, and Omaha's society matrons competed for the Foo family's rare downtime. These gatherings often included "several other Chinese friends" and augured future multicultural get-togethers that would become a mainstay of the Foo troupe's interaction with the outside world while off the stage.[36]

Foo's English-Language Skills

At this point it is useful to address Foo's English-language skills. While Foo used interpreters throughout his U.S. and other foreign tours, it was evident he did speak some English. Clearly, his career as a merchant dealing with foreigners and his entertainment career would have facilitated the acquisition of this skill. As to how good Foo's English was, we can make some surmises.

It appears from the record that Foo could, when he wanted to, attempt to converse in English. However, he seemed to save these efforts for the relatively comfortable environments of conversations with friends, close professional colleagues, or dealings with old business partners.

Foo's habit of using interpreters when dealing with journalists may have been reinforced by the less-than-flattering assessments that emerged from his initial attempts, during his first tour of the U.S. to communicate with reporters directly. These initial efforts resulted in reports highlighting Foo's limited English skills, compounded by his stutter, rather than focusing on his magic. Typical of this sort of result was a 1900 report in the Richmond *Times*, which informed its readers, "Ching is not a fluent conversationalist in English. He is acquainted with but a few words and stutters at that."[37] It would not have taken many of these sorts of reports for Foo and his promoters to recognize that the best way to maintain his mystique and have the media focus on the magic was to use an interpreter.

It was understandable, then, that Foo would in the future save his efforts in English for more comfortable environments, kibitzing with fellow magicians at Martinka's famous New York magic shop or the friendly rooftop Chinese dinners and lunches he would come to regularly host for fellow performers and journalists.[38]

Meanwhile, the media focus on all things Foo, generated by his success in Omaha, accelerated, with stories about the colorful conjurer being picked up by the national newspaper wire services and distributed across the country. The Omaha *World-Herald* was the source of one such humorous report that centered around "a well-known society matron of Omaha" attending the Chinese Theater, hoping to better understand Foo's conjuring act. She reportedly approached Hong Sling, the Chinese-American manager of the Chinese Village, but since the woman had never met a Chinese person before, she relied on her knowledge of 'Chinglish' garnered from a few "funny newspaper columns." Her sing-song request, peppered with phrases such as "What allee samee is that?" and "What he say?" while pointing towards Foo, received the following reply from the popular and very Westernized Hong Sling: After listening patiently to the woman's request, he bowed courteously and replied in perfect English, "The performer is explaining that he has appeared before our emperor and performed feats of magic, and that he has been given several medals for his proficiency in the art of legerdemain. You will observe, madam, that he has no confederates and does not use any mechanical appliances in the performance of his tricks."[39,40]

Foo Performs the Chinese Decapitation Illusion

By the time the Exposition was in its last month, the excitement engendered by the Foo troupe, as well as the warmth the audience felt towards the charismatic family of performers, was at its peak. News that Foo, that "wonderful man," would be performing a number of new tricks resulted in a "packed to overflowing audience" at the Chinese Theater, and according to the Omaha *World Herald*, being "astonished and mystified" was only the start of their theatrical experience that night. The real magic had only just begun. Soon they were "awe-stricken and dumbfounded" when Foo, before their very eyes, cleverly severed his assistant's head "from his shoulders." The audience, for a moment believed that perhaps the performer had been killed. "But in a moment Ching Ling Foo stopped the flow of blood, placed the head back on the shoulders, and the boy walked off the stage very much alive."[41]

With startling performances like these, the fame of the Foo troupe continued to spread. According to the local media, thousands from

Recreation of 1898-style poster promoting Foo's decapitation Illusion. (Scobie)

across the country were regularly inquiring about the times and locations of Foo's performances, while the crowds at the Chinese Village were such that "it looked more like a thickly populated city" than a village. "The restaurant, the joss house, the bazaar, the theater and every other building were crowded from morning until night."[42]

THE OMAHA FAIR'S TRAFFICKING CASE

One of the first intercultural fumbles involving the management of the Omaha Chinese Village involved a lawsuit brought by a Chinese businessman, claiming that the Mee Lee Wah Village Company intended to engage in human trafficking with the over 50 young Chinese women brought in for the Fair. The ensuing court drama, which seemed to originate out of a business conflict that occurred after the Chinese Pavilion changed hands, received national attention.[43]

In the first instance, the local judge the matter was raised before ruled that three girls (representing the 50 girls working at the Fair) should be placed in the custody of a female missionary from Kansas, who claimed expertise in things Chinese and had given as evidence of incipient immorality the fact that she had seen some of the Chinese men speaking with the Chinese women. However, the girls—aged 14 to 16 years, and described as "giddy, frisky young celestials" and "likely good at gum chewing" if they had grown up in the U.S. by the local press—refused to quietly surrender themselves to the guardianship of the female missionary. For her part, the missionary, after briefly having the girls in her care, admitted she did not want the situation to continue before retreating back to Kansas.[44]

Brought back before the local judge who had put them in the custody of the missionary, the less-than-pleased magistrate ordered the girls imprisoned for not following his orders. This closely watched judgement inspired widespread derision, and a federal judge brought into address the issue immediately rescinded the local judge's orders and freed the girls.

> In his judgement, the federal judge noted that the evidence presented revealed nothing untoward in the situation of the girls working at the Chinese Village, and that the girls were evidently well-treated. He also noted that it was an odd thing to imprison the girls while the man accused of wrongdoing was free. Finally, in reference to the missionary's earlier provided 'evidence' of immorality, he responded, "It's never been immoral in this country for men and women to talk." He therefore freed the girls, who "evinced the greatest delight" at the happy turn of events. They then thanked the people who had looked after them at the jail for the past weeks and happily returned to their work at the Chinese Theater.[45]

President McKinley, Chinese Minister Wu Ting Fang, and the Peace Jubilee

On October 12th, 1898, on the last scheduled month of the exhibition, President William McKinley visited Omaha to attend a "Peace Jubilee" and give a speech to commemorate the end of the Spanish-American War. The event was also designed to signal America's emergence as a new power in the Pacific with its acquisition of the Philippines, Guam and Hawaii. The Philippines and Guam were acquired as a result of the war; Hawaii had come under U.S. control through an insurrection directed by foreign plantation owners that led to the kingdom becoming a U.S. territory. As a result, on June 11th, 1898, what had been the independent Hawaii exhibit at the Omaha Fair was moved from the International Building into the Agricultural Building, as the former kingdom was now a U.S. possession.

Accompanying President McKinley to Omaha was Wu Ting Fang, China's powerful ambassador to Washington, who had trained as a British barrister in Hong Kong.[46] Wu Ting Fang met with Foo as part of his responsibilities during the Omaha Fair, which included a speech of Wu's own on world peace and lobbying McKinley to ensure the U.S. would not apply the restrictive immigration rules of the China

Chinese Minister to Washington Wu Ting Fang. In 1900, the storied American publication *Harper's Weekly* described Minister Wu as one of America's most popular after-dinner speakers and published the illustration above of Wu addressing a gathering of New York merchants.

Exclusion Act in its newly acquired territory of the Philippines.[47] Wu also found time to engage in an interaction with new cutting-edge technology when he participated in a phone call from the ground to a team of "ascensionists" in a hot air balloon a thousand feet off the ground.

As a result of their meeting in Omaha, Foo and Wu would become lifelong acquaintances. Foo would meet with Wu again a few years later when the Foo troupe's engagements took them to Washington and Wu, the Chinese minister to Washington, would play a key role in mediating a dispute Foo was having with his American business partners at the time.

The relationship the two men developed was a signal of the importance with which the highly influential Wu, who would later serve as China's Foreign Minister and rise as high as acting Premier of the Republic of China in 1917, took the good work Foo was doing rehabilitating the image of Chinese in America.

Foo's Last Days in Omaha

As the Trans-Mississippi International Exposition continued to wind down, Omaha proved reluctant to let go of the Foos—and the Foos, on their side, seemed in no hurry to leave either. After the close of the Exposition at the end of October, the Foos lingered in Omaha into early November. On November 7th, the beloved Foo was guest of honor for a well-covered tour of the offices of the Omaha *Daily Bee* wherein Foo, ever interested in new technological developments, paid great interest to his introduction to the newspaper's ultra-modern typesetting process and printing presses.[48]

Interestingly, during his tour of the newspaper facilities, Foo seemingly filled in some gaps in his past while commenting on the relative hospitality of Americans. The cosmopolitan Foo, in speaking with his hosts, claimed he had "spent one year in France, one in England, and some months in Germany." The conjurer, ever the diplomat, then went on to state that the welcome he had received in those countries paled compared to what he had lately received in America; Foo, auguring much of what he would encounter in the near future, stated, he "never met such friendship as has been extended to him in America." It was not clear from this statement whether Foo was referring just to his time in Omaha or the earlier time he had spent in San Francisco.

Did Foo and William Robinson Cross Paths in Omaha Before Robinson Became Chung Ling Soo?

A few days later, on November 9th and 10th, Leon Herrmann, nephew of the more famous and beloved Alexander Herrmann, appeared for an engagement in Omaha after taking over his now deceased uncle's show. An account in the April 1909 edition of the magical periodical *The Sphinx* by David P. Abbott claimed, on the basis of second-hand accounts, that Foo had attended a Herrmann performance in Omaha, seated prominently in a box seat surrounded by his Chinese troupe. During the performance, Herrmann supposedly spotted the now-famous Chinese magician and moved towards Foo to demonstrate his skills with the Chinese linking rings. According to Abbott's sources, an unsportsmanlike Foo supposedly "looked on coldly without enthusiasm."

Worse yet, the same informant claimed days later that Foo, no longer performing at the Chinese Theater since the Fair had closed down, rented a hall of his own and gave a performance wherein he purposely performed some amazing feats with the linking rings then contemptuously tossed them aside with a dismissive "bah" as "utterly below the standard of his art." According to the story, all this occurred while an undoubtedly chagrined Leon Herrmann and his entourage looked on. This, along with an account in the same *Sphinx* article of Foo blowing up when another magician attempted some tricks during a social gathering in Omaha, were brought together by Abbott to emphasize an alleged point about Foo's personality: "He would tolerate no rivals."[49] Abbott's account of Foo was otherwise quite positive.

Christopher Stahl, in his piece "Outdoing Ching Ling Foo", finds these second-hand accounts of Foo's crossing paths with Herrmann and Robinson—and Foo's alleged intolerance of competitors—suspect. He rightly argues that they appear to be part of a post-1905 London Foo-vs.-Soo contest effort to paint Foo as in some way disagreeable and as an overly competitive foreigner. In Stahl's thinking, this portrayal was designed to render Foo a less sympathetic figure than he otherwise would have been, given the highly questionable post-contest liberties taken by his great imitator William Robinson/Chung Ling Soo during and after that contest.[50]

Indeed, scheduling realities eat away at Abbott's premise that Leon Herrmann and William Robinson would have stayed on in Omaha for several days, waiting for Foo to rent a theater to perform his own show and thus face the alleged humiliation. Touring demands ensured the Herrmann troupe spent not an extra day in Omaha after their performance. The Herrmann troupe was on the way to Lincoln, Nebraska the evening of November 10th; by November 16th, when Foo actually held his going-away show at the Boyd Theater, which was the only time on record Foo had rented a hall in Omaha, the Herrmann troupe was already performing in Cedar Rapids, Iowa, more than a day's train ride from Omaha.

Beyond these temporal issues, the ideas that Foo was somehow cantankerous or that it was his nature to "tolerate no rivals" seem to be belied by the numerous instances during his first and second tours of his camaraderie with fellow magicians and the many enduring friendships he developed with so many of them—and of the honors their associations would bestow on him. These long-term friendships included a young Nicola, who, while still a teenager, got his start in professional conjuring at the 1898 Omaha Exposition. Years later, the now-"Great Nicola" spoke fondly of the friendship with the ever-amiable Foo that began there.

Indeed, what seemed to most impress the populace of Omaha, and most of Foo's audiences, during his run at the Omaha Exposition was the magician's evident good nature.

The Foo Troupe Farewell to Omaha

When the Foo troupe finally said goodbye to Omaha with a one-night "Grand Farewell Performance" held at Omaha's Boyd's Theater on November 16th, 1898, the Omaha *World-Herald*, which had repeatedly referred to Foo as "this wonderful man", made note of Foo "having made a host of friends" in Omaha and the consequently "large circle of his acquaintants" present at his celebratory going-away performance.

Demonstrating his capacity for invention, novelty and getting the audience on his side, Foo, for this last exhibition, "performed many new feats not seen at the Exposition," including the production, from what would become known as "Foo Cones", of "a large vase filled with carnations, roses and chrysanthemums, which were thrown to the ladies in the audience."

For the troupe's final performance in Omaha, the core elements of the Foo troupe act and its particularly appealing familial nature were all in evidence. Foo's wife Hai Quai contributed a song, while his son Foo Quai provided "a splendid exhibition of plate spinning,

> **BOYD'S THEATER** PAXTON & BURGESS
> Mgrs. Tel. 1919.
> WEDNESDAY EVENING, NOV. 16.
> ## Ching Ling Foo Troupe
> (Late of the Chinese Theater on the Midway.)
> In their **Grand Farewell Performance.**
> CHING LING FOO — The Greatest of all magicians, in wonderful feats of magic and his troupe of
> Acrobats, Jugglers, Wire Walkers, Bar Performers and Wonder Workers.
> ONE NIGHT, WEDNESDAY, NOV. 16f
> POPULAR PRICES - - 25c and 50c

Foo's farewell to Omaha. "The Greatest of all magicians."

acrobatic, and contortion feats." Chee Tai, the emerging star that was Foo's daughter—"the only baby Chinese performer in the world and certainly a wonder to all Americans"—sang "a baby song in her native tongue." And finally, Harry Foo, Foo's humorous assistant, did some "extraordinary juggling." The audience for Foo's final performance, as they had been during his entire run in Omaha, was "appreciative in the extreme", calling out for "frequent encores and curtain calls."[51,52]

For this final Omaha performance, Foo was touted as "The Greatest of All Magicians," an assessment shared by newspapers that had for months been singing his praises across the country. As a result, by the time they left Omaha, Foo and his troupe, with their stage presence, charm and family appeal, had captured not just the imagination of "the Gateway to the West", but of people across the country.[53]

However, despite the tremendous boost their Omaha engagement gave the Foo troupe, it would not be all clear sailing for the adventurous ensemble. Foo's initial foray into the American entertainment market had ended, but the roller-coaster ride that would be his first American tour had just begun.

CHAPTER THREE

AFTER OMAHA—HOPKINS HELPS FOO'S TROUPE FIND A LARGER STAGE

Despite their great success in Omaha, it was not an entirely smooth trajectory to greater fame and fortune for the Foo troupe upon finally leaving Nebraska. The prescient observer in Singapore years back who'd suggested Foo would need "European" management to truly succeed in the West proved not far off the mark.

The first known planned engagement the Foo troupe post-Omaha was a one-week engagement beginning November 21st, 1898, at Koster & Bial's Music Hall in New York. The venue, which was famous for showing the first film to a paying audience (Edison's first Vitascope "moving picture" in April of 1896) was located at Broadway and 34th Street, and had a seating capacity of almost 4,000. At the time, Koster & Bial's specialized in what they termed "foreign" vaudeville—essentially, acts that originated outside the U.S. This, of course, made the Foo troupe a natural fit.[54]

The Foo troupe, according to some reports, was paid $260 for the week's engagement, not including railway fares. This was an excellent salary for the time, but nothing compared to the more than $1,000 per week plus private railway cars Foo would be enjoying only eight months later.

Unfortunately, little record is left of the anticipated Koster & Bial's engagement. Koster & Bial's, at the time, did not promote in their newspaper advertisements acts other than their absolute headliners, and used the catch-all "foreign vaudeville" to advertise that they were presenting entertainers from overseas.

Indications that the Brooklyn performance did indeed take place are provided in articles published some 15 years later, when Foo was in the course of his second, highly successful U.S. tour, and references were made to Foo's 1898 performances in "the old Koster & Bial's Music Hall" that had evidently still left an impression.[55] Regardless, the fact the Foo troupe did not stay on in New York and left seemingly little record of their first performances there indicates that the act, most likely for lack of promotion, did not catch fire the way it had in Omaha or subsequently would in Chicago.[56]

December 1898, Chicago: The Foo Troupe Takes Off

After their late November Koster & Bial's New York engagement, there is no record of further Foo performances until the week of December 12th, 1898, when the Foo troupe played Chicago's Star Theater. At the time, the Star Theater was a smaller theater whose lack of relative success in the vaudeville game would soon prompt its owners to transform it into a boxing venue.[57]

Nonetheless, playing the less-than-top-of-the-line Star Theater proved the turning point at this stage of Foo's career. While playing the Star, Foo and his troupe were talent-spotted by theater scouts from Hopkins, the dominant Midwestern vaudeville theater chain. Hopkins management soon signed the promising Foo troupe up to play at the larger and much more prestigious Chicago Hopkins theater chain. The Hopkins chain was run by Colonel John D. Hopkins and, at the time, had major theaters in Chicago, St. Louis, and New Orleans, among other cities, mostly west of Chicago. The shrewd Colonel, recognizing the potential the Foo troupe represented, signed a special management agreement with the troupe and took a special interest in their development and promotion.

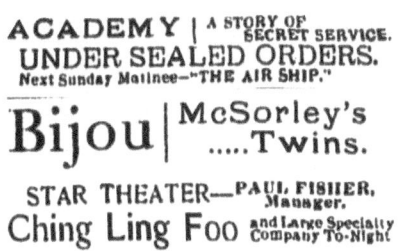

The Foo troupe's post-Omaha engagement at Chicago's Star Theater brought them to the attention of Col. John Hopkins, who, recognizing a good thing, soon acquired the troupe for his Hopkin's theater circuit. While at the Star, the Foo troupe were competing with an espionage thriller, *Under Sealed Orders*, playing at the Academy.

With this move to the Hopkins circuit, with its professional management and promotion skills, the Foo troupe's ascent to the American vaudeville stratosphere had begun.[58]

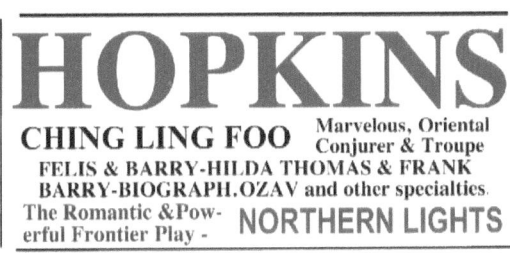

The Foo troupe comes under Col. John Hopkins' management and the proper "booming" of the "Marvelous Oriental Conjurer & Troupe" begins.

The Foo "Booming" Begins

On the promotional side, Hopkins management wisely picked up where the Omaha exhibition left off. Foo was once more touted as "magician to his Imperial Majesty the Emperor of China."

However, the Hopkins circuit "boomers" were not to have things entirely their own way when it came time to set the Foo narrative in the press. As we would see more than once during Foo's initial American tour (and his second tour from 1912 to 1915), there was seeming confusion in the media regarding just how to describe Foo's appearance. Did his face have the strong lines of American Indian chief, or the face of a "statesman", or was he "rather unhandsome", as one of the early Chicago critics claimed?[59] Regardless of this interesting lack of agreement on how to assess Foo's appearance, which we will revisit, at this early stage of his U.S. vaudeville career, one thing all could agree on was that he was doing "marvelous" work and demonstrated "wonders in legerdemain."

On stage in Chicago, steadily gaining in fame and popularity, Foo performed the tricks he did in Omaha, including an illusion where the Chinese magician turned "paper frogs into living ones."[60] In a sign of strongly favorable reaction, the troupe continued its run at the Chicago Hopkins theater into a second week, right through until Christmas. At the theater, as part of a "Cinderella promotion", the Foo troupe, in what would be the first of a series of similar promotional challenges, invited women in the audience on stage to "see if they can put on one of the shoes of Mrs. Ching Ling Foo"—and, not surprisingly given foot-binding was not a practice in America at the time, all who tried failed.[61]

January 1899, St. Louis

After their very successful Chicago engagement, the Foo troupe appeared in St. Louis early in the New Year of 1899, at the Columbia Theater. During this engagement, the Hopkins management began to spin their version of how the Chinese magician came to be under their management. According to the Hopkins "front men," after leaving the Omaha exposition, the Foo troupe had some difficulty navigating America's vaudeville business and were in a "sad predicament." Foo's English was not the best, and as he would not "associate" with the "common" Chinese of Chicago—and despite obtaining an engagement with the Star Theater—it was not until Foo "wandered up into the Orpheum vaudeville offices and conferred with Colonel Hopkins" that he ceased to "despair of an existence in the New World."[62] So ran Colonel Hopkins' version of the commencement of Foo's post-Omaha career.

Hopkins would not be the last theater owner and promoter to take credit for launching Foo's stellar vaudeville career, but the wily Colonel who first recognized Foo's potential post-Omaha and properly promoted him would remain the man with the most credible claim to that title.

Colonel Sam Moy and an Early Extortion Effort

CHINESE MAGICIAN'S TROUBLES

During Foo's engagement in St. Louis, the magician ran into another colonel, who turned out to be a bit more overtly menacing than the affable Hopkins. While performing in that city, Foo came into conflict with one "Colonel" Sam Moy, a Chinese businessman from Chicago. Moy presented Foo with the claim that as he had secured for Foo the engagement with the Hopkins circuit, he was entitled to some ten percent of Foo's earnings. Furthermore, Moy employed lawyers to seek Foo out and harass him on the matter in St. Louis, where Foo was at that moment performing.

An exasperated Foo, not fully familiar with the ways of American vaudeville management, turned to Colonel Hopkins for clarification on the matter. Informed of these developments, Colonel Hopkins advised Foo to ignore Moy's demands and that he would make clear in any resultant court case that Foo had secured his position with the Hopkins theater chain "on his own representation." Foo is quoted in news coverage of the incident as praising Colonel Hopkins for looking out for his interests.

The story of this pecuniary conflict was embellished in typical turn-of-the-century "booming" fashion by the St. Louis newspapers, which, imaginatively added references to a family feud between Foo and Moy stretching back to China where Foo's brother apparently held "an important position in the imperial cabinet" and had banished said Moy from China years earlier.[63] The idea that Chinese conflicts, and in particular any involving Ching Ling Foo, were quite exotic and stretched back decades, if not hundreds of years, would become a recurring theme in Foo's promotional efforts, and a cornerstone of Foo's legendary conflict with the pretender Chung Ling Soo in the so-called "World Championship of Chinese Magic", which would take place almost six years later.

Meanwhile, in St. Louis, the now quite profitable Foo troupe were the principal features on the Columbia Theater bill and performed before standing-room-only crowds. As was the case for their Chicago Hopkins theater run, they were reengaged for a second week.

Foo's Secrets Revealed!

But Colonel Moy's failed intervention was not the only cloud on the Foo troupe's otherwise sunny horizon. Another unwanted side effect of their increasing popularity, beyond the emergence of characters like Moy, was the publication of the first of what would become a stream of newspaper articles "revealing" the secrets behind Foo's illusions. Most of these were written or sourced from other professional magicians perhaps a bit miffed at Foo's success and eager to take him down a peg or two.

The first such piece to reveal the alleged secrets behind Foo's popular "production" and fire-eating tricks was published in the St. Louis *Dispatch* and was accompanied by helpful (if not too flattering) illustrations.[64,65] The article was soon picked up by the wire services and published across the country. As with all these articles, the authors put forward how they would have done the illusions, not necessarily how Foo himself performed the tricks.

As the Foo troupe moved into 1899, however, managing their post-Omaha career and the related illusion revelations were not the worst of the Foo troupe's problems. Since the Fair officially closed, the clock had been ticking on the three-month grace period Chinese performers were granted before they had to return to China. Foo and

Note detail of bowl production, where the bowl used is depicted as hollow with only a thin layer of water on top. As the bowls Foo produced evidently contained gallons of water carefully ladled from them after production, clearly, this was not how Foo performed the illusion.

his management had appealed the Foo troupe's current visa status to the U.S. Treasury Secretary, but that office responded that they could do nothing given the nature of the related special legislation passed by the U.S. Congress for the Exposition back on June 30th, 1898. That act excluded Chinese performers from the scope of the China Exclusion Act for the purposes of the Omaha Fair, but did so only temporarily. The Exposition legislation clearly required all Chinese who were in the U.S. for the Omaha event to leave the United States by the fast-approaching date of February 1st, 1899. That the whereabouts of hundreds of Chinese workers who had been brought in for both the 1893 Chicago World's Fair and subsequent 1898 Omaha World's Fair were currently unaccounted for with whereabouts unknown did not assist the atmosphere surrounding Foo's case.[66]

January 1899, New Orleans

While their management worked on the immigration problem, the Foo troupe completed their two-week run in St. Louis. They then moved on to the New Orleans Academy of Music for a week's engagement as the main attraction. The Foo troupe, which arrived in the city several days before their engagement, gave some insight into their early promotional methodology when they used this time, prior to the commencement of their performances, to wander the major streets of the city and mingle with its crowds. During these forays, Foo would perform small up-close magic tricks, and members of the troupe would display their acrobatic and contortionist skills, thus generating interest in their upcoming performances.

Foo's Fire-Breathing Act

As in Chicago and St. Louis, Foo's performances in the Big Easy were well-received by their audiences. Particular attention was paid to Foo's "very extraordinary" fire breathing act which, in the version he presented in New Orleans, took up a large portion—about 20 minutes of the performance. Local media reported that Foo "eats fire" and "in some mysterious way retains it in his mouth for minutes and minutes and then puffs out smoke and flame until the odor fills the whole theatre."

Foo's fire act would start by drawing an endless length of multi-colored "streamers" from his mouth which sparked, cracked, and flashed like fireworks. He would then begin to place handfuls of "punk" (the material used to create firework fuses) and sawdust into his mouth until his cheeks bulged. A great thirst was then feigned, and Foo would express a need for a tall glass of water, which an assistant—and sometimes his toddler daughter, little Chee Tai—would quickly provide. Foo would then begin to emit small but ever-increasing amounts of dark vapors from his mouth until the theater itself seemed filled with the black, fragrant smoke. Choking back the fumes, Foo would rub his stomach as if in pain, and then suddenly begin spitting out fireballs that sailed across the stage, each larger than the one before. Then the last and largest fireball would be expertly aimed from his mouth across the boards into a very large pot of fireworks that would explode into an enormous pyrotechnic display, dramatically illuminating the theater.

FOO'S FIRE-EATING ACT IN DETAIL

Foo usually introduced his fire act near the end of his performance. The stage would be bare except for a table, upon which would rest a large bowl of what could be mistaken for sawdust. Foo would enter the stage carrying half a dozen wisps of paper in one hand and a single large match in the other. He would then take his place behind the table and light one of the wisps of paper with the match, and then use that lit piece of paper to light another as the small wisps burst into flame then expire seemingly at his command. Foo then appeared to eat the half-dozen small pieces of paper while they were aflame.

Foo would then engage in a bit of theatrical 'business' wherein he would smile broadly and rub his chest and stomach as if he was thoroughly enjoying digesting the flaming paper. Then tiny Chee Tai arrived on stage carrying a large glass of water. Foo gargled with this water and rinsed his mouth. Here he would use some of his rare stage English, telling the crowd, "No fire, all gone out." Foo then would commence to fan his head and stomach as if he were getting very hot. He would then reach into the bowl of what appeared to be sawdust on the table, take great handfuls of the material in his hands, and let it run through his fingers back into the bowl like sand to demonstrate there was nothing else hidden in the bowl. Foo would then rapidly gulp down several large fistfuls of the material.

The magician would then fan his ears and mouth with rapid motions as if he was getting very, very hot. Out of his mouth, "great volumes of a thick, pungent and aromatic smoke which has the odor of incense" would billow. It floated "gracefully out over the crowd" packing the theater. Foo emitted these profusions of smoke about six times, and the end of each emission of smoke, he spat out a hot and flaming substance from his mouth, indicating what was left of the materials from the flammable materials just consumed.

The final part of the act was the expulsion of streams of ribbons that exploded like firecrackers from Foo's mouth, followed by a narrow red-colored tube pulled from his mouth, stretched by an assistant almost across the stage.

> All this material, as it was produced, was tossed, seemingly carelessly, upon the stage floor by Foo and his assistant. Then, just as casually, it was gathered up and tossed to the center of the stage. Foo then consumed another fistful of the sawdust-like material and breathed out his largest outpouring of smoke and flame yet, spitting the final burning ember from his mouth into the yards of ribbon and materials now piled at the center of the stage. Upon contact with the burning ember, the materials exploded into an enormous pyrotechnical display almost matched by the crowd's explosion of applause.[67]

Foo's standard production illusions also entertained, and during every performance at the New Orleans Art Academy, Foo invited audience members on stage to observe his work up close. But despite this, the *Times Picayune* reported the true secret of "his bowl and water trick remain a mystery."[68] Attention was also paid to the wider Foo troupe and the Foo family, consisting "of a wife, a little boy and a mere tot of a daughter" who were described as "quite as full of tricks as Foo himself."[69]

During the New Orleans engagement, the Foo troupe once more employed the Cinderella promotion, and at a Tuesday matinee focused on women and children, ladies in the audience were once again invited to try on Mrs. Foo's shoes. This was seen as particularly noteworthy as "Chinese women were rarely seen in New Orleans."[70] Chinese women in the U.S. were even rarer than Chinese men. The Page Act of 1875, which was the first restrictive federal immigration law passed in the U.S. prohibited the entry of Chinese women. Seven years later, the Chinese Exclusion Act would ban entry of Chinese men as well.

Foo's Appearance Revisited

Even by the time the Foo troupe reached New Orleans, however, the burning issue of just how to describe Foo's physical appearance remained unresolved. In stark juxtaposition to those pushing the handsome and stately narrative regarding the conjurer's countenance, one particular New Orleans theater critic had an entirely different take. Foo thus received some of the roughest press coverage he would encounter regarding his personal appearance.

The New Orleans critic, while otherwise giving the troupe a quite positive review, took pains to point out to his readers that Foo, "this tall ungainly individual", is "about as awkward ugly-looking a Chinese person as could be found in all the oriental empire." He went on to describe the magician as "all out of proportion physically" and "very stalky ugly."[71] Fortunately for Foo, this was mostly the last gasp of the Foo-as-an-unattractive-Chinese narrative, and due to his own chiseled natural bone structure, deep soulful eyes, and winning smile, coupled with some able advance men, Foo's appearance going forward, would no longer be subject to such uneasy nativist revisionism.

Once again in New Orleans the Foo troupe's popularity with the crowds led to its being held over for an additional week, and they performed at the New Orleans Music Academy through early February of 1899.

February 1899, Cincinnati Fountain Theater

By February 18th, the Foo troupe was performing at the Fountain Theater in Cincinnati, and the family element of the show, which played such a key role in the troupe's appeal, was now front and center in its promotion. Foo and his "high caste" family were billed as "the wonders of the century."[72]

"The Wonders of the Century", Ching Ling Foo "and Family."

March 1899: Back in Chicago

Finished with Cincinnati, a week later, the Foo troupe was back in Chicago, where the legendary dancer Isadora Duncan performed at Studebaker Hall while Foo provided a "remarkable, mystifying and original entertainment" at the Olympic Theater.

Staying in Chicago, the troupe moved on to the Haymarket Theater, where they continued to attract large West Side audiences. After the Haymarket, the troupe, still capable of drawing crowds, moved on to the Chicago Opera House, where their success continued.[73] The troupe reached its final Chicago venue in March 1899 when they were booked at the Great Northern Theater, "Chicago's Coziest and Safest", whose auditorium was proudly promoted as "absolutely fireproof." At the Great Northern, the Foo troupe was presented as part of a Weber & Field's Pousse Café Company extravaganza, advertised as featuring the best of a series of specialty acts.

Foo's "competition" in Chicago. The legendary Isadora Duncan, founder of modern dance, in her iconic Greek tunic and bare feet. As always with turn-of-the-century promotional ads, correct spelling was optional, but the seats were expensive.

CHAPTER FOUR

THE SENSATIONAL DEPORTATION TRIAL OF CHING LING FOO

"The Emperor Wants Him Back"

Before the Foo troupe had completed the first week of their engagement at the Great Northern, Foo, his family, and the Foo troupe's trusty juggler, Harry Foo, were all arrested and detained by U.S. authorities in Chicago. Charged with violating the 1882 China Exclusion Act, they were ordered deported from the United States.

The subsequent sensational deportation trial would not only become one of Foo's greatest triumphs, but also provided the burst of notoriety the act needed to become the most popular and highest paid troupe in American vaudeville.

Given Foo's fame at the time of his Chicago arrest in late March of 1899, news of his imminent deportation and the trial it sparked received prominent coverage across the U.S. The initial jocular coverage of the arrest and imminent deportation was influenced both by the date the news was published and the ever-nimble public relations and booming instincts of Foo's managers.

EMPEROR WANTS HIS MAGICIAN.

CALLED BY THE EMPEROR.
Chinese Magician Given His Walking Papers by Request of His Ruler.

CHING LING FOO IS DEMANDED.
Chinese Emperor Wants Back His Magician.

MAY DEPORT CHING LING FOO.
Chinese Juggler Charged with Having Overstaid the Time the Government Gave Him in America.

HE WANTS LING FOO.
Chinese Emperor Desires the Return of a Magician.

Across the country Foo's arrest for deportation was front page news in cities large and small.

So it was that the initial breathless reports of Foo's Chicago arrest, published across the country on April 1st, 1899—April Fool's Day—carried banner headlines claiming the Chinese emperor had demanded the return of his court magician and the U.S. government was complying.

That more people than one might think took this version of the story seriously, rather than as just an expression of April Fool's hijinks on the part of American newspapers at the time, was revealed by the fact the venerable New York *Times* ran essentially the same story on April 2nd on its front page.[74] The *Times* headline read "Chinese Magician to Go Home, The Emperor Wants Him, and an American Official Arrests Him."

In fact, "the Emperor wants him back" angle continued to be employed in coverage of the story long after April 1st had passed. This was surely a partial tribute to both Foo's management team's talent for "booming" and the American public's thirst for a colorful story.

These "the Emperor wants him back" pieces were spread about the country at the exact same time another well-timed piece loudly singing Foo's praises and providing a comprehensive review of Foo's time in the U.S. since his arrival for the Omaha exposition and the unprecedented success he and his troupe had enjoyed to date was also widely published.

It seems this latter piece, which extolled the Foo troupe and described it as the biggest hit in vaudeville for over a decade, was placed

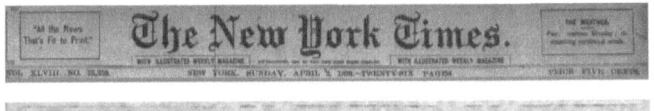

"All the news that's fit to print." Even the venerable New York *Times* reported Foo was going back to China, not due to something as mundane as an expired visa, but rather at the command of the Chinese Emperor. The story with the headline above appeared on the bottom left side of the front page of the April 2nd edition.

by E.F. Albee prior to Foo's arrest. Mr. Albee got his professional start with P.T. Barnum and was the senior manager at B.F. Keith's theater circuit. Headquartered in New York, Keith's was the largest and most powerful vaudeville circuit on the East Coast. The Keith's theater group vigorously sought the best talent and had been in negotiations with Midwestern theater power Colonel Hopkins about introducing the Foo troupe to East Coast audiences just before the Foo troupe was arrested.

Colonel Hopkins had been amenable to the transfer of Foo to the East Coast Keith's circuit, as he was in the midst of negotiations with Keith's to join forces with his Midwest chain of theaters.[75] In addition, the Keith's theaters had outbid the Chicago theaters, who were also anxious to engage the Foo troupe if they were able to somehow evade their pending deportation order.[76,77]

The Keith's-generated article promoting Foo and his troupe's great talents also helpfully noted the Chinese conjurer's next tour stop would have been at a Keith's circuit theater. These promotional articles were designed to orbit newspaper reports of the troupe's deportation trial and amplify the "sensation" that was already surrounding Foo.

The effusive article trumpeted that "competent judges" had declared "that the hit of the decade in vaudeville has been scored by the Ching Ling Foo troupe." Foo was described as surpassing all Chinese conjurers before him, and that beyond that, he performed feats that had "never been duplicated by any magician ever hitherto

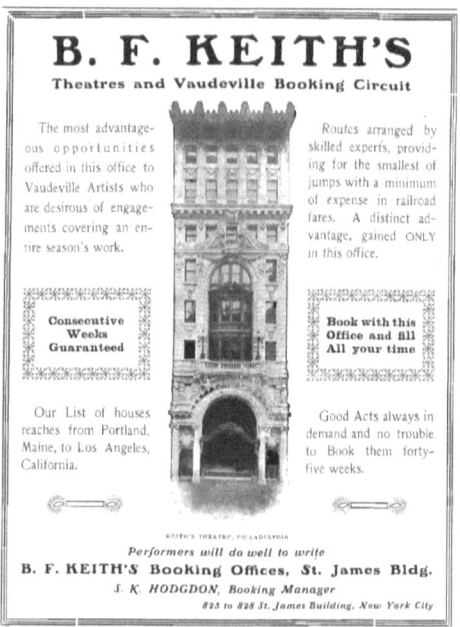

Above: an ad setting out the B.F. Keith's "pitch" to "good acts" to come and join the Keith's circuit. Keith's offered top performers a number of services, including booking them for an entire season at vaudeville theaters across the country and the expert logistical support to assist performers, who navigate often draining multi-city, multi-month tours.

seen in America." Foo's ability to draw and entrance audiences was touted by the fact the Chinese conjurer's "salary was tripled" by theater managers at the end of his first post-Omaha engagement due to the tremendous crowds he drew. This was a clear reference to the $260-a-week salary Foo reportedly earned at Koster & Bial's and, no doubt, Chicago's Star Theater before Colonel Hopkins took the troupe under his wing and began booming them and their (mind-boggling at the time) salary of over $1,000 a week. Well-advertised high salaries for top acts was all part of the "booming."78

As Foo was now evidently under engagement with B.F. Keith's chain as the result of a mutually beneficial deal negotiated with Colonel Hopkins, neither of these powerful show business tycoons had any intention of allowing their most popular current headliner to be sent back to China. Suitable investment in the best legal talent to address the problem followed. Thus Adolph Marks, a prominent Chicago entertainment lawyer who advised Warner Brothers, Ringling Brothers, and other major vaudeville entertainers, was engaged to argue the case for the Foo troupe.[79]

America Focuses on the Foo Trial

A wire service report published on April 5th, 1899 mixed fact and fiction in reporting that the Foo troupe had been arrested on a Saturday night just before their scheduled performance at Chicago's Great Northern Theater. The fiction part came in when the article went on to note by way of explanation that "the emperor had made a peremptory demand for his return, and this government was under a moral obligation to see to it that the command was obeyed", given the understanding that the Chinese "court magician" was being lent to America solely for the purposes of the Omaha Exhibition. The piece concluded that Foo, when faced with the prospect of returning to China and giving up his splendid salary, expressed his feelings regarding the emperor's actions in the pidgin phrase "Him hellee."[80] One wonders what went through the minds of Chinese diplomats sitting in Washington, such as Minister Wu Ting Fang, when they read such reports.

It was only when it became apparent that Foo was not going back to China voluntarily, and that Foo and his management had engaged the full majesty of the U.S. legal process to challenge the deportation order, that most newspapers settled down to focus on the genuinely fascinating, unembellished legal drama that was unfolding in Chicago.

In short order the public was informed Foo was picked up not because the Chinese emperor was missing his favorite conjurer, but rather because Foo and his troupe had violated the terms of the visas they had been granted to perform at the Omaha Exposition. As noted earlier, these visas allowed only for their holders to stay in the U.S.

while performing at or engaging in the business of the Omaha Exposition. Holders were required to leave the country within three months of the close of the Exhibition. By extending his troupe's stay in the U.S. beyond this period to perform in vaudeville, Foo and his troupe had violated the terms of their visas and were to be expelled.

Given the national interest in Foo's trial, almost-daily reports were published in the press regarding its progress. Great interest was taken in Chicago when the prominent and greatly influential Chinese-American businessman known as the unofficial leader of Chicago's Chinatown, Hip Lung—a bit of a local celebrity himself—testified in support of Foo. This, of course, was the same Hip Lung who had played a key role in the creation of the Mee Lee Wah Company, which had financed and managed the Chinese Village in Omaha.[81]

CHINESE FAMILY IN COURT.
Ching Ling Foo, a Magician, Resists Deportation.

Two Interpreters; One Too Many

By April 5th, Foo's legal team, working with not one, but two interpreters, was pleading its case. Two interpreters were required given the fact Foo spoke a northern Chinese dialect, Mandarin, while the Chinese court appointed translator spoke a southern dialect of Chinese, Cantonese. A second translator would have likely been required to translate Foo's Mandarin into Cantonese, which would then be translated into English by the court translator. Foo, according to the report, swore an oath to tell the truth and "wore a worried countenance." When he began testifying, the conjurer "made several passes with his hands and talked so fast that commas and other points of punctuation were overlooked entirely." Multiplying his troubles was the translation system, which, with its multiple translators, resulted in Foo reportedly (and not surprisingly) not fully understanding some of the questions.[82]

While Foo gave testimony, a newspaper at the time describes him as being surrounded by his family, who were "seated in a semi-circle around him." The Foo family itself was supported by "several sympathizing members of the local Chinese colony."[83]

In a clear show of her standing and status among the group, and to Western reporters' surprise that matters should unfold in this manner, Hai Quai, or "Mrs. Foo", was cited as repeatedly and aggressively breaking into the discussions to add her own thoughts to the proceedings "with remarks that sounded like hurried pickings on the low and high strings of a mandolin." While all the testifying was going on, one Western court observer reportedly passed a handful of licorice gum drops to a thankful little Chee Tai. Meanwhile, Foo Quai, Foo's son, also drew attention when the young contortionist, no doubt out of boredom, got his leg stuck between the rungs of his chair while playing with it and then required the assistance of Foo's right-hand man, Harry Foo, to extricate it.[84]

The Multi-Talented Foo Argues He is an "Authorized Merchant"

In their first set of arguments, Foo's legal team presented for observers what appeared to be a novel defense. They argued that the Chinese magician was not only a performer for the Omaha Exposition, but also a Chinese merchant and businessman who held a "certification of identification", which authorized him as a Chinese to do business in the U.S. Foo, it was claimed, had received the document as a result of his work with the Wah Yuen Lung trading company, a Chinese firm based in San Francisco, which he had joined in 1890.

Commissioner Mason, on April 6th, ruled it was clear to him that Foo, at one point, was indeed a "duly authorized merchant" holding the required document; but he also found Foo had returned to China without declaring any interest in returning to the U.S. sometime between 1885 and 1898. Foo, in Mason's judgement, returned to the U.S. in 1898 for the Omaha Exposition under the system that allowed the World's Fair performers to come to America. Commissioner Mason, therefore, while publicly stating he wished he did not have to, ruled that Foo, having stayed in the U.S. more than 3 months after the Fair had ended, must leave the country under the law governing those documents and the 1882 China Exclusion Act.

However, the Commissioner also found that Foo's fourteen-year-old son, Foo Quai, had been born in the U.S. during the period Foo was a resident, and Foo Quai therefore could remain in the country.[85]

Interestingly, the trading company listed as the one Foo worked at appears to have been linked to Hip Lung, the major Chinese entrepreneur who dominated the Chicago Chinese community and had played a major role in organizing Chinese participation in both the 1893 Chicago and the 1898 Omaha Expositions. Also of interest was the address provided for Foo's San Francisco place of business: 739 Commercial street. This building, located in San Francisco's Chinatown, has an interesting history and linkages to the intrigue that often linked the overseas Chinese community in the U.S. to the politics of its mother country. Just a year before Foo would appear in Omaha, a complicated dispute between some "reform-minded" overseas Chinese based in San Francisco and the Qing government had resulted in the property of several Chinese, whose U.S. address was provided as 739 Commercial Street, having their property seized by the Qing government and then released after an investigation proved the charges made against them by the Qing government representative in San Francisco of fomenting rebellion could not be substantiated. Over the years, the 739 Commercial St. building seems to have retained its connection with international intrigue. These days it functions as a representative office of the Taiwanese government.

Colonel Hopkins then directed Foo's legal team to appeal Mason's decision to the Chicago District Court, where a Judge Kohlsaat would review the matter.[86] The next day, on April 7th, Foo was issued a $5,000 bond and was allowed to travel to San Francisco to seek the papers which would demonstrate he was still indeed a "Duly Authorized

CHING LING FOO RELEASED.

United States Commissioner Mason expressed regret yesterday, when sitting in the office of Marshal Ames, that he ordered the deportation of Ching Ling Foo. Mrs. Foo and their baby daughter. A son, Ching Ling Qual, could remain, he said, but the other members of the family, under the statutes, were not permitted to stay in the country. In explanation, Commissioner Mason said he had carefully examined every statute he could find relating to the case and had failed to find one that gave him the slightest excuse for rendering any other decision. As for Ching Ling Qual, the son, it was apparent that he had been born in this country and was not amenable to the Chinese exclusion act.

CHING LING FOO AND HIS FAMILY

The courtroom sketch of the Ching Ling Foo deportation proceedings before U.S. Commissioner Mason.

Merchant" working for the Wah Yuen Lung wholesale merchants' firm he joined in 1880.[87]

Upon their release, Foo and his family had been in custody for one week. The hearing would be resumed on April 14th. When it did so, the court learned Foo, unfortunately, was not able to locate the document.[88–90]

Left: Christian Cecil Kohlsaat, Judge, U.S. District Court, Northern District of Illinois. Right: Adolph Marks, prominent Chicago entertainment lawyer engaged to defend the Foo troupe.

However, when Chicago District Court Judge Kohlsaat made his final decision on the matter on April 26th, 1899 he did not refer to Foo's claimed "duly authorized merchant" status, but rather judged the matter on broader terms. In interpreting the 1882 China Exclusion Act, which basically banned Chinese "skilled and unskilled" workers from entering the U.S. and prevented most Chinese in the country from becoming American citizens, Kohlsaat ruled that the act applied narrowly to laborers. Therefore, Ching Ling Foo, as a gentleman and an artist, as well as his troupe, came under the "learned professions" exemption of the Act. Given this, Kohlsaat ruled that the 1882 China Exclusion Act did not apply to Foo and his troupe, and they could tour and perform in the U.S. as long as they wished. Newspapers of the time trumpeted that Kohlsaat had judged Foo an "artist", not a laborer, and that he was thus entitled to stay in the U.S. as long as he pleased.[91,92]

AN IMPORTANT DECISION.
Chinese Actors Can Remain in This Country as Long as They Choose.

CHINESE CONJURER TO STAY.
Ching Ling Foo Discharged from the Custody of Federal Officials.

The judge's ruling, like Foo's arrest and trial, was treated as front page news across the U.S. While most of the coverage seemed to be neutral or favor the decision, there were those that found fault with the decision.

ANOTHER LOOPHOLE MADE.

Not surprisingly, one of these rare voices disappointed with the result emanated from California, home of much intolerance directed towards the Chinese. An editor for the Stockton *Evening Mail* headlined a wire piece setting out Judge Kohlsaat's decision as "Another Loophole Made"—referring, of course, to the China Exclusion Act.[93]

> THE CHINESE EXCLUSION ACT,
> The Chinese exclusion act is being shot so full of holes these days that it is rapidly coming to resemble that kitchen utensil known as a collander.

A more surprising dissent emanated from, of all places, Omaha. The Omaha *World-Herald*, in a lengthy editorial, took issue with Kohlsaat's judgement as providing yet another loophole for what it argued was already pervasive evasion of the Exclusion Act. In the wake of the decision, the newspaper conjured the spectacle of a wave of Chinese proceeding "to learn how to perform a few sleight-of-hand tricks, spout a few lines from some Chinese playwright or thunder across the boards in a tin suit and fierce demeanor. Then he will come to the United States and proceed to open a laundry, enter some kitchen or engage in one of the many vocations pursued by his brethren."[94] The author of the editorial also indicated the likely source of his skepticism when he noted that, of the 300 Chinese admitted under special legislation for the Omaha Exposition, some 225 remained unaccounted for somewhere in the country more than three months after their deadline for return to China.[95,96]

Foo's deportation trial and its outcome even captured the imagination of the English. Britain's premier big theater magazine, *The Era*, noted that "unusual interest has been centered on these performers" and wisely observed that this attempt to deport them and the subsequent trial provided the already extremely popular Foo troupe with added publicity and goodwill.[97]

CHAPTER FIVE

MAY 1899–JANUARY 1900—POST-DEPORTATION TRIAL; PEAK FOO: ACME OF FAME AND FORTUNE

May 1899: New York Keith's Union Square Theater: Foo Troupe Becomes Record-Breaking Sensation

With the Foo troupe now at peak fame, E.F. Albee and B.F. Keith decided to have it forgo the planned initial engagement at their Philadelphia theater and begin Foo's East Coast engagements at Keith's Theater in New York, the entertainment capital of the U.S.[98]

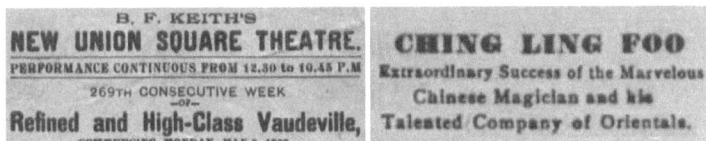

The playbill from Foo's New York debut at Keith's Union Square Theater. "Refined and High Class Vaudeville", "Extraordinary Success of the Marvelous Chinese Magician and his Talented Company of Orientals." Also on the bill: Joe Welch, "the unique Hebrew impersonator."

Thus, within a week of having the deportation charges against them dismissed, the Foo troupe was the leading attraction at Keith's famed Union Square Theatre in New York.[99]

In Foo's second crack at the New York market, his promoters at Keith's made no mistakes. Through an artful combination of talent, timing, and expert promotion, Foo quickly became even more of a "sensation."

Foo was praised for keeping his act fresh by always introducing new tricks. Reviewers gushed that "very few of his illusions ... have ever been presented before by any other magician", and that he kept the audience in "a state of nervous excitement for the entire act."[100] Not long after his Keith's debut, a headline blared "Ching Ling Foo Beats Herrmann." The accompanying article claimed Foo's work had been judged superior to the work of the legendary and beloved Alexander Herrmann, long considered America's greatest magician. Herrmann, who in many ways created the modern, slightly demonic template for a Western stage magician, right down to the moustache and goatee paired with a tight tuxedo, had passed away just two years earlier in 1896.[101]

Struggling for Comparisons to Foo's Impact on the Public, the Press Reaches out for Li Hung Chang

The public adoration of the Foo troupe reached such a peak that the Boston *Globe*, eagerly awaiting the troupe's arrival in Beantown, carried a piece claiming that Foo had created as much of a sensation in New York as Li Hung Chang had when he arrived in the U.S.

Li Hung Chang, envoy of the Chinese Emperor created a stir three years earlier in 1896 when he visited the U.S. Then-President Cleveland met Li personally on Governor's Island when his steamship arrived in New York. Li was feted with a major parade and hundreds of thousands were drawn to the public events and—for the American crowds—exotic pageantry surrounding his visit. *Harper's Weekly* and

Harper's Weekly, September 1896: *The Visit of the Ambassador of China* (T. Dart Walker) and to the left *Yellow Kid* illustrator and cartoonist Richard F. Outcault's cheerful depiction of Li's visit. In Outcault's depiction, the Chinese characters above Li are the Chinese characters for his name Li Hung Chang (李鸿章).

the popular and pioneering Hearst Newspapers' social commentary laden comic strip, the *Yellow Kid*, even got caught up in the excitement surrounding Li's 1896 visit.[102]

Foo Touted as Evidence that the Chinese Exclusion Act May be a Mistake

A week later, the Boston *Herald*, not wishing to be outdone in their professed adoration for Foo, proclaimed, "Ching Ling Foo, the Chinese magician, is proving every day that the immigration commissioner who held him up in Chicago as an alien made the biggest kind of mistake. Ching has turned out to be one of the greatest finds that a theatrical manager has ever run across. He is doing feats of magic that are said to be far ahead of anything yet seen in this country, and New Yorkers are having lots of fun trying to figure out how he does it." The piece ends with the happy news that Foo is billed to appear at Boston's Keith's Theater in the "very near future."[103] In fact, Boston would have to keep waiting, as the Foo troupe's stay at Keith's

Boston papers were flush with ads promoting Foo's imminent arrival. Foo's great friend Kellar would also soon be appearing in Boston. It was truly the age of the stage magician.

Union Square Theater in New York would run for an unprecedented seven weeks.

A further example of the promotion Foo was receiving prior to his troupe's highly anticipated arrival in Boston can be seen in the way his name was peppered through the Boston *Globe*'s entertainment page before Foo even arrived in the city. Similar coverage was appearing in Philadelphia and the other major cities on the American East Coast.

A Top Reviewer Marvels at the Foo Troupe's "Art" and "Tone", "So Absolutely Superior to Others in the Same Line There is No Room for Comparison"

The unprecedented booming of the Foo troupe continued. In its May 1899 edition, the theatrical trade publication *Dramatic* magazine devoted several pages, accompanied by several photographs, to the Ching Ling Foo phenomenon sweeping American vaudeville. The author notes a public lately jaded to stage magic and "grown too wise to be surprised by anything" had made the Foo troupe the vaudeville sensation of the year. Emphasis is given to the fact that Foo's conjuring involves "no mirrors, cabinets, or elaborate accessories." The "extreme simplicity" of the Foo troupe's act was a drawing card. The critic further observed that it is not just Foo's "deftness of touch and rapidity of motion" that captures the audience, but also the fact that the illusions provided by "these Celestials in their rich, flowing robes, and with their strange impassive faces, mystic motions and low-toned foreign utterances" will "savor so strongly of the occult orient", providing a "weird and uncanny" effect.

Foo, "a tall gaunt old magician", is cited as the "cleverest" of the troupe, whose act, in parts "seems to verge upon the supernatural." Praise is also provided for the acrobatic and contortionist work of Foo's "lithe and supple as a snake" 14-year-old son, and the "soubrette role" taken by the toddler Chee Tai, "who sings and poses like a veritable 'Pearl of Pekin.'" Meanwhile, "Madame Ching Ling Foo" is cited as the primary focus of attention of the women in the audience, who marvel at her sensational wardrobe with its "priceless embroideries and silks of exquisite texture." "Madame was a celebrated beauty in the land of far Cathay, and even with our Western standard of loveliness to judge her by, there is an undeniable charm about her delicate olive skin and soft dark eyes and shy, fleeting smile."

Most interestingly the *Dramatic* magazine critic, relatively expert as he was in what worked and what did not in the American vaudeville theaters of the time, recognized that the success of the Foo troupe, while partially attributable to their "extreme novelty", owed much more to other intangible factors. He importantly noted that prior to the Foo's troupe's arrival on American shores, the country's theaters had engaged other "oriental performers", who never caught on in the way the Foo troupe had and "ended their careers in a country circus." He attributed this difference to the "art" of the Foo troupe being "so absolutely superior to the others in the same line that there is no room for comparison." He went on to rhapsodize about the "'tone' and exclusiveness" the Foo troupe have about them, "which show the effect of their imperial environments and introduce us to a new social order of the Chinese." He prophetically concluded "success is sure for these favorites of the 'Son of Heaven.'"[104]

Foo the Technology Pioneer: The First Recordings of Chinese Singing and Music are Made

In the midst of the almost universal adulation accompanying their latest New York tour, Foo, ever eager to uncover and work with new technologies, reportedly partnered with the National Gramophone Company to produce "fifteen Chinese records." These records would later be determined to be the first recordings made of Chinese music and singing. The achievement was chronicled in the nascent recording industry's premier magazine, *The Phonoscope*. The magazine for the new technology proclaimed, "Although these particular records may be unintelligible and unappreciated by most Americans, they are said to be highly entertaining and artistic from a Chinese standpoint."[105] Foo, the polymath and eager adopter of new technologies, thus became the first person to record Chinese music and singing.[106]

Foo Warmly Welcomed Among the Fraternity of Conjurers

The unprecedented level of acclaim being awarded a Chinese magician naturally attracted the attention of America's premiere publication devoted to the conjuring arts and its editors. The venerable *Mahatma* made note of Foo's very successful fifth week as the main attraction at Keith's Union Square Theater. It also noted that the Chinese magician had found time during his busy schedule to make a pilgrimage to New York's famed Martinka's Magic Shop, where he was rightfully impressed by the quality and range of illusions on offer and spent time chatting with the shop's craftsmen and managers. After purchasing several items, Foo then entertained the Martinka employees with some well received impromptu legerdemain.[107]

"Magician's headquarters in America." An ad for the venerable magician apparatus manufacturer.

William Robinson, Soon to be "Chung Ling Soo," Struggles for Success While Foo Soars

The June 1898 edition of *Mahatma* is notable in that in these pages, we see the first pairing in print of Ching Ling Foo and the man who would become his archrival, Chung Ling Soo. While Foo was enjoying unprecedented success on the prestigious 'big time' Keith's circuit, William Robinson—the man who, out of professional desperation, would become Chung Ling Soo—was performing to much less acclaim as "the Man of Mystery", "entertaining New Yorkers with his spiritualistic séances" in far lesser venues. Robinson turned to spiritualism after finishing up a stint just prior to that in Philadelphia, serving as the backup act for the magician Fredrick Powell.[108]

June 1899, Rhode Island: "Chinatown is Stirred to Its Depths"

After seven record-breaking weeks in New York and prior to heading to Boston (the still-eager Bostonians would have to continue to wait), the Foo troupe was booked for the Keith's theater in Providence, Rhode Island the week of June 12th.

Chinatown is stirred to its depths

Prior to his arrival in Rhode Island, the Keith's promotional team seem to have outdone themselves in cleverly reimagining Foo's recent past for best promotional effect. The June 8th, 1899 *Pawtucket Times* carries a major piece with a headline describing Foo the "Great Magician" and "Oriental Wonder" as "a Prince of the Blood" who holds the position of "conjurer to his majesty the Emperor of China." They add a local angle to the story through news of an outreach to the local Chinese community, which they claim is "stirred to its depths" by the Foo story and puzzled that Foo, being a "prince and conjurer to the Emperor", "should have been permitted to come here at all."[109]

CHING LING FOO GREAT MAGICIAN
The Oriental Wonder Will be Seen at Keith's Next Week.

A PRINCE OF THE BLOOD
Conjurer to the Emperor, who Tried Vainly to Force His Return to China.

The article also rewrites Foo's participation in the Omaha Exposition as something that was "secured through the 'pull' of the aforementioned Li Hung Chang", and that after Omaha, Foo was "induced" to appear on the Chicago vaudeville circuit, which was around the time the Chinese Emperor "yearned again to see the wonderful tricks of his conjurer, and through the Chinese embassy, efforts were made to force Ching Ling Foo to return to China." The deportation trial is then fairly accurately described as determining that Foo, as an "artist", was permitted to remain in the country. However, the author playfully added, this was "altogether independent of any understanding that he might have had with the Celestial Emperor when he left home."

The payoff for the Keith promoters in this piece comes next, when the article informs readers that, all this having occurred, the "amazement and interest" of the local Chinese "know no bounds, now that perhaps the greatest conjurer the world has ever known is actually to be here at Keith's next week."[110]

A Word from Boston's Chinese Community

CHINESE MAGICIAN.
Cleverest of All Oriental Wizards Soon to be Seen in Boston at Keith's.

Still patiently waiting for Foo to arrive and eager to run more stories about him, the Boston *Sunday Globe* did its own outreach to Boston's relatively substantial Chinese community. The paper sought to gauge the local Chinese community's feelings about the soon-to-arrive conjurer from their native land, attracting so much attention and confirming rumors that the Boston Chinese community was going to greet Foo with a welcoming feast when he returned to the city.

The responses recorded by the *Globe* ring a bit more authentic than the observations of local Chinese allegedly recorded by the Pawtucket *Times*. While the quoted responses in the Boston paper were recorded in Chinglish, the observers did come off as better informed on the general issues surrounding Foo and his troupe, but not necessarily the details, which may say more about the reporters than the alleged interviewees. One Chinese observer, a major Boston Chinese business figure, noted that there was indeed a "big time" dinner planned for Foo; he was also aware of the problems Foo had had in New York working his children into the act due to child labor laws, and noted—shades of Wu Ting Fang!—that the Chinese Consul of New York had provided Foo with a declaration praising his performance and contribution to U.S.-China relations.[111]

For the rest of the article, what seemed to be the Keith's promotional version of Foo's past was laid out. This included the basics about Foo being a wealthy businessman, which was true, and his work with a major Chinese trading firm with offices in Beijing, Tianjin, and San Francisco. Where the story began to diverge from more credible accounts was in its discussions of when Foo began performing magic professionally and when he took up the study of the art. However, the overall idea that Foo fluctuated between magic and business as a focus for his career, or that the two careers may have in fact supplemented each other, remained correct.

The competing Boston *Herald* newspaper, unwilling to surrender the Foo promotion laurels to the *Globe*, continued its booming with an item claiming Foo, in New York, was achieving what "Herrmann or Kellar never dreamed of doing." Foo was supposed to have been in Boston months ago, but he had "been packing Keith's Union Square Theatre to the doors at every performance and has been subject of columns of attention by the press." The notice then advised that Foo would appear at Keith's Boston theater a week from that Monday.[112]

The piece went on to say that, during the Omaha Exposition, "nobody drew larger crowds than the wonderful" Foo, and that he was quickly deemed "the greatest artist ever sent out from the Orient." "People who had seen all the great magicians looked on in wonder." Then, in an interesting diversion targeted at those articles allegedly revealing Foo's secrets, it addressed the issue of just how Foo's tricks might have been done.

"Investigators went home and tried to figure out how he performed some of his most remarkable tricks, but when they came to see Ching next time, he did the tricks in an entirely different way, and the mystery was greater than ever." The alleged revelations of Foo's methodology and his remarkable success at the Omaha Exposition was once more touted. "Everybody who attended the Omaha Exposition saw Ching Ling Foo. His fame spread throughout the state, and a person who missed his performance at the Omaha Exposition was considered in the same category with the man who went to the Chicago fair and neglected to take a walk through the Midway."[113]

Where the Boston *Herald* account really got interesting was how it recounted what happened during Foo's deportation trial. In this telling, it is B.F. Keith and "his manager Mr. Albee" who saved the day by using their influence to have the case brought up before Judge Kohlsaat, who heard testimony from Foo's many supporters as well as observing a special demonstration of his talents put on for the court. "That was enough. Judge Kohlsaat instantly decided that instead of being an alien, and objectionable, according to the reading of the law, Ching was an artist and a gentleman, whose presence in any country should be considered an honor. He lost no time discharging him from custody, and Mr. Keith at once made arrangements to have the magician journey to New York."

Commenting on Foo's record-breaking success since the deportation trial, the reporter noted that Mr. Keith and Mr. Albee expected good things, but even they "were not prepared for the wonderful enthusiasm of New Yorkers over the startling new feats of magic, with which he made his bow at the Union Square Theatre." The reporter concluded that this unprecedented success and the constant extensions of Foo's New York engagement are what kept him from Boston so long.[114]

The article concluded with yet another interesting diversion into Foo's physical appearance and its impact on his appeal. In this assessment, we have come a long way from the views expressed by the reporter with the New Orleans *Times Picayune*. Here, the Boston reporter notes, "Ching's personal appearance is said to be greatly in his favor. He does not in the least resemble the ordinary Chinese who comes to this country to work in a laundry, but on the contrary, suggests the higher class, and has an air of refinement and dignity about him which at once commands respect."[115] Once more, turn-of-the-century American audiences in the cradle of the world's democracies indicated their preference for foreign performers, at least purportedly sprung from other countries' higher classes or 'castes'—ideally royalty.

June 1899: The Foo Troupe's Providence and other Rhode Island Performances

Ching Ling Foo Is a Wonder and Other
Acts Are Very Pleasing.

Meanwhile, over in Rhode Island, where the Foo troupe was appearing at the local Keith's theater, the local theater critic broke down just how many items Foo "produced" during his first performance in their town. After describing Foo's magic shawl as "an embroidered cloth perhaps four feet square", the author noted that Foo not only made things appear out of nowhere, he actually could make them disappear just as rapidly using the same technique. At Foo's first performance, the Providence audience was treated to the production out of thin air of six different plates of "cakes and bon-bons," a "good sized" bowl of water, and later, "a large vessel containing more than two pails of water."

The review, however, didn't just praise the Foo act. The article also, like similar articles before it, addressed the issue of the problematic "recent alleged exposé" of the magician's work. The author was careful to emphasize that the actual methodology Foo employed to present his illusions "make the recent alleged exposé of his methods seem absolutely absurd."[116]

By this point on the tour, Foo's assistant and juggler was winning audiences and beginning to enjoy his own recognition. Harry Foo had, been working on his English during his months in America, and now could provoke "several laughs by his unexpected discharges of English slang" during his juggling exhibition, which was rated "marvelous." Harry's act involved tossing an "immense earthenware vessel that would hold at least half a bushel, throwing it high in the air" and catching it, still spinning, "upon his forehead, where he balances it in various positions." Foo's son Foo Quai further entertained the crowd with his plate spinning, acrobatics, and contortion feats that were "the best ever seen here."

In one variation of the act, which does not seem to have been repeated often, Harry and Foo Quai even sang a few Chinese songs accompanied by "weird" Chinese instruments. Chee Tai, for her part, reliably "captured the hearts of ladies by her cuteness and her singing of several songs in English." Once again, the Foo troupe's supporting cast was judged as being "quite as remarkable as is Ching himself in his own field."

At the conclusion of the act, the Providence crowd could not get enough. "Foo was recalled again and again to respond to the enthusiastic applause that greeted the marvelous work not only of himself but of his entire troupe."[117]

Pioneering Journalist Mildred Irving Calls on the Great Chinese Magician

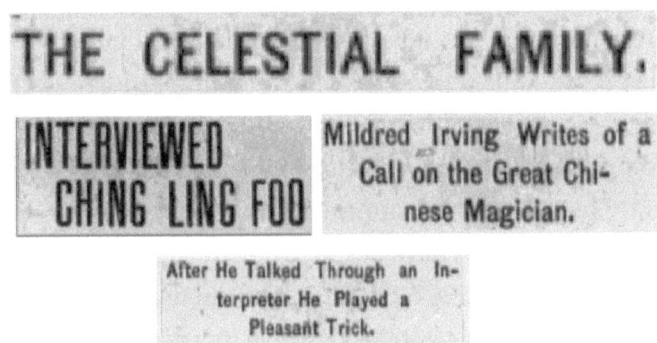

While in Rhode Island, the Foos granted what would become one of their iconic interviews. Well-known reporter Mildred Irving began by describing the "delicate aromatic odor" that greeted her nostrils when she arrived at Foo's dressing room at the Keith's theater in Pawtucket. She noted that "it was no laundry smell" and "there is nothing 'dopey' about these bright, high caste" Chinese. Indeed, she described Moy Frederic Sang, who is still on hand to provide translation services, as an "interesting" man who speaks so many languages "he is kind of walking higher education."

She began the interview by utilizing the Mandarin Chinese phrase for "How do you do?": "How lah mah?" Her apt usage of the phrase, taught to her by Moy while she was arranging the interview, pleasantly "startled" Foo and set a good tone for their talk.

In Irving's eyes, Foo, although he was "a giant in stature ... has the grace and polish of a Chesterfield."[118] Foo's status as a wealthy businessman in China was extolled, as were his many shops in Shanghai, Beijing, and Tianjin, along with his "heavy interest in a large concern in San Francisco." The San Francisco company referred to was likely the already-noted Wah Yuen Lung Trading Company. Once more, Foo's professed noble blood was put forward. The magician, Irving's audience learned, had "the bluest blood in the Celestial Empire" and moved in the "inner circle of its '400.'" Foo's wife, for her part, was described as "one of the first ladies of the land."

Partially in response to this, Irving then raised the delicate question as to whether it was not somewhat "inconsistent" for a man of Foo's purported "financial and social standing" to be "performing in public as a magician." Moy, responding to this query, explained that Foo's personal wealth was not inconsistent with his performing, as in China it was not unusual for wealthy men to dabble in magic. While this might have been true, Moy then went a bit too far when he claimed that in China, Foo performed only at the pleasure of "the Emperor or other notables." While this may have warmed the hearts of those in the cheaper seats at the Shanghai Lyceum, it was clearly not the case. Moy may have come closer to the truth when he described Foo as a man who had a passion for magic and had learned to profitably "combine business with pleasure." There was no question Foo was both a skilled successful businessman and a master magician.

As the interview ended, Foo took his leave and stated the reporter was a bright and "pretty young lady." Irving, deciding to return the compliment, replied that Foo was "the most refined and cultured and remarkable" Chinese man she, within her "wide circle of acquaintances," had ever met. After Moy translated these thoughts, according to Irving, Foo smiled "a smile so broad" that even the great magician himself could not have concealed it on his person.

Irving rose from her seat to leave and discovered a box of sweets as big as a hat box had magically appeared on her chair. The "little Chinese family chattered and laughed." After exchanging goodbyes at the door Harry Foo, the juggler-comedian, looked out, and with a "jolly laugh and a comical gesture" cried "Search me!" On her time spent with the Foos, Irving concluded, all in all, that even without the bon-bons "It was one of the most pleasant interviews I ever had."[119]

That same day, the industrious Irving filed yet another story on the Foo troupe, this time providing a review of the stage performance. After declaring she had seen each performance the troupe had provided in Providence, she lauded Foo's conjuring work as done differently each time and added although they may have appeared simple, his tricks were actually the "most wonderful and difficult" illusions that had ever been offered for Rhode Island's "mystification." Fulsome praise was also directed towards the rest of the troupe.[120]

"A Man of Culture": A Boston Globe Reporter Declares Foo "Gives One a Better Idea of the Chinese Than I Have Ever Had Before"

Meanwhile, the Boston papers, still waiting for their crack at the Foo phenomenon and breathlessly waiting for his premiere on June 19th, continued to provide yeoman like service in promoting the magician. The latest item to find its way into the Boston *Globe* on June 17th reported "a New York man who visited Ching Ling Foo ... in his dressing room" and assessed that Foo is "one of the most intelligent" Chinese men he has ever met and "a man of culture." The paper's correspondent went on to add that Foo "gives one a better idea of the Chinese than I have ever had before." He even noted that the incense Foo burned was "the real stuff" and not the "imitation we get in this country."[121]

Foo, "whom all the other magicians and illusionists bow to as the master", "does the same trick differently each time you see him." These ads for the Foo troupe appeared in the Boston papers on the eve of Foo's engagement.

Not to be outdone, the Boston *Herald* the same day informed its status-conscious readership that the "giant", "very imposing in appearance" Foo, who was a "leading merchant" in China, had performed before the Emperor, and sprang from one of that country's "best families."[122]

The next day, the Boston *Globe* informed its eager readers that Foo, "who has a quiet dignity that commands respect and admiration", would appear in Boston the next day. It was anticipated that if he generated as much of a sensation in Boston as he had in New York and Omaha, he would likely remain in their city over the summer.

Further information was also provided on what transpired immediately after Foo's deportation trial, and it was reported that the Keith's theaters outbid the Chicago theaters who were also anxious to engage the Foo troupe after the burst of publicity that attended the deportation trial.[123]

For the Children

That same day in the Boston *Sunday Post*, an interesting promotion for Foo's imminent engagement in the city focused on the Foo troupe's appeal to children, who, along with their mothers, were an increasingly important and devoted portion of the "polite" vaudeville audience. The writer noted that while Foo was generally conceded to be the greatest magician ever to come to the U.S. from the Orient, Foo "himself seems to be more interested in pleasing the children" than anything else.

The reporter went on to recount the story of one of Boston's few Chinese children, in this case "the son of a leading merchant on Harrison Avenue," who had written the conjurer a letter a week earlier and was delighted when he'd received a reply—which the reporter, having come into the possession of, published with this article. The Chinese script written by Foo in reply to the boy was translated "I, Ching Ling Foo, prince conjurer to the Emperor of China, will soon appear in Boston at Mr. Keith's Theatre to make happy the men and women and little boys and girls by doing strange things that I do for the Emperor of the Celestial kingdom, and more wonderful than any other magician of any race has ever shown to the good people of the United States. Come and see me and my troupe. Ching Ling Foo."[124]

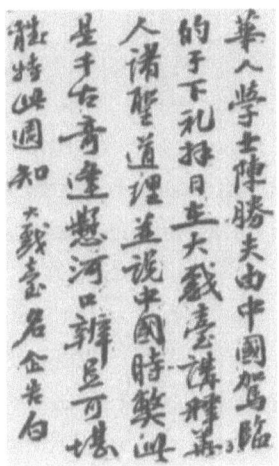

"I, Ching Ling Foo, prince conjurer to the Emperor of China, will soon appear in Boston ..."

To emphasize the novelty of the letter, the author went to great lengths to explain that, to that date, Foo had never allowed any document he had written in Chinese characters to fall into the hands of anyone outside his circle. So, the letter shared with the Boston *Sunday Post's* readers was therefore an object of great value and interest.

Addressing potential questions that might arise in a cynical mind as to whether Foo's management was involved in the Boston newspaper getting hold of the letter, the author stated "Its present possessor does not admit that it was secured from Ching Ling Foo with any collusion between himself" and the Chinese person to whom it was sent. The reporter, realizing that the best booming is a mutually understood collaboration between the targets and the perpetrators, then added with a wink, "but there are press agents and press agents, and no one can be denied a right to an opinion."[125] For those rare vaudeville habitués prone to such things, a cynical "opinion" might have been formed rather quickly if they had learned that the exact same letter and surrounding storyline had been published in Rhode Island papers, promoting Foo's show at the Providence Theater a few weeks earlier. Clearly, as the *Post* reporter warned, "there are press agents and there are press agents", and when it came to "booming", the Foo troupe had some of the best.

No doubt one of the reasons the Foo troupe performance did have a particular allure for the little ones was because two key members of the famed troupe were, in fact, children themselves.

Foo's son and daughter were described as "two of the most amusing members of the troupe", who, with their colorful costumes and delightful acts, had become "great favorites with the little folk" during their recent record-breaking New York run. Foo's daughter Chee Tai was especially popular because of her demure manner, her surprising capacity for mimicry, and her impressive rendition of popular English songs.

Cissy Loftus: Chee Tai's Early Role Model

Interestingly, given Chee Tai's evident talents, it is fascinating to learn at this early age—natural mimic that she was—the little girl felt a special bond with the performer Cissy Loftus, whose fame was on a par with Foo's at the time and whose specialty was mimicry. While

Chee Toy's early role model: vaudeville star, Scottish singer, and mimic Cissy Loftus (1876–1943), painted by Toulouse Lautrec and adored by Max Beerbohm.

the Foo troupe was performing in New York and sharing a bill with Loftus on several occasions while she was in the midst of performing, little Chee Tai would toddle out on stage to join the act. Loftus would take the adorable child into her arms and the audiences were sent into "raptures of delight."[126] As far as mimicry went, little Chee Tai, always eagerly watching from the wings, learned from the best.

Foo's Illusion Secrets (Allegedly) Revealed Again

Amidst all this positive media coverage, there were some outlets—not at the time on the positive end of B.F. Keith's advertising dollars—that seemed keen on spoiling the party. The day before Foo's much-anticipated opening in Boston, some newspapers in other parts of the country, also eager to cash in on the great interest generated by Foo, published illustrated exposés of some of Foo's major tricks, including the "great bowl trick."

The very same day, the Boston *Herald* directly addressed the spoilsports. The paper acknowledged that most people believe the objects produced by Foo are hidden earlier somewhere on the magician's person, but noted that in a recent performance, Foo "astonished" the audience and stage hands by sporting tight-fitting clothing and pulling

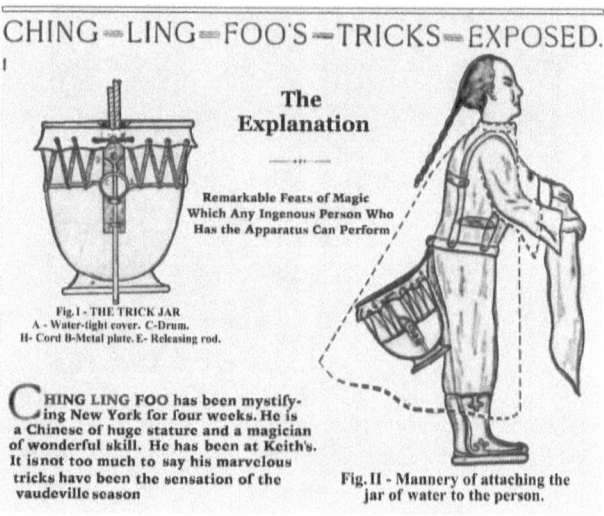

Enhanced composite drawn from a Foo "exposé" of June 1899.

it close to his body to illustrate it could contain no bulky objects. Foo then did a running somersault in the tight-fitting clothing, leapt into a few somersaults on the floor, and came up holding a big bowl of water containing goldfish. It was then stressed that Foo changes his method of doing the same trick nearly every performance.[127] The Boston *Post* filed a similar rebuke to the revelationists.[128]

At Long Last, Foo Finally Opens in Boston, Takes City "By Storm"; "Orientalism"

All this coverage only heightened anticipation for Foo's opening night in Boston, and when the long-awaited event finally arrived on June 20th, 1899, it did not disappoint. The Boston papers were unanimous, based on the evidence of what they had seen, that the Foo troupe would take Boston "by storm" the same way they had taken New York and other cities. Particular note was taken of the "surprising gracefulness" with which Foo performed his illusions. Also noteworthy was the performance of Foo's son, who managed the trick of juggling while standing on his head. Due note was also made of Harry Foo's ability to spin an "immense bowl in the air" and catch it "on his chin all while it was still going around at a good rate." Little Chee Tai merited mention as well, mostly because of her endearing "coyness" "that made the ladies and children applaud", while "Mrs. Ching", alongside her "big husband", proved to be "a very pleasant and good looking Chinese woman with feet so small she seemed to walk around with difficulty." The Boston reviewers were unanimous in concluding that Foo, regardless of what spoilsports in other cities may have claimed, "is a wonder" and "those who miss him are losing a treat."[129]

The warm embrace of the Foos in Boston continued into the following week, when the Boston *Herald* published a tribute to the Foo troupe awash in Orientalism. First, informing his readership of the received knowledge that "it is out of the Far East that marvels come", the author acknowledged the "oriental" as "master" of the "cleverest tricks of legerdemain" and "the graceful magic that baffled and mystified their ancestors when the world was much younger than it is now." The author went on to note that the "oriental atmosphere" of the show added greatly to its "charm" and that the "solemn and priest-like" Foo, "who might be Confucius himself", transformed the stage "with the richness and splendor of his accessories" into a "picturesque scene" which was only amplified when the other members of the troupe joined him.

Taking a breath, the journalist took a more quotidian interest in the quality of porcelain the troupe was transporting across the country with them. "Collectors of rare porcelain will be loath to let those Chinese jars which the juggler tosses about as if they were made of paper out of Boston. I would like to know where Ching Ling Foo keeps that black and white one with the vermillion decoration nights."[130] But in keeping with the Orientalist theme, the vases were not the only thing the author coveted for her curio cabinet. "The Chinese baby that sings and dances ... is a darling little object that the spectator wants to secure for her cabinet of treasures."[131] She notes that one of Foo's prettiest tricks was the production from beneath the cloth of "little Chee Wai", who "makes a hit every performance."[132]

Evidently not wishing to leave out any turn-of-the century trope concerning the Chinese, the author concluded with a nod to the (very popular at the time) concept of "Chinese stagnation": "anything seems possible with these extraordinary people, who advanced far beyond this era, and yet have stood still hundreds of centuries."[133]

Dangers of Hosting Fire-Breathing Acts in 19th-Century Theaters

In Boston, Foo, as during his previous engagements, treated his audiences to his salamandrine fire-breathing act, much to the delight of the crowds—and in one precarious instance, no little excitement for the back-stage crew.

During one demonstration of this talent, according to a man who was a teenage usher at the time, Foo was at the edge of the Keith's theater stage in the midst of his fire-breathing demonstration, spitting fireballs from his mouth when some of the burning projectiles sprayed so far from the conjurer's mouth they landed underneath an "apron" placed on the edge of the stage where (popular at the time but highly flammable) palm-leaf fans were stored. The observant usher, witnessing what was transpiring from his unique angle up on the theater's second gallery, leapt unseen from the balcony onto the far edge of the stage, slipped under the stage apron, and smothered the nascent flames with his coat. The show went on, the crowd was none the wiser, and the heroic usher later received the commendations of Foo and a hand-written letter from the old man, B.F. Keith himself.[134]

By the second week of Foo's engagement the growing crowds that come to see the troupe only seem to result in more crowds. The remarkable capacity of the troupe to generate return business week after week was put to the troupe's capacity to continually vary their act providing "a surprise at almost every performance" despite performing twice a day.[135]

Foo Troupe Members Develop Their Own Fan Base

This capacity to always offer something new led Foo to begin the third week in Boston sharing the stage and billing with the Boston

Symphony Orchestra. The supporting members of the Foo troupe were now known so well to the Boston crowds "each now receives a welcome on his or her appearance."[136]

In a testament to little Chee Tai's growing fame, it was acknowledged that the Boston crowds loved Ching Ling Foo, but "it was not until little Chee Tai toddled in on the stage, with a hop skip and a jump, that the enthusiasm and laughter reached the limit." The "so cute" Chee Tai had become "the special favorite of all the ladies and children."[137] In fact, the Foo troupe's popularity with children was such that theater parties made up exclusively of large numbers of ladies and children "were a fad" during their Boston engagement.[138]

As a testament to Chee Tai's increasing popularity and fame, stories setting out the legal issues surrounding her ability to perform on stage in light of recent child welfare and work laws were published across the country.[139]

Soon the Foo troupe was into an almost unprecedented fourth week of their Boston engagement—one of the longest engagements Boston's Keith's Theater had ever had. With regard to Foo's production tricks, people, despite the plethora of explanations, were happy to understand that the only solution was that he was "in some inconceivable way" concealing these articles on his person. They knew they were being fooled, but they also knew they were being fooled by a charismatic and engaging master of deception. The mechanics of the illusions were secondary to the joyful experience the troupe put forward, and the Boston audience, happy with the bargain, continued to pay well and repeatedly for the privilege.

Each member of the Foo troupe received their time in the spotlight and in their fourth week in Boston it turned to "Mrs. Foo." Hai Quai was deigned one of the most interesting members of the troupe even though reports acknowledged she does not do much due to her clothes and her tiny feet; "probably the smallest that have ever been seen on a grown woman in Boston."

While in Boston the Foo troupe only added to their appeal when they charitably participated in a fund raiser for Boston's Holy Ghost Hospital which thousands attended.[140] Both of the Foo troupe's U.S. tours would be marked by ready tendency to contribute their services to worthy causes.

July 1899, Philadelphia

After spending fourteen weeks in Chicago, seven weeks in New York, and six weeks in Boston, the Foo troupe arrived in Philadelphia. The Philadelphia *Inquirer* welcomed the Chinese magician to their city by proclaiming "never in the history of vaudeville has any performer created more of a sensation than has Ching Ling Foo." The paper then went overboard, no doubt with the eager aid of Keith's promotional department press agents, in claiming Foo "for a decade" was the "chief entertainer" for the Emperor of China, and that the same Emperor "declares that all the magicians China has produced in a thousand years have not equaled the work of Ching." The paper touched another Chinese cornerstone in the Philadelphia public's limited knowledge of China when Li Hung Chang was, as in Boston, also brought into the promotional mix.

"The Greatest Magician in the Universe", "The Most Popular Child That Has Appeared on Any Stage"

Readers were somewhat fancifully informed that after the aforementioned Li Hung Chang's triumphant tour of the Europe and North America, wherein the famed senior Chinese diplomat sampled the best magicians of both continents, he urged Ching Ling Foo to come to North America to demonstrate China's leadership in the conjuring field. The paper added that Foo had duplicated "all his predecessors' most marvelous feats" as well as having "tricks not in the repertoire

1899 Promotional Keith's ad and photo of the Foo troupe. Tiny, adorable "Chee Tai" stands between Foo and her mother.

of any other conjurer", and, considering all this, he was "probably the greatest magician in the universe."[141,142] Who could argue with that?

Foo's shows in Philadelphia were once again met with record attendance, with crowds being turned away when even standing room was no longer available. People even travelled from Atlantic City to attend the performances. One such "Foo party" consisted of 23 people.[143] Chee Tai, the ever-absorbent mimic, now not only sang English songs but also does the latest Western dances during her performances. She is declared "the most popular youngster that has ever appeared on any stage."[144]

Harry Foo, Foo's "humorous assistant", also continued to increase in popularity and was described as "a whole show in himself." Sharing the bill with Foo, "the Herrmann of the Orient," in Philadelphia were the Robert Downing company performing an excerpt of the popular play *Gladiator* and a one-man show in which the performer H.V. Fitzgerald took on 30 different parts, including "a whirl of costume changes." The bill was filled out with "Irish character impersonations," comedians, hand balancers, a mimic, a "comic instrumentalist," and what was sure to have been a crowd favorite: "those intrepid acrobats, the Four Florences."[145]

The Cinderella Promotions Continue

One particularly high-profile aspect of the Foo troupe's Philadelphia engagement was a continuation of their highly successful "Cinderella" promotion that played upon that popular fairy tale and the American fascination with Chinese 'small feet' women. Mrs. Foo's feet, which had been bound in the traditional manner, were just five inches long. Once more, articles calling upon "all you modern Cinderellas" were placed in the press, offering a one-hundred-dollar reward to the woman who could successfully wear the tiny silk slippers worn by Ching Ling Foo's wife.

The articles, of course, emphasized Mrs. Foo was a "high-born" Chinese lady and that—not entirely accurately—"in the land of the Celestials the small foot is a sign of noble birth." The notice concluded that while the hundred-dollar challenge was open to all "American women", this did not include "any freaks, such as a woman of mature years who is only twelve inches high."[146] It would be left to Foo's second American tour to address the more serious implications of foot binding.

"Now All You Modern Cinderellas!" Enhanced, reconfigured Cinderella promotion from the Foo troupe's August 1899 Philadelphia engagement. The paper printed the shoe "life-size".

All this success—and the subsequent attention Foo had been receiving—naturally tweaked the interest of European theater promoters always eager to showcase an exceptionally popular act. Expressions of interest to engage Foo for a European tour were received by Foo's managers in America.[147]

Foo's second week in Philadelphia included an entirely new supporting bill, including entertainment inspired by one of America's newly acquired territories. The "Hawaiian Queens" performed a unique 18-minute operetta, entitled *King Moo's Wedding Day*. In addition, theatergoers were treated to a "little comedy" called *One Wife Too Many* and, in a nod to the new technology disrupting the entertainment world, "American Biograph" moving pictures.[148]

August 1899: Back to New York

By mid-August, Keith's management had the Foo troupe back at their New York Union Square theater. Once the troupe was ensconced in the theater, one of the odder instances in the Foo troupe's history unfolded. During their first week back, "Little Charlie," the lead singer of the popular Rossow Lilliputian little people act, caused much discussion among the press and the public when he was deemed to be taking too much of an interest in little Chee Tai. Charlie's attention to Ching Ling Foo's daughter "created no little comment."[149]

Lafayette would well profit from his time sharing a stage with Foo. The great mimic would develop a Foo "travesty" that would become a mainstay of his act for years. The list of those who shared a stage with Foo and then developed a parody of him due to his popularity is quite long.

Others on the bill with the Foo troupe in New York included John Rice and Sally Cohen who performed a musical comedy called *The Kleptomaniacs*.[150] Foo's return to New York was so successful, the troupe was granted a continuation of an "indefinite period" by Keith's management.[151] Most of the acts surrounding Foo at Keith's theater at this point consisted of skits or "short plays."[152]

Also during this period, it was reported that Ted Marks, a well-established theater agent, had been in New York continuing European theater managers' efforts to secure some British and European dates for the Foo troupe. Negotiations, however, finally fell through, and Marks returned to England unsuccessful.[153]

Foo Still Making at Minimum a Thousand a Week

A piece appeared in the Washington *Times* in mid-September relaying the startling news that Foo's salary was at minimum $1,000 per week (approximately $31,000 a week in 2020 dollars).[154] On the same page announcing Foo's imminent arrival in Washington, ads are prominently displayed for "Prof. Gentry's Famous Dog and Pony Show", comprising "100 acting dogs, 75 performing ponies, 25 grimacing monkeys, and Pinto and Satan, the two smallest performing elephants in existence."[155]

"The Hit of the Decade": Private Performances by Foo Status Symbol for the New York "400"

The Foo troupe's popularity was sustained and even magnified during their triumphant return to the New York stage. The Foo troupe was now regularly referred to by people in the vaudeville industry as "the hit of the decade."

Similar to what happened during the troupe's tenure in Omaha but on a grander scale, the social elite of New York—what was known as the "Gotham 400"—not satisfied with having to witness Foo's wonders while rubbing shoulders with the hoi polloi, arranged private showings inviting Ching Ling Foo and his assistants to their homes to entertain family and friends.[156]

Chinese in Popular Entertainment: "The King of the Opium Ring" and Others—A Profusion of Chinese-Themed Plays

Things Asian now being a bit of a fad, a Broadway theater near the Keith's offered those who missed a seat at Foo's performance a chance to take in *King of the Opium Ring*. This play was originally produced a New York's Academy of Music and promised much-sensationalized revelations of "what really happens" in America's Chinatowns.[157] Throughout the Foo troupe's tour of the U.S., *King of the Opium Ring*, like a moon to the Foo troupe's sun, could be found doing a run not far from the theater in which the Foo troupe was performing its act. Beyond *King of the Opium Ring*, there were several other of these allegedly thematically Chinese plays attracting good audiences during the Foo troupe's first U.S. tour. One could experience *A Night in Chinatown* or *French Maids in Chinatown*, which presented itself as a satire on the more popular *King of the Opium Ring*, to list but a few.[158]

King of the Opium Ring was set in 1890 San Francisco. It featured some Chinese performers and purported to present a broad view of Chinese life, and very importantly, "the Chinese character as it is." However, it was actually more focused on the depiction of how opium is smuggled into the U.S. by Chinese gangs of "highbinders" and how the "opium fiends" consume it.[159,160] Meanwhile, the lead performer in *A Night in Chinatown*, billed as "Ling Ching Foo", precedes William Robinson by several months in adopting a name that would easily be confused with Ching Ling Foo. *A Night in Chinatown* ran for 200 nights on Broadway. As regards the play, it again played to the Chinese tropes of the times.

A review of the play in Harrisburg, Pennsylvania noted that many of its principal scenes take place in Ling Foo Ching's "opium joint, showing society's elite (to use the vernacular) hitting the pipe." Police arrive to make arrests and everything is dramatically transformed into a Salvation Army prayer meeting to deceive them. This scene allegedly "created a furor in the metropolis."[161]

Things got worse with *French Maids in Chinatown*, which apparently had the dubious honor of making *A Night in Chinatown* seem refined. Billed as a "celestial spectacular," a burlesque, and a satire on the more popular *King of the Opium Ring*, *French Maids in Chinatown* told the story of a 16-year-old girl from small town America, the daughter of a wealthy silk manufacturer and about to be married to a bank cashier, who flees her drab Midwestern life for New York and the excitement of Chinatown. Her father and fiancé then travel to New York to find her, but once physically in the locale, they too are caught up in the seductive whirl of Chinatown.

"Degenerates of All Classes"

Maids was promoted as introducing a "genuine novelty" through its presentation of an "opium joint in full operation, wherein the degenerates of all classes congregate to indulge in the flowing vapor of the Poppy plant and other midnight orgies." Apart from "degenerates of all classes", the play also featured the "Joss House," "the police raid," and a very popular at the time anti-Chinese trope: a young white woman from a good family under the hypnotic spell of a Chinese villain. "Soubrette" was a term used at the time to refer to young attractive woman playing a lively role in theater play or opera. At that time, opium and proximity to Chinese men were thought to be particularly dangerous for young European women.

In the context of all this reimagining of the Chinese "other" in Chinatown, one review of *French Maids in Chinatown* interestingly

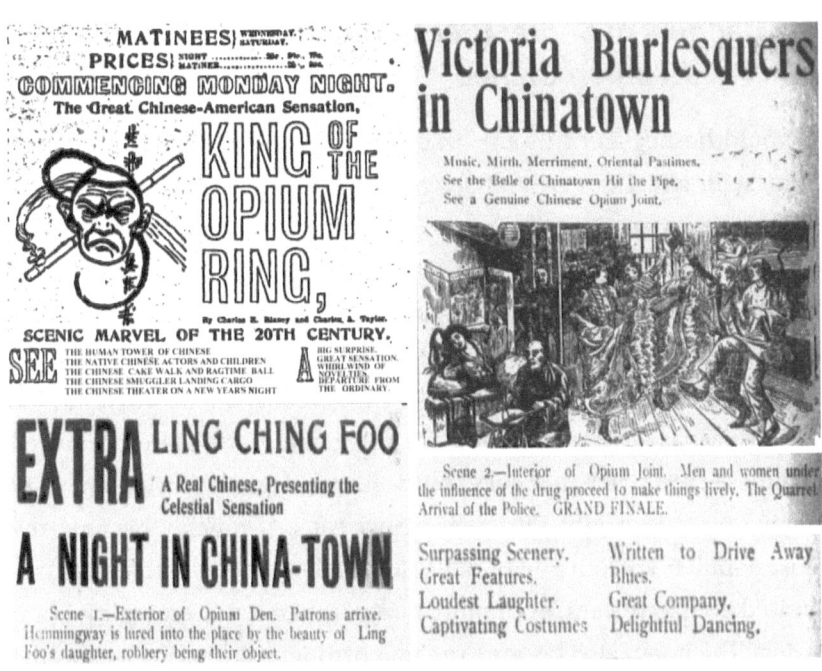

A Night in Chinatown and *King of the Opium Ring*, just two of the China-themed entertainments that tended to orbit the Foo troupe's performances.

refers to Chinatown as a place where "you lose your own identity."[162] "A night in Chinatown means for you to lose your own identity" and disappear into its "mysteries." Clearly, for many Americans at the end of the 19th century, losing "your own identity" had a certain appeal.

Reviews of *French Maids in Chinatown* tended towards the harsh. One reviewer referred to it as "a third-class burlesque, rendered very poorly." The assessment was made in the context of a comparison to *A Night in Chinatown*, which was in comparison promoted as something for a more "refined taste" than the apparently crude *French Maids in Chinatown*.

However, A quick glance at the ads for *A Night in Chinatown* and *The Opium King*, below, demonstrate that even these entertainments, when it came to representations of the Chinese in the late 1890s, as far as refinement went, had not set the bar too high.

The Dangers of Satire: Bret Harte and "The Heathen Chinee"

It would be negligent in any assessment of the presentation of the Chinese in late 19th-/early-20th century American popular media the Foo troupe encountered to ignore the influential ur-text of American popular attitudes towards the Chinese: Bret Harte's phenomenon "Plain Language from Truthful James". This was the hugely popular spoken poem better known to history as "The Heathen Chinee".

This post-Gold Rush tale was first published in 1870 in the California-based *Overland Monthly* Magazine. Harte's poem featured a Chinese card sharp, not very subtly named Ah Sin, putting one over on two not-too-bright European Americans. It quickly became the most popular "spoken poem" of its time and made Harte the most celebrated poet of the era, even more popular than a still-emerging Mark Twain. The poem also became the touchstone for America's—and the broader English language-speaking world's—view of the Chinese for over 50 years.

Given its enormous popularity, "The Heathen Chinee" was omnipresent in late 19th- and early 20th-century America. Above: two images from an illustrated version of the popular poem used in 1872 to promote the Rock Island and Pacific Railroad are employed to frame the full text of the poem. The actual Rock Island illustrated version of the poem, provided free to travelers, comprised eleven illustrated panels.

The wildly popular "Heathen Chinee" was published and republished, often with helpful stereotypical illustrations, in newspapers and magazines around the U.S. and Europe for years. Unfortunately for the Chinese, Harte's satirical tone for the poem, intended as a critique of what he considered the irrational anti-Chinese sentiment of the time and prevalent in his home state of California, flew over the heads of the vast majority of its readership. Harte, who was also the editor of the *Overland Monthly* Magazine and a rare critic of the ill treatment of Chinese in his home state, instead saw the poem read as confirmation of prevailing anti-Chinese sentiments, which saw the Chinese as alien, duplicitous, immune to assimilation, and dangerously crafty.

The poem's general readership, most of whom would never actually meet a Chinese person in their lives, blithely ignored the fact that Bill Nye, the rougher ("white labor" representative) of the poem's two European-American characters, with his sleeves "stuffed full of aces and bowers", clearly intended to cheat Ah Sin out of his money, and that Nye's companion, the more urbane Truthful James, was more than willing to participate in the scheme. Ignoring this, most readers in the economically uncertain 1870s instead fixed on Nye's claim that "we are ruined by Chinese cheap labor" and Truthful James's general assessment of Chinese character, which would be endlessly quoted for the decades that followed: "That for ways that are dark and for tricks that are vain, the heathen Chinee is peculiar."

In the years that followed, bolstering stump speeches with select snippets from "The Heathen Chinee" became standard practice among politicians and representatives of groups like the Working Man's Party when rallying public opinion to support various anti-Chinese policies. The anti-Chinese sentiments thus fueled included the many anti-Chinese laws passed in the California state legislature, and culminated in the Chinese Exclusion Act of 1882, passed by the U.S. Congress and reluctantly signed by President Chester A. Arthur.

> **Shea's Garden Theater.**
> "For ways that are dark and tricks that are vain."
> The Heathen Chinee is peculiar.
> When Bret Harte penned these immortal lines he had probably never seen Ching Ling Foo, the Chinese magician who has filled Shea's Garden Theater for a week and is just starting another record-breaking dozen performances. Ching Ling Foo makes Bret Harte's Chinese sentiments look like a half-hatched chicken compared to a full grown turkey gobbler. Mr. Ching Ling Foo defies description. He mystifies beyond explanation. At the end of the present season it is said he will go back to his heathen country and live in luxury on his American-made money in the mysterious city of Pekin. If the Empress of China is looking for a new juggler for the throne, or for some one to fill the shoes and yellow jacket of Li Hung Chang, Ching Ling will be open for a job. If his Buffalo performances can be taken for a criterion, the Russian bear would do well to beware, for if he hangs around Ching Ling he may suddenly find himself converted into a dish of chop suey.

"These immortal lines." A typical sample from late in Foo's first tour of the almost reflexive references to the Heathen Chinee Foo's presence elicited.

Thirty to forty-five years, later during both Foo's tours of America, rare would be the local or national reporter who would be able to resist the temptation to reference the "Heathen Chinee" with his "ways that are dark" and "his tricks that are vain" when writing of Foo.

Harte, lionized as a national poet and once considered the equal of his more enduring contemporary Mark Twain, in his later years continued writing voluminously, if not as commercially successfully as before, and died in England in 1902.

Harte's final assessment of "The Heathen Chinee": "trash" and "the worst poem I or anyone else had ever written."[163]

The Chinese Government Officially Recognizes Foo's Contribution to U.S.-China Relations

In the face of this sort of constant negative representations of Chinese in American popular culture, it is no wonder Foo's old friend from Omaha, Wu Ting Fang, the Chinese Minister Plenipotentiary in Washington, found the wholesome Foo family-centered troupe, with its focus on "magic, mirth and melody", such a relative breath of fresh air and its warm reception across the U.S. such a relief.

Given the Foo troupe's success in presenting a somewhat more positive view of the Chinese, it was not surprising then that official Chinese government recognition for Foo, no doubt directed by Wu came Foo's way. In late August of 1899, the *New York* Times

The imperial flag presented to Foo would have looked something like this.

would report the Empress of China had an imperial dragon flag presented on stage to Foo by Chinese officials in recognition of his achievements while in the U.S.[164] Meanwhile, Foo's tenure at Keith's New York theater was once more extended. Foo, as the New York *World* newspaper reports, having "proved worthy to remain as long as he wishes."[165]

William Robinson, Apparently Not Understanding 19th-Century Vaudeville Promotion Methodology, Accepts Foo's Bowl Challenge, is Disappointed When Turned Down; Mahatma Shares His Sorrow

It was while in New York during this tour that Foo would have his first pivotal conflict with the aforementioned William Robinson that would, according to some observers, serve as the essential trigger to Robinson's later decision to transform himself into Chung Ling Soo, the 24-hour travesty of Foo and his family Robinson constructed in London.

It was during this New York engagement that Foo's promotion team issued the fateful challenge offering $1,000 to anyone who could duplicate Foo's great bowl trick.[166] At the time, it was seemingly a risky gesture. $1,000 was an enormous sum and several versions of how to do Foo's bowl trick were already in circulation amongst professional magicians, and available for modest price.

"Ching Ling Foo offers $ 1,000 to anyone who can duplicate his great bowl trick."

According to *Mahatma*, the industry bible of professional American magicians, the ever-enterprising William Robinson seized on the apparent opportunity to make some fast money and took Foo up on his aforementioned public challenge. The way *Mahatma* recounts the tale, William Robinson approached Foo's management at the Union Square Theater and offered to duplicate the bowl production feat, but his offer was refused. The magazine reported that witnesses had seen Robinson do the trick and that he did it as well as Foo.[167,168]

Not satisfied with this turn of events at all, the somewhat jingoistic *Mahatma* editors felt compelled to keep addressing the matter in multiple later editions of their publication and additionally directly called upon *Mahatma* readers who had the gear to take Foo's money and "call his bluff."[169] Despite the encouragements of *Mahatma*, no other formal challenger appeared to come forward.[170]

In that same month, the furor surrounding the bowl challenge having subsided, *Mahatma* reported that the newsworthy Foo would soon add to his act a new illusion wherein "knives and other hardware will protrude from his mouth nose and eyes." However, when Foo performed the illusion before his New York audience, it was seen as more distasteful and disturbing than entertaining. Interestingly, Foo's original audiences in the Midwest responded to reports on this alleged sensitivity of the big-city "Eastern audiences" to these new illusions with amusement. "The Eastern people objected to his realistic trick of a sharp knife being run through his nose and the act was cut out."[171,172]

As to the matter of passing objects through parts of the body, in describing Foo's use of the magic rings, Guy Jarrett, a preeminent designer of illusions who had met Foo on several occasions, wrote that Foo, apart from an uncanny ability to manipulate them in the normal fashion—having them merge and separate, turn in the air, and return—also had the ability to appear to run Chinese linking rings through a hole in his cheek. However, this, like his attempts to incorporate an illusion where he passed a knife through his nose, apparently proved too graphic for East Coast audiences.[173]

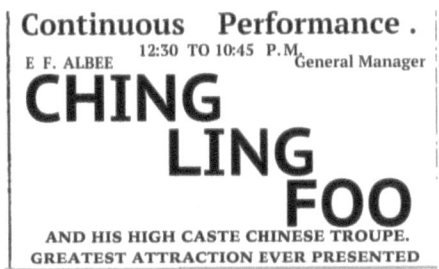

Foo's "High Caste Chinese Troupe." In the bustling, ambitious, and ever-expanding America of the 1890s, average Americans liked to think of themselves on par with foreign royalty. Hence all the foreign "nobility" populating the vaudeville stage.

The "Exceptionally Graceful" Foo's Performance Style and Appearance: Draped in Fabrics "Unknown to Bargain Counters"

At the beginning of Foo's last week in New York, the New York *Times* provided an interesting take on Foo's presentation style and how the Chinese conjurer's act had evolved. In the piece, Foo's presentation pace was described as "deliberate", even "exasperatingly so at times."

But once he decides to move, the reviewer claims Foo is "like chain lightning" and, for such a large man, "exceptionally graceful."

The reviewer added an additional detail on Foo's appearance that had been missing to date. He wrote that Foo, a large, big-boned man, "so spare he might be called gaunt", had a large mouth and an abundant smile "made rich by the presence of a large gold tooth in the center of the upper row." He was also much impressed by Foo's fabulously expensive and wondrously embroidered clothing of silk and satin, of the "sort that are unknown to bargain counters."

FOO'S HANDS

An observer of Foo's up-close magic expertise wrote of the Chinese magician's "curious" hands. The author felt it strange, given what they could do, that they looked like the hands of an aged man. They were "long, well-shaped, and with plenty of flesh on them, but they are very wrinkled and shiny, and when using them in the ordinary way" they can look "feeble". However, once engaged in trickery, they are deft and move at an unbelievable speed.[174]

Fall of 1899: Foo Troupe Act Maintains Its Popularity Despite Emerging Copycats; Europe and Australia Come to Call

The vaudeville crowds surging to see the Foo troupe in the fall of 1899—in a continuous vaudeville format where their performance would be framed by a long bill of other acts—enjoyed a performance from the Chinese wonder-workers that typically lasted only 30 minutes. In this half hour, they would see Foo's conjuring act and all the Foo troupe supporting player routines. The relatively short time required for Foo's act in this format, compared to the almost two hours their act could take when appearing in a theater as the solo attraction, was a product of the system of continuous vaudeville, which was designed to have a constant flow of acts to maintain the interest of theatergoers in the audience. The goal was that anyone entering the theater at any time could be assured something to suit their tastes would be coming up soon.[175]

By October 1899, the Foo troupe's grip on the American market was showing no signs of abating, and *Mahatma* magazine continued to evince an evident discomfiture with the success of Foo in the U.S. market. In a pithy note to its readers, the periodical, seemingly having given up on its call to arms to with regard to Foo's production bowl challenge, huffily informed its readers: "An imitator of Ching Ling Foo, calling himself 'Clung Ling Too,' under the management of Chas. Carter, duplicates Ching Ling Foo's tricks. Any person with the necessary apparatus can easily perform these tricks."[176]

The *Mahatma*, of course, was right; "anyone" could easily duplicate Foo's tricks, but as many had discovered and would discover, duplicating Foo's popularity was a far more difficult proposition.

By October, English and European interest in booking Foo for tours of their lands continued to build, but an agent for Keith's Theaters over in London warned the eager European theatrical men that while he wanted to negotiate a deal with them, it would be a lot more expensive now than it would have been for them before the almost unprecedented success of Foo's first U.S. tour.

As Foo was already commanding a minimum of $1,000 a week in the U.S., the Keith's agent in Europe went on to rightly assert, it would take "a big price to tempt" Foo, but "he is worth all he gets and stands absolutely alone for his novelty as a performer."[177]

The offered engagements would reportedly keep Foo in Europe for at least two years, and the Australian market was making similar pleas. Theatrical managers in Paris, which was having an international exposition, claimed to have a letter from Li Hung Chang, never far from a Foo promotion, recommending the Paris engagement, and the organizers offered to build a special theater to house Foo's act.[178] Foo, unswayed, elected to stay with Keith's.

In 1899 Only Admiral Dewey, The Hero of Manila Bay, Rivaled Foo in Popularity

Part of the success of the Foo troupe at Keith's theater in New York is attributed to the ongoing celebrations and celebrity of Admiral Dewey, "the Hero of Manila Bay." Dewey played a major role in the very successful Spanish-American War. Keith's, as part of its bill, was running "biograph" films that depicted "superb views of the naval parade and military parade that was held in honor of Dewey" and scenes from the war. In this way, the author claimed the Admiral, who was so popular many were clamoring for him to run for president, was Foo's only "rival."[179]

The Mahatma Continues Its Somewhat Adversarial Foo Coverage

As Foo continued his record-breaking engagement at Keith's New York theater into November, *Mahatma* magazine continued its somewhat prickly attitude towards the Chinese conjurer. In a November 1899 report, they claimed Foo's "tricks" had been duplicated, "with improvements" no less, by Frank Hewes. Hewes was a magician also known as "the White Yogi."[180]

Not content with this knock, the editors further repeated once again, in their "Flashes" news section, the story they already published the previous month.

"We hear from good authority that Robinson, the Man of Mystery, accepted the challenge of Ching Ling Foo of $1,000 to any person duplicating his tricks. The wily Chinese backed out and his challenge was taken out of the papers."[181]

These repeated reports on the challenge and how they were couched are important because the Foo team's refusal to accept Robinson's response to the bowl production challenge often, in the storied history of the Foo-William Robinson/Chung Ling Soo rivalry, is put forward as some sort of "wrong" that was done to Robinson and thus a basis for Robinson's future ill treatment of Foo.

The difficulty with this argument is that these sorts of promotional "challenges" for general public consumption were the bread and butter of magician promotion at the time and no one, particularly fellow magicians, took them terribly seriously, especially if they involved big money. Furthermore, at the same time this "challenge" was out, as noted above, sophisticated magic shops were already selling devices to duplicate Foo's tricks. It is highly unlikely given all this context that anyone could have expected Foo or his management to take someone who wanted to respond to the bowl production promotional challenge seriously.

Furthermore, despite what *Mahatma* had written regarding Foo's withdrawal of the bowl challenge and the evident means with which it could be met, Keith's management cheekily kept the challenge in the ads for the Chinese conjurer after dismissing Robinson's challenge, and even upped the ante by throwing in Foo's imperial Chinese flag along with the promised $1,000. The public challenge was even extended beyond the bowl production trick to anyone who could duplicate "any of his tricks other than those of simple legerdemain."[182]

The James Thornton Incident: Big Laughs for Thornton Xenophobia for Foo

In discussing these negative elements of the otherwise positive professional atmosphere Foo enjoyed during his first tour of the U.S., another now legendary incident involving Foo and a then-prominent Irish-American entertainer, one James Thornton, needs to be addressed as part of any assessment of the backlash Foo's overwhelming popularity and success generated. The much-told tale was often put forward as an example of Thornton's legendary 'wit' and the story of this popular Irish-American entertainer putting a Chinese man 'in his place' became a touchstone of vaudeville lore among many.

According to the triumphantly ethnocentric story, Thornton and Foo were both performing on a bill at the same theater. A report in *Genii* Magazine claimed it would have occurred at Keith's theater in Boston sometime in 1899.[183] Somehow Foo, during this engagement, had "appropriated" the best dressing room in the theater, which by rights should have gone to Thornton, who was the headliner. According to the tale, Thornton "stood it for three days"; then, having had his fill of this foreigner's impertinence the fourth night, walked on stage, interrupting Foo in mid-performance. Once Thornton had the audience's and Foo's attention, Thornton reportedly "stripped off his shirt, flung it at Ching Ling Foo with the sharp order, 'Have it back by Friday!'" Thornton then "stalked majestically out of the theatre." And the audience roared.[184] So goes the legend.

While the Thornton anecdote has a certain bracing quality for those who appreciate such things, there are some issues. Firstly, it is hard to imagine a theater either during Foo's first tour or his second that would have placed John Thornton at the top of a bill in a theater where the hugely popular Ching Ling Foo was playing. During Foo's first tour of the U.S., Thornton was, while a popular singer and comedic monologist who was the author of many popular songs such as "My Sweetheart's the Man in the Moon," rarely set at the top of the bill of the larger venues.

In fact, at the time of Foo's first tour, Thornton often reached no higher than third or fourth in the billing of the larger houses. So, while a dispute over dressing rooms could have occurred, it is unlikely Thornton's act would ever have been placed above the Foo troupe on a bill at any theater Foo would have been playing. Thus, the whole basis for the Thornton story anecdote appears highly improbable.

Further bolstering the above argument, an idea of the relative status of the two acts during the period they were both performing can be adjudged from the promotional ads being run for Foo's appearance in the Boston *Globe*, on the very same page, for the week of June 5th, 1899.

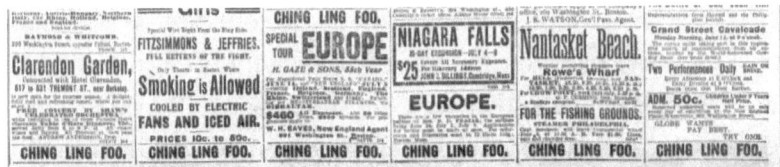

Two weeks before Foo arrives at Keith's Boston theater, management is already investing heavily in his promotion.

In addition, while the two performers could have certainly shared a bill and performed at the same theater at the same time, in the course of researching this book, no such overlapping engagement was uncovered, either during the period of Foo's first U.S. tour or his second tour. It appears while they sometimes performed in the same city at the same time, the closest they got to appearing in the same theater at the same time was when Thornton was fourth on the bill at Keith's theater in Boston for the week of June 5th, 1899, and Foo—at the peak of his popularity—was scheduled to be headlining the same theater June 19th, some two weeks later. Even the September 1938 report in *Genii* Magazine of the incident appears to be based on little more than the accounts relayed in the obituaries that were published months earlier.

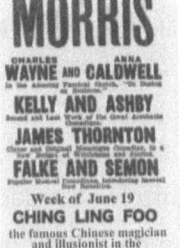

On the same page, the same day, the advertisement for the current array of performers at Keith's Boston theater lists Thornton fourth on the bill. Below was an announcement of Foo's upcoming headline engagement at the theater. To the right, Thornton's 1938 New York *Times* obituary, where the Foo anecdote is prominently presented as an example of Thornton's "celebrated wit".

So, it is highly probable this storied 'confrontation' was an apocryphal product of a comic monologist known for his fertile mind and 'witty topical sayings.' Either way, the story served Thornton well. It was a significant part of his vaudeville legend. Variations would be featured in Thornton's obituary published almost 40 years later in newspapers such as the New York *Times* and Philadelphia *Inquirer*.[185]

November 1899: Foo Moves On to Philadelphia and Goes Over Better than New Fad, Hot Waffles

In November 1899, Keith's announced the last week of Foo's current New York run, the first sign of Keith's management being willing to relax their recent monopoly control of the Foo troupe and lend him out to other theater chains. By special arrangement with Keith's. the Weber & Fields music hall would feature the Foo troupe, who would now headline that venue's Sunday entertainment.[186]

After New York, the Foo troupe moved on to Philadelphia, arriving November 13th. They had been the leading earners on the Keith circuit for over six months.[187]

Foo's first entrance upon the stage on his return to Philadelphia "was the signal for a breathless hush which continued till the magician had made his first remark." Contemporaneous with the Foo troupe's appearance, the theater was apparently introducing a new audience snack service selling so-called "hot waffles"—essentially hotcakes. A prominent reviewer, however, judged them not so "hot" and reported that unlike Foo, overall, they did not have much to recommend them.

Once more in Philadelphia, the more thoughtful reviews addressed Foo's charisma and graceful manner. One reviewer noted "the genial way in which he smiles and his peculiar idea of American slang captures the house at once." The reviewer also notes that a major difference from the Foo troupe's act presented last summer is that the rest of the Foo troupe, "of which there are four", carry much more of the act now, and they too are "quite remarkable."[188]

Another "Ching Ling Foo" Is "Interviewed" Regarding His Role in French Maids in Chinatown

In what appears to be some additional negative blowback in response to Foo's enormous success in the popular press, an odd article appears in the Harrisburg *Telegraph* in Pennsylvania, not far from where Foo is appearing in Philadelphia. It is an "interview" with a "Ching Ling Foo," the star of the aforementioned almost three-hour-long vehicle labeled *French Maids in Chinatown*. In earlier reporting his name had been given as Ling Ching Foo, but seemingly emboldened, the show's promoters were presenting their lead performer to the press as "Ching Ling Foo" with no concern as to the confusion it would cause with the actual Ching Ling Foo, who was currently performing in nearby Philadelphia.

The Harrisburg interview with this other Ching Ling Foo, in the guise of humor and promotion of the *French Maids in Chinatown* play, proceeded to present the worst negative stereotypes of the Chinese. The fake Foo's responses to the reporter's questions were presented in pidgin English. This "Foo" is initially described in a manner similar to the actual Foo: He is a "very progressive gentleman much superior in taste and manners to his celestial brothers." Then the *French Maids in Chinatown* Foo reportedly states, when asked his opinion of Americans, "You lie, me steal, Me cheatee like hell, Me be like Mellican man." The aspiring humorist, apparently stung by the genuine Foo's popularity among women and children, concludes that these musings of *his* Foo "would not look good in the columns of the *Ladies Home Journal* or *Scribner's* Magazine."[189] Clearly, they would not and that seems the whole point of the article.

The Europeans Still Want Him, Repeat Business Helps Foo Break Attendance Records

Approaching the end of 1899, British and European interest in getting Foo across the Atlantic continued to be strong. European theater managers watched closely as the Foo troupe broke more audience records, including the one-week audience attendance record, in Philadelphia. Crowds packed the Philadelphia theater "from pit to dome daily" and no day of the week had less than capacity audiences for both afternoon and evening shows. Even "orchestra seats", which cost a dollar to reserve, were being snatched up. "Hundreds have been turned away and thousands have willingly accepted standing room."[190-192]

Repeat attendees were a key part of the Foo troupe's secret in continually breaking theater attendance records. People apparently returned again and again to see the shows, and the troupe varied the act enough that Foo's repertoire was described as "apparently inexhaustible", to make such multiple viewings worthwhile. Reportedly, "people who see the act a dozen times are as enthusiastic as those about them who have been dumbfounded but once."[193]

Foo Family "Probably from Respectable Bourgeois Classes"

As the troupe finished up their engagement in Philadelphia and prepared to enter their final week, a piece written under the name "The Call Boy" was written for the theatrical section of the Philadelphia *Inquirer*.

"The daughter and wife of Ching Ling Foo, who are now at Keith's, are, contrary to the general occidental idea of Chinese females, an attractive pair. The little girl who, not quite three years, old can sing 'She's the Only Girl in the World', do the 'split', and say a few words in English, is a charmer, with the softest and richest Oriental eyes, plump olive cheeks and the sedatest and most polite of manners. Her dress, with its loose surface, richly patterned and picturesque headdress of long black strings, is a little gayer, but much the same character as that of her mother, a handsome and serious woman, who looks cheerful although she is seldom seen to smile."

The author feels it is unremarkable to note that the "general occidental idea of Chinese females" is that they are unattractive.

The author informs the readers that the Foo family is from Peking and notes they are "probably from the respectable bourgeois classes, for their manners are good without being grand, which would at once exclude them from the coolie and the aristocrats." Foo, however, given "his tall figure and scrupulously polite, although rather cool, demeanor," could easily pass for "an aristocrat of the first water."

The profile concludes by noting that despite the fact that Foo's current repertoire of illusions was judged to be among the best seen in this country, according to the Chinese conjurer, many of his best tricks were damaged while being shipped to America. Foo therefore, reportedly, planned to return to China in September, restock his wares, and return to America with a whole new slate of illusions.[194]

"Queen of Chinatown": "The Gambling Den, the Opium Joint and the Dance Hall Are Here"

Once again, the Foo troupe's presence in a new city brought with it a trailing competitive or symbiotic "China experience." This time, Philadelphians who couldn't get enough the of the Chinese mystique had a chance to see *French Maids in Chinatown* in nearby Harrisburg or take in a performance of a new Chinese-themed melodrama, *The Queen of Chinatown*, at Philadelphia's Gilmore's Auditorium.

Much like *King of the Opium Ring*, *French Maids in Chinatown*, and *A Night in Chinatown* before it, in *Queen of Chinatown* there is a lot going on, but it all seems fairly familiar. It is a story of homicide, robbery, and romance in "the murkily mysterious locality known as Chinatown." A place "where the Highbinders, the yellow-skinned gamester, the victim of the deadly and degrading poppy juice, and the poorer classes, who have to seek cheap shelter, hide, plot, prey, swarm" and, very importantly for a turn-of-the-century audience, "intermingle."

"The gambling den, the opium joint and the dance hall are here. But there is a comic lining to the cloud and wickedness is sunnily offset by the breezy manliness of the jolly tar, the pranks and peculiar dialect of the bootblack and the newsgirl, the oddities of the strapping

Irish washer-woman, and the dilemmas of the Dutch cobbler." So, the Philadelphia punters basically got "wickedness" and "humor" in Chinatown, and apparently liked the deal.[195]

Once again, the family-focused and relatively wholesome Foo troupe presented both in their performance and promotional activities with the media a whole other picture.

The Foo Troupe Keeps the Act Fresh and Chee Tai Continues to Win Hearts

With an eye to keeping the record crowds coming even after they have seen the show an initial time, a piece published in Philadelphia mid-December notes how the Foo troupe performers and their acts have evolved over the past year. According to the report, the juggler Harry Foo's English has become much better and is now part of the comedian's already startling juggling act, which also has become only better. Little Chee Tai has added several new English hit songs to her repetoire, and it is said she "dances in the cutest way imaginable."

The "tot" is also reportedly still produced from underneath her father's empty shawl and she is the "biggest hit" of the show. "Ladies and children are entirely unwilling to part with her." Meanwhile, Chee Tai's mother, in her "picturesque garb and tiny shoes", is "both attractive and winsome" while "Ching Ling Foo's bright son" has improved his acrobatics and contortion work.[196]

Another Iconic and Widely Distributed Interview: The Foo Family Provides "A Very Different Idea of the Chinese", "A New and Interesting Picture"

Amidst the competing views of the Chinese championed by the Foo troupe on one hand and the myriad and lurid *Night In Chinatown*-style entertainments in mid-December 1899, a hugely important and perceptive piece would be carried by the wire services across the U.S.

that recognized the enormous impact the Foo troupe was having on American popular perceptions of the Chinese.

At the outset, the author stated that Foo "has accomplished much, though without effort, since his arrival in this country in the way of giving Americans a very different idea of the Chinese people from that previously entertained."

The author went on to note the "American ideas of the 'heathen Chinee' have been formed, of course, from what has been seen of the ordinary Chinese laundryman, and the advent of a high-caste Mandarin, who now for a year has been constantly within the observation our people, has afforded opportunity to realize the difference between the two castes." Now we know Foo was not in fact "a high caste Mandarin", but he and his family were certainly members of the Chinese upper-middle class and certainly emerged from different social circumstances than the simple Chinese laborers who helped build America's railroads and perform so many other onerous tasks.

The author claimed the result of this observation had been "that in the estimation of intelligent observers the Chinese has been raised materially."[197] The reporter continued, "Aside from the revelation afforded by his marvelous skill in legerdemain and conjuring and the interest aroused in his bright children, Ching Ling Foo is showing American theatre-goers something else that is equally as novel. It is his wife. The sight of a Celestial matron, with her bright almond-eyed children about her, is a new and interesting picture. Indeed, the most winning part of the performance of the children and the assistance of their mother is the genuine pleasure they all seem to take in it."

Again, what was popular and novel was the "family" nature of the Foo act and the way it joyously combined "mirth, melody and magic"—the key selling points of the act. The opportunity to experience "mirth" and enjoy a happy, talented family were really a large part of the troupe's appeal. It is important to remember at this point that the onstage Foo troupe consisted of only four people in addition to Foo: Foo, his wife, son, daughter, and Harry Foo.[198]

The female reporter then described the way Foo's wife Hai Quai had altered the apartments they occupied near the theater to make them more Chinese and the manner with which she was occupied with her family during the troupe's downtime.

"Bits of scarlet silk and satin embroidered in gold designs hung upon the walls, and there were scented silk divans and fragrant sandalwood boxes, pearl inlaid about the room."

"With her head prettily poised, Mrs. Foo sat doing what most other good mothers might have been found engaged in at that time of day. She was busy with her needle fixing things for the children. Little Chee Tai squatted in a divan, toyed with her queue and hummed something in Chinese in the 'ragtime' that she has acquired."

The gracefulness of Mrs. Foo's manner was then noted. "A Delaarte graduate would like to know how to make a bow similar to the one that came from Mrs. Foo as she greeted the writer, and she did it, too, standing on shoes that are only four inches long. These, though ugly in shape, were things of beauty in the matter of exquisite embroidering on the white satin … Mrs. Foo's house costume was in silk of sober tones. The upper garment was long, square cut, of glistening black satin. The trousers were of dark blue."

As the interview commenced, tea was served, with sugar forgotten momentarily, with apologies offered. Some pidgin English appears: "I forgettee—Melican people like sugar. Spoilee tea but you like—you like that allee."

Chee Tai was then asked to sing a song. "Chee Tai clapped her little hands. Without the slightest show of embarrassment, she reeled off her 'ragtime' airs that sound so quaint from the tiny geisha … Patting the little girl's cheek, Mrs. Foo said fondly that the child would have a great future, and little Chee Tai lisped that she loved the stage, the lights and all the people. Her father and brother liked it too. She made a pretty little bow of respect when she spoke of her father."

Then Foo's wife demonstrated her American outfits, dresses, and hats she bought, modeled some, and commiserated with the reporter about the constricting nature of corsets. She refused to squeeze herself into those, then dismissed the corset, tossing it to one side, and said "something short in a high key, the correct translation of which is probably 'Not I.'"[199]

This article, and others like it about the Foo family, were critically important in that while they did perpetuate stereotypes, they, in their relatively positive portrayals, stood as strong arguments against the very prevalent claims that the Chinese were incapable of assimilation and/or adaption to the American way of life.

December 1899–January 1900 January, Boston: Foo's Unprecedented Keith's Tour is Coming to an End; "Ching Ling Foo's Success in Vaudeville has Never Been Equaled"

With their engagement in Philadelphia complete, the Foo troupe returned to Boston. After a successful run in Boston through December, the Foo troupe entered a new century full of technological advancements and shrinking borders at the Keith's theater in Boston, playing out their last week.

This last week in Boston also marked the end of the Foo troupe's unprecedented nearly one-year run within the Keith's theater circuit as a headlining act. In assessing this and his earlier success, the Boston *Herald* rightly noted "Ching Ling Foo's success in vaudeville has never been equaled." This is a fact that could sometimes be lost in the sometimes over-the-top promotion the troupe was given.[200]

Harry Houdini Appears, Potentially Foo's "Greatest Rival" for Public Acclaim

Another noteworthy event in the Foo troupe's last week in Boston was a new act sharing the bill. He was "a remarkable young man from Budapest" who had been making some waves himself in the world of

A very young Harry Houdini on the cusp of his legendary career. He would become a close friend and confidante of Foo, and the Chinese conjurer, on his death, would bequeath a large part of his considerable magic library to Houdini.

conjuring. The young man, "who has been astonishing audiences in New York during the past week by releasing himself from the entanglements of several pairs of police handcuffs" and "beats all records in escaping from a trunk", was Harry Houdini. Prescient observers already marked him as a quality performer who combined a rare level of charisma and talent who had the potential to prove Foo's "greatest rival" in attracting public interest and acclaim.[201] In fact, some claim Houdini's escape from a bound trunk illusion in which he was placed bound in a sack was already "a way ahead of anything done by the noted Chinese magician Ching Ling Foo."[202]

January 1900, Washington, DC: "The Costliest Vaudeville Act in the World"

As they approached two very successful years touring in America, Foo's exceptional salary at the princely sum of at minimum $1,000 a week—including, in some instances, a share of the gate plus the use of a private railcar to transport his troupe to engagements—was increasingly a key element used in the promotion of the troupe. Foo's weekly salary was reported as "the largest sum paid any specialty performer in this country."[203]

When the Foo troupe arrived in Washington, D.C. for an engagement, there was much discussion in the Washington papers regarding how the manager of the Washington New Grand theater could make this kind of outlay for Foo's engagement beginning the week of January 15th.[204]

"The Costliest Vaudeville Act in the World." If one reads the fine print it is evident telephones developed to commercially usable form just ten years earlier were already becoming a staple of American life, and one was advised to "phone in advance and avoid waiting in line."

The Diabolo

It is during the engagement in Washington that Foo's demonstration of his mastery of the Diabolo spinning top, allegedly gained in his childhood, became one of the performer's most admired feats. Diabolos, in form, looked like two tops joined at their tops along a string controlled by two sticks. The devices went through several periods of great popularity at various periods in the 1800s. In the right hands, they could be manipulated to make the tops perform startling feats, including some that seemed to defy the laws of gravity.

In some cases, they were also constructed so that their rapidly spinning motion would draw air through a network of passages inside the Diabolo, producing varying piercing or sonorous sounds. For the initial Washington audience, the manipulation of the Diabolo, which came at the end of their performance, was thought to be the best trick of the act. A Washington theater critic noted Foo's "control of the top is nothing short of marvelous."

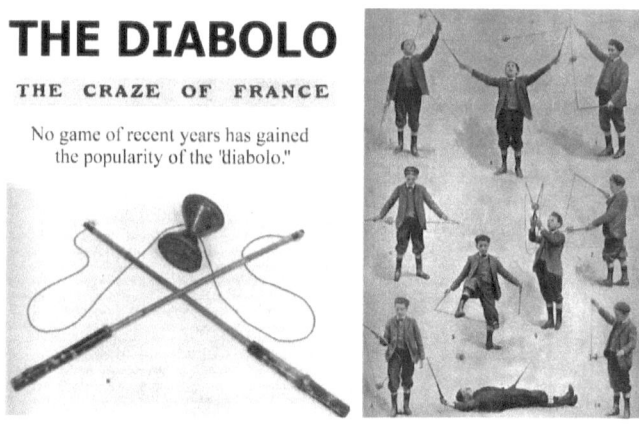

The ancient Chinese toy known as the Diabolo went through several phases of mass popularity over time. To the left, a classic Diabolo. To the right, child juggling star Marcel Meunier demonstrating various Diabolo tricks.

The exact time of the Foo troupe performances, "3 o'clock in the afternoon and 9 o'clock at night", were now provided in the Washington advertisements so those who did not want to sit through the other six acts on the "continuous vaudeville" bill could come directly to see the "Costliest Vaudeville Act in the World."[205] The Foos played to standing room only signs for their entire Washington engagement.

Wu Ting Fang Returns

In recognition of the enormous impact the Foo troupe was having on popular U.S. entertainment, Foo's old acquaintance from Omaha, China's Minister to Washington Wu Ting Fang, and a group of senior members of the Chinese legation took in the Foo troupe's performance on the night of January 16th.[206]

An Enduring Curiosity Concerning Seldom-Seen Chinese Women

Chee Tai's increasing popularity was given a nod when the reviewer noted the young singing diva "captivates all" with her "cunning sweetness" and songs.[207] Demonstrating the Foo troupe's appeal was not just about magic, it was once more acknowledged that the audience's interest in Mrs. Foo and Chee Tai, particularly among young children and women, was as great and sometimes greater than interest in Foo.

In the America of 1900, due to restrictive immigration laws such as the 1875 Page Act that had essentially banned Chinese women from the U.S. seven years before the Chinese Exclusion Act of 1882 would also ban Chinese men, Chinese women were a rarity in the public domain, and particularly on stage. Chinese women's views of America and adaption to its ways, not to mention their fashion choices, were thus subjects of great curiosity. They were also considered to be highly relevant to the great ongoing debate as to whether Chinese could or wanted to assimilate into a broader American culture. In this context, the Washington *Evening Star* noted of the female members of the Foo troupe, "These feminine celestials have been wonderful at adapting themselves to American ways" and that while Mrs. Foo "is a refutation of the stories that Chinese women cannot be graceful because their feet are small", she has "ceased to rejoice in her tiny feet and professes admiration for the feminine feet of the No. 6 or 7 order" while firmly on the "against" side when it comes to corsets.

There was also great interest in the Chinese women's clothing and jewelry and detailed descriptions of their outfits were often published. Mrs. Foo was described as "a very picturesque figure in her soft silk robes in every conceivable color" and "exquisitely decorated jacket" with "very long pointed nails but no rings" and wrists "loaded with bracelets of various sizes and materials."

Chee Tai, A "Prima Donna" Who "Breathes the Perfume of Childhood Sweetness"

Chee Tai, whose popularity at this point in the U.S. tour now rivaled that of her father, was presented as a "miniature of her mother" and a born mimic who "spends a great deal of time in the wings of the stage picking up bits of songs and dances."[208] "The tiny soubrette breathes the perfume of child sweetness about the stage like some dainty bloom from an Asiatic conservatory. She has none of the trite mannerisms of precocity. She is as natural as sunshine and as autocratic as a prima donna, for it was she who compelled the management to change the hour for the company's appearance from 9:30 p.m. to 9, in order that she might retire at her accustomed hour."[209]

Nellie Gilliand's Iconic Interview: The Foo Family, Like Your Average American Family, If Not a Bit Better

> **MME CHING LING FOO**
> **WIFE OF A CHINESE MAGICIAN**
> A Visit to a Family, Who Have Been Interesting Washington Theater Goers Recently.

This interest in the female component of the Foo troupe and their lives continued with yet another key long-form article about the Foo family that would do much to break stereotypes and improve the image of Chinese in America.

The in-depth report on the Foos at home was done by a pioneering female Washington *Post* journalist who visited the Foos outside the theatrical environment to give readers an introduction to the Foo's home life that, in contrast to entertainments like *King of the Opium Ring* or *A Night In Chinatown*, presented the visiting Foo family as

The Riggs Hotel in Washington, located at the corner of 15th and Pennsylvania Avenues, where the Foo troupe stayed during their 1900 engagement. Individual rooms were adorned with richly upholstered lounges and chairs. Noise between floors was muffled by thick velvet carpets.

like an average American family, if not a bit better—and, seemingly contrary to much of the ongoing "China Question" debate, once again, infinitely capable of assimilation.

Nellie Gilliand's Washington interview with the magician's wife at their suite at the Riggs Hotel begins with her being greeted by "Mrs. Ching Ling Foo." "Two black, shiny eyes, peering at you from under bands of blacker, shinier hair, ears half-hidden by the kettle-like head-dress," a woman with "a smile as radiant as a Celestial sun" who "fairly beams with content."

The journalist informed her readers that seeing Mrs. Foo on stage in her Oriental finery with her children is one thing, but to "visit her in her temporary hotel home where she 'mothers' her baby girl, sews buttons on her boys' trousers and mends her husband's socks, is quite another story. And a much prettier one."

Foo and Hai Quai were reported to have just returned from a "call" they "had that morning made on Minister Wu." By Minister Wu, Gilliand was referring to the aforementioned Wu Ting Fang, the Chinese ambassador to Washington at that time. As noted earlier,

Wu had travelled to the Omaha Exposition with President McKinley for the Peace Jubilee celebrations held there, and undoubtedly met with Foo while in Omaha.

Gilliand described Hai Quai as a bit of a magician on her own, "for with the magic of her love she transforms into a fallacy the theory that the woman who marries a genius lives an unhappy life", and noted when the genius in question "draws a cool thousand a week" it must have no small impact on said happiness.

She then described Mrs. Foo telling Foo that Chee Tai required a new pair of shoes and some new English books, and Foo smilingly revealing "every gold tooth in his head" while reaching into his pocket to provide the necessary funds.

Gilliand then informed readers Mrs. Foo, who referred constantly to her husband, played the traditional maternal role in the family, mending the clothing of her 12-year-old son Foo Quai, who, with his "manly spirit", served as the family's translator and thus "takes the stand between his parents and the pushing driving American business world." The reporter also observed Mrs. Foo ensuring little Chee Tai got the English books she needed for her studies, all while the proud mother admitted the two studied the language—including reading and writing—together, and her daughter was the far better student. In their hotel room turned home, little Chee Tai wore a combination of American and Chinese clothes and happily sang the current popular hit "Hello, My Baby" for Gilliand. She noted Foo Quai was "gentle and respectful to his father and mother, and is quiet and tender with his little sister, whom Americans are doing their best to spoil."

When Hai Quai was asked how she liked America, she crossed her legs with a grace "even the most elegant American girl might sit up to practice in vain" and enthusiastically bubbled "with rhetorical bouquets" for the country in which she had spent the last two years. For Mrs. Foo in her emerging English, America was "nice, so nice," "cars and bicycles," "nice," so "good to me and my children." She went on to explain she has purchased Western women's clothing but prefers her own. Gilliand noted that "two years in America have won this interesting little woman a great many friends among her own sex and have taught her many American customs." Her modesty was displayed in the way she "speaks deprecatingly of her part in her husband's performance" and admitted her main goal in being on stage is "only to be near her children whose every move she watches with unaffected pride and pleasure." Then, just before Gilliand takes her leave, precocious Chee Tai sang "Because I Love You."

Ms. Gilliand closed her report on the Foo family by revealing once more the source of so much of the enormous appeal of the Foo troupe: the fact the adventurous, talented troupe is a family, and more importantly, a happy one. "You feel it would be a joy to linger indefinitely in the friendly atmosphere of this happy travelling home circle."[210]

Rarities: Among Reviewers Some Foo Skeptics; "One of the Blandest Wizards That Ever Pulled a Bowl of Goldfish Out of Nowhere"

In the midst of all this positive coverage, another rare negative review of the Foo troupe emerged. It occurred buried in an otherwise positive review of the troupe's performance during their last week in Washington. No doubt the article's tone was no little influenced by the reaction of some American magicians, as evidenced in the editorial positions of *Mahatma* and others that seem to have developed some resentment against this overly successful and very much praised "foreign" magician.

First, the writer expressed a little bit of discomfort at Foo's high earnings. He grudgingly acknowledged that Foo's "patronage"—essentially, the large audiences he had been drawing—"justified" his enormous salary. However, the Washington correspondent was compelled to add that regardless, "Ching is one of the blandest wizards that ever pulled a bowl of goldfish out of nowhere. His tricks are few and not at all out of the ordinary." That major blow having been landed, the Washington, D.C.-based reviewer lauded the rest of Foo troupe, whose feats "are in their way unsurpassed." But shots had undeniably been fired.[211]

Foo Once Again Seen Through the "Heathen Chinee" Lens

This percolating, somewhat contrarian sentiment towards Foo accelerated with the publishing the next day of a humorous or satirical poem in the Washington *Times*. Not surprisingly, the author, when composing a satirical poem about a Chinese magician, was drawn irresistibly as source material and inspiration yet again to Bret Harte's aforementioned "Heathen Chinee," then the fountainhead from which all presentations of Chinese in American popular culture sprang.

The poem, taking up almost a third of the front page of the entertainment section and stretching from top to bottom, borrowed liberally from Harte's work to address the Foo phenomenon.

Of course, it led off with the infamous lines, "That for ways that are dark, and tricks that are vain, the heathen Chinee is peculiar." Interesting comments within the knockoff poem point to Foo or his management's deft use of that relatively new species known as "press agents" and their habit of blanketing the streets "with posters and three-sheets" promoting the wizard. In its most amusing thrust, the poem turned one of the complaints of Harte's "Heathen Chinee" on its head when he asserted Foo's enormous salary of, at minimum, $1,000 per week as an instance where American vaudeville managers were being "ruined by Chinese high labor", as opposed to the reference to the "Chinese cheap labor" referenced in Harte's original poem.

Friends of Last Week

Which I wish to remark
    And my language is plain
That for ways that are dark
    And for tricks that are vain
The Heathen Chinee is peculiar
    Which the same I would rise
    to explain.

Ching Ling Foo was his name,
    And I shall not deny
In regard to the same
    That it sounds like a "guy."
But it finally got on the billboards
    In letters a foot or two high.

It was August the third,
    And the neighboring heaths
Were not plundered or stirred
    For garlands or wreaths
Ching was almost alone in his glory
    On the day that he opened at Keith's.

Which the house it was small,
    And it pains me to say
That its members were all
    Of the species called "jay"
They had breakfasted a la the camel,
    Intending to stay through the day,

Ching's long robes were stocked
    In a way that I grieve
And those yokels were shocked
    As you'd scarcely believe
They reported from Troy to Elmira
    On the ease with which Ching could
    deceive.

By the game that was played
    Through the press agent beast
Ching Ling was displayed
    As a sort of high priest:
A mixture of Herrmann and Kellar.
    Or Kellar and Bancroft at least.

Then they named figures four
    As a fit salary.
And the managers swore,
    And said: "Can it be?
We are ruined by Chinese high labor!"
    But they went for that heathen Chinee.

In the hit that ensued
    Ching had a small hand,
For the town and the streets were strewed
    Like the leaves on the strand
With posters and three-sheets and printing
    Of the class that is known as "the
    stand."

Folk came early and late,
    And when they could speak,
They voted him great
    In a manner most meek.
Because his feats really were clever
    And he drew just a thousand a week.

Which is why I remark,
    Though booking men fain
Would have it kept dark.
    That for tricks that are vain
The heathen Chinee is peculiar
    Which the same I am free to
    maintain.[212]

Making the Case for America's Own Great Illusionists

Once complete, the author claimed this "parody" on Bret Harte's most famous work is "intended merely as a jest a pleasantry" and went on to say "Ching Ling Foo really is a remarkable fellow" due to his ticket sales and capacity to improve on the great Alexander Herrmann and his other predecessors. But in a telling presage of arguments to come, the author then balked at reports Foo had outstripped the great American magicians of the day, including Kellar, with his "mechanical ventures", and Herrmann, who focused on "cabinet illusions."

The reporter asserted any claims Foo might make to being superior to these home-born magicians would be "great exaggerations." He cited the additional challenges American magicians faced by working in tight-fitting clothing and their habit of often inviting men up on the stage to examine their efforts. In this, the author seemed to forget that Foo often would perform in tight-fitting clothes to address the criticism his flowing Chinese-style clothing provided an advantage, and Foo also often invited spectators on stage to closely examine his work.

The author also found fault with the fact that Foo's act was only, at most, 40 minutes sometimes 30, whereas the American greats were asked to keep a stage show going for "several hours." Again, in response, one must note the modern "continuous vaudeville" format, not Foo, determined the length of Foo's act. The author then made the assessment he was waiting before he took up pen to write. While it was "undeniable" Foo is "a wonderfully ingenious fellow", there was "no reason for our compatriots to look fearfully at their laurels."

Finally, and lastly, he finished off his worthwhile analytical piece on the Foo phenomenon, rightly focusing on the essential role the American hunger for the exotic and intensive marketing played in promoting Foo's success and adding value to the Foo troupe's act.

"Ching's act is worth the $1,000 a week paid him principally because of the manner in which he was advertised. His hit on the Keith's circuit, curiosity concerning his nationality, and the number of his assistants all count in that figure."

Parts of this were undoubtedly true, but mere interest in things Chinese or exotic, or even the best "booming", could not explain the record-breaking success of the Foo troupe. Many, many other outlets featuring Asian-themed entertainments existed, and greatly increased as the Foo troupe triumphantly toured America; and none of these other entertainments enjoyed anywhere near the popularity or demonstrated the staying power of the Foo troupe when it came to ongoing success. On this point, one has to go back to the fact the Foo and his troupe, from all evidence available, were indeed something inherently special and not just a promotional or "race act" phenomenon.[213]

"Fool Foo Ding-a-Ling": An Oriental Burlesque

Even after Foo left Washington, his effect was still felt. The Bijou Theater, hoping to capitalize on the still-strong demand for more things Foo, put together *Fool Foo Ding-a-Ling*, an "oriental burlesque" that ran for a week. "A mélange of jollity," it was made up of "sketches culled from the brightest and wittiest lines of *The Geisha* and *The Mikado*" while an actor in yellowface provided a "laughable and entertaining burlesque on Ching Ling Foo."[214] There is no indication of how commercially successful this effort was but it appears after its Washington run to have never been heard from again.

January 1900: Brooklyn, New York

For the last week in January 1900, the Foo troupe returned once more to New York to head the bill at New York's Hyde & Behman's Theater in Brooklyn. The long gone and lamented Brooklyn *Daily Eagle* welcomed the Foo troupe to the neighborhood—Keith's New York theater was in Manhattan—with this gem.

"The wonders performed by this Oriental border on the marvelous and savor strongly of the stories told of Merlin and other magi of

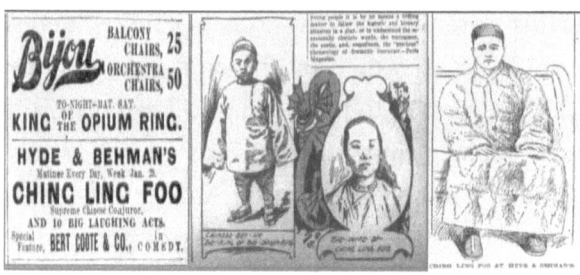

Foo appears a bit forlorn in this Brooklyn *Times* depiction, while the Brooklyn *Citizen* prefers to run an illustration of his wife and a young Chinese actor from the popular play *King of the Opium Ring*, which always seemed to be playing near a Foo troupe show.

other days, and were it not for the fact we are living in enlightened times there would be danger of his being set down as a disciple of the cloven hoof."

Once again Foo was able to continually sell out his shows in a market in which he had already appeared due to his capacity to add novelty to his act and the desire of the public to see the Foo troupe performances over and over again, the way one enjoys a popular song.[215]

The second weekend of Foo's engagement at Hyde and Behman's was as successful as the first.

Once more, the Foo troupe's popularity and box office success resulted in an engagement for a second week at the theater they were performing at, and once again, it was noted as "a rare privilege." Chee Tai remained a standout, and at each performance she was "liberally encored." Sharing the bill with the Foo troupe were a dancing act, acrobats, and "the High-Toned Burglar," a sketch by James F. Dolan.[216]

Foo Imitators Begin to Multiply; "Ching Ling Foo Rag" Released

While Foo is in Brooklyn, the very talented mimic the Great Lafayette, who had just recently performed as a supporting act to the Foo troupe and subsequently developed a Foo act parody, or "travesty", which was now the biggest draw in his act, publicly warned anyone who would dare to parody his Foo parody that "imitators will be severely dealt with." Interestingly, apparently neither Foo nor Foo's managers had any objections to Lafayette's travesty, as it was developed with "all due courtesy" to Foo.

"Lots of counterfeiting imitators but not the real." Lafayette is quite proud of being the "originator & first to produce travesties on Sousa & Ching Ling Foo" and suffers no cognitive dissonance whatsoever when deriding "counterfeiting imitators" of his act.

This incongruity in attitudes towards the sincerest form of flattery would persist as a key element of the Great Lafayette's business practices throughout his storied career. One could understand the *mimitique*'s concerns, however, as he was at this point making some $500 a week imitating Foo.[217–219]

Meanwhile, Foo's stint in Brooklyn had gotten off to a good start. The Foo troupe was described as one of the venue's best acts of the year. Chee Tai continued to sing her popular songs, which were now referred to more and more as "Ragtime" songs and popular dances. The Ragtime genre of music, which was developed by Black American musicians in the 1890s, was characterized by a syncopated or "ragged" style of music that involved displacing rhythms in a manner such that strong beats became weak and weak beats or accents became strong. It was hugely popular at the time. An early overlap of the Foo troupe's popularity with the rise of ragtime would come with the release of the "Ching Ling Foo Rag", or the "Chinese Ragtime March", by Emil Katzenstein in 1899.

"The Ching Ling Foo Rag March and Two Step."

Harry Foo Demonstrates the Chinese Sense of Humor

The Foo troupe juggler Harry Foo's English continued to improve, and he continued to delight audiences with his injection of American slang into his act as well as singing some Chinese songs more or less for comedic effect—"they are not pleasing to the American ear"—than audience appreciation. Harry was otherwise given high praise for his clever "phrasing" and "comic antics" that "reveal the sense of humor that some people say his countrymen lack."[220]

Foo, at this point, was entering his second week headlining at Hyde and Behman's, "a resort for ladies and children," which was apparently unheard of for acts, given the notoriously picky Brooklyn audience. "There are but few artists who can so absorb their attention that they will stand for a two-week run." The Brooklynites were a sophisticated audience that had seen a lot of vaudeville and a lot of magic; so much so that they could appreciate the stellar elements of Foo's fire breathing act—blowing out of his mouth "red hot and blazing balls of fire" while recognizing "eating blazing paper" as a common dime-store "museum trick."

The "Joy" of a Foo Troupe Performance

As it was in other markets, Brooklynites were coming to see Foo and his troupe do their act again and again. As to why, the reviewer hit on something profound when he repeatedly made a soon-to-be-recurrent reference to the "joy" with which the Foo troupe performed, and how that feeling was shared with the audience.

In Brooklyn, Foo also continued to continually vary the act. The Brooklyn show was scheduled to run 30 minutes during each of their twice-daily performances. There was always something new with each performance, and the troupe's five performers had all become audience favorites. This applied even to "Mrs. Foo" despite the fact her role had evolved mostly into encouraging the other performers, particularly her children, and giving them suggestions of what to do.

Chee Tai was "produced" from her father's shawl daily and the Brooklyn audience was keen on Foo's Diabolo demonstrations. "Chee Tai", at this point, was now learning new ragtime songs at a rapid rate; her rendition of "I'd Leave My Happy Home for You" was the hit of the act the night she introduced it.[221]

A promotional ad for the Hyde & Behman's show. "Have You Seen Ching Ling Foo?" Hyde and Beham's, "A Resort for Ladies and Children." To the right, a photo of "the clever impersonator of male characters" Zelma Rawlston.

Features on the lower part of the card with the Foo troupe during their last week in Brooklyn included Miss Zelma Rawlston, "the clever impersonator of male characters."[222]

February 1900: Buffalo

Promotion for the Foo troupe's engagement in Buffalo began with a short piece in the Buffalo *Enquirer* wherein Foo's much-reworked background story was given yet another run. In this version, Foo, who was 46 years old at the time of the article, only began to study conjuring in his early thirties, but used it only to entertain friends and family, given he earned his trade as a merchant working for a large firm.

It was explained that Foo was in San Francisco for business at the time of the Omaha Exposition and joined the performers who were going to appear there. This rather fanciful version of Foo's immediate past, particularly his alleged presence in San Francisco, may have been necessitated by his recent and not completely resolved immigration problems. But this version did at least correct the previous version's statements with regard to Keith's management discovering Foo in Omaha, as opposed to Colonel Hopkins, who actually played that crucial initial role in the launch of the Foo troupe.[223]

CHAPTER SIX

JANUARY 1900 TO APRIL 1900—PEAK FOO CRESTS—THINGS COME APART

Chinese Diplomats Step In to Mediate Foo's Clash with Management

This disappearance of Keith's management from Foo's entertainment biography in the Buffalo story may have been related to a recent report out of Washington regarding a clash between Foo and "his managers." Interestingly, it was reported the clash had to be "settled" by Chinese Minister Wu Ting Fang.[224] It seems the earlier reported meeting of Foo and Wu while Foo was performing in Washington was no mere courtesy visit. Foo and four members from his troupe, including his wife, paid a visit to the Chinese legation on January 16th, 1900, to consult with their good friend, Chinese Minister in Washington Wu Ting Fang, to discuss the difficulties Foo was having with regard to his contract with the powerful Keith's theater chain. Foo explained to the Minister that when he had originally signed the agreement with Keith's, he understood it would be for a term of just two years. But the Chinese magician learned to his grief that the Keith's contract set out an obligation for Foo to tour as directed by Keith's management for a period of five years.

Beyond that, Foo complained that the terms of the contract were too generous for the Keith's group. As Foo's managers, they were entitled to a percentage of his very high salary, but Foo believed, given his success since the contract had been signed, it would only be fair to increase his share and decrease that allotted to Keith's.

Foo met with Minister Wu to see if these matters could be addressed or, in the alternative, how he could end his relationship with Albee and Keith's.

As a result of all this, the Chinese legation invited E.F. Albee, Keith's top manager, to come to Washington and meet with Foo while the Chinese Minister acted as a mediator.

Not long after this report, another notice would be placed in the media, this time no doubt issued by promoters working for both B.F. Keith and Colonel John D. Hopkins, announcing Ching Ling Foo "has signed a contract with B.F. Keith and Col. John D. Hopkins whereby his services are controlled by them for a number of years."[225,226]

This successful (for a time) intervention by Wu demonstrates the degree to which Foo was seen as important by the Chinese government, given his positive role in presenting the Chinese image in the U.S.[227]

At This Point, Foo is Making a Lot More Than Houdini

Foo's fluid contractual status was not affecting his capacity to obtain record-breaking salaries. For the year 1900, Foo was the highest paid act engaged by the management of Buffalo's Shea's Theater. Foo was recorded as making $1,046 a week. At this time, the highly touted and promising Houdini, still just getting started in his career, was making only $150 a week.[228]

The Buffalo engagement began the 2nd of February. In total running time, the Foo portion of the act ran about an hour, indicating there were not many other acts on the bill. As always, the Foo troupe

How Salaries Have Leaped		Edward Lattell	150
I was given permission in the office to examine the bookkeeping of Shea's as far back as 1899 and make known the weekly salaries of the prominent players and make comparison with them and now. Here is a list as I copied it, that will probably be cut out and saved by a small army of readers of The Courier who are ardent lovers of the stage and its people.		Robert Hilliard	600
		Lochhart's Elephants	400
		Classy Loftus	300
		Jack Norworth & Louise Dresser	150
		Blanche Ring	75
		Louise Gunning	125
		Dillon Brothers	150
		Ching Ling Foo	1046
		Houdini	150
		Elizabeth Murray	125
1900		**1899**	
Ezra Kendall	400	George Evans	150
Edward M. Royle	450	Bessie Bonehill	350
Four Cohans	360	Adelaide Herrmann	500
Montgomery & Stone	300	Camille D'Arville	750
Lottie Gilson	150	Fred Niblo	60
Ross Coghlan	550	Violet Dale	75
Press Eldridge	260	Irene Franklin	135
Williams & Walker	500	John Kernell	250
Pauline Hall	500	Carrie Behr	20
Elsie Janis	75	Howard Thurston	75
In 1901 this was raised to	135	Alcide Capitaine	425
In 1915 it was	2500		
McIntyre & Heath	350		
Digby Bell	500		

"How Salaries Have Leaped." A list of top weekly salaries of performers at Buffalo's Shea Theater. One can see how spectacular Foo can be seen to be making $1,046 while Houdini, who was at a relatively early stage in his career, was making only $150 a week.

was very well received. Foo was declared "the cleverest magician ever seen in this city." Chee Tai "sang popular songs in a remarkably sweet strong voice" while Harry Foo, the juggler, demonstrated "hardness of head".

Reviewers noted Foo continued to deflect criticism that his flowing Chinese robes assisted in his production feats by, at points during his act, stripping down to his shirt and then running across the stage to do a flying somersault, after which he landed, producing "a glass aquarium of goldfish fluttering in clear water."[229,230] In the end the Buffalo audience "could not get enough of the family."

Sharing the bill in Buffalo with the Foo family was the "Wormwood Dog and Monkey Show", and in Foo's second week in Buffalo, a Japanese group called the Tanakas that did magic and top spinning.[231–233]

HARRY FOO GOES OUT FOR A GOOD TIME AND GETS ROBBED

It was during this second week in Buffalo that Harry Foo made the papers for all the wrong reasons. Harry was robbed of $255 dollars on Clinton Street in Buffalo.

> "Bee" Wilson, a 21-year-old bellboy at the New Gruener Hotel, was suspected of the theft and arrested.
>
> According to accounts, Harry, after two weeks at the hotel in Buffalo, was getting a bit bored, so he set out to see what Buffalo had in the way of entertainment with Bee, the bellboy, acting as his guide. Harry did this without following the Foo troupe's standard procedure of notifying their manager when they left the hotel for any length of time to ensure their safety in unfamiliar surroundings.
>
> Apparently, Harry ended up on Buffalo's Oak Street with his guide. "By 5 a.m. Harry showed up at the police station, claiming earlier he had been robbed and was too drunk to stop it. In addition, he went back to the hotel and in the morning laid out what had happened to his manager."
>
> The bellboy at first claimed he took the money to keep it safe and gave it to his brother. The brother claimed he never had it. Harry says he had the wallet in an inside pocket, and they saw it when he paid for drinks. But he became too drunk at one point, and one of the brothers then took advantage of his incapacity and relieved him of his cash. Harry claimed the thief even waved the treasured wallet under Harry's nose, knowing Harry, in his state at that time, was incapable of regaining his savings.[234]

The Buffalo Crowds Hiss The King of the Opium Ring: "Such a Good Black-Hearted Villain"

As always, another allegedly Chinese-themed entertainment followed the Foo troupe to Buffalo and set up shop in a nearby theater. In this instance, it was the old staple, *The King of the Opium Ring*. It was a return performance to Buffalo for the play, and it promised new scenery and some new "specialties" in the acts. Reviews for the play were quite positive, and it was observed that John Laughney, who in yellowface played the evil Opium King, "made such a good black-hearted villain that on several occasions the gallery gods threatened to do him personal injury."[235]

Foo Gets Tied Up With Some Timely Geopolitical References

A piece on Foo in the Buffalo *Review* redeemed itself after a clichéd introduction referencing the Heathen Chinee and Li Hung Chang by then making actual reference to then-current, Chinese geopolitics. "If the Empress of China is looking for a new juggler for the throne or someone to fill the shoes and yellow jacket of Li Hung Chang, Ching Ling will be open for the job. If his Buffalo performances can be taken for a criterion, the Russian bear would do well to beware, for if he hangs around Ching Ling, he may suddenly find himself converted into a dish of chop suey." At the time, both Japan and Russia were threatening to take by force territory in China's north.[236]

While in Buffalo, it is reported that a businessman associated with Foo, an E.W. Davis, had signaled his interest in obtaining the Chinese Village concession for the upcoming Buffalo exposition. Davis was listed as the manager of the New York-based Ching Ling Foo company.

No more was heard of this, but it is interesting to observe that Foo, the ever-resourceful businessman, appears to have attempted to obtain a concession to run a Chinese Village at the Buffalo exposition. His failure to do so may have contributed to his decision, along with all the other difficulties that began to manifest themselves, with Foo's decision to return to China.[237,238]

A Planned Foo Engagement in Toronto Comes Apart

Foo ultimately ended up staying the first three weeks of February in Buffalo, as a planned and heavily promoted engagement in Toronto came apart due to his troupe's still-precarious immigration status in the U.S. Apparently, it was feared U.S. immigration laws regarding Chinese were such that if Foo left the U.S. to enter Canada, he and the

Chinese members of his troupe would likely be denied reentry into the country, and the Canadian authorities were unwilling to take this risk. Foo's inability to perform in Canada reportedly was met with great disappointment. His story was widely covered in Canada, and Canadian theater goers were looking forward to seeing the man "who had broken records" and "whose price is the highest, it is said, ever paid for such an act in the South."[239] Several attempts were made to appeal to the border authorities in the U.S., but they fell on deaf ears, and the much-hyped Canadian tour had to be cancelled.[240]

Shea's Toronto Theater, which had heavily promoted the upcoming visit of the Foo troupe, publicly apologized for "being unable to land Ching Ling Foo in Toronto." The theater explained that "owing to international questions on the bringing of Chinese into Canada, it was impossible for Mr. Shea to get Ching Ling Foo to Toronto." To assuage their distraught patrons, Mr. Shea promised them that he had "secured the biggest and best attraction that money could buy to take the place of the magician."

The alternate attraction to act as headliners for the week Foo was to be in Toronto was the Hungarian Boy's Band, a 40-member "musical organization said to be composed of the youngest musicians in the world." Shea management assured potential ticket-buyers "they are all boys and running down to tots whose feet do not touch the floor while sitting and vie with their instruments in size. In this is the wonder of the accomplishment."[241] Also included on the bill would, be operatic stars T.W. Eckert and Emma Berg who would be presenting a Japanese operetta, Wormwood's Monkey Circus, performances by the noted thespian Charles Leonard Fletcher, and George Evans's "Honey Boy" with new stories and parodies.

Shea's management hoped to be able to work around the difficulties and have the Foo troupe in Toronto by March 5th.

More scheduling confusion, perhaps homesickness, and a desire to remove themselves from an increasingly uncomfortable contractual situation in America seems to have confronted the Foo troupe when a London theatrical publication reported in early March that Foo had rejected a 12-week summer in London offer at $1,000 a week to return to the "flowery kingdom", which he prefers, according to the publication's editors, "to the land of the 'foreign devils.'"[242]

February–March 1900, Cleveland

More Legal Troubles in Cleveland: When Foo Comes, Lafayette is Cancelled

The Foo troupe exited Buffalo to play an engagement in Cleveland at the Empire for the last week in February. The Cleveland bill also included "Lew Hawkins, the producer of original songs and sayings", some "hard shoe dancers", and new biograph pictures.[243]

The Foo troupe encountered new copycat-related legal problems when their engagement in Cleveland resulted in a lawsuit between management of the Empire Theater, where Foo would be performing, and management of Cleveland's Star Theater. It seems the Empire might have broken a contract with the Great Lafayette when they managed to book Foo, and when Lafayette learned his contract was broken, the prideful illusionist got himself booked for the same week at the Star Theater, where he would be competing directly with Foo's act. The Great Lafayette's act was anchored by a Ching Ling Foo "travesty", and his advertising now included the phrase "The Man Who Mystifies Ching Ling Foo in His Own Tricks."[244] The Empire Theater tried and failed to get an injunction preventing Lafayette from presenting his act during the week Foo was engaged at the Empire.[245]

Despite Lafayette's proximate competition, Foo broke records in Cleveland with an attendance over 3,000 souls a day for his two shows at the Cleveland Empire, averaging 1,500 a show. The Foo troupe's two weeks in Cleveland is also represented to be the first time a vaudeville act headlined for two consecutive weeks in Cleveland. During his engagement, the Empire Theater had to "construct an additional box office situated in the front vestibule" which would be "used for handling seats ordered by telephone exclusively."[246]

While Foo was performing in Cleveland, thousands of miles away in far-off Brisbane, Australia, an audience was enjoying a Foo performance through the modern technological wonder of moving pictures. The Harry Roberts Cineograph and Stereopticon film of "Ching Ling Foo and his Troupe of Chinese Jugglers" was being shown along with another film of a "Commonwealth Swearing-In Ceremony" taken in Sydney, Australia.[247] By 1900 film had already begun to displace live performance.

March 1900, Richmond, Virginia: Things Begin to Fall Apart

Finally finished in Cleveland, the Foo troupe was booked for the week of March 5th at the Bijou Theater in Richmond, Virginia. The relatively small-market theater was more than pleased with signing the prestigious troupe. The proud theater declared "that no act in vaudeville is too good for the Bijou will be demonstrated this week" when Ching Ling Foo, "the Celestial Mystifier and his family and assistants", appeared the next week.

In the Bijou's promotions, there was also an indication of the pressure the frequent press "exposés" of the alleged secrets behind Foo's illusions had put on the act. According to one promotion, the mystifying Foo, in the face of all the so-called exposures of his methodology, "goes blandly on with the new and hitherto unknown tricks, calmly ignoring all the declarations from would-be experts in magic that they have discovered the secret of his trickery." Even better, Foo continued to offer "large sums of money to the person or persons who can successfully duplicate anything he does."[248] Of course, the general Richmond public would little understand the nuances of vaudeville challenges.

The plucky Bijou's gamble on Foo seems to have paid off as an "immense audience packed the Bijou last night and a large number of people were turned away." The Foo troupe's act lasted 40 minutes.

The Richmond press went into detail on the Foo troupe's order of performers and how that allowed Foo time to go back and prepare his next tricks. After Foo's first set of productions, the Chinese magician went off stage and his wife, son, and daughter came on stage. Harry Foo, working as a juggler and comedian, came on stage next; then Foo returned, and "after fooling around with Harry, produces a huge bowl of water from that wonderful blanket." Foo exited and then returned, and "after spending some time hopping around, spreads the blanket again and out comes little Chee Toy on the stage." The Richmond Times' assessment of the act? "Ching had won another audience."[249,250]

While in Richmond, Foo sat for interviews with the local papers. The contrasting themes that came out of the interviews, and sometimes less than flattering portrayals, hinted at the friction that were now undermining the current leg of the Foo troupe's U.S. tour.

In these interviews, Foo was once more positioned as a "high-caste" northern Chinese, which was intended to contrast him with the so-called low caste "coolie" class from southern China that had recently come to the U.S. in such great numbers to build the railways and engage in other arduous labor, creating great unease. These alleged caste distinctions mirrored in some ways race issues more familiar to audiences in the Southern U.S.[251]

Richmond readers were assured Foo was both engaged in the mercantile business and a mandarin, which was explained as a status "equivalent to that of city councilor." Foo's handlers from Keith's went on to provide the Keith's-management-friendly version of Foo's "discovery", omitting the role of Colonel Hopkins and replacing him with Keith's general agent E.F. Albee. They also misrepresented how much money Foo, as an established star, was likely making in Omaha and ignored his stint with the Midwestern Hopkins theaters prior to his deportation trial. There is no question Albee and Keith's, with their expert promotion machine, elevated Foo's fame to the next level, but they certainly did not, as this article implies, start from nothing.[252]

Further discordant, un-"joy-like" notes are struck towards the end of the interview, when it was revealed that a somewhat prickly Foo would likely return to China in May, that he had a second wife back in China, and that he and his assistant and comedic juggler Harry Foo now had a bit of a rivalry because of Harry's increasing popularity on stage.

This last point seemed to presage an attempt by Keith's management for Harry to break off from the increasingly uncooperative Foo troupe and tour on his own. Finally, in these interviews, which were conducted without an official interpreter, Foo was described as not being able to "speak English very well." We get a confirmation that Foo's speech impediment was still in place and that he did indeed, when communicating in English with the reporter, "stutter."[253,254]

Another story on Foo, published just as he was finishing his Richmond engagement, also combined some odd elements that would seem to have fit an earlier stage of his U.S. tour, as opposed to one near the end of it. But the tone of the article may have had more to do with Richmond's relative parochialism at that time compared to Foo's other venues. It also likely did not help that Foo appeared to be working without an official translator and had a fraying relationship with the powerful Keith's theater management group. After noting that Foo was indeed "the highest salaried act in vaudeville," the local reporter went on to usefully note that "Ching is not one of your ordinary, every-day Chinese, such as we are familiar with. He doesn't eat rats. That rat story is a libel on the Chinese, anyway, I believe. But Ching is not to be classed with the 'heathen Chinee,' who washes and irons shirts. Ching is a high-caste Chinese, and in his own land he is a mandarin."

The reporter, who seems to have seen what he could do to get a better idea of how Foo did his tricks, also noted that Foo had apparently increased security to protect the integrity of his "professional secrets." Foo now "allows no one (not even stagehands) on that side of the stage which is located his dressing-room." Anyone on the stage with him, stagehand or otherwise, was also is constrained as to what angle they could observe him work his magic.

It was also in Richmond that for one of the first times, Chee Tai, who "can speak English as well as any child her age", was referred to in print as Chee Toy and not Chee Tai. Foo Quai is noted as speaking English "very well, though he is not as apt as his little sister."[255]

Week of March 12th, 900, Washington, D.C.: Chinese Minister Wu Ting Fang Attends a Performance, Presents Foo with American and Chinese Flags

After a week in the smaller market of Richmond, the Foo troupe returned to nearby Washington to appear the week of March 12th at the New Grand Opera House, which had been renovated to provide more seats so that the crowds turned away when Foo last appeared would not be disappointed again. Promotions for Foo noted that such had Foo's fame grown since he was last in Washington that "one vaudevillian, Lafayette by name, since he began his clever imitations of Ching, has been getting a salary of $500 a week."[256]

Potential audiences were also informed that the theater's management had used the legal process to deal with "ticket speculators" that apparently plagued theatergoers who sought to see Foo the last time he was in Washington.[257] Not content to rely on simple legal solutions to address the waves of "ticket speculators" aroused by Foo's popularity, Manager Chase of the theater introduced some more direct techniques.

On nights when performances were being given, spectators outside the Opera House were treated to the "novel sight" of a "robust man wearing a long light coat and a pink silk high hat … parading up and down before the theater carrying a big banner upon which was painted the information that desirable seats to the show could be obtained across the street." Manager Chase's efforts received "remarks favorable" from "all sides." Foo, "as usual, created the greatest astonishment among the audience."[258]

In Washington, Foo and his troupe were once more granted a rare honor on Wednesday, March 14th, by the Chinese Minister Wu Ting Fang. The chief diplomatic representative to the U.S. and his legation not only attended Foo's performance in Washington, observing him from the box seats, but also, the Chief Minister himself presented Foo on stage prior to his performance with "two silk flags, one the star-spangled banner and the other the imperial flag of the Chinese Empire." The Baltimore *Sun* helpfully added that earlier that year while in New York, Foo had received "from the Emperor of China a flag which confers upon the bearer of it the freedom of any city within the walls of China."[259]

After Washington, the Foo troupe traveled to nearby Baltimore for a week's engagement heading the bill at the Auditorium Music Hall, beginning March 19th. Once again, the Foo troupe was well-received, and Foo's magic was referred to as "the strong card" of the act. Harry Foo's juggling attracted attention and care was given to describe "the small pad bound upon" Harry's forehead "by a twist of his queue" upon which Harry caught and balanced "a heavy jardinière" weighing some 35 pounds. Foo's production of Chee Toy (Chee Tai's new name) at the end of the act out of nowhere was judged the highlight of the act.[260]

Closing in On Two Years in the U.S.: Storm Clouds and Copycats Gather

As the Foo troupe approached the end of March 1900, however, and closed in on almost two years in the U.S., problems and challenges continued to accumulate. Bookings were not coming as quickly, and they were running just one week. Despite the earlier mediation of Chinese Minister Wu Ting Fang, friction continued to build between the Foo troupe and senior Keith's manager E.F. Albee at the same time the Foo troupe finally seemed close to exhausting itself in some of the major Eastern markets.

No little contributor to the threat of market saturation for the Foo troupe had been the accelerating proliferation of copycat acts. Foo's success had now generated imitators at both the high and low ends of the entertainment market.

Magicians like Lafayette and Robert Hewes, a.k.a. "the White Yogi", represented the high end of Foo mimicry, while a slightly chauvinist media—aided by American conjurers whose noses were a little out of joint—had begun, in some cases, declaring the imitators had exceeded the original. Both Lafayette and Hewes had, in some instances, wrangled this kind of coverage.

For instance, the March 1900 issue of *Mahatma* declared that Hewes, in his act, duplicated Foo's tricks "with improvements",[261] while the next month, the magazine deemed Foo's act "tame" compared to the performance of Lafayette. According to the *Mahatma*, Lafayette's "production of the bowl of water with two live geese and floating oranges left nothing to be desired from an artistic point of view." Then, as an encore, Lafayette produced a washtub containing a toddler of about three years.

Meanwhile, in some smaller venues, a magician known as "Speed" billed himself as "the only rival of Ching Ling Foo." Mr. Speed was not the first or last Foo copycat to bill himself in this way. Foo was fast becoming the standard by which all magicians, Oriental or not, would measure themselves—in their promotional materials, at least.[262] At the same time, "Ah Foon, the Oriental entertainer" had emerged and was "playing to large houses in the Eastern States." It seems *Mahatma's* earlier exhortations for magicians to go out and copy Foo's act was beginning to bear fruit.[263]

While Lafayette and Hewes may have represented the high end of the Foo act imitation business, with Speed and Ah Foon representing the middle tier, they did not cover the whole range of competition facing Foo. By this point in Foo's U.S. tour, given his fame, the Chinese conjurer and the theaters who wanted to make money from him were also facing a growing number of decidedly low-end "Chinese magician" imitators who could now be found at the numerous low-rent "dime museums" that dotted America's emerging cities and which, with their curiosities and bottom-rung performers, occupied the lowest tier of the American entertainment ladder.

April 1900, New York: Albee Overworks and Overbooks Foo

In the midst of all this, the Foo troupe returned to New York, site of their earlier triumphs. They would headline Miner's 125th Street Theater beginning the week of April 2nd. On the bill with them were Adolph Zink, "The Lilliputian," and George Evans, "The Honey Boy".[264]

Meanwhile, E.F. Albee, looking for new ways to use the Chinese wizard after his Miner's engagement, announced that Foo was to appear as a performer in the Broadway musical comedy *From Broadway to Tokio* (or *From Broadway to Tokyo*, as it was sometimes called). Foo's participation started April 9th, which was seemingly the last week in the play's run prior to most of the cast—not including Foo—taking the play to Paris for the Exposition.[265] In yet another first associated with Foo, the writer behind *From Broadway to Tokio* was the first to coin the term "Broadway" as the word for the geographic center of American theatrical life. The appellation soon took fire.

In keeping with the constant stream of troubles emerging for Foo, the staging of *From Broadway to Tokio* came into conflict with the New York theater venue's commitment for a presentation of *Quo Vadis* during the same time period. The conflict was ultimately resolved but not without some difficulty.[266]

Simultaneous to his commitment to a role in the last week of *From Broadway to Tokio*, Foo and his troupe were booked the week of April 9th at the Bijou Theater at Broadway and 30th Street to do his regular vaudeville act. At the Bijou, Foo split the bill with Tim Murphy starring in *The Carpet Bagger*. Murphy's show played only in the evenings while Foo appeared only in the afternoons. This "Stars of Two Hemispheres" approach allowed Foo to honor his *From Broadway to Tokio* engagement in the evenings but no doubt made things rather hectic. Interestingly, Foo, in his afternoon vaudeville show was sharing the bill with the Kawakami troupe of Japanese performers.[267,268]

Very Meta: Across the Street Foo Faces Himself

Now, in one of the more meta developments in Foo's career but not the last, the wave of copycat competition facing Foo seemed to reach an apotheosis when the Comique Theater at Broadway & 29th Street, directly across from the Bijou Theater in which Foo was then performing, advertised as one of its features "Ching Ling Foo in moving pictures."

So, New Yorkers could either see Foo in the flesh for between 50 cents and a dollar at the Bijou or cross the street and see him in "moving pictures" at the Comique Theater for between 25 and 50 cents.[269]

These films of Foo appeared to be the product of the Lubin Film Company of Philadelphia, which produced the films of Foo's performances made in that city in early 1900. This film of Foo was also advertised in the New York *Clipper*, a weekly entertainment industry newspaper, the same week the Comique was showing the Foo film. In the ad, the Lubin Company promoted its "cineograph with stereopticon combined", a complete system involving both cameras and film. They also promoted their "own exclusive product—the only moving picture of the original and wonderful Chinese conjurer Ching Ling Foo and his entire company of artists." The ad went on to state "the film shows Ching performing his wonderful tricks, clear, sharp and brilliantly distinct in every detail, just as he was seen on the stage." The length of film—the measure used at the time for films—was given as about 300 feet.[270] The ad also makes clear the film is "copyrighted."

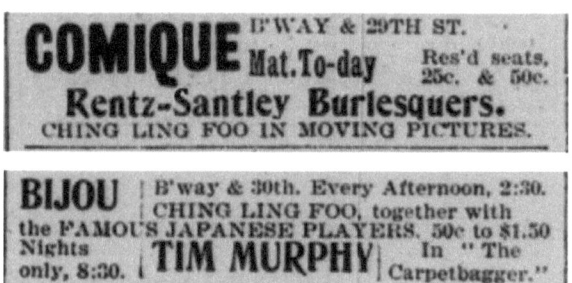

Foo encounters the disruptive nature of the new film media and its impact on live performance. In the New York *Times*, April 4th, 1900, ads appeared side by side for theaters across the street from each other: the Comique at Broadway and 29th and the Bijou at Broadway and 30th; both theaters were promoting bills featuring Ching Ling Foo. The Comique was promoting a film of Ching Ling Foo performing his tricks, while the Bijou had the real thing. See Foo live for 50 cents or cross the street and see him enlarged on the screen for half that price in "crisp, sharp, and brilliantly distinct in every detail" film.

As noted, these films of Foo made it all the way to Australia. In one instance, Foo's filmed performance was the undercard to a film of the world heavyweight boxing championship battle between the cerebral James J. Corbett and the rugged brawler James J. Jeffries. The fight and the Foo films were touted as "actual reality."[271]

The Lubin Company, given its focus on the production of unique filmmaking technology and systems as well as content, naturally took a deep interest in both understanding and applying emerging intellectual property laws designed to encourage innovation and creativity. The Lubin Company understood clearly the essential role these nascent laws could play in protecting a company's entertainment products, technical innovations and content. Thus, the company's advertisements in industry journals took pains to warn the numerous "pirates" and "infringers" that plagued the industry that they would be "vigorously prosecuted to the fullest extent of the law." Clearly, the film industry's notorious intellectual property protection problems were with it from the onset.[272]

During this period, apart from Lubin's work, several other short, pioneering films inspired by Foo were made. These included efforts by the Edison Manufacturing Company (EMC), including *Ching Ling Foo Outdone*, copies of which still exist, as well as other Chinese conjurer films inspired by Foo and made by French and German film makers that have unfortunately been lost to us.

Advertisement for Australian film bill including 1900 world championship boxing match, with Foo "the great Chinese juggler" as an undercard. To the right, promotional photo of Corbett and Jeffries. (Corbett won.)

CHAPTER SEVEN

AS CHUNG LING SOO EMERGES AND THE BOXERS UPEND TIANJIN, FOO RETURNS TO CHINA

To make matters worse for Foo, although he did not yet know it, it was around this time that Foo's ultimate copycat, Will Robinson's Chung Ling Soo, began to make his theatrical debut.

Within the tight-knit community of professional magicians, Robinson's plans to duplicate Foo's act over in Europe was an open secret. No less an authority than the industry bible *Mahatma* published in its "London Notes" of April 1900 that, "It is rumored that W. E. Robinson, the late Herrmann's assistant, is coming over to present the 'Ching Ling Foo' act. Several Frenchmen have the apparatus, and should he prove the success anticipated, the tricks would be performed more or less skillfully, all over the city."[273]

Robinson would, of course, go forward with his plans to copy Foo's act. First trying them out at the Folies-Bergère in Paris to work out any kinks in the act using the name "Hop Sing Loo" prior to heading to London for the big time, his troupe, while evidently plagued by some initial difficulties, is evaluated by knowledgeable European critics for what it was: a "clever act on the lines of Ching Ling Foo".[274]

One Parisian *Mahatma* correspondent made a historic blunder, however, with his evaluation that Robinson would have fared better if he would have presented "an evening dress performance and exhibited some of his admirable hand and mechanical illusions, as he is out of his element in Chinese business."[275] Little did the *Mahatma* correspondent realize how much in Robinson's element this "Chinese business" would become.

Ironically and fittingly, the initial American press report of Robinson's inaugural run in London at the Alhambra Theater as "Chung Ling Soo", which began in April of 1900, was misreported in the New York *Clipper* as a "Ching Ling Foo" engagement. This would be the first of generations of these sorts of mix-ups. Robinson's intent in ultimately selecting such a similar stage name to Foo's would serve him well. Apart from the name error, however, the report was accurate in identifying the act as an "Ike Rose import." It was Ike Rose who was responsible for bringing Robinson over from the U.S. to Europe to do a Ching Ling Foo act.[276]

The British papers reviewing Soo's premiere performance may have got Robinson's new stage name right, but of course, even in London at this time, no mention of the Chinese could go by without a reference to Bret Harte's aforementioned "Heathen Chinee".

Thus, we learn from a British review of Robinson's performance that "His name is Chung Ling Soo, and he has a duplicate smile to that which Bret Harte tells us was in the possession of Ah Sin, attired in gorgeous raiment with a little Chinese dame as his assistant." The "little Chinese dame" was "Dot" Robinson, Robinson's wife, who would take on the Chinese name Suee Suan.

Examining the reviews of Soo's act at this early stage and the illusions presented, it is clear as regards the tricks performed, the Chung Ling Soo act was a straight copy of the Ching Ling Foo act, right down to the production illusions, humorous sidekick, and acrobats hanging from queues. Although, to be fair, one cannot guarantee Foo's queue hangers also juggled flaming torches as they hung from the flies.

In London, 1900, William Robinson became Chung Ling Soo, and "Dot" Robinson became Suee Suan.

April 1900: An Early Chung Ling Soo Performance

The jocular *Sporting Times* laid out Soo's act for their readers in the following fashion. Soo "produces a great a basin of water out of a bundle of flags and also two low-comedy ducks. His finest feat is to swing a fishing line in the air and one after the other live goldfish appear on the hook and are put into a glass bowl." The *Sporting Times* correspondent also noted the act included a "wild untamed creature of a boy, who looks more like a Javanese" than a Chinese man, who passes his queue through a ring and swings from his hair from the flies as he juggles two torches, making patterns of fire in the air.

Soo's assistant also played the comedian role originated by Harry Foo, right down to punctuating his act with the use of popular English slang, a technique that always amused the audience. Again, Robinson was a very shrewd observer of what, beyond the magic, made Foo's work so remarkably and enduringly popular.[277,278]

Looking on from across the Atlantic, *Mahatma*, still pulling for Robinson, noted of Robinson's debut as Chung Ling Soo: "Wm. E. Robinson, tired of making fame and fortune for other performers, has crossed to Paris on his account, presenting a Chinese act. His success here and later in London more than justified the predictions of his friends and well-wishers." To add insult to injury, later in the same edition, in its review of the theatrical season to date, *Mahatma* added, "At the beginning of the season the oriental act of Ching Ling Foo was no doubt the sensation of the hour, but of late his star is on the wane. Houdini, the handcuff manipulator, has become a top-liner in our leading vaudeville houses, a place his act merited some years ago."[279]

The World's Greatest Mystifier	**HOUDINI,**	THE KING OF HANDCUFFS
The Times Philadelphia. Pa. Houdini, the "King of Handcuffs," created a profound sensation by his remarkable feats. He even in the unexplainable. character of his performance surpasses the doings of Ching Ling Foo."		Boston Herald, Boston, Mass. "Houdini is indeed the most baffling prestdigitator who has been with us for a long day. This man is like nobody or nothing in his line of performance, and one scarcely knows where to place him.

Houdini "surpasses the doings of Ching Ling Foo."

On their assessment of Houdini, the *Mahatma* is proved correct when the young magician plays the Richmond Bijou he is billed as "surpassing the doings of Ching Ling Foo."[280]

April 1900: Foo Steps Up to Help a Women's Hospital When His Own Wife Falls Ill

Foo, still in New York, found time in his busy schedule in late April 1900 for more charitable work when he stepped in to replace a major actor who was on tour to add to the entertainment package for a benefit raising money for the Hospital Guild of the New York Medical College and Hospital for Women.[281] Interestingly, and perhaps it was no coincidence, the very same week he stepped in to support the hospital, Foo's own wife had a bout of illness that resulted in not only her absence from the troupe's show, but Foo's absence as well. One suspects the somewhat frantic nature of the Foo troupe's recent performance schedule may have played its part in his wife's illness. Newspapers as far away as Washington reported the Chinese conjurer's decision to forgo his stage performances for a week to be with his ill wife.[282]

Yet Another Headache: Carter the Great Comes out of Nowhere to Claim He Owns Foo's Act

Just out of this charity engagement, Foo would encounter, to his surprise, the fascinating claims of an emerging magician, Carter the Great. Carter, it appeared, like the Lubin Company, was quite keen on the emerging practice of intellectual property rights. Just prior to opening an engagement in at the Philadelphia Grand Opera House, Carter billed himself as no less than "the originator of the Ching Ling Foo tricks."[283] Carter in his promotional bills and advertisements even attempts to copyright the phrase "The World's Greatest Magician" so it could only be applied to himself.

Carter helpfully explained to the Philadelphia press that under U.S. copyright law, he was "the only man who owns the rights to produce the Ching Ling Foo tricks." Carter claimed to have secured his rights to these illusions from one Shang Ling Ta, a Chinese conjurer who allegedly performed at the Chicago Exposition. The Chicago Exposition took place in 1893, preceding the Omaha exposition by some five years.[284] The questionable solidity of these claims was evidenced by the fact that after this brief but ambitious volley, not much more is heard of "Shang Ling Ta" or Carter's alleged unique "rights" to produce the Foo tricks. One hopes Carter received a refund from his lawyer—or Shang Ling Ta.

Yet More Woes: The Boxer Threat Emerges

If all this was not enough, amidst Foo's other amassing woes, what would be a serious threat to all his worldly goods in his home country began to emerge in China. A grass-roots Chinese anti-foreigner spiritual movement, "The Righteous and Harmonious Fists," soon to become known around the world as the Boxers, was gaining strength daily in and around Tianjin, home base for Foo's family and business interests.[285]

In late April of 1900, reports of what would become known as the Boxer Rebellion detailing horrors against Westerners and the targeting of missionaries were just beginning to appear in the British newspapers. Soon such reports would soon make their way to America, fueling and elevating already existing anti-Chinese sentiment.

With all this going on, the Foo troupe continued to deal with their increasingly chaotic bookings courtesy of a seemingly increasingly hostile Albee-led Keith's management team. They returned to New York for an engagement at Miner's 125th Street theater less than a month after they last played there. On the bill with Foo could be found Frank Cotton's Donkey Circus.[286] In the midst of all this, Foo also managed to work in yet another charity benefit in the second week of May for the Manhattan Institute of Holy Angels.[287]

DID ALEXANDER HERRMANN ORIGINATE THE BOWL PRODUCTION TRICK?

A dig from the dead comes to Foo by way of an article carried on the wire services claiming Alexander Herrmann, the beloved (and deceased since 1896) American magician had his own version of Foo's bowl production trick in his day wherein he, like Foo, would produce a glass bowl filled with water in which a number of live goldfish were "complacently swimming." This account includes the now-standard humorous mishap part of the story when the rubber lining malfunctions.[288] If this was indeed a significant part of Herrmann's act, it seems unlikely Foo's version of the illusion would have created such a furor or so many copycats that had not bothered when Herrmann was allegedly doing the trick. In addition, it is mostly conceded that Herrmann, if he did do the illusion, likely picked it up from a Chinese magician.

1900 May: In the Face of Multiple Frustrations and Rumors, Foo Contemplates Heading to London

As mid-May of 1900 approached, relief appeared to be in the offing for the Foo troupe when news came that Foo was soon to concede to the British entreaties he had been receiving and accept a London engagement. Reportedly, the only thing holding the Chinese conjurer back was indecision with regard to his choice of London venue, as he "hesitates between two great West End variety theaters." The source of this story, indicating further confusion in the Keith's management camp re: Foo, was H.H. Feiber, the Keith's representative in London. Feiber, no doubt, was very aware Robinson, as Chung Ling Soo, was already doing Foo's act in London, where the "Oriental magic" craze was just beginning to catch on.[289]

Foo's booking travails and tensions with Keith's management peaked when B.F. Keith launched a lawsuit against H. B. Sire and his Greater New York Amusement Company. Keith's had "leased" the Foo troupe to Sire's company to appear at the Bijou Theater for two weeks at $1,000 a week, and after the first few performances, Sire's company ended the performances without explanation and refused to pay the agreed sum.[290]

Clearly, after Foo's epic record-breaking runs in the city, the passion for Foo was ebbing in the immediate New York market and hurting due to the plethora of copycats, cheap imitations, and even competition from at least one widely circulating film version of himself.

The managers of the Bijou, in the face of all this and Foo's imposing weekly salary, were the first to wave the white flag. E.F. Albee then tried to book the Foo troupe elsewhere. But Mr. Sire reportedly "refused to release the wizard from his two weeks' contract, which kept him idle." Finally, Sire refused to pay for anything, and the result was Keith's lawsuit to recover.[291] Not surprisingly, in the midst of all this, rumors began to swirl that Foo had finally had enough and would soon return to China.[292]

May 25th, 1900: Foo Heads Home

This latest professional misfortune appeared to be the last straw for Foo and company as regards their U.S. tour. By May 25th, they were occupying a private luxury railway car heading from New York to Vancouver, where they would board a steamer back to Asia. Given that the Canadian rail system at that time was the only one that offered direct, uninterrupted rail travel from one coast to another, Foo and his family first headed from New York to Montreal. They would then take the Canadian railway to Vancouver, where they would board a steamer to Asia. During the trip from New York to Montreal, Chee Toy reportedly entertained the other travelers by singing ragtime songs and spoke English "to perfection."[293]

The Last Interview of Foo's First American Tour

The Chinese magician and his family once more appeared in the press prior to their departure from North America. They were halfway to Vancouver when a reporter in the Midwestern Canadian city of Winnipeg, Manitoba, during their train's stop at that city's train station, attempted an interview. The industrious reporter, having been alerted to news that a Chinese family travelling in a private luxury railway car was going to have a brief stop in his city, knew this unusual circumstance would likely lead to a story.

Thus, when the Foos arrived at the Winnipeg station for a brief pause in their journey, the reporter, thinking the Chinese visitor might be a "Mandarin" or "at least an agent of the government of China", sought out an interview. He managed to board the train and approach Foo in his luxury car. According to the reporter's account, Foo, once approached, apologized for his English, and the interview was on the edge of being lost. One suspects, however, Foo was just keen to avoid yet another interview. The journalist's luck then turned when young Chee Toy popped out from under one of the bunks on the other side of the railway car and demanded in perfect English "What do you want?"

A quick interview was had with Chee Toy (now regularly going by that name) as translator. Unfortunately, Chee Toy's acknowledged lisp and the reporter's ear got in the way of a proper transcription. When the reporter published his story later, headlined "A Smart Boy", he incorrectly quotes the gender-misidentified Chee Toy as saying her father worked as a "musician", not "magician", in New York. Too bad for the reporter. If he realized he had the legendary Chinese wizard Ching Ling Foo on his hands, he would have had a much bigger story.[294] So ended the last interview to be had with Foo on North American soil for twelve years.

Three days later, Foo and his wife, along with Chee Toy and Foo Quai, boarded the *Empress of India* in Vancouver, bound for Yokohama and Hong Kong.[295] The ship would arrive in Yokohama around June 19, 1900 and then sail on to Hong Kong. Although their intentions were likely otherwise, it would be more than a decade before the Foo troupe would return to America.

Summer of 1900: Real World Intrudes Upon the Illusions; the Boxer Revolution Hits Home

In the midst of all this cashing in on the popularity of Foo and mania for Asian magic in general, the geopolitical realities surrounding the rise of the Boxers continued to percolate. As events in China reached a boil, the first major coverage of the Boxer uprising and their targeting of foreigners and symbols of perceived Western oppression, such as the railways, began to make its way onto the pages of American newspapers.

In July of 1900, the Philadelphia Pier Theatre, which did great business in the hot summer because of its location near the beach and the cool breezes it enjoyed, showed not only films of Foo's act, but also the latest film addressing what was happening in

Sample U.S. headlines and editorial cartoon coverage of the Boxer Rebellion, July 1900. The Boxers represent "murder" and "anarchy", while the "Allied Powers" are driven by "civilization."

China with the increasingly notorious Boxers. These films were played during the intermission required for the popular opera *Olivette*.[296]

The news coverage and film depictions of Chinese and the Boxers being produced exhibited the xenophobia and racism of the times. Typical of the Boxer films made at the time were *Rescue of a White Girl from the Boxers* (1900), *How the Artist Captured the Chinese Boxers* (1900), and *An American Soldier Tortured by Boxers* (1900).[297]

A July 1900 page one article and accompanying cartoon from the Philadelphia *Record* addressing ongoing negotiations with the Chinese regarding the Boxer situation focused on perceived Chinese duplicity, with the almost inevitable reference to and quotation from Harte's poem "Heathen Chinee."

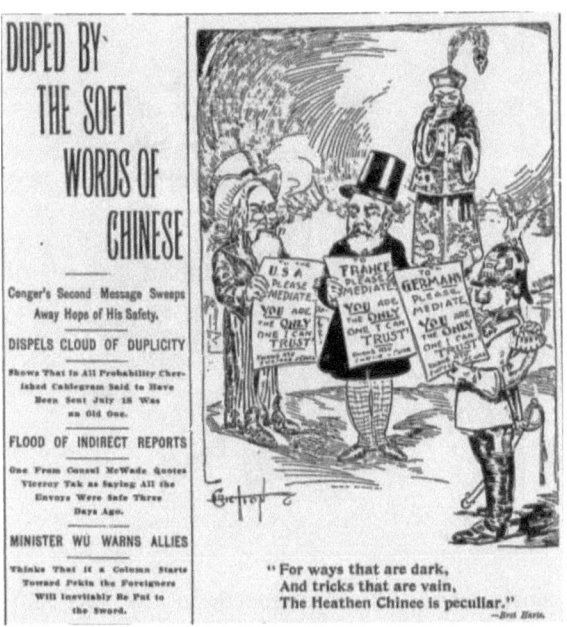

"Duped by the Soft Words of the Chinese." A July 1900 cartoon from the Philadelphia *Record* warning against being "duped" by the Chinese includes the almost inevitable reference to Harte's poem "Heathen Chinee."

Amidst all this, one of the tamest cartoons addressing the Boxer situation appeared in the Washington *Evening Star* and drew marked attention across the U.S. The editorial cartoon featured Uncle Sam and Ching Ling Foo representing their respective countries. In the cartoon, Foo is stands on a stage producing large bowls from underneath his magical shawl. Foo has already produced the message from America's besieged ambassador and the latest Chinese government statement on the matter. Foo is in the course of producing a bowl containing the Chinese appeal for mediation as Uncle Sam says "Very good so far—now produce my minister."[298]

In his production demand, Uncle Sam was referring to the diplomat Edwin H. Conger, the U.S. Minister to China, who, with other foreigners, was at the time under siege by the Boxers in the foreign compounds of Beijing.[299] The cartoon is remarkable in its relative balance

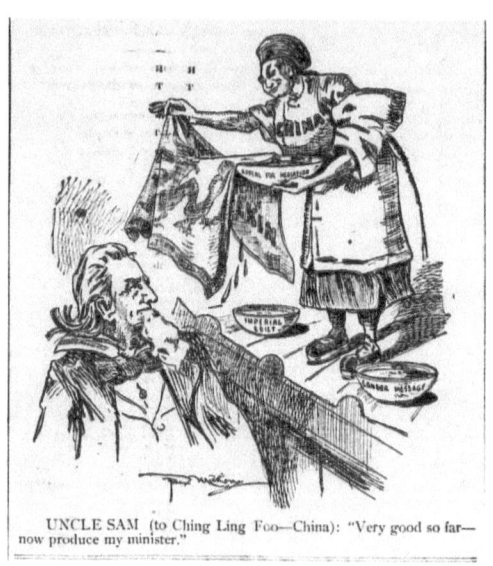

UNCLE SAM (to Ching Ling Foo—China): "Very good so far—now produce my minister."

In this composite of elements drawn from the July 26th, 1900 edition of the *Washington Evening Star*, Ching Ling Foo, representing China and mimicking Chinese communications to date, produces "the Conger Report", "the Imperial Edict", and the "appeal for mediation" for Uncle Sam, which is all well and good, but Uncle Sam wants the Chinese to "produce" his ambassador to China, who, with the other members of the Foreign delegations in Beijing, has been under siege.

and relatively inoffensive depiction of the Chinese. Not surprising in this context is that an editorial cartoon advocating cool heads and negotiation with the Chinese, as opposed to the much more common suggestion of violent retribution, ethnocentrism and jingoism seen in other editorial cartoons, used a depiction of the well-thought-of and dignified Ching Ling Foo to represent China. Foo's friend Wu Ting Fang, who is referred to as "Minister Wu" in the article and was liaising with the U.S. government on this issue, would have been pleased.

June to August 1900: News of Foo Comes from Amidst the Boxers

Then, in the midst of all this news of the turmoil in China in August of 1900, the world received its first word on the fate of the Foo troupe since they set off to return to China some three months earlier.

> Ching Ling Foo and the Boxers
>
> CHINESE MAGICIAN WRITES A LETTER
>
> ## A LETTER FROM CHING LING FOO.
>
> Chinese Conjurer Fears His Parents Have Been Killed.
>
> *THE MAGICIAN AND THE BOXERS*
>
> ## CHING LING FOO HEARD FROM
>
> The Necromancer Is Worried About His Assistants

August 1900 headlines generated by letters from Foo setting out his and his troupe's current circumstances in the midst of the Boxer uprising.

E.F. Albee, the senior Keith's executive who had played a major role in managing Foo's career in the latter stages of Foo's time in America, had received a letter from Foo. Albee shared with a curious America the letter Foo had sent from Shanghai dated June 23rd. In it, Foo set out what had happened to the troupe since they left America.

Clearly, initially, Foo, like the wider public, was unaware of the extent of the Boxer upheaval and the potential chaos to come when he left America back in May 1900. From the limited selection of translated excerpts from Foo's letter provided by Albee, we learn that Foo, upon returning to China, first headed to Hong Kong to pursue some business. Unaware of the extent of the unrest brewing, the rest of his family had gone separately to their home base at the time, the northern Chinese city of Tianjin. There, Foo's family soon became caught up in the emerging Boxer chaos, as Tianjin was essentially the epicenter of the conflict, while Foo, in Hong Kong, was wracked with worry while he waited to reestablish contact.[300,301]

American interest in Foo's travails with the Boxers proved strong. Days later, a longer translated excerpt of Foo's letter was carried by the wire services and published in papers across America as front-page news. This excerpt from the letter, dated June 23rd, includes the information that Foo's hometown is indeed Tianjin, and that the extent of the Boxer outbreak and unrest there took Foo and most of China by surprise. Foo states he had travelled to Hong Kong for business, then returned to Shanghai, and now does not know the fate of his wife and children, who had travelled separately to Tianjin. The conjurer writes of the enormous destruction caused by the Boxers and their claims of supernatural powers, concluding that the outcome of all this unrest remains very uncertain.[302]

U.S. news outlets gradually begin to focus more on the tumult roiling northern China as more news of the unsettling Boxer Rebellion came in. Reports claimed that in just one battle between Western forces in China and the Boxer rebels, more than 1,250 Western-allied country forces were killed and wounded, while three times that number of Chinese were killed or wounded due to the Western side's superiority in weapons. The report indicated that the Allies had 16,000 soldiers in the battle, and that it lasted over seven and a half hours.

The report went on to note that "the Allies" and the Chinese continued to "fight stubbornly" along the rail lines linking Tianjin and Beijing. Most of the casualties reported were of Russian and Japanese troops, who were already jockeying for influence in and control of northern China before the hostilities started. Western papers also reported that two senior members of the Chinese Foreign Office were put to death for "alleged friendliness to foreigners," signaling the dissension within the Chinese leadership on how to deal with the Boxer revolt and its goal of driving foreign forces out of China.[303]

As the resolution of the Boxer Rebellion in August and September of 1900 approached, note should be taken of the relatively principled stand America took in the face of the Boxer crisis. Debates raged in the youthful country regarding the cause of the uprising and the morality of European imperialism and colonialism. America's "Open Door" policy towards China took a middle ground by requiring China to remain open to trade but opposing the wholesale carving up of the country by the European powers, Russia and Japan. This attitude was reflected in the use America later made of its share of the overly onerous reparations charged to China after the uprising by dedicating those sums to a fund used to sponsor Chinese students to come and study in America—a foresighted policy if ever there was one.

August 1900: In the Midst of the China Turmoil, Soo Continues to Hone His Act in London

News of Foo's fate in the midst of this turmoil was also published in the theatrical journals of London, where, importantly, William Robinson—now masquerading as Chung Ling Soo—would have read them. These letters no doubt laid the seeds that would enable Robinson to construct Soo's own public relations campaign to ensure the growing resentment against the Boxers did not impact the popularity of his own "Chinese act."[304]

Apart from preparing his response to the Boxer threat to Chung Ling Soo's popularity, William Robinson continued to demonstrate his deep understanding of what made the Foo troupe a hit beyond just the skill of Foo and its other performers. Soo recognized that a key part of the Foo act's appeal was not just Foo's magic, but the way it was presented, particularly the way the Foo troupe was promoted as a genuine Chinese family. Soo, in promoting his act in London, followed in kind.[305]

October 1900: Albee Receives More News of Foo

In October, the worst of the Boxer crisis now over, Albee received more news of Foo in a second letter, which the magician wrote from Hong Kong, dated August 18th, 1900. Translated excerpts appeared in newspapers across the U.S. under the headline, "Ching Ling Foo Heard From."

In these excerpts, Foo explained he was now in Hong Kong and that he went to Tianjin from Shanghai with his assistants. In Tianjin, some sort of Boxer-induced commotion occurred, and Foo and members of his troupe were separated and had to run for their lives. Foo explains he made it safely back to Hong Kong, where he has been living for about a month. Foo would return soon to Tianjin to see if he could locate the members of his troupe lost in the tumult. He closed his letter indicating he hoped he can find his troupe members, but feared in the chaos he well may not, and thus would have to rebuild and retrain a team if he was to return and tour the U.S.[306]

Despite the emergence of the telegraph, obtaining reliable news regarding the Boxer revolution out of China—particularly during a time when the Boxers were destroying Western telegraph systems surrounding Beijing and Tianjin—proved difficult. This is why Foo's letters had such an impact. In the absence of solid information, speculation, misinformation, and rumors ran rampant. In this environment, *Mahatma* published a report in January of 1901 that Foo's wife and two children, as well as the troupe's juggler Harry Foo, had been killed by an enraged Boxer mob.

"From China comes the news that Ching Ling Foo, who returned to Pekin from this country last June, has lost his wife and two children through the Boxer uprising. It seems that at the start of the trouble, they were sent to a suburban town, under the protection of Harry Foy, the juggler and comedian of the troupe. An outbreak occurred here, and Foy incurred the hatred of the mob by attempting to defend the missionaries, and a few days later the rioters murdered Ching Ling Foo's wife, son and the little girl and soon after beheaded Harry Foy."[307,308]

This account was not corroborated at any time later by any other source, including, importantly, Foo, so one should believe it reflected the reality of events on the ground as they unfolded. Also, the reference to Foo's two children in the story would have likely been to Chee Toy and Foo Quai, who clearly survived the upheaval surrounding the Boxer Rebellion. Finally, the idea that Harry died protecting missionaries, while not inconceivable, seems to comfortably fit a Chinese-magician-friendly narrative that would, importantly, put Foo and his troupe on the side of the "good" Chinese who sided with the Westerners and opposed the Boxers. This is precisely how Albee and Keith would want to position Foo, whom they seemed to anticipate bringing back to America soon. This narrative that Foo was on the "right side" of the Boxer Rebellion would also soon inspire Chung Ling Soo's approach to the matter.

February 1901: "Ching Ling Foo's Hard Luck" Continues

Confirmation that the beheading of Harry Foo tale was not completely accurate came almost a month later with the publication in late February of 1901 of yet more translated excerpts of Foo's latest letter to Albee. In the Foo letter excerpts reported in the New York *Times*, Foo relates that since his return to China, "his lot has been to meet untold troubles." Members of his family as well as friends had lost their property and sometimes their lives. Foo's third brother was reported dead at the hands of foreign troops, while his mother

Ching Ling Foo's Hard Luck.

CHING-LING-FOO'S WOES.

The Conjurer Writes to Manager Albee from China That He Has Suffered Greatly.

The Sorrows of a Magician.

SOME INSIDE NEWS OF BOXER OUTRAGES

Ching Ling Foo Writes a Letter of Chinese Troubles

For the American public, Foo's fate in the midst of the Boxer Rebellion was a point of major interest.

had fled to Chong Chou, about 200 miles from Tianjin. The paper further reported that Foo's "daughter is with her mother, and only through the aid of the Red Cross Society and their meagre knowledge of English where they enabled to reach Shanghai, leaving everything in their native town behind them"; while Foo Quai, Foo's son, is reported to have taken refuge in the country. Meanwhile, Harry Foo, the juggler, survived the upheaval only due to the "assistance of a European suit" and the good fortune to fall in with some English troops.[309]

Finally, the magician related that all his property and business interests had been destroyed while up to 50% of Tianjin's population, "rich and poor", had abandoned the city due to the chaos.[310]

Only about a week later, a notice appeared in papers across the country from E.F. Albee announcing that Foo would return "soon" to America and "fulfill his contracts." This clearly did not happen, but it did demonstrate that at least Albee, at that point, was ready for Foo to return.[311]

"Unless he says 'twee'": In the midst of the Boxer furor and the interest in Foo's fate, a housing supply retailer integrated Foo and his magic into its advertising campaign, a move that would be replicated many times in the future.[312]

Apart from his use in advertising campaigns, the memory of the now-absent Foo was also retained in the American sports pages of the

> day, where the magician is often invoked. A typical instance appears in the description of a 1901 baseball game wherein the visitors bested the locals with their superior ball handling skills. "You should have seen the visitors juggle. Ching Ling Foo ain't in it with them."[313]

March 1901: Foo's Last Letter

Weeks after Albee's announcement that Foo would be returning to the U.S. to "fulfil his contracts", the latest letter from Foo was published across the country via the wire services. In it, Foo outlined the catastrophic events of the past months and the significant toll they had taken on his physical health.

In the letter Foo informed Albee "my health has been much impaired by the serious losses I have sustained. At the present time, I am under medical treatment and I am in hope to soon recover. As soon as my health is fully restored, I shall hasten to act, looking to fulfilling my agreement with you. My failure to do so was only due to troubles which are so well known to the world. I do perfectly realize the kindness you have shown me, which I heartily appreciate. If you are still desirous of my services, I shall feel myself in duty bound to live up to my contract without fail, no matter where you desire I should go. If you will kindly inform me of the address of such place as you desire to have me go, I shall be pleased to be at your services."

This latter part of Foo's letter echoed the earlier letters from Foo released for publication by Albee, in that all seem to include a reference to Foo's contractual obligations to him. In this most recent letter from Foo, the language regarding contractual obligations was even clearer. With the publication of these letters, it seemed Albee was sending a message that he still controlled Foo's bookings and that Foo was under his control. In so doing, they echoed the contractual difficulties Keith's management had with Foo before the Chinese conjurer returned to China, and those Foo would have with them when Foo would ultimately return to America some ten years later.[314]

May 1901: Meanwhile, in England, Chung Ling Soo Prospers

Meanwhile, in England, Soo—whose renown was growing by leaps and bounds—had taken his act outside London and was performing both in "the provinces" and on the Continent. At the Brighton Alhambra in May 1901, Soo, "in gorgeous native dress and amid typical Chinese scenic surroundings", was basically still presenting a Foo "travesty" in all but name. All Foo's staples—the production tricks, fire-eating, flower-producing, "Ching Ling Foo Cones", and even his live bird manipulation illusion—were duplicated by Soo. The supporting troupe Soo had assembled also mimicked, to the extent possible, the supporting performers of the Foo troupe. Soo's troupe numbered contortionists, plate spinners, and wise-cracking acrobats who made liberal use of English slang. In one instance, a young acrobat finished his hanging-by-the-queue act by being lowered back to the ground and exiting the stage with the remark "There's hair!".

Later that month, Soo took his act to the Continent, where he had a successful run at *La Palais d'Ete* in Brussels, where he was billed as "*le fameux magician chinois.*"[315]

These early Chung Ling Soo posters demonstrate how the early Soo act copied Foo so closely, and the lifelong investment in high-quality promotional posters Chung Ling Soo was going to make a cornerstone of his promotional materials. These Soo posters are today highly collectible, with some samples priced in the tens of thousands of dollars. Soo clearly had a good eye.

March 1902: More Rumors of Foo's Return

Ching Ling Foo Coming.
It is reported that Ching Ling Foo is coming to this country again, but the rumour is all in the air.

In early 1902, reports were published across the U.S. wire services that Foo was returning for another American tour.

New rumors of an imminent Foo return, inevitably placed by Keith and Albee, hit the U.S. papers in March of 1902.[316] The topic was picked up by Henry Evans over in London writing for the English magic trade periodical *Stanyon's Magic*. According to Evans, Foo was supposedly finally getting his footing in China as the repercussions of the Boxer Rebellion died down. Foo was reportedly hard at work putting together another act and securing the equipment and paraphernalia he would require prior to another tour of the U.S.[317]

Soo's Scheme to Become the European Foo Succeeds

In discussing Foo, given Evans was based in London, the subject of "Billy Robinson, the Chung Ling Foo of the London Music Halls whose Chinese make-up has deceived so many people", naturally comes to mind, and Evans noted Soo is among the many "imitators" of Foo. Interestingly, Evans, like so many commentators, garbled the two men's names, calling Robinson "Chung Ling Foo", not Chung Ling Soo. Evans also praises Robinson as a wily inventor of card tricks, but someone who is sometimes too eager to expose their mechanisms to non-professionals. This interestingly presages complaints about Robinson that would arise years later, when it was learned that an ongoing series of articles in the lauded journal *Scientific American* that revealed how certain tricks and illusions were done came from the pen of William Robinson.[318]

The Sincerest Form of Flattery

Of all Foo's imitators, it was Soo who most completely captured the Foo troupe's act. Everything Foo did was mimicked, including performance style and promotion methods.

Like Foo, Soo remained mute on stage but purported to struggle with the English language in smaller settings like an interview. But the alleged effort involved supposedly caused Soo to speak very slowly, which gave a journalist working for the Leigh *Chronicle* and others the impression that Soo's knowledge of English may not be "as extensive as a college professor", but that "he can express himself without leaving the listener confused." While performing in Leigh, Soo, like Foo, relies on a "son" ("Prince Fee Lung") to handle any English announcements required.[319]

Not content just to appropriate Foo's act, performing style, and promotion techniques, Robinson even appropriated Foo's own personal history.

Like Foo, Soo threw out various versions of his backstory over the years.[320] Soo's earliest versions of his backstory, not surprisingly, resembled those of Foo. Early on, Soo claimed to have spent a "score" of years travelling Asia and that he grew up in the south of China, the son of a physician and worked with his father in that field until wanderlust took him and he travelled to America just in time for not Foo's Omaha Exposition of 1898 but rather the Chicago Exhibition of 1893. Soo further claimed he had originally started work as a doctor in Chicago but was soon drawn to perform as a magician after complying with startled colleagues' demands he follow his true calling and demonstrate his skills with cards and legerdemain to a wider public. This then led to his career launch and great success at the 1893 Chicago Exhibition.

Soo also informed reporters he returned to China between engagements and was always working on new tricks. Echoing the intentions Foo voiced while in America, Soo stated his "intention to organize a company composed of some 30 or more Chinese and tour round with it, giving an entertainment which will illustrate life in the Flowery Land."[321] Of course, this version of Soo's backstory, like his stage name, was clearly intended to sow confusion with regards to Ching Ling Foo and Chung Ling Soo.

December 1902: Despite Chung Ling Soo's Success in Europe, He Will Never Be Seen as "the Original Chinese Conjurer" in America

Despite all Soo's efforts, however, it appeared one major audience was clearly aware of who the "Original Chinese Conjurer" was and who was the copycat. As early as December 1902, the well-known American magazine *The Cosmopolitan*, with a circulation in the hundreds of thousands, published an article entitled "The Best Tricks of Famous Magicians", which included references to the still-fondly remembered Foo, who by that time had been out of the U.S. for almost three years.

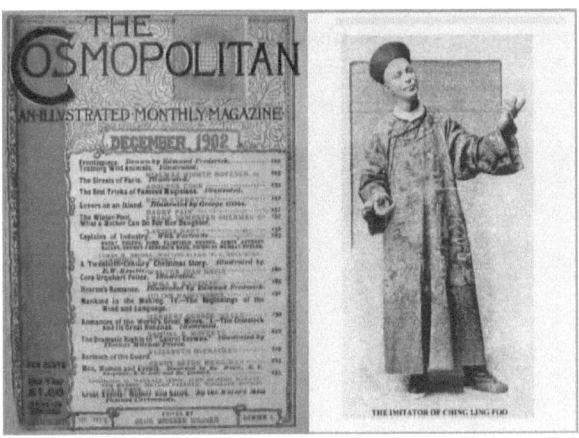

"The Imitator of Ching Ling Foo": So says *The Cosmopolitan* its December 1902 story, "The Best Tricks of Famous Magicians." In the 1900s, *The Cosmopolitan*, a hugely popular general-interest magazine, had a circulation in the hundreds of thousands.

In words that would have been painful for William Robinson to read, *The Cosmopolitan* clearly laid out who, in fact, Chung Ling Soo really was.

"There is no more conclusive evidence of Ching Ling Foo's greatness than is to be found in imitation, that sincere flattery paid to the Asiatic giant by Mr. William E. Robinson, for whose valuable services as an assistant Mr. Herrmann and Mr. Kellar bid against each other for so many years. Mr. Robinson is now playing in Europe as Chung Ling Soo. He does the complete act of the Chinese, and dresses in Chinese costume even on the street."[322] *The Cosmopolitan* added to the bluntness of their assessment of the relationship between the two conjurers in the text accompanying a promotional photograph of Chung Ling Soo.

"The Imitator of Ching Ling Foo": Not exactly the way Chung Ling Soo preferred to promote his act. This clarity in the U.S. regarding just where Soo's act came from no doubt heavily influenced the proud performer's decision to never tour in the U.S., where memories of Foo and knowledge of his actual background would completely deconstruct his claims to be Chinese, let alone "the Original Chinese Conjurer." Robinson a.k.a. Soo well realized, as regards America, it was best for him to keep to his newfound side of the Atlantic.

CHAPTER EIGHT

SOO'S FAME GROWS AS FOO BACK ON HIS FEET IN SHANGHAI PREPARES FOR HIS NEXT TOUR

December 1902: Foo is Back to Playing the Theaters of Shanghai

As Soo's career, so heavily indebted to Foo, prospered in Europe, Foo, the now-recovered original Chinese conjurer, was just now back to playing theaters in Shanghai. One of Foo's earliest returns to the stage was at the Shanghai Lyceum for the holiday season on December 31st, 1902.

Having observed that performance, one Shanghai entertainment critic, jaded to Asian magic, conceded that while Foo's tricks and the troupe's acrobats are excellent, they are nothing not seen quite often from Chinese conjurers and acrobats by anyone who has been in China any length of time. Chee Tai, however, who would have been seven or eight years old at the time, is singled out for particular praise, presaging the great triumphs she would see in America some ten years hence, as a "little girl remarkable for her 'mimical' singing." Chee Tai was crowned "the hit of the night."

The impressed reviewer noted that Chee Toy's "coolness and self-possession and the engaging way in which she put herself at once on good terms with her audience would have done credit to a musical artist four times or five times her age." Her performance, consisting of the singing of popular Western songs including ragtime numbers, was "encored again and again" and she "responded most cheerfully", once more indicating that the Foo troupe was something special even in Asia. The "audience applauded madly when it was announced the troupe would do another show New Year's Day."[323]

By early 1903, the Foo troupe's return to the stage continued apace. The current act, still doing shows at the Shanghai Lyceum, admittedly drew a "scanty crowd." But the reviewer well noted that the Foo troupe would find much more appreciative audiences outside the treaty ports of China, whose Chinese and foreign citizens had seen the work of more than a few Chinese conjurers in their time. The new act Foo was still busy putting together included, of course, Foo's production tricks and "trained sparrows" that "appeared, disappeared, died and revived as obediently as he could have wished." The audience, "scanty" as it was, was still appreciative, however, and "asking for more" at half past eleven.

Once more, "the undoubted favorite of the evening was tiny Chee Toy." The young singer's renditions of popular American and English songs again delighted the audience and "her final appeal for an 'all together' chorus fetched the gods mightily." Also featured in the act was a "strong-haired trio" whose "extraordinary maneuverings while dangling from their queues from the ends of swinging ropes" fascinated the crowd, while the usual contortionists, acrobats, and plate spinners did their parts well.[324]

As he did in the U.S., Foo in China supplemented the troupe's income by providing private performances. In one such instance, he and his troupe provided the entertainment for the George Washington birthday celebrations at the U.S. Shanghai Consul General's house on February 24th, 1903. All the important people from the international and Chinese communities attended, and it was a gala affair. The Foo troupe's performance ran an hour and a half, and in-between Foo's feats, Chee Toy "very much amused the guests by singing ditties."[325]

April 1903: More Rumors of Foo's Imminent Return to America

By April of 1903, more news was heard of Foo's impending return to America to tour the U.S., and this time it was made very clear that if this event did take place it would be under the management of John D. Hopkins and B. F. Keith. The report, again carried across the U.S. wire services, reads, "Ching Ling Foo, the Chinese conjurer, who went back to China just before the Boxer outbreak and was lost for several months, has been heard from. He will return to America and play under the management of John D. Hopkins and B.F. Keith."

This back-and-forth on the dates for Foo's return tour, and Hopkins and Keith's very public repeated assertions that they are Foo's managers, seemed to reflect some distance between Foo and his alleged American managers. It also raised questions regarding the exact nature of their contractual relationship and the legal implications of the management contract Foo supposedly signed after a deal had allegedly been mediated by China's Chief Minister in the U.S., Wu Ting Fang, between Foo, E.F. Keith, and Hopkins just before Foo left America. It should be remembered that the contract reportedly put Foo under Hopkins and Keith's managerial control for "many years."[326]

> Foo's enduring fame in America is once more exhibited in May of 1903 when "beautiful" Luna Park, "the heart of Coney Island", promotes its new exhibitions, which include a Chinese Theater with the claim that they have a "New Ching Ling Foo."

With Foo's anticipated return very much a topic of the hour among professional magicians, it was not entirely surprising for the *Sphinx*, the reputed professional magicians' periodical, to republish information outlining how Foo allegedly performed his bowl production tricks and portions of his fire-eating and -breathing act. This exposé basically repeated, down to the accompanying diagrams, what was published earlier in some regional newspapers when Foo was in the U.S. years earlier.[327]

August 1903: Foo's New Management Team — Meet the Moosers

With regard to the tortured issue of just when Foo might return to America and the various reasons for the delays, a relevant article appeared in the popular San Francisco-based periodical *The Wasp* in late August 1903 that may have shed some light on the rationale for all those publicized claims by Colonel Hopkins and B.F. Keith that they had Foo under contract.

The *Wasp* article relates the story of the "Brothers Mooser in China." These (to the editors) "well-known former residents of San

Francisco" were now active in the entertainment and circus business and based in China. According to *The Wasp*, Leon Mooser, not Hopkins and Keith, were then managing Foo, and Mooser was planning on taking Foo to London. This seemingly new, chaotic contractual situation for Foo, along with new, tighter U.S. immigration laws affecting Chinese entertainers, may have played key roles in delaying Foo's return to America.

As to the Mooser brothers, *The Wasp* informed its readership that George Mooser, originally a newspaper man, got his start in Shanghai when he took a job there from San Francisco to take charge of *L'Echo de Chine*, but he gave that up to join his brother Leon in the exciting world of circus management. Apart from representing the Foo troupe, the Mooser brothers currently were also managing Baroufsky's Imperial Russian Circus and Chatres' Indian circus. The periodical importantly notes the brothers were fully aware of the difficulties "the Exclusion Act" presented to any efforts to bring these acts to the U.S.[328]

November-December 1903: Soo Publishes a Book of Chinese Fairy Tales

Chung Ling Soo the wonderful Chinese conjurer, sends per his manager, Mr. J. Rose, a little booklet to "Quiz," containing fairy tales of the Flowery Land. The booklet, which is mailed from Cardiff, Wales, contains the best known Chinese legends amongst them the famous "Willow Pattern Plate." Included is a sheet giving an illustrated interview with Chung Ling Soo, who is assisted in his entertainments by Prince Fee Lung, his son, and a pretty Chinese maiden, Suee Seen. C. L. Soo is now booking for 1904 and onwards, so managers better get in early and avoid the crush.

To the right: cover, enhanced from fragments, of Chung Ling Soo's book of Chinese fairy tales published in late 1903. To the left: a quote from Australia's *Quiz Magazine* regarding the work. Works translated include *The Willow Pattern Plate*, a tale which Soo used as the inspiration for one of his later illusions. The Chinese characters read "Chung Ling Soo, Magician".

Promotional shots of Soo appearing in the January 1904 edition of London's *Tatler* magazine.

Meanwhile, in London, the end of 1903 arrived with new efforts by Soo to extend his brand. This time it was with a book of Chinese fairy tales. Soo produced the book just prior to the booking season for 1904 as a vehicle to promote himself. News stories covering Soo's production of the book, which is sent to entertainment reporters and editors in major theater markets around the world, helpfully inform recipients that Soo is "now booking for 1904 and onwards." So, theater managers are encouraged to "get in early and avoid the crush." Soo was nothing if not a world class promoter.[329]

In another money-making move predicated on Soo's keen understanding of the public's appetite for all things Asian, Soo appears, from business notices in *The Stage*, a London theatrical trade newspaper, to be leasing stage space to a Japanese magic act, the Lukushima Troupe of Japanese acrobats heading the bill at the Oxford. William Robinson is listed as the lessee of the theatre.[330]

March 1904: Lazern Brings News of Foo

Perhaps in reaction to rumors of Foo's imminent return to the U.S., we see yet another exposure of a major Foo trick. This time it is Foo's famous paper-shredding and reassembly illusion. In the New York *Times*, the author of *Later Magic* explained for the paper's readers how Foo's famous trick works. Readers were informed how the trick involved tearing a strip of paper held by the magician into small pieces, rolling them between the fingers, and reproducing the single strip whole without a tear as it was before. The author informed them that the trick was a second strip of paper hidden between thumb and finger. He explains that the act of holding the paper to be torn hides, through the positioning of the hand and finger, the second strip of paper. Then, the pressed-together torn bits of paper are replaced by the hidden whole roll when the cut strips are placed in the hand. People also used false thumbs or flesh-colored tubes hidden between fingers to conceal the second roll of paper.[331]

Fresh news of Foo was heard in the pages of *The Sphinx* when Emile Lazern, a prominent Australian magician, reported having met with Foo when he was performing in Shanghai, and how Chee Toy and Foo's son participated in Lazern's act while he was there.[332]

May: 1904: Rumored to be Going to London

By mid-1904, rumors of the ever-impending U.S. Foo tour are replaced by rumors Foo would now be going to London and Europe. *The Sphinx*, in May of 1904, reported that Foo had been booked at the London Empire, adding the definitive-sounding detail that he would be paid $1,075 per week. In the same edition of *The Sphinx*, it was stated that "W.E. Robinson (Ching Ling Soo) is on the Stoll Tour, doing as well as ever." *Sphinx* editors added that rumor had it the ever-ambitious Soo planned "to enlarge his own show and go out on his own account." One can only assume that "rumor" came directly from Soo.[333]

A month later, additional information emerged that Foo would likely perform in South Africa *en route* to London. The headline in London's *Music Hall and Theatre Review* reads Foo to go to South Africa "in the immediate future." The review also mistook the Foo troupe for Japanese performers.[334]

In London, Soo Alters the Act, Develops His Own Illusions

Meanwhile, by late 1904, Soo had moved on from simply imitating Foo's tricks and had engaged his considerable design and organizational skills into setting up his own workshop, reminiscent of his old one at Martinka's in New York, where he, with his specially-trained workmen, developed new and impressive illusions.[335]

What is noteworthy here is that Soo had begun using the wealth he was accumulating to develop new tricks and larger-scale illusions that would characterize his later career. Of course, in this, Soo had already demonstrated a great talent when he worked in developing illusions, first at the legendary magic shop and illusion factory of the Martinka's, and then later as a chief illusionist technician in the elaborate magic workshop foundries of the great American magicians Herrmann and Kellar.

This piece also contains a mention of Soo's ill-fated bullet capture trick, designed to establish for British audiences that Foo was on the right side of the Boxer conflict.[336] In the article, Soo was rightly described as not only a magician but "an artist." The author duly noted "he recognizes the value of creating an 'atmosphere.' The beauty and realism of his costumes and scenery, the pageant of his Mandarin's procession" are as carefully thought out and presented as the greatest works of art. Much of this probably originated from Soo's promotion department, but that did not make it untrue. Soo, along with Lafayette, shared with Foo an artistic quality and charisma that benefited all their magic.

July 1904: Just Before Foo Heads to London, an Odd Report on His Life in Shanghai

Just on the verge of Foo's anticipated arrival in London, *Mahatma*, never an enormous proponent of Ching Ling Foo and seemingly forever in the corner of Chung Ling Soo, published an interesting but quite ethnocentric piece on Foo and his family, penned by performer and manager Max Berol. Berol had met with Foo while recently performing in Shanghai with the Konorah Company, which was headed by his wife, Madame Konorah. Madame Konorah was billed as a Modern Witch and Mystic Calculator. In Shanghai, Berol reported they performed before "the better class Chinese, the mandarins, compradors, and shroffs."

Berol's piece in *Mahatma* was interesting, as it purported to provide a description of Foo's home and home life in Shanghai; but one suspects, given *Mahatma's* ongoing bias for Soo and its not unrelated, somewhat chauvinistic attitude towards Foo, the account was perhaps intentionally rather unflattering. Information to be discussed later regarding the relatively wealthy Foo's multiple homes in Shanghai and Tianjin would cast doubt on Berol's assumption below that the rather ramshackle abode he described was indeed Foo's primary residence in Shanghai. One suspects any understanding that it was is best understood as a communication error between the two.

That said, the overall tone of Berol's piece, in keeping with previous *Mahatma* coverage of Foo, was condescending and read like it was penned by a supporter of the "no" side of the then-ongoing, at the time, US. debate of the "Chinese Question" as to whether the Chinese could assimilate into U.S. culture or not.

Berol began by recounting the numerous and varied reports of Foo's demise that had been reported since the conjurer returned to his homeland in the midst of the Boxer uprising. In some accounts, he had died at the hands of the Boxers; in other accounts he succumbed to the plague in Tianjin. Happily, though, Berol discovered Foo in 1904 alive and well, family intact, and performing in Shanghai.

Once communications were established, Foo invited the Konorah troupe for tea. After meeting with Foo, his wife, and Chee Toy, Berol concluded from his assessment of the location at which Foo had tea with them that, despite the fact "Ching Ling Foo is no doubt very rich", the magician, "on return to his native land, has gone back to the Chinese way of living." Berol—an expert, it seemed—helpfully added that this return to "the Chinese way of living" was something "all Chinese do, no matter how long they have been absent or what their fortune."

Clearly, Berol was not aware of the magnificent garden homes of the Shanghai silk merchants or other magnificent dwellings easily seen in Shanghai and throughout China. Regardless, Berol continued with a deprecating description of the venue in which they shared tea with Foo. It was "a small house of two rooms, one on the ground floor and the other one above it." It was "shut off from the street by a high wall, and this court, some five by nine feet in area, is partly filled with broken down furniture, old lumber, a tumble-down rickshaw and other discarded property."

In Berol's account, everything was "cheap and dusty," including a "six-dollar mantle clock" and "greasy photo albums." The walls were decorated with "photos of the Ching Ling Foo Company which had evidently seen better days in the lobbies of American vaudeville theatres." Among the photos was an image of the great American magician Kellar "signed in autograph and dedicated to 'his friend, Ching Ling Foo.'"

What this building actually sounded like, in the context of Foo's life and significant post-Boxer disruption of commercial holdings, including theaters, is, without being certain, a venue containing a piano and other theatrical materials near the downtown Shanghai theaters that was used by Foo and his troupe as a practice and storage facility. One suspects it was not a home, but rather a rehearsal space.

Once he had set the stage by describing Foo's surroundings, Berol turned his descriptive talents to Foo and his family and discovered that, while what he understood to be their home may not have been up to standard, their clothing and jewelry incongruously marked them as extremely wealthy.

"Ching Ling Foo received the members of the Konorah Company all dressed in the finest and heaviest of Chinese silks. He looks somewhat older than he did while in America, but there is still the massive, bulging forehead, the health, though pockmarked cheeks with their high Mongolian cheekbones, the cunning, inquisitive eye, and the luxuriant, jet-black queue. His wife likewise dressed in the most expensive Oriental finery, and like himself bedecked with diamonds of enormous size, looks pretty much the same as years ago."

The real interest in Berol's reports came from his later observations, particularly concerning Chee Toy—now around nine years old—and her apparent rebellion against the lot of being a girl in turn-of-the-century China.

"It seems that Chee Toy hates to be a girl, which to a Chinese child is even more natural than in the Occident, and prefers to dress as a boy and wear the pigtail in regular boy fashion." Wisely, the Foos allowed the clearly headstrong young girl to "indulge in her caprice." Chee Toy sang, according to Berol, "not badly" for their guests. He then noted that the piano which she used to accompany herself was likely kept in the building for her "benefit." He wrote that when Chee Toy sang, Foo, "who undoubtedly takes a great deal of pride in Chee Toy though she is only a girl," accompanied her on a "snake-skin Chinese banjo." To close their impromptu performance, Foo also provided a demonstration of "some very clever top spinning with a new kind of whistling top."

Foo Begins Working with Film

Berol provided other useful information when he informed the readers that Foo told him the troupe was booked for engagements in Europe for the coming season and would, on the first stage of the tour, initially honor engagements with the Moss and Thornton theater circuit. Foo's troupe for this tour would consist of some 11 performers, including his wife and Chee Toy. Most interestingly, Berol included information that, in addition to the live performers the troupe would tour with, there was a young Chinese man in the company, evidently an early cinematographer, who had compiled about 8,000 feet of film depicting everyday life in China and views of some of its scenic sites. Clearly, Foo had paid attention to the rapidly emerging role film was taking in the American entertainment world and wanted to be ahead of the curve in China. According to Berol, the new Foo act would blend this film footage with the live performances, allowing the audiences to get a fuller picture of China and its people. The addition of this footage in the Foo act would also easily enable the troupe to potentially hold the stage for nearly two hours all on their own.

After the tea, the guests were invited by Foo to attend a performance at a theater he had a financial interest in the next night, as two of the performers would be travelling with him to Europe. Berol was generous with his praise for the performance, but his account contained yet another dig at Foo describing the conjurer as "jealous" of a magician who was performing, who Berol claimed outdid Foo in production illusions.

Foo, according to Berol, "threw a bamboo shoot from a plate in the box at the rival Chinese magician and said: 'No man likee him.'" This somewhat suspect account of Foo's behavior towards a competing magician seemed nicely timed prior to Foo's arrival in London and his pending confrontation with Soo.[337,338]

CHAPTER NINE

FOO VS. SOO THE 1905 WORLD CHAMPIONSHIP OF CHINESE MAGIC

December 1904: The Buildup

By December of 1904 it was confirmed. Ching Ling Foo was definitely going to London. Foo's engagement at the venerable London Empire Theater would set in play a series of events that would soon lead to the legendary, in magic circles, 1905 World Championship of Chinese Magic.

The buildup to the contest began with a notice, no doubt the work of the Mooser Brothers, as adept a pair of act "boomers" as ever worked in vaudeville, in the London *St. James Gazette* pointedly noting that Foo, who would be making his first appearance at the London Empire supported by a company of "ten celestials" on January 2nd, 1905, was a "veritable" Chinese, and not a mere 'American imitation.'"[339,340] The opening salvo in the World Championship of Chinese Magic had been fired.

Fortunately for Soo, for the purposes of comparison, his act had evolved over the last five years from its early days and was no longer an almost pure imitation of Foo's act. Much of this evolution had to do with Soo (William Robinson)'s long-acknowledged genius as a designer and developer of illusions. Soo would not sit long on the same act, no matter how successful and regardless; the crowds always demanded something new. So, it is not surprising that the London crowds thronging to see Soo would enjoy not only the Foo-inspired traditional Chinese magic staples, but also being treated to some Western-style illusions distinctly and decidedly of Soo's own making.

A Typical 1904 Chung Ling Soo Performance

A typical Chung Ling Soo performance circa 1904 opened with the production of real chrysanthemums from seemingly empty cones which would then, echoing Foo's 1898–1900 performances in the U.S., be distributed among the ladies of the audience. Soo's wife, the tiny "Suee Suan" a.k.a. Dot Robinson, would then be placed up on a stand where she would be covered with a large cone which, when lifted, revealed she had been transformed into a large burst of flowers. Soo would then turn to the Chinese rings, displaying with great speed and skill how they could be juggled, tossed, reconnected, disconnected, and then tossed again.

Chung Ling Soo's Cannon Illusion

Then, in the first break from a Foo-style traditional Chinese conjuring performance, a large cannon would be wheeled out on stage by a team of more than four men. The cannon would be turned and positioned until its muzzle pointed threateningly over the audience.

The cannon barrel would then be packed down with gunpowder and Suee Suan, after some "business" where she would be chased around the stage, would reluctantly be pushed down the cannon's mouth with a ramrod, followed by a cannonball larger than she was. Then, with much fanfare, the cannon would be fired out over

Chung Ling Soo on stage performing the cannon illusion and an illustration of the trick published in a London newspaper.

the audience, which would shrink in horror as the large cannonball came roaring towards them. Then, at the last moment, the ball—hesitating just before contact—would spring back quickly to the stage. In the same instance, Suee Suan—now inexplicably standing at the other end of the theater—would wave to the crowd while tossing out Chung Ling Soo promotional cards to the "much relieved" audience.[341]

The cannon illusion would be followed by a traditional Chinese magic staple: fire-eating. In presenting this part of his act, Soo would follow the manner in which Foo had performed the act back in Omaha.

For his finale, Soo would sometimes perform his show-stopping (and ultimately deadly) "Condemned to Death by the Boxers" illusion, a bullet-catching trick Soo had first developed in 1900 at the peak of the Boxer Rebellion. The illusion was developed to convey to Soo's Western audiences that he, Chung Ling Soo, was on the "right side" of the Boxer conflict—the Western side. In Soo's elaborate rendition of this illusion, his assistants, dressed as Boxers, would form a firing squad. After the rifles had been checked by volunteers from the audience with knowledge of such things. Soo's assistant, Frank Kametaro, would give the order and the squad would fire the rifles at Soo, who would catch the bullets exploding towards him on a plate held out in front of his chest. Upon striking the plate the bullets would spin noisily but harmlessly around the plate until Soo plucked them, still spinning, into his hand.[342]

Above: a promotional poster illustrating Soo's "Condemned to Death by the Boxers" illusion.

December 1904: Foo Challenges Soo

Foo, in late December of 1904, was now in London and busy under Leon Mooser's management engaging in a series of promotional interviews prior to his premiere performance in England. Foo's salary of over £250 a week (over $1,000) had drawn interest, as had his management's declaration that he was "the greatest magician in the world." When Foo was asked his opinion of the current popular self-styled "original Chinese conjurer" resident in London, he disparagingly replied, "Ah, you know that foreign devil!" I can smell he is a foreign devil."[343]

In an additional attack on Soo, Foo referred to Soo's choice of Chinese garments and pointed out that only members of the Chinese royal family can wear robes featuring a five-claw dragon, and that if this imposter Soo dared to wear these garments in China it would, in quick order, result in his execution.[344,345]

One can speculate whether Foo and his management, in other circumstances, would have let Soo get away with mimicking Foo's name and his act so closely. Others had done this before Soo, but, most were operating in the U.S. where, regardless of public declarations, they were widely known as mere imitators of Foo. Soo, on the other hand, was by design operating in an environment where the general public was relatively unaware of Foo, and importantly, Soo was engaging in no mere theatrical travesty. Soo was copying Foo's persona both onstage and off.

Soo unabashedly did all this and even had the chutzpah, as the consummate copy, to appropriate Foo's customary promotional sobriquet "the original Chinese Conjurer" as his own. To top it off, upon Foo's arrival in London, Soo had the additional temerity to claim it was Foo that was copying his tricks and that it was he that had been "plagiarized in America, Australasia, China and elsewhere."[346]

Confronted with this level of effrontery and appropriation when premiering in as important a market as London—particularly when a tour of the American market, for both immigration and contractual reasons, remained problematic—Foo and his management had no choice but to go hard at Soo. Thus the emergence of the legendary "challenge", or more properly, challenges.

RIVALS IN ART OF MAGIC
Two Chinese Fakirs Mystify London and Quarrel Over Their Pretensions to Skill

Foo's Three Challenges

The challenges formally presented by Leon Mooser and the manager of the London Empire, M.J. Hitchings, to Soo's management team began with a challenge that cut to the root of Soo's success and credibility with the British public: Soo's claim to be Chinese.

First, the Foo side requested Soo render himself to representatives of London's Chinese Legation so they could make a determination of whether Soo was, in fact, as he claimed, truly Chinese. If Soo successfully established that he was, in fact, Chinese, the Foo camp would donate the equivalent of $500 to the charity of Soo's choice. The second element of the Foo challenge was in response to what had to be Soo's historically ill-advised claim that Foo had copied his tricks. In response to this claim, the Foo camp predictably countered that it was Soo who plagiarized Foo's entire act, using Foo's performances from his 1898–1900 tour of the U.S. as a template. Furthermore, the Foo camp offered the equivalent of $2,500 to a deserving charity of Soo's choice if the magician could prove he ever used the name Chung Ling Soo or performed his current act prior to Foo's acknowledged, enormous, and well-published successes in the United States, beginning in 1898.

While the preceding two challenges may have been the most important to Foo, it was the final and third challenge issued by the Foo camp that fired the newspapers' and the general public's imaginations. In this final challenge, the Foo camp claimed Soo's illusions were but "poor imitations" of Foo's work and invited Soo to "a contest of magic" "at any hall or theatre in London" for any amount up to the equivalent of $5,000. Foo agreed to forfeit the agreed sum if he was unable to perform any Chinese trick demonstrated by Soo, or if Soo could successfully perform 10 out of 20 Chinese tricks that would be demonstrated by Foo.[347]

Very importantly, Foo and Leon Mooser, who had attended one of Soo's London performances shortly after their arrival and seen Soo perform some of his impressive Western illusions, ensured it was understood that the magic skills portion of the proposed challenge was limited to "Chinese" magic.

Who is "The Original Chinese Magician"? Readers of The Sphinx "Know Who is Who"

Back in America, the editor of *The Sphinx*, in setting out for its readers the probable origin of the conjurer conflict, acknowledged that

The 1905 London version of the Foo troupe. Their manager, Leon Mooser, is in the back row in a black top hat. In another photo from that era, Chee Toy and her mother pose along with another performer from the troupe.

"Foo's anger was likely aroused by the management of the Hippodrome, which sent out circulars to newspapers, etc., informing them that the original Chinese magician was Chung Ling Soo." The editor then added, in a sly observation that serves as a clear nod to Foo as the premier Chinese conjurer and acknowledged popularizer of Chinese magic in the West, "It is needless for me to proceed further; as the readers of this letter know who is who."[348]

This knowledge of "who is who" when it came to "who" was truly "the original Chinese conjurer" among professional magicians, theatrical people, and major media in United States (such as the aforementioned *The Cosmopolitan*), may explain more than anything else why Soo never, ever, during his long successful career wherein he toured the world from England to Australia, ever returned to tour his native country. Too many Americans knew the truth behind Chung Ling Soo's glorious deception, and once that illusion was fully and duly pricked, much of the appeal of Chung Ling Soo fell away.

Furthermore, the now-comfortable, wealthy, and famous Chung Ling Soo had no desire to go back to being the somewhat less exotic William Robinson. Europe—England in particular—was Soo's turf, and ultimately, he would spare no effort to defend it.

Pressure Builds on Suddenly Difficult-to-Find Soo to Submit to Contest

Meanwhile, Foo's management team was increasing the pressure on Soo to submit to the challenges. In a clever move, Mooser ensured that Foo's intent to make a courtesy call on the Chinese Legation in London to meet with China's ambassador to England was widely publicized. He also simultaneously brought attention to the fact this was something Soo has not done once in his almost five years in London.

When London *Daily News* reporters brought these observations and consequent challenges to a suddenly difficult-to-locate Chung Ling Soo, Soo was declared unavailable for interviews. Soo's management relayed that the great man "absolutely refuses to be drawn into any discussions with persons connected to rival shows, and states positively that he is the only 'original' Chung Ling Soo and no other." With regard to the Foo camp's claims that Soo was not actually Chinese, Soo's management, perhaps without informing Soo, replied the Foo camp could "stick pins" in Soo all day and never get a word of English out of him. Soo's management representative added, as an additional reason for Soo's reticence in the face of this situation, that his client's "dignity is too sublime to allow him to descend to the ordinary showman's methods of 'puffing' himself."[349,350]

Ignoring these initial attempts by Soo's management to sidestep the challenges, an eager local media, recognizing a circulation builder, continued to do all they could to promote the challenge. Soo, increasingly under siege, continued to keep a low profile. Newspapers responded by reporting Soo had "made himself invisible." But even in seclusion, Soo's combative personality caused him to insouciantly feed the fire by continuing, in his public statements on the matter, to refer to Foo as a mere street-corner conjurer and himself as the "the only original Chinese necromancer" and "the original Chinese conjurer."[351]

By late December, as Foo's first performance in London drew ever closer, both sides appeared to up the ante in their confrontation.

> **HIPPODROME. CHUNG LING SOO.**
> THE ONLY ORIGINAL CHINESE NECROMANCER
> THE WORLD'S GREATEST JUGGLER
> AND MYSTIFIER.

Still uncommitted to the contest Soo dangerously ups the ante by proclaiming himself "The Only Original Chinese Necromancer."

Leon Mooser, using the technique of an "open letter", called out Soo once more for having the temerity to use the phrase "the only original Chinese conjurer" in his advertising. Mooser repeated the claim that Soo's real name was Robinson and that it was Foo's performance, not Soo's, that had been "plagiarized by imitators" around the world. Finally, Mooser once more offered large sums to charity if Soo could prove to the Chinese Legation he was Chinese "or if he can bring forward any proof of his ever having used this name or attempted a Chinese act until after he had seen Ching Ling Foo perform in America in 1898."[352]

Mooser then further ramped up the challenge by suggesting that far from being copied by imitators around the world, Chung Ling Soo was not even worth copying. Mooser, in his open letter published in the *Music Hall and Theatre Review*, continued, "I will further pay to the alleged Chinese magician, Chung Ling Soo, the sum of 500 pounds if he can bring proof that any artist in America, Asia or Australia has plagiarized his name." Ouch! Mooser was clearly, once more, establishing for the record that it was Foo's act that had been plagiarized and it was the Ching Ling Foo name that had been stolen around the world, not that of Chung Ling Soo.[353]

The very next day, eager to keep the pressure up, the Foo team released ads in the London newspapers once more directly challenging Soo's promotional claims to be "the Original Chinese Conjurer." The ad for Ching Ling Foo in the London *Evening Standard* read "Ching Ling Foo the Original Chinese Magician", and in case the point had not been absorbed, another ad nearby proclaimed "Ching Ling Foo the Real Chinese Magician Challenges All Imitators".[354]

Chas Aldrich, "the Tramp Juggler", was also on Foo's bill at the Empire with no word whether he would be doing the Foo travesty he profitably developed soon after Foo's departure from the U.S. in 1900.[355]

EMPIRE	CHING LING FOO.
	The REAL CHINESE MAGICIAN.
	CHALLENGES ALL IMITATORS
	MONDAY NEXT AT 9.45

EMPIRE	The ORIGINAL CHING LING FOO.
	Chinese Magician and his Company
	MONDAY NEXT at 9:45

In the London papers Foo promotional advertising notices refer to Foo as "The Real" or "Original" Chinese Magician" who "Challenges All Imitators"

1905 January: "War Between Rival Wizards" The Contest is On!

Unable to further resist the pressure to answer the challenge, Soo submitted to the inevitable and reluctantly accepted the challenge—with conditions. Terrified that Foo might attempt to test his Chinese or tear off his fake queue, Soo asked that a glass panel be used to separate the two combatants, claiming this to be a question of caste.[356] Soo, with his legendary sharp elbows, continue to position Foo as a mere "street corner juggler" hardly worth the notice of his high-caste mandarin self, further infuriating the genuine Chinese magician.

The date for the contest was set and the two were to meet at the editorial offices of the *Weekly Standard* the afternoon of January 7th, 1905. A panel of judges, including prominent London stage managers and Houdini—always eager to participate in a high-profile publicity stunt—would rule on their performances.

The contest being set, the London press continued to have a field day working with the rich material a world championship of Chinese magic between bitter rivals provided. Some scribes, encouraged by promoters on both sides, gave free range to their imaginations in spinning the purple prose that kept the media frenzy surrounding the upcoming contest going. One journalist went so far as to report, echoing what was seen as Foo's difficulties back in St. Louis in 1899, that the rivalry between Foo and Soo was intergenerational and went back hundreds of years. Other reports posited that, once faced with each other, they might transform into animals and devour each other. Regardless, the "War Between Rival Wizards" was on.

WAR BETWEEN RIVAL WIZARDS.

Through this headline, the *Yorkshire Evening News* demonstrated that its editors knew what caught the public eye.

Building up the fast-approaching confrontation, the *Yorkshire Evening News*, on the day of Foo's first performance in London under the headline "War Between Rival Wizards", emphasized Foo's eagerness for combat and his considerable pride. "There is no false modesty about Ching Ling Foo. He is very proud of his social position in China. 'I belong to the Manchus,' he explained. 'I was the court magician. The Empress-Dowager liked me very much. She said I was very clever. And, he added, with delightful solemnity, 'I am.'"[357]

Chinese Magician Challenge "Stirs Music Hall London to its Depths

Interest in the contest was not confined to England. The Scots were also keeping a close eye on the nabobs of necromancy down in London. The Edinburgh *Scotsman* even offered some useful historical context to the Foo vs. Soo stage challenge by referencing promotional challenges of a similar nature that had earlier captured the public attention and stirred "music-hall London to its depths." Only a few years ago, according to the paper, "all London was ringing with the challenges and counter-challenges of wrestlers, and all, of course, were world champions." One is sure "music-hall London" would not have had it any other way.

A Reviewer Assesses the Two Acts: Foo Troupe Better Value for Your Money

The paper then went on to compare the two acts provided by Foo and Soo and makes some perceptive comments regarding what might lead one to lean to—for pure entertainment value—the superiority of the Foo troupe act over Soo's late-1904 derivative version of the Foo act. The paper noted that the Soo act was primarily focused on conjuring and in that, arguably, on a par with Foo. However, the paper went on to note as far as the manner in which the two acts were currently constituted, the highlights of Foo's act were not limited to his conjuring. The reviewer rightly noted that the Foo troupe "has quite a number of native performers", the feats of which were quite as uncanny as those of Foo.

The author then referred to the contortionists, acrobats, and jugglers who made up the Foo act, reserving special praise for "a young fellow who is sent flying all over the stage suspended by his own pigtail from a long-hooked rope which descends from the 'flies.'" This "strong hair" act with an "iron-haired gentleman" swinging across the stage hanging by his queue is acknowledged as providing "a particular surprise for the audience"—especially the sardonic reviewer, observes, "for those of the audience with whom hair is not a particular strong point."[358]

Special mention was also given to an adult Chinese contortionist of the Foo troupe who, standing on a stool at least 18 inches high, bends himself backward and picks up a coin off the floor with his teeth. There were also "winsome" girls spinning plates to be marveled at. But even with all this supporting talent, the reviewer concluded Foo was "the head and foot of the whole business."

Even in 1905, Foo's signature illusion remained his production tricks, and the author deemed these to be done very well and mystifyingly quickly. Foo's best trick was judged his production act finale, where he stripped down to his undershirt, bounded across the stage before launching himself into a somersault and coming up with a large splashing bowl of live goldfish.[359]

Even If the English Audiences Have Seen the Illusions, Foo Invests them with "A New Interest and Charm"

As regards to the appeal of Foo's performance, the reality was that after five highly promoted and successful years of what was essentially Chung Ling Soo's "travesty" of Foo's act playing London, the English provinces and Europe, there was very little of Foo's magic act, including his signature bowl productions and fire-eating, that would be seen as "startlingly new" by British or European audiences. Despite this, Foo's performance still received strong praise. Reviewers judged that Foo did what he did during the almost 45-minute act exceedingly well and in "a highly entertaining manner." Some reviewers even found some of Foo's tricks to be novel, "drawing gasps from the audience" and claimed "those that are not, like fire-eating, are done so dexterously and with such a jolly air they have a new interest and charm." Once more, the Foo troupe's presentation skills and ability to transfuse their work with joy seemed to transmute what in other circumstances might have been perceived as ordinary into something special.

It was indeed a tribute to Foo that in yet another environment awash with copycat Chinese magicians and similar acts competing for the theatergoing public's money, Foo was still widely described in the press as drawing large crowds, well worth the fortune he was being paid, and "incomparably the greatest artiste of this kind ever seen here."[360–363]

The rest of the Foo troupe, consisting of ten other Chinese performers, was actually seen as presenting the more novel elements of the act. The acrobats, jugglers, and contortionists presented things reportedly not yet seen by the London audiences. In particular, the troupe's young contortionist, with a "false head attached to the rear of his garments so that it shows conspicuously when he is reversed", was praised as providing "a number of comical effects." The young man was deemed "quite an artist."[364] As noted earlier, this two-headed boy act had been a sure-fire hit from its long-ago inception with the Foo troupe, both in China and abroad.

January 1905: Chee Toy "the Tiny Diva" Repeatedly "Wins All Hearts"

Finally, Chee Toy's steadily ascending popularity was once again confirmed as she was showered with applause and repeated demands for encores by the London audiences. The tiny diva was considered by many the biggest hit of the London premiere, with one critic claiming "nothing so delighted the audience" as Chee Toy's rendition of "Because I love you", which was "rapturously received."[365–367]

The Foo troupe's London success was even followed with interest back in Shanghai. One of the *North China Herald's* London correspondents sent back periodic dispatches covering the troupe's reception. In one dispatch, he noted that while the Shanghai audience would be familiar with the magic Foo performed, Chee Toy was "winning all hearts" with her singing solos and her endearing technique of singling out "someone in the box" and singing "her song to him or her in a manner that is quite irresistible." The London correspondent concluded, "I think she will soon be quite the rage or perhaps I should say 'The Talk of the Town.'"[368]

What Made the Foo Troupe's Performances So Special

First made evident in America during the latter stages of their first tour, the mystery ingredients of the Foo act that allowed it to stand apart from all its numerous imitators were becoming clearer. They included Foo's charisma, a quality that young Chee Toy, "a fascinating little person," was also clearly demonstrating the troupe's creativity in working with and adapting what were admittedly historic staples of the Chinese conjuring and entertainment world, and very importantly, the apparently infectious joyfulness of the Foo troupe's performance.

Many an imitator would discover to their grief that these elements were not as readily replicated as the Chinese illusion mechanisms, costumes, or backdrops one could order from the mail.

FOO'S 1905 ACT IN DETAIL

A typical Foo performance circa 1905 played out as follows. The curtain goes up, and Ching Ling Foo is standing on stage surrounded by the approximately ten other performers in his troupe. They are dressed in colorful Chinese clothing and surrounded by Chinese-style stage settings and elaborate embroidered hangings. Each performer has a special talent or act he or she will perform. The other performers' acts are ordered in such a fashion as to occupy the time that Foo requires to return backstage to prepare for each of his successive illusions.

All the performers leave the stage except Foo and his assistant. Foo, attired in his flowing robes, pulls out a colorful Chinese-style embroidered silk cloth approximately four feet by four feet—previously draped across his left shoulder—and shakes it out before the audience to demonstrate there is nothing hidden on either side of the fabric or inside its folds. Foo and his assistant's arms and shoulders disappear well under the cloth, and after some busied activity, produce a dinner plate piled up full of oranges.

The top few oranges are genuine and can be lifted from the pile, peeled and tossed to the audience, but one cannot be certain of whether all the others are real or not. Then, another cloth of similar size is placed over the plate of oranges so recently made to appear, and they disappear.

Then, using the same cloth, the plate of oranges is made to appear once more. But Foo is not finished with productions from that cloth. The plate of oranges is taken away, and Foo then waves the cloth once more and produces a large china basin full of water.

Foo and his assistant receive sustained applause and leave the stage as a member of their company takes the stage and commences his plate-spinning act. For this performance, a rice bowl is spun upside down at the end of a long stick. The stick is placed inside the basin of the bowl. The momentum of the spin is initially generated by the performer theatrically striking the side of the bowl with his fingers. The performer holds two sticks and is able to toss the spinning bowl from one stick to the other without interrupting the bowl's spin. The bowl is then tossed very high in the air and caught on the very same stick, then thrown under the performer's leg and caught again on the same stick. While spinning the stick in left hand, the stick is passed behind the performer's back and the basin is thrown across to the stick in the right hand, then back to the stick in the left hand. The prettiest effect is judged to be where the performer throws the basin from the stick, hits it on its side, and catches it on the same stick. This is done repeatedly while the basin rings out like a bell.

The troupe's juggler then does some very clever throwing and catching of a very large and heavy pottery bowl. He tosses it high into the air and catches it, still spinning, on his forehead. Once on his forehead, the jug's position is altered by the juggler—just using the movements of this head and without use of his hands—and tosses the large, still-spinning bowl back up into the air several times.

As the juggler retires from the stage, two Chinese girls emerge from the curtains and commence spinning small saucers on the end of sticks. The tea-style saucers are again spun at the end of long sticks with a definitive wobble. One of the performers takes her companion's stick from her hand so that she is now spinning one saucer in each hand, and she has done so without interrupting the spin of the saucer on the stick she has just taken into her hand. An expert observer notes that this passing of the stick, upon which a saucer is still spinning, to another performer without interrupting the spin is a particularly difficult feat. The girl then multiplies the difficulty of her feat by crossing her arms, holding the two sticks with the spinning saucers, kneeling down, turning head-over-heels, and returning to a standing position, all without interrupting the spin of the two saucers still wobbling at the ends of the two long sticks she still holds.

Next, a young acrobat appears and does the now-classic Foo troupe contortionist act, involving a dummy head that is a very good imitation of his own attached to the lower bottom of his back. The false head is revealed when the contortionist walks on his hands and creates the illusion that his arms are his legs and his feet his hands, while doing the opposite with his legs, which now act as arms. "Some excruciatingly funny poses on a chair are obtained with the aid of this dummy head."

Next on stage after the contortionist is Chee Toy. She sings two popular English songs, "Because I Love You" and "Just One Girl."

An adult Chinese acrobat then appears, performing contortions—a key element of which is when he stands upon a chair about 18 inches high and manages to bend backwards right to the floor and pick a silver coin up with his teeth.

By this point, Foo has prepared for his next illusion and enters the stage where he, with the aid of his multi-colored cloth and assistant, produces an even larger bowl of water than he did the last time. This time, a card is produced and placed by the very large bowl, which reads in large letters "85 Pounds", which is the weight of the bowl and the water. Foo, bowing to the applause, then leaves the stage, as several assistants with small ladles empty the water "slowly for effect" out of the bowl and into about 4 pails.

Foo then returns after the bowl and pails have been removed and begins patting his body to demonstrate to the audience there is nothing underneath his clothes. To make the point even clearer, he begins to remove all his outer garments, until he is left wearing only a tight tunic and trousers. Foo then humorously feigns considering also removing these items, then thinks better of it. Once more, the cloth is produced, shaken, and shown from both sides. Foo drapes the cloth over his left shoulder, then suddenly bounds across the stage with the multi-hued cloth billowing behind him, and leaps into a somersault from which he emerges standing holding a very large bowl brimming with water and goldfish.

After ample applause, Foo disappears behind the curtain to once more change into his full attire before he retakes the stage armed with his Diabolo apparatus. Foo spins the large top as it moves along the cord, stretched out between the sticks he holds in each hand. The top is made to run up and across the cord and jumps over Foo's foot when it is placed on the cord. The Diabolo, seemingly even defies gravity by climbing up the cord when stretched vertically.[369]

A Chinese Dinner at London's Hotel Provence

With the magicians' confrontation set, Foo, working with a "courteous" Leon Mooser, invited London newsmen for a well-received introduction to Chinese cuisine. The London theatrical trade newspaper *The Stage* reported that Ching Ling Foo acted as host to a Chinese dinner at the Hotel Provence days before the contest. Ching Ling Foo himself assisted in the preparation of the broad menu, which

The Hotel Provence was a favorite hotel for entertainers performing in London.

comprised over a dozen courses. Foo's actual participation in the preparation of these promotional meals, introducing Chinese cuisine to foreign friends and journalists, would become a signature promotional move for the conjurer for years to come.

Guests gathered for the feast apparently included those who were unfamiliar even with the hybridized concoction "Chop Sooey," which actually arose in America and few Chinese claimed as a native dish. In this iteration, it was described as consisting of "bamboo, mushrooms and onions."

Typically, the culinary cultural exchange drew much good-natured coverage. Chopsticks were provided to the attendees "and the gaucherie of the guests in manipulating them caused much merriment to Chee Toy, Ching's talented little daughter." However, one of those attending demonstrated "considerable address in this direction and the manner in which he negotiated the elusive pea was a source of wonder and envy to his neighbors." Foo closed the event with some close-in magic, including "extraordinary feats of palming" at the end of the dinner.[370]

January 1905: London Faces a Congestion of Chinese Conjurers

All the attention Foo and Soo were attracting through their contest naturally stimulated the competitive juices of another noted magician seeking his own path to increased ticket sales performing in London at the time. Horace Goldin, the American magician/humorist, was at the Palace Theater and must have been feeling left out amidst all the Foo-versus-Soo furor. Goldin responded by trying to get in on some of the publicity being generated through the challenge by sharing with the gentlemen of the press that he too had some "Chinese jugglery tricks of his own", and that Foo and Soo were "not to have it all their own way" when it comes to capturing the attention of London's theatergoing public. Goldin's publicist noted with pride that Foo had already taken in one of Goldin's performances and was suitably impressed.

Goldin then confided to reporters that he would be using his new Chinese performance name, "Gol Din Poo", when he returned to the stage at the London Palace the following week.[371] Goldin, of course, was not speaking lightly as he had, like so many others, developed his own Foo travesty back in 1900 at the height of the American fascination with Foo.

In the same report, the author draws attention to yet another noted performer currently in London who had attended the Goldin show at the Palace: "Coco the Monkey." It seems Coco "occupied the front seat in a box, into which he shrank in the manner of one of those very old and wicked financiers whom the French comic artists draw." It seems even the animal acts were anxious to get in on the free publicity generated by the Foo-versus-Soo circus.[372]

What had by this time been aptly termed by the London press a "congestion of Chinese conjurors" in London's theatrical district ratcheted up with the addition of yet another Chinese act to the London theatrical scene in early January 1905. A "quaint troupe" of "Chunchusen" conjurers with "gorgeous" native costumes and scenery arrived in London under German management from Dresden and joined the fray. One of the troupe was an expert at knife throwing, and another an exemplar of acrobatics, while the third was a contortionist.[373,374]

The London 1905 "Invasion of Chinese Jugglers."

The Contest

Finally, at 11 a.m. on January 7th, 1905, the time for the much-touted "War of the Wizards" had arrived. At the appointed hour, Chung Ling Soo, the challenged—transported in his magnificent red open-top Panhard motor car, which always drew a crowd—appeared with his colorful entourage at the *Weekly Dispatch* offices, which were serving as a venue for the contest. Soo and his entourage were escorted to the newspaper's great room.

There, waiting for the necromancers, were those appointed to judge the affair, which included many editors from various newspapers and fellow magician Harry Houdini—a friend of both men, who, knowing a good publicity stunt when he saw it, had volunteered to be a judge at the event.

Chung Ling Soo and his entourage travelling through London in a touring vehicle designed to attract attention. This is likely the same vehicle he used to arrive at the January 7th challenge.

Foo Fails to Appear; Soo Seen to Triumph, Renders Foo "Invisible"

All that had been gathered then waited in excitement for the second combatant to appear. But as the minutes passed, it eventually became clear that Ching Ling Foo would not be participating. In *Mahatma*'s retelling of the accounts published in London papers, "Soo's almond eyes twinkled, but never a word said he. The journalists and guests discussed the situation. An eerie feeling was present among the assembly. Half-past eleven struck. Where was the challenger? It might have been that Chung's grim mouth relaxed—certain is it that the light in his eyes danced more rapidly than ever. Then the conclusion suddenly flashed upon the minds of everyone present: Chung had rendered his hated rival invisible."[375]

To hear the *Evening Mail* tell it, at this point, Soo's "face broke out into laughter and he uttered an unearthly yell of triumph. What an ordeal for poor invisible Ching Ling Foo!"[376]

Telephone calls were made to both Foo and his manager Leon Mooser to no avail. By 11:45 a.m., Foo had still not yet made an appearance. The challenge, in accordance with the rules, would continue in his absence.

A much-relieved Soo was then invited to replicate Foo's Chinese tricks. He did so with, according to those in attendance, apparent ease. "Right in the midst of the assembled company, and without any preparation whatever, Chung tore in pieces a long strip of paper, and even as he ripped them asunder, they joined together again. A table cover was given him, and, laying it on the ground, he produced fruit-pies, joints—enough, in fact, in the eatable line to keep the *Dispatch* staff from entering a restaurant for a week … More wonders were to come. Suddenly he rolled over on the ground, and when he regained his feet, he had brought from nowhere a glass bowl full of water, in which live goldfish were merrily swimming about." Foo's signature act was duplicated. Next, Soo performed Foo's fire act and worked with Chinese linking rings. When he was finished, Soo had, as required, successfully performed ten of Foo's Chinese tricks. The performance over, Soo then, with his colorful entourage, left the *Weekly Dispatch* offices in triumph, waving to the large crowd waiting outside for news of the contest's outcome.[377]

What Was the Reason Behind Foo's No-show?

It was not till after seven o'clock that night that a message was received by the *Weekly Dispatch* from Leon Mooser, indicating that Foo would have only participated in the challenge if all conditions as originally laid out for the challenge by Foo and his management had been followed.

As the current contest ignored the first two elements of Foo's challenge—the establishment of Soo's ethnicity and whether Soo had used his current stage name or performed his act prior to seeing Foo's act in 1898—Foo did not participate.[378]

These, of course, were two reasons why Foo would not have appeared for the contest of skills. Surprisingly, however, in the aftermath of the aborted contest, Foo did not continue to press Soo and continue to make his case to the newspapers that Soo was not, in fact, Chinese, and evidently had thoroughly copied Foo's act. Certainly other magicians in the U.S. and Europe had taken similar steps when their acts had been copied.

Why, then, would Foo back away from what were undeniably two guaranteed wins, at least in the court of public opinion on both these matters?

It is possible both Foo and his management were just fatigued by the whole matter and eager to move on from what was, from a Chinese conjurer's perspective, a crowded London which, after all, was Soo's home territory. But given the richness of the market, the pride, and the known combativeness of both the Mooser Brothers and Foo, the possibility that they just abruptly gave up seems unlikely.[379]

So, why, then, would Foo and his management forgo the Chinese magic skills contest in which they certainly would have at least equaled Soo—and foregone pressing the points on Foo's true ethnicity and just where he got his act from which they were sure to win?

One credible possibility for Foo's seemingly inexplicable decision to suddenly back away from the contest and his related challenges to

Soo was a geopolitically motivated intervention by the Chinese Legation in London to influence Foo's approach to the matter.

For all his excesses and cultural miscues, the popular Chung Ling Soo had a net positive impact on Chinese interests in England, and more broadly, Europe. Soo, like Ching Ling Foo and his troupe earlier in America, presented a rare positive image of the Chinese to the British and European public, likely evaluated to be sorely needed given the plethora of negative Chinese tropes that surrounded the public in those countries at that time.

Furthermore, the precedent for interaction between Foo and China's representatives abroad, including Foo's good friend the Chinese Minister to Washington Wu Ting Fang, had already been set in the U.S. during the Omaha Exposition and Foo's subsequent tour of major American cities on the U.S. East Coast from 1898 to 1900.

Given this, and the fact that Foo had met with the Chinese Legation in London not long after his arrival, it is not beyond the bounds of possibility that China's London representatives, whose opinion would have held enormous influence over Foo (and who were already dealing with issues relating to overblown assessments of the insidious influence of Chinese in the Limehouse area of London, the usual opium and gambling scares, and addressing concerns about low-wage Chinese sailors taking the jobs of British seamen), might formally or informally request that Foo, in the larger interests of his homeland, go easy on one of the few promoters of a positive image of the Chinese they had in London.

It is important in this context to remember that Soo had wisely made a habit of investing heavily in developing positive relations with the London Chinese community, and indeed the various Chinese communities he encountered while touring.

In the end, however, it is impossible to know definitively why Foo did not show up for the challenge. But what can be known for certain is that once the deadline for the challenge passed, even in the face of repeated goading by Chung Ling Soo, neither Foo nor the Mooser

Brothers again publicly challenged Soo's clearly egregious claims to Chinese ethnicity or his patently false claims regarding how his act originated and the evident influence Ching Ling Foo had on his career.

For a man as prideful as Foo to stand down in such a situation and not further engage on these matters, very powerful arguments must have presented themselves.

Soo Exalts in His Victory; Foo Soldiers On

Given how things looked for Chung Ling Soo at the start of Foo's challenges, Soo was justifiably much more than just relieved when it appeared he had escaped the whole process not only with the first successful stage act he had ever concocted still intact, but with Chung Ling Soo as the evident undisputed champion of Chinese magic.

It was no surprise, then, that Soo positively exalted in his "victory" over Foo. Neither was it at all surprising that, consummate self-promoter that he was, he began to use his "victory" over Foo as a key part of his promotional materials going forward. He did not limit his gloating to Europe, either. Ever mindful of his status in America just weeks after the contest, Soo placed a large ad in the major American theatrical periodical of the day, the New York *Clipper*. The text of the large ad proclaimed:

"Chung Ling Soo: They said he couldn't, but he did. The Original Chung Ling Soo, Marvelous Chinese Conjurer, who has been mystifying British audiences for the past five years and is now playing the second engagement of three months at the London Hippodrome, in a sensational magic show, was challenged by Ching Ling Foo from the Empire Theatre London, for £1,000, to perform Ching Ling Foo's tricks. Chung Ling Soo most successfully accomplished these tricks on Saturday, January 7th, 1905, at the *Weekly Dispatch* Office, London, where the challenger and his money failed to put in an appearance and have not since been heard of. Chung Ling Soo! Chung Ling Soo! Ching Ling Soo! The Original Chinese Conjuror, at the London

Hippodrome. Sole Agent E. De Vere, Waterloo Road, London, England."[380]

It is interesting Soo felt compelled to publicize his victory in his homeland, but at the same time, as noted earlier, never dared to venture to America to perform as Chung Ling Soo. Needless to mention, Soo, in his victory proclamation lists only the trick-copying portion of the challenges and not the still-unmet challenges to prove his Chinese identity and establish he had not plagiarized Foo's act. Similar ads were placed in both general newspapers and theatrical journals across England.

By the end of 1905, Soo had even adopted the sobriquet "He of the One Button, favorite of the London Hippodrome audiences,

In ads following the contest Soo declares, "Some time ago, a certain Ching Ling Foo challenged Chung Ling Soo to do ten out of twenty of his tricks, agreeing to forfeit £1,000 in the event of failure. Chung Ling Soo, the challenged, turned up to face the music; at the last-minute Foo, the challenger, failed to put in an appearance and nothing more has been seen or heard of him … He said I couldn't but I did." In another ad, Soo repeats "an old Chinese saying" for the benefit of his "rival Chinese conjurer": "Don't throw mud at your neighbor or your hands will ever remain dirty." The ad on the right was published shortly after the contest in both the *Music Hall and Theater Review* and *Entr'acte*.

vanquisher of the dreaded Ching Ling Foo, and the honored sorcerer of the Dowager Empress of China."[381]

Despite Soo's promotional claims to the contrary, however, Foo had not "disappeared" or "not been heard of" since the challenge. Almost two weeks after the failed contest, Foo was still successfully performing at the Empire and completing his engagement. In fact, by all reports, Foo was a big hit at the Empire, and he and his troupe, as always particularly Chee Toy, were receiving laudatory coverage in the major London entertainment press not more than one week after the challenge. Nowhere in that reporting was the challenge mentioned.[382,383]

February-March 1905: The Magic Community Addresses the Contest

While the regular press may have been willing to let the challenge pass into obscurity, the magic journals of the time were understandably especially interested in assessing and evaluating what had transpired. The nature of their coverage varied considerably according to whether a particular journal was more favorably disposed to one combatant than another.

For example, the American magic journal *Mahatma*, in examining the contest for its readership, was not surprisingly primarily interested in covering the "contest in magic" element.

The question of Soo's true ancestry was dismissed by *Mahatma* in the following fashion. "It has been sought in some quarters to change the issue into one of the nationality of the rivals. This is a mistake. The public is not interested in the ancestry of Soo or Foo; it is interested in their conjuring, and this is the question the *Weekly Dispatch* wished to solve."[384]

It is also curious that, given the passion with which the magic community had so recently described the proprietary nature of illusions and tricks, no discussion was had regarding Foo's claims that Soo had plagiarized his act. Once again, *Mahatma* avoided discussing these more disconcerting, still-outstanding elements of Foo's challenges.

It would come as no surprise, then, that *Mahatma* made no mention that it was Soo's refusal to address these other two challenges that led, according to many, to Foo's decision not to participate in the magic skills part of the challenge. To hear *Mahatma* tell it, Foo had challenged Soo to a contest of magic skill, and at the last minute the Chinese conjurer backed out of the very confrontation he himself had instigated with his rival.

Stanyon's Magic, London-based and therefore even closer to Soo, was even more demonstrative in their support of the Soo side of the conflict. The editors of that journal reveled in Soo's triumph and were positively bursting when he survived what they recognized as an existential challenge. "We backed our pal 'Billy' to win and he won easily by a length and a half." They even noted the *Daily Mirror's* suggestion that it had been "hinted that Soo had borrowed Foo's soul, and thus was enabled to do Foo's tricks with such ease", and repeated the question raised by the *Daily Mail* and others: "Can Soo sue Foo?"[385,386]

John Northern Hillard Admirably Addresses the "Ethical Aspect" of this "International Dispute": "This May be Good Showmanship But It is Not Fair Play"

In the midst of this outpouring of support for Soo from the professional magician's community, *The Sphinx* did distinguish itself by publishing an article raising questions about the ethics and propriety of Soo's behavior both during and after the contest. Writing in the March 1905 edition of that conjuring journal, one John Northern Hillard, a journalist and expert in magic who had, among other things, witnessed Sitting Bull's surrender to American troops, was not as inclined as his fellows to uncritically celebrate the triumph of "our pal Billy." In his impressive essay, Hillard, after first acknowledging the ethereal—and, perhaps, ultimately none-too-serious

"While we do not take the controversy with undue seriousness, there is an ethical aspect to the case that invites discussion."

and even "mildly amusing"—nature of such promotional challenges, nonetheless took the time to address what he saw as some of the ethical and moral issues surrounding this international dispute.

"Adroit Manipulation of the Press"

Hillard, as a newsman and somewhat of an expert on promotion, began his analysis with a nod to the fact that if the goal of the participants in the Foo-versus-Soo challenge was to gain publicity through "adroit manipulation of the press," they both succeeded beyond their wildest dreams. At this level, he observes, once the "smoke of battle has rolled away, the *entente cordiale*" between the two conjurors should not have been more than a few shared Guinness stouts away, while "a judicious blending of chartreuse and absinthe might inspire them to vows of eternal friendship."

With that humorous introduction out of the way and with a recognition that perhaps the contest not be taken that seriously, Hillard signaled he did have something serious to say about what he perceived as "the ethical aspect of it," which he convincingly argued "invites discussion."

Hillard posited that "Mr. Robinson (Chung Ling Soo)", in "commenting disparagingly on the professional ability" of Foo and "belittling his originality and his achievements in the magic arts", is "really throwing stones at his own crystal dwelling place." Despite everything else and what the press agents may say, Hillard argued, "one naked truth shines out as clearly as a frosty star in a turquoise sky." If it was not for Ching Ling Foo there would never have been any Chung Ling Soo. Foo is the originator, "as far as the Western hemisphere is concerned at least, of this peculiar act, and Robinson is merely an imitator."

Hillard then noted Robinson's earlier lack of success in his stage career and rightly concludes "the success of Ching Ling Foo in this country was his opportunity." Everything else followed, including copying Foo's look and his act and moving to Europe, "where the act was a novelty, and scored a success." Hillard, in assessing the situation, then rightly notes "in light of what the American magician really owes to the great Chinese conjuror, it is ridiculous for Robinson to pose as 'the original Chinese magician'" and to claim Foo was a mere street performer while he was a court magician to the Empress Dowager "may be good showmanship but it is not fair play."

Brushing off some contemporary claims that Foo himself might be difficult to deal with and overly fond of his own talent, Hillard noted "the devil himself is entitled to his due."[387]

Hillard's attitude towards the contest and Soo was shared by many in the magic profession including Houdini, whose superior knowledge of the facts surrounding the related events made him more than a little uneasy with the manner "Chung Ling Soo" had conducted himself during the challenge and his unseemly preening after he realized he had gotten away with it.

Soo, for his part, if he saw such criticism from his professional peers for his handling of the affair, chose to ignore it.

March 1905: Foo Tours the Continent; Soo Tours the Provinces

Having completed their engagement in London, the Foo troupe, continuing on its world tour, moved on to Europe.[388] In March of 1905, it was performing in Prague. As part of its promotional efforts, it

These photos were taken during the troupe's engagement in Prague.

donated some Chinese clothing and other items to Prague's Náprstek Museum. The Náprstek still has these objects.

After Bohemia, the Foo troupe moved on to Berlin, where they appeared with the Circus Schumann and performed in the center ring. As part of the promotion for his Berlin engagement on April 1st, Foo gave a private performance to Berlin press representatives, resulting in "much well-earned praise in the Berlin papers", which generated great interest in his act. After a month in Germany, the Circus Schumann moved on to shows in Vienna.[389,390]

Meanwhile, back in England, in the aftermath of the challenge and perhaps to avoid the "Chinese conjurer congestion" so recently remarked upon, Soo had also left London and was touring Britain's provincial halls. During Soo's stop at the Plymouth Palace Theatre, it was reported that the theater went to "enormous expense" to get him there and Soo was paid the "largest salary ever paid locally to a music hall star." Soo's Plymouth performance lasted about 30 minutes.

1905 July: Soo's "Robes of His Ancestors"

A key element of Soo's act was now his new illusions, such as the cannon trick. Much promotional use was also made of the fact that Soo's "gorgeous" Chinese clothing was insured for the startling amount of £6000.

STRANGE EXHIBITION.

Headline promoting Soo's "Strange Exhibition", or what would become known more widely as the Robes of His Ancestors.

This clothing, along with other Chinese objects and artifacts Soo had studiously collected along the way, was now, as noted earlier, being put on display by the canny Soo as an additional promotional element of his act. "Robes of His Ancestors," essentially a Chinese curio museum, was now installed in the lobby of each of the theaters Soo played prior to his performances. During Soo's engagement, viewing the display usually set up in the theater lobby was free of charge and served as a means to both promote his act and draw potential ticket buyers into the theater.

The collection consisted of 40 or more main objects and 15 cases containing smaller objects, such as jewelry and small carvings. Within the collection were war drums and banners, arms and weapons of war, opium pipes, and temple pieces, as well as joss house hangings, a river houseboat carved out of a nut, and table covers and bedspreads. There was even a carved ivory ball that contained 19 other balls, all carved from a single piece of ivory. Most were collected by Soo from antique and Chinese curiosity shops during his travels.

One of the most prized elements of the collection was an intricately embroidered robe described as a birthday present to a high-ranking Beijing judge. The garment was made from the finest red silk and embroidered with green and gold, as well as black and white patterns including faces demonstrating various emotions.

The centerpiece of the exhibit was a large palanquin, a conveyance typically designed to carry one person, consisting of a portable chair mounted on two poles and carried upon the shoulders of two or more men. Soo's palanquin was claimed to have at one point been a gift to him by the Dowager Empress and worth over

Artist's rendition of Ching Ling Soo's "Robes of His Ancestors" theater lobby installation. (Scobie)

£1,000. The palanquin was constructed of solid ebony, inlaid with thousands of solid gold sequins, and with a copper cover polished to a mirror finish. Soo used to delight in using the palanquin to arrive, with much pageantry, to his performances. He would wave from his perch in the palanquin at the curious crowds that would surround the vehicle.

In Soo's promotions, it was alleged some of the objects in the Robes of His Ancestors displays were from the Imperial Palace in Beijing. However, given public sensitivities regarding the "carnival of looting" which the Western Allies reportedly engaged in after their victory over the Boxers, Soo's promoters made clear that none of the objects on display were looted from the Chinese palace. However, this did not mean that the objects might not have been looted from the Boxers, who themselves had supposedly engaged in looting of their own—the idea being that taking loot already looted by the Boxers was fair game.[391]

For many British, Soo's travelling exhibition of Chinese artifacts would be their only exposure, limited as it was, to Chinese culture.

November 1905: Foo Troupe Back in Shanghai

By September of 1905, the Foo troupe was back in Shanghai and nine-year-old Chee Toy was performing, independent of the Foo troupe, in a patriotic Chinese Student Federation Concert featuring Western classical music, including Beethoven's *27th Sonata*, Handel's *Lago*, madrigals, and patriotic drills featuring the Chinese imperial flag.

The only Chinese music at the event was a number of patriotic songs sung at the start of the concert along with the patriotic drills. The event was a first of its kind, but the talents of "Miss Chee Toy" were already well-known in high-toned Shanghai music circles, and she was "always a favorite." A glowing report noted "since her last appearance in Shanghai she has travelled much and sung to very large Western audiences in Europe and South Africa. She has grown considerably, and her voice is more under control. The charm of her singing lies in the only just-perceptible accentuation of the mannerisms of music-hall singers of the West." Another critic in attendance noted Chee Toy's "low notes were excellent; and the dramatic manner in which one so young rendered her songs was highly amusing and delighted the audience", which was primarily Chinese with a sprinkling of British.[392]

At the conclusion of the concert, "it was announced that the organizers had decided to present to Miss Chee Toy a silver medal to go with the one already given her by H.E. the Governor of the Transvaal" (His Excellency, Governor of South Africa), which Chee Toy would have received when the Foo troupe were performing in South Africa prior to their arrival in London.[393]

CHAPTER TEN
1906–1911, THE INTERIM YEARS: A PROLONGED VICTORY LAP FOR SOO AND A GOLDEN ERA FOR FOO IMITATORS IN AMERICA AND ELSEWHERE

1906: A Prolonged Victory Lap for Soo

Back in England, still basking in equal parts relief and "victory", Soo continued into 1906 much as he had in 1905, trumpeting his triumph over Foo and taking his act on the road to parts of Britain such as Gloucester, Bolton, Derbyshire, and Chesterfield. Even in June of 1906, a year and a half after the contest, one of Soo's promotional ads read, Soo "recently proved his claim to be the greatest Chinese Magician before representatives of the *Daily Mirror, Evening News, Weekly Dispatch*, and representatives of London's best newspapers, having accepted and won Ching Ling Foo's challenge of £1,000."

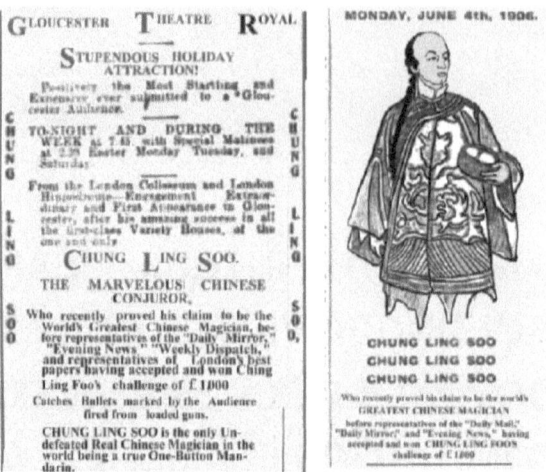

In the years that followed their clash, Soo's victory over Foo became a key part of this marketing campaign. "Chung Ling Soo is the only Undefeated Real Chinese Magician in the world, ... having accepted and won Ching Ling Foo's challenge of £1,000." In more candid moments with the media, Soo was less boastful and presented a more sympathetic figure who gave voice to his fear that Foo "had come to England to run him out of business."

"The Yankee Who Fooled All London": Soo's "Shrewd Ruse" Revealed (Again)

In the midst of this prolonged victory lap, in June of 1906 the American press published its first major coverage and revelations regarding the true identity of Chung Ling Soo. This time, the story of Soo's deception was not tucked in as a not-too-remarkable side point of a larger article on magic in a popular general interest magazine, as it was in a late 1902 edition of *The Cosmopolitan*. This time the secret behind Soo *was* the main story.

The reason this apparently remarkable revelation may have been incorporated as a not-too-noteworthy element of a larger story in the 1902 *The Cosmopolitan* article is that the author was undoubtedly a magician, and as a magician, he would have been part of a fraternity that had always been very aware of William Robinson's venture in

England since he first left the U.S. At that time, Chung Ling Soo's secret identity was an open secret within U.S. magic circles; thus, the power that revelation would have on an uninitiated public was likely lost on the author.

Fueled by Chung Ling Soo's ever-growing success and fame, and a good nose for sensational news, the articles in question were prominently featured in major mainstream American daily newspapers published across the country. A piece with the jingoistic title "The Yankee Who Fooled All London" appeared in the Boston *Herald* and other newspapers across the United States on June 17th, 1906. This time Chung Ling Soo's secrets, with regard to his true identity and origin, were given the prominence they deserved.[394]

At the onset, the piece recounted Foo's challenge to Soo and the fact that Foo did not appear when the time came for the test of conjuring skills. However, like so many of these accounts of the contest published in this era, it importantly left out the other elements of the challenge Foo's team put forward that Soo refused to address. In particular, the question of whether Soo was indeed Chinese was reported as having been dismissed at the time of the contest as an "unusual

Reworked composite of design motifs used to accompany June of 1906 Soo revelation stories in the U.S.

proviso" that, while it generated some interest, was "thought to be merely a question of caste, and soon died away."

Then, after recounting the outcome of the challenge and Foo's failure to show up for it, the writer informed his audience that suspicions of Soo's nationality resurfaced not long after the contest. Reportedly, stagehands who had been observing the odd goings-on backstage at a Soo performance for some time gradually leaked the truth. Soo was, in fact, an American named William Robinson. As to why this revelation, when it broke, did not have more of an impact in England, where Soo had his base and actively performed, the American journalist observed that while this new information did indeed invoke "consternation" among the British press, by the time these revelations were made known, Soo was "too firmly established in the hearts of his English audiences to be ousted by exposure of his shrewd ruse."[395,396] So, essentially, the British press, with whom Soo had worked closely for over six years, mostly sat on the story.

1907–1911: Soo Preemptively Alters His Progenitors, Offers New Version of Ancestry

Soo's seeming ongoing cockiness in the aftermath of his victory over Foo, even after the revelations regarding his identity were widely published in the U.S., belied the canny conjurer's perception of the risks his very profitable act now faced. Soo well understood that while the revelations printed in the United States might currently have little impact on his career in London and Europe, it would be best for him to begin altering his storyline to respond in a more credible way to claims the Foo team had made regarding his background that had by now been vindicated in the U.S. press. Thus, not long after the contest, Soo began admitting in some interviews that he might not be one hundred percent Chinese after all.

During this phase, Soo, apparently none too concerned about consistency, at various times provided various versions of his new and revised ethnicity. Gradually, however, he seemed to settle in on and let it be known in select interviews with friendly journalists, that his father was actually a Scotsman by the name of Campbell. Mr. Campbell was, in Soo's early tellings, a missionary in Canton, deceased when Soo was a child in China, and his mother, whose surname was Chung, was Chinese. Soo, embracing his newly concocted heritage, claimed this mixed Scot-Chinese background was a good blend for a conjurer; combining "the mysticism of the Oriental with the practical canniness of the Scot."[397] In some versions of this story, he added that the "Ling Soo" portion of his name meant "extra good luck", as he was the first boy born after four girls.[398]

After further thought on the matter in a later interview, Soo altered his imaginary father's profession, making him an "engineer." In this telling, Soo claimed absent his father's death, he would have likely followed his "father's footsteps" and gone into engineering. In a nice touch, he then invited the interviewer to examine his hands and "feel the dirt", claiming he had "just come from the lathe."[399]

Given Soo's evident and widely admired technical abilities, this later origin tale fit better with Soo's actual inclinations than claims he was the son of a missionary. Soo, at this stage in his career, had constructed a large, free-standing workshop behind his palatial English home in which he and a professional crew of technicians were constantly at work to develop new illusions.[400] Even before the contest, Soo had been broadening his act from his initial basic replication of Foo's tricks, and playing to his evident strengths and interests by adding more and more grand-scale, Western-style mechanical illusions to his act. At one point, Soo boasted of being capable of creating a new illusion every day, all of which furthered the argument that Soo's performance was no longer a mere copy of Foo's act.

In discussing some of these Western-style illusions, like the reanimating cauldron, the corded arrow shot through a body, and, of course, the bullet-catching illusion, Foo prophetically noted, "the tricks are dangerous and we are sometimes injured, but we carry on."[401]

Soo Responds to Those Who Wonder Why He Does Not Return to China

In the wake of the questions raised by the contest, Soo also moved to address the issue of why he did not return to China more often by spinning a tale whereby he was banished from the Middle Kingdom for rescuing some unfortunates from a terrible torture which Soo, being "enlightened," would not allow to take place. But by rescuing these unfortunates, Soo, according to the story, incurred the wrath of the fearsome Dowager Empress. As a result, Soo, who barely escaped with his life was afterwards banned from returning to China. Safe in enlightened England, Soo "thanks his lucky stars" that "he is alive to tell the tale."

Soo further embellished the yarn by adding he was summoned to see the terrible ruler for punishment for his good deed, but only by adopting a number of disguises was he able to smuggle himself safely out of the country and back to England.[402]

Soo Introduces "Bamboo Flower", His Very Own Chee Toy

Yet, even as he was in the time since the contest distancing himself in some ways from Foo's act by introducing more new and large-scale mechanical, Western-style illusions, the magpie-like Soo saw in Foo's London performances one other element of Foo's act he wished to emulate. The rapturous reception Chee Toy, the adorable and talented little daughter of Foo, had received in London had not gone unnoticed by Soo. So, not long after Foo departed London, Soo went to work on developing his own "Chee Toy."

Given that Chee Toy's transcendent singing talent was not something that could be easily replicated, and understanding the absolute

A BABY CONJURER: BAMBOO FLOWER, DAUGHTER OF CHUNG LING SOO, THE FAMOUS ILLUSIONIST.

necessity of trust if the child was to be presented as his own daughter to the public, Foo naturally turned to Frank Kametaro, his Japanese right-hand man, who was married to an English woman and had a young daughter: Nina Kametaro.

Thus "Bamboo Leaf", a.k.a. "Bamboo Flower", was born and joined Soo's "Chinese" family alongside Soo's Chinese "son." Unlike Chee Toy, Bamboo Flower's special talent was not singing and music, but rather magic. She was promoted as a "baby conjurer", free to ply her trade with exquisite skill in China but conveniently barred by the child labor laws of England from demonstrating her prowess on the London stage. She was reported to be unable to understand why she could not perform in England and saddened by her predicament. Her contribution to the Soo act was therefore mostly on the publicity and promotion side, appearing at the opening of performances and handing out lucky Chinese coins to big spenders. She also reportedly

The adorable "Bamboo Flower." There is a story of a magician performing decades later in London and noticing a stylish older woman in the front row, entranced by the show. She lingered after the crowd had left and he approached her, asking her if she liked magic. The woman replied that she did and revealed, as her eyes lit up, that when she was a child she had been Chung Ling Soo's Bamboo Flower. She passed away on April 29th, 1978.

performed some minor sleight-of-hand tricks to limited audiences of select friendly reporters making coins disappear and multiply all while she "chuckled in infantile delight."[403]

Soo Continues to Tour; Foo, in the Face of Immigration Issues, Focuses on Other Things

Meanwhile, in contrast to Soo's almost constant promotional and touring activity in the three to four years since their London confrontation, there is little evidence that the Foo troupe, once returned to Shanghai, continued to perform onstage in a significant way during this period.

It appears Foo used this time to rest up, enjoy some of the wealth he had accumulated abroad, and focus on his other entertainment-related business ventures, including his expanding interests in the emerging movie theater and film sector and other business ventures he likely jointly invested in with the Moosers, including a Chinese circus. Thus, according to theatrical sources of the time, Foo in 1907 was now "retired from the stage with a large fortune" and was a "prosperous businessman of Shanghai."[404]

In late 1906, Howard Thurston, one of the great emerging American magicians of the time, was touring through Asia, including Saigon, which he found—with its "boulevards, cafés, music and beautiful women"—truly a "miniature Paris," and met with Ching Ling Foo in Shanghai. Thurston noted that Foo, along with Chee Toy were contemplating a return visit to America.[405]

Part of Foo's decision to focus on matters other than international touring in this period may well have been influenced by what appeared to be the increasing strictness with which the ban on Chinese entering the U.S., including performers, was now being enforced. Having most recently toured Britain, Europe, and South Africa, the natural next move for the Foo troupe after a period of rest and recuperation in Shanghai would have been a tour of the United States. However, indications of just how difficult it was for Chinese performers to obtain immigration papers and perform in the U.S. at this time was evidenced when the Tschin Man troupe, in March of 1906, was refused entry by immigration authorities. This is the same group of Chungchausen performers who, just one year earlier, had performed successfully in London at the time Foo and Soo were engaged in their legendary contest.[406]

CHINESE PERFORMERS BARRED.

In the U.S., a Golden Era for Foo Impersonators

So, with Foo "retired" in China, Soo seemingly deciding it might not be in his best interests to tour his homeland, and with the continued ratcheting up of barriers to Chinese wishing to enter the U.S., a flourishing market for genuine homegrown Chinese and yellowface magic acts emerged in a post-Foo America. Performers ranging from those who would be fortunate to earn a spot on the bill of a dime store museum to some of the most successful stage performers of the time rushed to fill the vacuum created by the absence of Foo and the trepidation of Soo.

Just a partial list of the Foo copycats and mimics that emerged during the period from 1906 to 1911 included Ah Ling Foo, Ching La Foo, Rush Ling Toy, Okito, Carter the Great, Ah Foon, Madame Chung, Sing Toy, and even two performers—one in America and another in Australia—who actually appropriated not only Ching Ling Foo's act, but his name as well. This list includes both genuine Chinese magicians and yellowface performers, as well as magicians who incorporated an impersonation of a Chinese magician as a major part of their act.

As to the success of these Foo impersonators, the case of Ah Ling Foo, the E.F. Albee/Keith's Theater-backed Chinese conjurer, is instructive. Ah Ling was introduced to the theatrical market as the comedian who had originally worked as Foo's comic assistant on Foo's first tour. Albee had laid the groundwork for the introduction of this Foo replacement in earlier interviews, where he indicated that Foo's comedian assistant was one of the discoveries of the worldwide Keith's talent-scouting network. Albee claimed that Ah Ling, a "natural comedian", had been talent-spotted in a small city in the interior of China.

Albee's promotional bumpf to one side, it was never clear just who "Ah Ling Foo" really was. But one thing was certain: He was not Harry Foo, Foo's most famous comedic assistant from troupe's first tour. Nonetheless, Keith's management, under Albee's direction, claimed Ah Ling at first to be both a nephew and a student of Foo. By 1911, Ah Ling's backstory included the claim he had taken over the Foo troupe after Foo died. His absence from America up to that point was explained as due to tour obligations in Europe and Asia during this period.[407]

Despite the alleged links to Foo and the support of Albee and the powerful B.F. Keith's network, professional critics, for their part, were pretty much united in deeming Ah Ling Foo a "very poor imitation of his former employer." Ah Ling's work was described "as transparent as glass" and, at best, suitable for the "small time" theaters.[408]

For Ah Ling, attempts to play before the vaudeville crowds in the larger urban centers were fraught with risk. In one notable instance in early 1907, Ah Ling Foo was performing as part of the bill at Keith's New York Union Square theater when scheduling problems forced the theater manager to ask him to repeat his act only 45 minutes after he had already performed. Unfortunately for Ah Ling, who was brave enough to face the notoriously volatile Union crowd again after such a short interval, the audience lying in wait for him reportedly was not too keen on his performance the first time he "struggled through" his "tiresome "act. Discovering they would be subjected to Ah Ling's tired conjuring once again, the Union Square crowd erupted in "heartfelt jeers and hisses."[409]

Despite Albee's best efforts, Ah Ling did in fact ultimately spend most of his time performing merely as an "added attraction" for troupes such as the "Bohemian Burlesquers" in the smaller venues.[410]

Carter the Great Plays Foo in Australia

Meanwhile, down in Australia, Carter the Mysterious and/or Great, depending on his mood, devoted like Lafayette before him a large part of his stage act to an imitation of Ching Ling Foo. Carter performed his Foo imitation "dressed in Chinese fashion" and, according to a Brisbane paper, "using a humorous stage Chinese patter."[411,412] During his world tour, Carter even made appearances in both Singapore and Shanghai, where the mixed Asian and Western audiences, clearly very familiar with Foo's work, reportedly appreciated his imitation of the Chinese conjurer.[413,414] By this point Carter had wisely abandoned his aforementioned claims of ownership with regard to all Foo's most popular illusions.

Albee Tries to Replace Foo with a Chinese Play, with Chinese Actors, in Chinese

Back in the U.S., E.F. Albee had not yet given up on his attempts to develop another Chinese act to rival the success of the Foo troupe. In June of 1910, his latest venture was a three-act play entitled *The Dragon's Wrath*, involving five Chinese principals. The play was set in a Chinese palace. Madam Chung, one of the stars, was a petite actress reportedly from the Pekin Imperial Theater, and was appearing for the first time in the U.S.

The play was positioned as a headline act at Keith's Boston theater, running about 40 minutes. The principals were all Chinese and were supported by seven Chinese attendants and four "American girls" who danced in some of the numbers. A Chinese actress called "Sing Toy," reminiscent of Chee Toy, played a "Chinese piano" and sang. However, Sing Toy sang in a manner U.S. audiences reportedly found "odd." Even worse, the dancing of Hung Lou, "the fat prince"—which was probably similar to what one would have seen in Beijing Opera performances—was considered "grotesque."

Remarkably, the play was all in Chinese except for the end, where Madam Chung recited some poetry in English and threw flowers to the audience. Unfortunately for him, Albee had struck out again, and neither the "diminutive" Madam Chung nor the actress "Sing Toy" demonstrated any of Foo or Chee Toy's magnetic appeal.[415]

Rush Ling Toy, "The Greatest Portrayer of the Chinese Character in America", Gets His Turn

About the same time as *The Dragon's Wrath* was appearing in theaters, Rush Ling Toy, the "greatest portrayer of Chinese character", emerged with his act: "A Night in the Orient."[416] As part of his promotional efforts, Rush solidified the always promotionally important and treasured links to Ching Ling Foo by claiming he was given a "letter" by the conjurer saying he was Foo's true successor in talent and "well qualified to succeed him at the Royal Court of Pekin." Rush was, in fact, one George F. Reuschling, who, not content to mimic Foo, would also later in his career perform a travesty of the Great Lafayette under the stage name the "Great LaFollette."

Rush, as befit his name, adopted a performance style wherein he performed his tricks very, very quickly. He aimed to not leave a minute between stunts and did none of the smaller variety of tricks.[417] There is no record if "Rush" had any relationship with the earlier Foo imitator who, shortly after Foo's first U.S. tour, adopted the stage name "Speed". Regardless, Rush would later play a significant part in Albee's and the UBO's attempts to undermine the success of Foo's second American tour.

Ah Foon's Unfortunate Accident

Another follower in Foo's footsteps, the Chinese magician "Ah Foon", only made headlines when he was hospitalized for three weeks due to complications from a trick involving swallowing some needles and thread separately and then, after a brief display of focused manipulation of the mouth, removing the needles already threaded. Reportedly, an X-ray revealed Foon still had two of the needles "that must have missed their cue" lodged in his stomach. Reporters, seeing a comic angle to the story, also noted that Ah Foon's manager, Joe Raymond, was still owed his commission and was "wanting" to use this new X-ray technology to discover if Ah Foon had "secreted his commissions" elsewhere. Newsmen reported Raymond wanted Foon "to cough up the commission, not the needles."[418]

Editors of Magicians' Journals Unite in Condemnation of Fake Foo and His Managers

Foo's ongoing continued absence from America, despite all the intermittent touting of his imminent return, emboldened one performer to simply forego imitating Foo's act and appropriate Foo's name as well as his tricks. So it was we saw the emergence of the first and only fake "Ching Ling Foo" in America. He first appeared in late 1907 at the Orpheum Theatre in Ohio. This fake Foo and his "high class legerdemain" were not even at the top of the bill of the small-town Ohio venue at which he appeared, where seats went from 10 to 15 cents.[419]

The plethora of copycat Foos with similar-sounding names were generally tolerated and acknowledged as to-be-expected outgrowths of Foo's tremendous success and indications of just how enduringly popular the Foo troupe and its style of Chinese entertainment remained. But the emergence of this fake Ching Ling Foo in Ohio was, for the professional magician's fraternity, a step too far, and drew the critical attention of the editors of the *Conjurer's Monthly* Magazine.

Given "the Great and Original" Ching Ling Foo's fame and preeminence among magicians in the U.S., no less an authority than Foo's then-current manager Leon Mooser was contacted in Shanghai to confirm whether the highest-paid magician in U.S. history was now touring the minor circuits of Ohio playing in ten-cents-a-seat houses.

Mooser quickly responded that, as suspected, the real Foo "is closer to Canton, China, than to Canton, Ohio."[420]

Even as his activities drew attention from professionals, the fake Foo continued to tour, and in early 1908 he was the undercard to a "long awaited" bachelor auction in Monessen, Pennsylvania.[421,422]

From Monessen, the fake Foo moved on to various entertainment meccas across small-town America, including Rockford, Illinois and Sheboygan, Wisconsin. In Sheboygan, he found himself billed under "The Three Sunbeams" at the town's Unique Theater.[423] The fake Foo and his managers doubled down on their duplicity when, in 1909, they distributed promotional material targeting the smaller venues in New York state proclaiming that this fake Foo "had been the cause of more talk than possibly any other single foreign act that has appeared upon the American vaudeville stage."[424]

But the fake Foo's promotional material continued to promise a level of performance that was not forthcoming. Try as he might and despite aggressive promotion, he continued to languish, none too successfully, in the smaller markets. By the time 1910 rolled around, theaters were actually partially apologizing for engaging this counterfeit Chinese conjurer. In one notable instance in Kentucky, where the fake Foo was engaged by the Lexington Hippodrome, the promotion for his appearance read, "This show will be a good one—well worth the money but not a big as last week. We think you will like it just as well. If ever you saw a better show for the money it was at the Hipp, and you know all of them cannot be the biggest and the best." Faint praise indeed.[425]

This may have been the last straw for the people at *The Sphinx*, then one of America's premier publications for professional and amateur conjurers. In its January 1910 issue, the venerable periodical went on record as being aggrieved at the assault on Ching Ling Foo's reputation, occasioned by the ongoing fraud being perpetrated by this false Ching Ling Foo and the theater managers who seemed quite happy to employ him.

The respected journal first established that it was evident the gentleman then playing in Toledo, Ohio "is not the genuine Ching Ling

Foo", and perhaps even more importantly, that "it is equally evident the manager must know that fact." The bible of American magicians went on to assert "It is altogether likely the genuine Ching Ling Foo may never show in Toledo, not even at a first-class house, but if he should, his reputation would have been spoiled by the rank imitator of his name and makeup who played the 10, 20, 30 house three times week days and four times Sundays." In this context, it is important to note that one of the distinguishing features of 'big time' vaudeville was that its top performers only performed twice a day, while the smaller, cheaper 'small time' vaudeville houses required their lesser acts to perform three times a day.

Then, with a nod to its less successful readership, *The Sphinx* added a codicil to its condemnation of small-time vaudeville and its practices. "Not that good men and good magicians do not play the cheaper houses, but magicians like the original Ching Ling Foo have attained a greater reputation and command a larger salary than such houses can possibly afford to pay."[426]

Alas, immune to shame, the fake Foo and his manager continued touring, appearing in smaller and smaller venues until the act found itself billed after even Tambo and Tambo, a singing roller-skating duo. Unable to meet audience expectations but reluctant to leave the stage, over the handful of years of its existence, the fake Foo act declined into farce.

Likely this mocking comedic approach was the safest angle for the apparently inexpert performer to take. A reviewer from a September 1910 performance in Portsmouth, Ohio—a town of approximately 20,000—noted of the fake Foo's act that the magician "excited not a little mirth, but not by his tricks. His petulant perambulations before the footlights in putting through his tricks bring down the house."[427]

The end for this fake Foo seems to have come in 1911, when he made his last appearance in his last small venue and a combination of professional embarrassment and commercial failure finally drove him from the stage.

Foo's Tricks Could be Delivered by Mail; His Stage Presence and Charisma? Not So Much

What was most evident from the overall audience reaction to this crowd of Foo imitators was that duplicating the allure, popularity, and success of the Foo troupe was not as simple as the numerous ads hawking Ching Ling Foo 'kits' to would-be Chinese conjurers might have suggested. Nor was it enough to simply be authentically Chinese; most of these duplicate Foo acts, while they initially might have succeeded at smaller venues and the dime museums of the time, were unsuitable and even unwelcome before the much more demanding audiences of vaudeville's big time.

The Foo troupe's engaging and elegant execution and audience-charming charisma and dash, as exemplified by Foo and an emerging Chee Toy, could not, unlike facsimiles of Foo's tricks, be obtained through the mail. Regardless, during this period of Foo's exile, Albee and other theater managers in America continued their efforts to recreate the box office magic that the Foo troupe had engendered.

1907–1908: Rumors of Foo's Imminent Return Proliferate

Not surprisingly given Foo's continued popularity in America and the sustained efforts by theater managers to find Chinese acts to equal the Foo troupe's allure during Foo's absence from America, rumors continued to emerge in the popular and theatrical press indicating that the original Chinese conjurer's return to America was imminent.

The first of these rumors appears in January of 1907, when the magician Howard Thurston related a story of meeting Foo in Shanghai during his recent global tour in the magician's periodical *Conjurer's Monthly Magazine*. In this note, Thurston claimed Foo, who was apparently "looking very old and becoming bent with age," shared that he was preparing to come back to America. Interestingly, the piece was careful to point out that if Foo and his troupe did return to the U.S., they would be managed by E.F. Albee, who, according to the article, has Foo and his troupe "under contract."[428] This reference to Albee and his contractual relationship with Foo in an otherwise small note on the possibility Foo would soon return to the U.S. was unlikely to be incidental.

Albee, who, as seen above, had spent the last few years trying to put together and/or promote a Chinese-themed act with an appeal similar to that of the Foo troupe, seemed keen on once more declaring his contractual control over them in the event they returned to tour America. Furthermore, this declaration seemed almost a warning to the Mooser Brothers, who were currently managing Foo. These actions by Albee also resurface memories of contractual difficulties with Albee and the Keith's circuit he represented that preceded Foo's rather abrupt return to China at the close of his last American tour.

Almost six months later, another reference to Foo is made in a May 1907 notice. *Conjurer's Monthly Magazine* reminded its readers that Foo was the first magician to make the grand sum of $1,000 week. Importantly, in this very short piece, Colonel Hopkins is forgotten, and this auspicious wage is attributed solely to the good work of E.F. Albee.[429] It seemed this reference to Albee's expert management skills was, once again, no coincidence. It appeared Albee had become aware of efforts by the Moosers to bring Foo back to America for a return tour.

Albee's early warning proved prescient. In October 1907, London's *Music Hall and Theatre Review* noted Leon Mooser "is about to arrange an American tour for his principal" Ching Ling Foo. These 1907 efforts would ultimately be unsuccessful.[430]

Then, taking a somewhat different tack, the Mooser Brothers, in the next month's *Conjurer's Monthly* Magazine, countered persistent rumors that Foo had passed away during the Boxer Rebellion or met some other fate, and shared with the magazine's readers that Ching Ling Foo was indeed alive and well in China, but might never return to America. However, they were careful to add, one could still contact the Moosers if they wanted to see if they could arrange something.[431]

In 1909 the Foo Troupe is Performing in Shanghai

In the midst of all these new U.S. tour-related machinations, the Foo troupe appeared at the Shanghai Lyceum Theatre in January of 1909. Reportedly, a large audience enjoyed Foo and Chee Toy. Foo was not on stage long, but reportedly, his tricks still "mystified." "Little" Chee Toy, now a young teenager around 15 years of age, sang "Because I Love You" and "Just One Girl" and was "loudly applauded for her quaint rendering in a good contralto voice of the well-known songs." Of special interest was a requested encore wherein she treated the audience to "a Chinese ballad to her own accompaniment on the piano." A new member of the troupe, San Tow "the Chinese Hercules", who showed himself the equal of any European strongmen, was also on the bill, as well as a juggler.[432]

Memories of Foo at the 1898 Omaha Exhibition

All the talk of Foo returning to America kindled still-strong memories of the huge impact the Chinese conjurer's tour from 1898 to 1900 had on the American public. In the April 1909 edition of *The Sphinx*, the magician David Abbot, stimulated by all the rumors of an imminent return tour by Foo, reminisced about seeing the great magician for the first time at the Omaha Fair back in 1898.

According to Abbot, the Chinese pavilion in Omaha was "quite a miniature Chinese city", where you could experience daily Chinese life. A Chinese theater was part of that, and Foo was by far the theater's most popular act.

FOO'S INNOVATIVE PAPER-TEARING TRICK

Of all the tricks Foo demonstrated, Abbott was most taken by Foo's paper-tearing trick, wherein Foo would seemingly tear up in his hands a strip of paper and then have it magically reassemble after he massaged

> it in his fist while all observed. Abbott knew all the techniques normally used to execute this maneuver, but even with this knowledge, he could not explain the way Foo did it. Foo exposed his fingers and hands in a way that would have revealed the methods familiar to Abbot, as no doubt set out in the earlier 1904 New York *Times* exposé of the trick addressed in Chapter 8 of this book. Unable to determine the methodology, Abbot and another magician speculated that Foo perhaps actually did what he claimed with some form of specially treated paper and did not resort to mere substitution or sleight of hand.[433]

Foo "Would Tolerate No Rivals"

After a very favorable review of Foo's conjuring skills, Abbot's reminiscence then moves to the part of his story that tends to get picked up on by those favoring Soo in the Foo-vs.-Soo narrative.

Abbot notes that Foo, during his last days in Omaha, was invited to dine with the high families of the city, as he had a habit of doing during the entire exhibition. As noted, Foo, during his engagement, had become quite a favorite of the local gentry, and he and his family were often invited to special dinners. During one particular dinner, a rival Western magician had also been invited and performed after Foo.

According to this rival magician, a "wrathful" Foo "fairly raved in Chinese" with regard to the presumption of another magician performing at the same venue as he. The local Chinese consul, also in attendance, was apparently required to calm Foo down. This story was, Abbot said, illustrative of one element of "this Oriental's disposition": "he would tolerate no rivals."

This unsubstantiated tale of Foo's prideful intolerance of other magicians is of a piece with the earlier debunked story of Foo's dismissive treatment of Leon Herrmann, who reportedly had come to see Foo in Omaha.[434]

June 1909: The Foo Troupe in Hong Kong

As excitement escalated regarding a potential return of the Foo troupe to America, the troupe, perhaps polishing their act in anticipation of a long, lucrative international tour, appeared in Hong Kong in June of 1909. The Foo troupe, with the now adolescent Chee Toy, was reported to have performed in various theatres in Hong Kong and was thoroughly appreciated by the Chinese, foreign, and mixed audiences they appeared before. Reviews of the performances once more single out Chee Toy for the quality of her singing and the many awards and medals she had received for her singing ability in Europe and Asia. The article notes the Foo troupe planned to leave for Europe within a week.[435]

July–August 1909: Ching Ling Foo to Return

While all this Foo mimicry and impersonation was going on, a piece in the new American show business bible *Variety* made clear what many had long suspected. Tightened U.S. immigration laws with regard to the Chinese had been the major reason that Foo had been kept out of the American market these past four years. Seeking to work his way around these restrictions, Leon Mooser was examining getting the Foo troupe into the U.S. as part of the upcoming Seattle exhibition.[436]

A month later, Mooser appeared to change gears, with a plan for Foo to first tour France and go on from there to London and then America to play the United circuit. Foo's tour organizers were certain they would succeed this time. They went so far as to publish Foo's

> **THEATRE ROYAL**
> Friday, 4th June 1909, at 9p.m.
> THE GREAT MAGICIAN CHING LING FOO And His Troupe
> Miss Chee Toy: (His Wonderful little daughter.) Singer of English Songs.
> Piansit - - - - - - - - - - - Mr. L. David
> PROGRAMME
> 1. Overture   (Ten Minutes' Interval)
> 2. Eight Volumes of Magical Longevity   10. Western Magic.
> 3. Flying Plates and Bowls.   11. Playing with Flower Pots.
> 4. Revolving Plates.   12. Transformation of Clothes.
> 5. Foreign and Chinese Songs.   13. Piano Solo -- Valse - Rubenstein
> 6. Sudden appearance of persons from   14. Triple Juggling.
>   underground   15. Drums and Bowls.
> 7. Scientific Juggling.   16. Flashes of Various Colors of Lights.
> 8. Playing with Vases.   17. Somersault with a bowl filled with
> 9. Foreign Songs, with Piano   95 lbs of water. God Save the King.
>   accompaniment. Miss Chee Toy.

The program for Foo troupe's Hong Kong performance of June 4th, 1909. (Enhanced and reconfigured.)

schedule for the planned upcoming tour in the August 1909 edition of *The Sphinx*. The Foo troupe for this tour was to comprise 12 Chinese women and 8 men. It would begin in Austria in September, then Paris in October, followed by London in November and December, and finally the U.S. in January. The U.S. leg of the tour would begin in New York with an indefinite stay. But once more Foo and Mooser's plans were thwarted, and the proposed U.S. portion of the tour fell through.[437-439]

During this period of uncertainty regarding the timing of a U.S. tour, the Foo troupe continued to play Hong Kong, Shanghai, and other Asian venues.[440] November of 1909 found the Foo troupe still playing the Shanghai Lyceum Theater.[441]

Interestingly, by this point, even the English-language Hong Kong newspapers found it difficult not to confuse Ching Ling Foo with Chung Ling Soo. Some coverage of Foo's performances in Hong Kong incorrectly claimed the Foo troupe, in July of 1909, had just returned from Australia. This reporting misstep was the result of confusing Foo rival Chung Ling Soo's 1909 Australian tour with Ching Ling Foo's Asian engagements.

Australia 1909: Down Under Insurrection— Soo's Illusion Secrets Leaked

Fascinatingly, the 1909 Australian tour by Soo had a pivotal role in the most meta of all Foo impersonator tales.

By the end of 1908, Soo, having extensively toured Britain and Europe, was looking for new markets to conquer. A tour of Australia presented itself as a fine option. So it was that in 1909 Soo arrived Down Under to begin what would be a months-long and hugely successful tour of that continent.

As Soo's tour came to an end, some of the key technical staff he had engaged for his tour, both on the illusion design and manufacturing sides, decided there was no reason for them not to profit from their newfound knowledge after Soo returned to England. These former Soo technicians then hired out their services to Jean Hugarde, one of Australia's premier stage magicians, and assisted him in creating his own Chinese magician act.

Hugarde's new act, "Jean Hugarde's 'All Star Performers,'" included not only the standard Foo tricks and illusions that Soo had incorporated into his act, such as fire-eating and bowl productions, but also copies of most of Soo's newer Western-style illusions. The former Soo technicians now working with the Australian magician had provided Hugarde with the knowledge needed to recreate, among others, Soo's famous Mystic Cauldron illusion, bullet catching act, and the trick where Soo seemingly shot an arrow with a cord attached to it through a woman standing in front of him, which pierced her body and then traveled straight on to its target. Armed with this new act, "Jean Hugarde's 'All Star Performers'" began touring Australia not long after Soo left in late 1909.

In his "All Star Performers" revue, Hugarde had as a special guest star a Chinese magician he unashamedly billed as Ching Ling Foo. Then, in a move that caused Chung Ling Soo even more irritation, Hugarde not only repurposed Soo's illusions as his own, he also even reworked Soo's promotional materials for promoting his fake Ching Ling Foo act.

Post-Soo Australia Tour Indignities Part II: The Case of the Purloined Posters

In a very meta twist, in 1909 Australia, a fake Ching Ling Foo appropriates Foo copycat Chung Ling Soo's posters. He only had to change the "U" to an "I" and the "S" to an "F".

Hugarde, who would later move to the U.S. bought a small theater on Coney Island and performed as Ching Sung Loo. Later in his career Hugarde became a well-respected chronicler of stage magic, penning over 30 books on the craft.

It would have been poetic justice—and more than a little amusing—if the genuine Ching Ling Foo had, in fact, been touring Australia using repurposed versions of Soo's own tricks and slightly altered pirated Chung Ling Soo promotional materials; one only had to convert the "S" in Soo on the posters to an "F" and the "U" to an "I." Yet, sadly, this was not the case.

Instead, we had the very meta situation of a copy of an original being itself copied, and the second-level copy then calling itself by the name of the original. This was certainly the final slight to Chung Ling Soo by both his former technicians and Hugarde, who in doing this subtly flagged Soo himself as a pilferer of intellectual property, and who, in complaining, would only reveal himself as such.[442]

November 1909: Ironic Indignation—Soo Fumes About Hugarde's Act Theft to Houdini

The poetic justice of Chung Ling Soo being the victim of an act thief in another country, given what he had done to Foo, was lost on Soo. In a November 14th, 1909 letter to Houdini, who was planning a tour of Australia, Soo warned his off-and-on friend, of the perfidy of some of the continent's inhabitants and bemoaned with a straight face his helplessness to deal with copycats of both his posters and his act through legal action.

"Now, whatever you do, send a copy of your lithographs to the Copyright Office at Bristol, and also New Zealand, and have them registered. Since I left, Hugarde, a man I warn you of, has deliberately made exact reproductions, simply changing the name, calling himself Ching Ling Foo, and I cannot do a thing in the matter, as English copyright does not hold good."

Soo went on to complain of the untrustworthiness of another man called Breton, who, although presenting himself with recommendation letters from the magicians Thurston, Carter, and Dante, betrayed Soo, selling his illusion methodologies to Hugarde after Soo left Australia. This after Soo had specifically implored Breton to "Do me a favor and don't make up any of the show." Soo notes that despite this, "As soon as I left the country, he was in with Hugarde."[443]

1910 May: Foo Rescues His Friend the Great Nicola from a Traitorous Translator

The summer of 1910 found Nicola the Great, an old friend of Foo's from the 1898 Omaha Exposition, opening his tour of China with a big show in the southern Chinese city of Canton, now known as Guangzhou.

Foo had first met Nicola 12 years earlier at the Omaha exhibition, when a young Nicola was serving as an apprentice magician to his own father, who was also a magician working at the fair. Decades later, Nicola the Great would fondly remember how his friend Foo had come to his opening show in Guangzhou and rescued his act.

Nicola's promotional team had done good promotional work in the city and there was an audience of over 3,000—predominantly Chinese—in the audience on opening night. To assist in his performance, Nicola had sought out and engaged "the best interpreter obtainable."

About 15 minutes through his opening performance, Nicola believed all was going well, but he was made uneasy by the "outbursts of laughter and purring celestial tongues that followed each and every trick." Despite the fact that he was successfully performing each of his tricks, Nicola could not avoid the sense he was being laughed at.

All would become clear when his great friend Foo suddenly leapt from his seat, ran up to the stage, and proceeded to drag Nicola's interpreter by the ear to the edge of the stage and send him sailing off of it with a well-placed kick to the rear.

Foo quickly explained to a startled Nicola that the traitorous translator not only explained what Nicola was about to do to the audience, but also how he was going to do it. According to Nicola, he "might as well have delivered an autographed blueprint" of his methodologies to the huge audience in attendance that night. Foo then volunteered

Foo with Nicola in front of Foo's Fun Ming Theater in Tienstin/Tianjin in 1910.

to act as Nicola's translator for the rest of the show and everything went "swimmingly" before one of the most "appreciative audiences" for whom Nicola had ever perform.[444]

During that tour of China, Nicola would also travel North to Tianjin for an engagement at Foo's Fun Ming Theater.[445]

June 1911: Chinese Audiences Also Adored the Foo Troupe

Foo's success with Western audiences would sometimes result in the perception that the Foo troupe was a Chinese act designed for Western audiences. It was anything but. The Foo troupe emerged first and foremost as a Chinese act for Chinese audiences and gradually evolved to tailor elements for foreign audiences when appearing before then.

For over two decades in Asia, the Foo troupe had tremendous success, not just with Western audiences, but with mixed Chinese and Western audiences, and in theaters devoted to an exclusively Chinese clientele. Evidence that the Foo troupe was still a strong draw for Chinese audiences came in late 1911, when the Foo troupe performed many shows in Chinese theaters throughout mainland China, Hong Kong, Macao and the Straits Settlements, including Singapore. During this period, the Chinese news coverage of the Foo troupe was as laudatory as their Western coverage.

Three Chinese-language articles published in Hong Kong praising Foo and the Foo troupe performances.

Foo was a significant celebrity in Hong Kong, and Chinese language newspapers of the time kept track of his comings and goings. In one instance, a Hong Kong paper published a story entitled "Where is Foo?" and informed its readers the magician would have an engagement in Macao soon and his fans should be sure not to miss his act.[446]

In the summer of 1911, in another piece from the Chinese press, Foo was proudly acknowledged as being famous both in the West and China and was lauded for his steady work for needy causes and charities. Foo's close integration with both the Chinese and Western elites in Hong Kong was demonstrated by his decision to forgo embarking on a new tour out of Hong Kong to instead perform, free of charge, for numerous charity events, including the upcoming Coronation celebration for the British monarch and some Hong Kong children's charities. All of these events would be attended by the Governor of Hong Kong and other local luminaries, while the ticket receipts were provided to charity.[447]

The accompanying prominent coverage and its tone demonstrated the very important point that the Foo troupe was not simply a 'race novelty' act whose appeal depended on foreign audiences and a commodification of "otherness." There were certainly elements of that to their success in Western countries and before Western audiences, but at the core of the popularity of the Foo troupe and its key components—Ching Ling Foo and later, Chee Toy—was undeniable talent and charisma that crossed all cultural boundaries. If this was not the case, the myriad copycat acts, both yellowface and actual Chinese, would have ultimately overwhelmed the Foo act, drowning it in a sea of fungible competitors.

The fact that never happened, but rather, on the contrary, that over the decades the long success of the troupe the Foo troupe continued to break box office records and elicit adulation from both Western and Chinese audiences, speaks deeply of very rare showmanship skill and ability that only Foo's great rival Chung Ling Soo, Lafayette, and a select few others were able to rival.

October 1911: More News of Foo Reaches the U.S.; He Would "Love" to go Back

In the fall of 1911, yet another troupe of performers on a world tour passing through Shanghai confirmed that Ching Ling Foo and his famed troupe were there. De Hollis and Velora, playing at the Shanghai Lyceum in mid-September, reported that Foo came to the theater almost every night and that he had a wonderful show. Their dispatch, however, divulged that Foo "can't do much in these parts", referring to China and the Far East, because of the relatively lower box office returns at the theaters in Asia. It was clear to all that the troupe's revenue potential in China paled in comparison to what they could make on a U.S. tour.

Foo was reported to have further confided to the touring performers that he would love to go back to America and that he has received all sorts of offers to perform in the U.S. but, alas, due to the strict laws restricting the entry of Chinese into their country, he and his management had repeatedly been unable to take up these offers due to these ongoing immigration difficulties.[448]

CHAPTER ELEVEN

OCTOBER–NOVEMBER 1911—FOO PRODUCES CHINA'S FIRST DOCUMENTARY, *WUCHANG UPRISING*; PLAYS SIGNIFICANT ROLE IN COLLAPSE OF THE QING DYNASTY AND EMERGENCE OF THE CHINESE REPUBLIC

The repeated delays dealt to Foo's plans to return for a second tour of America, and his subsequent increased focus on his China-based film- and theater-related businesses, would ultimately lead Foo into an environment where the magician would, in October of 1911, make a critical decision that would lead him—or more properly in this case, Zhu Liankui or Chee Ling Qua—to create what many claim to be China's first documentary, and certainly its first war documentary.[449]

In so doing, the Original Chinese Conjurer would play a pivotal role in the fall of the Qing Dynasty and the rise of the Chinese Republic, thus making no small contribution to a significant change in the course of Chinese history.

Towards the end of 1911, the Qing Dynasty, which had ruled China for over 250 years, was facing a multitude of challenges. It had repeatedly failed, over the last 100 years to protect China's interests in the face of repeated incursions by increasingly rapacious Western countries as well as Russia and Japan.

The list of the Qing failures was a long one that included the two Opium Wars in the mid 1800s and the Sino-Japanese War (1894–1895). Each war resulted in successive losses of Chinese territory to foreign victors, including Hong Kong, Taiwan, parts of northeastern China, and control of Korea—and in some areas where territory was not ceded, sovereignty was, resulting in the forced opening of numerous Chinese "treaty ports" such as Shanghai, wherein foreigners and their companies enjoyed extraterritorial status—meaning they were not subject to Chinese law.

In the face of this litany of humiliations, many Chinese at home and the millions living abroad felt the need to replace what they saw as failing, corrupt Qing rulers with a more modern form of government that would enable China to develop as it needed if the country was to survive. Sun Yat-Sen led the Revolutionary Alliance that strove to replace the Qing Dynasty with a republican form of government. There had been several earlier attempts to overthrow the Qing Dynasty, but all failed—until the autumn of 1911.

In October 10th of 1911, Ching Ling Foo, who by some reports was performing in Hankou at the time, first received news of a troop revolt led by the Revolutionary Alliance in Wuchang. This event became known as the Wuchang Uprising. It would later be widely acknowledged as the turning point in the overthrow of the Qing Dynasty.

The revolutionaries and rebellious Wuchang troops soon captured the city's armory and its mint. That Foo's sentiments were on the side of the rebels appears evident from both his decision and his capacity to reach out to their leaders to seek permission to film the uprising and related battles from within their lines. But Foo the businessman was, as his Western partners in the Meli Company certainly were at the time, clearly motivated by the pecuniary and promotional potential that war documentaries often achieved in the early years of film.

Foo had seen firsthand during his 1898–1900 tour of the United States that actual war documentaries and reenactments inspired by the Spanish-American War and the Boxer Rebellion were hugely popular with the ticket-buying audience. In fact, they were often more popular than the live entertainment on offer in the vaudeville theaters.

According to accounts from witnesses at the time, Foo and his crew, made up of Chinese and Westerners, were fearless in their push to capture the most dramatic and telling footage possible. Foo filmed from the tops of roofs and within firing distance of the battles, including from the roofs of the British Tobacco Company factory and the Daqing Bank. Their cameras captured rebel troops crossing the Yangtze River and brutal scenes of the Qing army burning houses.

Having shot the footage, by mid-October, Foo returned to Shanghai, where he and his team turned their hands to editing and putting the footage together.

On December 1st, 1911, *Wuchang Uprising* was premiered at the Bijou Theater of Moutrie and Company located just off Shanghai's Bund. It was shown as part of the Foo troupe's performance and played through January 12th, 1912.[450,451]

A surviving still from Foo's pioneering war documentary *Wuchang Uprising* with superimposed text explaining the risk Foo took in taking film of the battle from a nearby high vantage point.

The decision to integrate the showing of the film with the Foo troupe performance, of course, fit with a decision Foo had made years before. As early as 1904, Foo had a cameraman as part of his troupe, and had taken some 8,000 feet of film of Chinese life and scenes with the idea that the troupe, with this added cinematic element to their repertoire, would be able to provide a nearly two-hour entertainment just on their own.

Most importantly, the impact of the film—China's first authentic war documentary—was massive and immediate. The film proved immensely popular and was heavily advertised in the Shanghai papers as a film that brought the viewer into the battlefield and demonstrated the "martial prowess" of the "New Army." The "New Army" were the forces led by Sun Yat-Sen and others heading the rebellion.[452] The Chinese public had never seen scenes of Chinese battles up close, and Foo's editing and narrative techniques, including footage of the heroic leaders of the rebellion, Sun Yat-Sen, Huang Xing, and others captured the public's imagination.

A Beijing teahouse advertisement for the film in 1911 extolled the film's use of "real scenes" and editing techniques that enabled the viewer to follow "the chronology of the revolution."[453] According to the *Routledge Handbook of Chinese Media*, the documentary was "immensely popular." The "sensation it caused was due as much to its technological novelty as to the information the audience gained on the momentous revolution that had shaken the country." The *People's Independence Journal* (*Min Li Bao*), the largest newspaper run by the revolutionaries in Shanghai, published a special advertisement for the documentary, saying that watching this documentary would take viewers on to the battlefield and spread the spirit of the revolution. The film played until January 12th.[454]

Ultimately, the documentary was widely cited as raising support for the uprising among the general public, and thus playing a significant role in bringing down the Qing Dynasty.[455]

Sadly, no complete or even partial copy of *Wuchang Uprising* appears to have survived. However, a large number of now-treasured historical materials drawn from that documentary still exist. Many later printed materials and film and television products related to the Revolution of 1911 incorporated film clips or images that were drawn from Foo's original documentary. For example, *Portraits of the Great Revolutionaries*, a popular collection of commemorative photographs and memorial postcards printed by China's Commercial Press in the early years of the Republic of China—which included portraits of the leaders of the 1911 uprising—was produced using images taken from Foo's documentary. In addition, other fragments of the film Foo so courageously made live on in other preserved photographs and clips from the documentary that were later incorporated into other documentaries and films.

The year of 2011 marked the 100th anniversary of the Chinese documentary. On December 23rd, a major celebration was held in China's Great Hall of the People, in Beijing. The centerpiece of the event, organized by the Communications University of China and the China Documentary Research Center, was the unveiling of three bronze busts honoring the fathers of the Chinese documentary— Chee Ling Qua (otherwise known as Zhu Lian Kui/Ching Ling Foo), Sun Mingjing, and Joris Evans.

Three busts of the founding fathers of the Chinese documentary. Zhu Lian Kui a.k.a. Ching Ling Foo, is first to the right.

CHAPTER TWELVE

NOVEMBER 1912—"HE'S BACK!" FOO RETURNS TO AMERICA TO TRIUMPH AT HAMMERSTEIN'S

February 1912: Foo's Return—The Buildup

Not long on the heels of his *Wuchang Uprising* triumph, rumors again rekindled that, at last, and this time for certain, Foo, with China transitioning from the end of the Qing Dynasty to the beginning of the Republican Era, would be returning to the U.S. for another tour.

In February of 1912 a report circulated that one of Foo's managers, George Mooser, has returned to the U.S. from the Orient. Mooser was noted as both a former newspaper man and a theater magnate in the Far East, where he managed circuses and cinemas. The report added that Mooser also represented several foreign attractions, "particularly, Ching Ling Foo, the Chinese magician who would like to reappear."[456]

Mooser's presence in the U.S. was an acknowledgement that given the intransigence of immigration laws it was going to require one of the Mooser brothers working diligently from the U.S. side full time to get the Foo troupe back in the country.

In a related development, E.F. Albee, who not too long ago was still claiming to have Foo under contract for U.S. work, was working feverishly to expand his control over 'big time' vaudeville through the expansion of the B.F. Keith's-controlled monopoly-in-waiting, the United Booking Office (UBO).

Albee's monopolistic instincts, popular in an era of the big trusts Teddy Roosevelt would later famously bust, were meeting only limited resistance from the more independent-minded theater owners and managers.[457] The Mooser brothers and Foo, who had a history with Albee, would walk right into the middle of this when they returned to the U.S. in late 1912. Foo, who just months earlier played a significant role in overthrowing the Qing Dynasty, would play, along with his managers the Moosers, another significant role in challenging the UBO.

With Foo's return to the U.S. all but assured, the booming regarding the conjurer's imminent return to the American stage reached top gear. U.S. papers began to run pieces indicating the "Chinese magician who created something like a sensation when he made a tour of the American variety theaters in 1899 is to return here next season." Readers were reminded that Foo's magical style was noted to be "quite apart" from the styles of Herrmann, Keller, and Thurston, the then-famous American proponents of the art, and his return to once more demonstrate his skills should be eagerly anticipated.[458]

Meantime, the Foo troupe, which now featured a teenage Chee Toy as a prominent element of the act, was appearing at the Shanghai Bijou Theater located on Nanking Road (now Nanjing Road) near the Bund.[459] This was the same theater where Foo triumphantly premiered *Wuchang Uprising* only two months earlier.

Soo Inserts Himself Into the Chinese Turmoils of the Time

Over in England, Soo, as was his habit, could not avoid inserting himself into the Chinese turmoils of the time. In 1912, Soo had several interviews with English papers wherein he spoke credibly of his close relationship with a senior aide to Sun Yat-Sen and his membership in the China Reform Association, which Soo allowed was "to a great extent responsible for the present movement in China."[460]

In these interviews with Soo, it is claimed that it was in Australia that Soo joined the China Reform Association. It was also on Soo's 1909 Australian tour that he met Tong Chai Chi, the editor of a Sydney Chinese newspaper, who was a close ally of Sun Yat-Sen, the Reform Association's leader. According to Soo, during his Australian tour the two men worked together, including engaging in various charitable works to improve the Australian people's view of China and Chinese people.[461] Most of this account, while self-serving in a promotional context, was quite probable. Wherever Soo performed, in England or elsewhere, he wisely worked to keep the Chinese communities on his side, and for the most part, the local Chinese communities where he performed were either indifferent or quite supportive of his act.

It was, therefore quite probable Soo met Tong, a leader in the Australian Chinese community and the head of an important Chinese language media outlet, during his long tour of Australia when he had quite a bit of interaction with the local Chinese community, and he was very well received by them. Tong was no doubt well aware, as were most of the Chinese in Australia and elsewhere, of Soo's subterfuge. But, like many other Chinese faced with Soo's deception, they perceived the Chung Ling Soo persona as a net positive for the Chinese community and welcomed the dignified profile the magician presented to Western audiences. In addition, of course, Soo's donations to the China Reform Association cause and other Chinese charities were well appreciated.

Once more, as it was with the Boxer situation, while Foo was actually living and creating Chinese history, Soo, the master of self-promotion, liberally borrowed from it to weave his backstory.

The great irony was that while Soo touted his tangential relationship with the reform movements in China, Foo's substantial contribution to the fall of the Qing Dynasty and the advance of the Chinese reform movement remain largely unknown outside China.

Soo Still Half Scottish: "He Takes his Pigtail Off ... At Night and Retires a Canny Scot."

Soo also took a moment from his discussion of his involvement in Chinese geopolitics to once again revise his background. Soo, who seemed pathologically unable to stick to the same story, now disclosed that his Scottish father died when he was seven, and his real name was Sandy McCluskey, not Campbell as he had indicated in 1905 in the wake of questions raised by the Foo challenge. Soo said he would later take Chung, the surname of his Chinese mother's family, when he began performing as a professional magician at nine years old, when his first job was to "stand in front of a board while his master threw knives round his head and limbs." Absorbing these latest fictions, the reporter wrote of Soo "He takes his pigtail off with his clothes at night, and retires to bed a simple but canny Scot."[462]

August–September 1912: On the Eve of Foo's Return to the U.S., Albee and Keith's Take Credit for Foo's 1899–1900 Successes, Tout Rush Ling Toy

Rumors of Foo at last returning to the U.S. compelled E.F. Albee to once more make reference to the Chinese sorcerer in print. In an August 1912 article in a Brooklyn paper outlining Albee's plans for the Keith's theater chain, Albee discussed the successful formula his group used to both identify and, importantly, manage up-and-coming vaudeville stars. He made a point of claiming the Chinese comedian that worked with the Foo troupe during their historically successful original U.S. tour more than a decade ago, Harry Foo, was discovered by Keith's talent scouts. Albee went on to describe Harry as one of the most natural comedians of the day and a Keith's group discovery.

Albee claimed Keith's agents "scouring the small inland cities of the various countries of the world for original acts for presentation in Keith's houses" came across the talented comedian in "a small Chinese city many hundreds of miles on the other side of Peking." Albee further cemented his role in the legendary success of the Foo act by going on to set out how important "the management side" was to the success of vaudeville acts. According to Albee, before Foo benefited from his management during his first tour, the Chinese magician was making only fifty dollars a week, whereas under Albee's tender tutelage, it "shot up to over a thousand dollars" a week.[463] Here, of course, Albee was omitting the key role Col. Hopkins played in Foo's rise.

Always careful to have a backup plan and constantly on the lookout for a Chinese act that could replicate Foo's success, Albee and the UBO had also been busy promoting Foo mimic Rush Ling Toy, "China's Imperial Mystifier". Toy—whose specialty, as noted earlier and indicated by his name, was Chinese magic at high speed—had been selected as the Keith's circuit's latest attempt to recreate the success of the Foo act. Toy's new act, "A Night in the Orient", then playing Washington, D.C., reportedly "condenses a whole evening's entertainment into about fifteen minutes."[464] In Toy's promotional material, he was billed as yet another real successor to Ching Ling Foo.

An interesting act sharing the bill at the Nesbitt Theater with Toy was "Felix", the famous newspaper cartoonist whose always well-received act consisted of rapidly drawing illustrations of "current events and prominent people."[465]

November 1912: "He's Back!" — "Ching Ling Foo, The Original Oriental Illusionist Is In!"

Promotional photo of the Foo troupe used at the beginning of their second US tour probably taken in late 1912. Chee Toy is third from the left. A fresh-faced Yee Dee is by father's left hand.

Finally, the moment the many copycat Foos, who so benefited from Foo's absence, feared, arrived, and in November 1912, after over ten years of false starts and announcements made too soon, *Variety* reported that Foo was definitely, this time for sure, returning to America.

The deal that finally paved Foo's way back to the U.S. stage was with storied theater impresario Oscar Hammerstein, who had reportedly booked Foo for 52 weeks at his theaters for the princely sum of $2,000 per week. The original plan was for Foo to open at Hammerstein's New York theatre on November 18th.[466]

On November 5th, 1912, the Foo troupe stopped over in Hawaii on their way to San Francisco. The Pacific mail liner *Nile's* manifest of passengers listed Chee Toy as "Mrs. Chee Toy", indicating she was now married.[467]

Foo, along with Chee Toy, his son Yee Dee, and eight other Chinese performers and personnel, arrived in San Francisco, sailing on the *Nile* on November 11th, 1912. Among this new troupe, only Chee Toy and Foo remained from the original 1898–1900 team that toured the U.S.

November 12, 1912: San Francisco—U.S. Landing of Foo Troupe Delayed Due to Smallpox Scare

LINER NILE IS IN QUARANTINE;

In an augury of the challenges and difficulties to come, the troupe's arrival in the U.S. did not go smoothly.

Not yet landed upon American shores, the performers faced their first hurdle when the *Nile* was ordered into quarantine after the liner's surgeon reported two cases of the dreaded smallpox upon the ship's arrival in California. In an era of emerging public health systems, urban overcrowding, and plagues, the use of quarantine facilities was a deadly serious business.

As such, given that two cases of smallpox had been detected, the ship and all 221 of its passengers were escorted to the Angel Island quarantine facilities off San Francisco. At the island, which was equipped with special facilities to address these issues both the ship's passengers and crew were vaccinated and given antiseptic baths. While the passengers received this treatment, their personal effects and clothes were given "a Russian bath" by the enormous sterilizers installed on Angel Island for just this purpose.[468]

News of the quarantine and Ching Ling Foo's and Chee Toy's presence on the liner appeared in newspapers across the U.S.

On the very same day the news was broken on the Nile quarantine, a separate piece was published and prominently featured in the San Francisco *Examiner* on Chee Toy's view of the quarantine situation.[469]

QUARANTINE ANNOYS CHINESE SONGBIRD

In the article, Chee Toy was described as a 19-year-old "Chinese opera singer and protégé of Oscar Hammerstein." "Garbed in a richly embroidered Oriental costume, Miss Toy and her small Chinese poodle were ready to walk down the gangplank." When they discovered they would be going into quarantine, "The young songbird insisted that she and her father and 12 members of their troupe be permitted to land." When this was denied, she "shed tears" and pleaded with George Mooser, their manager, who had come to meet them on the "customs tug *Golden Gate*" to let them land, but he could do nothing.[470]

Hammerstein, the opera patron and impresario, had first become enamored of Chee Toy's talent when he heard her "remarkable contralto voice" at the Berlin Opera House earlier that year. He followed up by negotiating her engagement with her father, Ching Ling Foo.

A collage of Chee Toy coverage. By November 1912, the Chee Toy booming had begun, and newspapers across the country carried stories regarding Ching Ling Foo's talented daughter. The "Melba" being referred to in some of the headlines was the Dame Nellie Melba, the stage name for Helen Porter Mitchell, enormously popular at the time. "Melba" was the inspiration for, and lent her name to, both "Melba Toast" (it was created for the Australian singer when she had an upset stomach) and the dessert "Peach Melba", both concocted by an admiring chief chef at the synonymous-with-luxury Ritz Hotel—still run at that time by the proprietor, Cesar Ritz, who with the chef, came up with the names in honor of Dame Nellie.

Hammerstein's purported plan was for Chee Toy is to become "the first opera star from the Orient", and he was certain she would be a "wonder." According to the terms of the agreement signed by Foo, after Chee Toy's U.S., tour she would study opera under the famous European opera teacher De Reszke in Paris for two years.[471]

If she developed as expected, the impresario will engage her as a star in his opera houses "for a period of five years." This story generated great interest across the country and was syndicated and published across the U.S., typically with a large accompanying photo of Chee Toy and Foo.[472-474]

The nascent diva and the rest of the Foo troupe did not have to wait long for the quarantine process to complete itself and, cleared of any concern of contagion, they were soon heading to New York by train.[475]

More Details Emerge on How Foo Finally Made It Through the Immigration Obstacles

With the Foo troupe scheduled to begin performing at Hammerstein's Theater in New York on November 25th, *Variety*, in its in-depth coverage of the story, sets out as background for its readers the immigration law challenges Foo and his managers encountered while seeking to regain the American stage.

According to *Variety*, George Mooser, who was already resident in the U.S. prior to Foo's return, "pulled the wires in San Francisco" to ensure a solution was found that would enable the Foo troupe to return to America. In these efforts, Mooser was reportedly "generously supported" "by important people of the coast."[476]

Given the significant obstacles they had to work around, Foo and Mooser needed all the supporters they could get. As of 1912, Chinese were only allowed in the U.S if they fell within one of four categories; tourist, merchant, missionary, or teacher. At this point, more than a decade since Judge Kohlsaat ruled otherwise, Chinese performers were deemed not to fall into any of these categories, artists and gentlemen or not.

However, there was a clear and ongoing demand from both the public and theater managers to allow these individuals, particularly Foo and his troupe, to enter the U.S. to ply their trade. After years of entreaties regarding this issue culminating in Mooser's most recent redoubled efforts, authorities within the U.S. federal government acknowledged the demand and sought to address the issue. The immigration officials in charge seized upon the idea of allowing the Foo troupe back into the U.S. if their departure after a specific time was guaranteed through a bond, which would be collected by the government and forfeited to them if the Chinese performers did not return as required.

Adopting this new approach, Foo and his troupe thus entered the country on November 12th, 1912, under a reported $50,000 bond guaranteed by his managers the Mooser Brothers. This enabled the U.S. Commissioner-General of Immigration in Washington D.C. to waive Section 6 of the Chinese Exclusion Law as it applied to the Foo troupe.

The bond system, thus structured, allowed the performers to work in the U.S. for up to one year from the time at which their bonds were registered.[477]

This special immigration arrangement, designed for the Foo troupe, would be used as a model for future Chinese entertainers being vetted to enter the U.S. Within the U.S. immigration bureaucracy, it would be referred to as "the Foo model". Once more, the Original Chinese conjuror had an impact on U.S. immigration law as it relates to Chinese.

WHEREAS, Ching Ling Foo a Chinese male aged 56 years who arrived at the Port of San Francisco, per Steamship "Nile", on the 11th day of November, 1912, ticket number 8597, made application to the United States Commissioner of Immigration of the the said Port for permission to temporarily land in the United States for a period of one year from the 11th day of November, 1912,

"KNOW ALL MEN BY THESE PRESENT … Excerpts from the bond issued for the admission of Ching Ling Foo. Note that the bond was renewed and "expires June 23rd, 1915."

Some 14 members of the Foo troupe arrived on the *Nile* and were, as Chinese citizens, individually bonded into the U.S.

November–December 1912: Contractual Conflicts

The anticipated competing rights snarl with regard to issues surrounding Foo's contractual obligations to E.F. Albee and others, stemming from contracts signed by Foo during his last U.S. tour, arrived when questions over just where Foo would perform, delay his much-anticipated New York premiere. As a result, Foo's opening performance in New York was initially rescheduled for December 9th, and various parties positioned themselves to court the act.

Representatives of the Shubert circuit at New York's Winter Garden Theater negotiated with George Mooser, who was asking for $2,500 per week for the Foo troupe for an engagement of 25 weeks. William Hammerstein, Oscar's father, was willing to release Foo from his 52-week commitment and take him on for 25 weeks at his Victoria Theater at $2,500 a week. On top of this, E.F. Albee, as anticipated, had raised his head to claim that the Keith's circuit managers already had Foo under contract for any American performances, and thus he must be dealt with before any other Foo engagements could be confirmed. Albee wanted the Foo troupe to perform at the Colonial theater.[478]

December 2, 1912: Under Many Flags—the Foos Attend a Performance of the Popular Pacifist Drama at the Schubert Hippodrome

As part of their courtship of the Foo troupe, on December 2nd, Foo and Chee Toy were the guests of Lee Shubert, who took them to their major spectacle *Under Many Flags*. The popular entertainment was an optimistic story of world peace playing at Shubert's massive New York Hippodrome.

Chee Toy was delighted with the spectacle and particularly impressed by the Ballet of the Flowers of Nations and the Silver Palace of Peace sequences.[479] The play was a colorful travelogue with singing and dancing and told the story of the creation of a terrible weapon—a dirigible that could travel at 200 miles an hour and carry a payload of

Excerpts from the playbill for *Under Many Flags*. The "extravaganza" ran for 445 performances at the Hippodrome, from August 31st, 1912 to May 17th, 1913, and featured songs such as "For Universal Peace." World War I would begin a little over year later, on July 28th, 1914.

deadly explosives. When this death-dealing device was displayed to world leaders, they were moved to sign a "Treaty of Universal Peace." In retrospect, the show was naïvely optimistic—World War I would begin a little over a year later.[480]

December 4, 1912: The Yellow Jacket—Foo and Chee Toy Attend the Popular Chinese-Themed Play

Only two days later, the still-idle Foo troupe and management, still in promotion mode, attended a performance of the very popular Chinese-themed play, *The Yellow Jacket*. The entertainment, written by George Hazelton, premiered in the fall of 1912 at the Fulton Theater. While written by a Westerner, the play incorporated elements of Chinese opera and was far less openly xenophobic than earlier works such as *King of the Opium Den* or *French Maids in Chinatown*. Several prominent New York Chinese joined the Foo party to attend the play.[481]

Foo and his management were not only demonstrating they were very good at synergistic marketing, but also that they could network with the top level of New York's Chinese community.

A CHINESE PLAY DONE IN A CHINESE MANNER IN THREE ACTS

"The Most Unusual Drama of this or any Other Season." The ongoing American fascination for things Chinese continued to play out with the success of the Chinese-themed play *The Yellow Jacket*. The play opened on November 4th, 1912.

"MIKE MCGRAW RUNS INTO THE DEVIL ON WEST FIFTY-FIFTH STREET"

"Mike McGraw runs into the Devil on West Fifty-Fifth Street." The image to the right, above, is an uncredited illustration from the New York *Evening World* depicting a performer from the play *The Yellow Jacket* walking to the theater in full costume and thus startling a passerby, who believes he has encountered a "devil." "Yes sir. He was a big devil too. He had great flowing robes with circles and rings on them and great gold dragons and flowers … And out of his head stuck a bunch of peacock feathers and underneath them Mike could see the horns. And the face of him! Oh, the FACE of him!482 Image to the left is a newspaper ad for *The Yellow Jacket*.483

FOO IN THE POPULAR IMAGINATION

Interestingly, given Foo and the Moosers' ongoing struggles with the UBO monopoly, Foo's hold on the popular imagination led to his being referenced twice in a major editorial decrying the Standard Oil trust, which despite President Theodore Roosevelt's best efforts, still—with an assist from the Supreme Court—seemed to manipulate prices to the detriment of consumers.

"Since the Supreme Court decision pretending to dissolve the Standard Oil trust, the cost of Standard Oil products has continually increased, and the value of Standard Oil stock has doubled … The

> people know this increase in Standard Oil prices and increase in Standard Oil wealth are due to a certain playful sleight of hand performance on the part of the Supreme Court, which goes through the motions of dissolving a trust without dissolving it. Just as **Ching Ling Foo**, the marvelous juggler, apparently causes your watch to dissolve into thin air and then restores it to your waistcoat pocket ticking just as regularly, faithfully and effectively as ever ... The people know that the Supreme Court read into law certain words that Congress had not put into law and had not intended to have in the law, and had even refused to allow the law, just as **Ching Ling Foo** takes out of your hat certain hard boiled eggs and rolls of ribbon and rabbits that you had never put in your hat and never intended to have in your hat and never expected to see come out of your hat: and the audience laughs at your surprise and embarrassment.
>
> "Just exactly in the way the trusts laugh at the people."[484] (Emphasis added)

December 6, 1912: Opening Night Anticipation Builds; "Ching Ling Foo American Reappearance Next Week!"

As the legal machinations were worked out and the Foo troupe's premiere approached, *Variety*, on December 6th, 1912, featured a huge ad for the "American reappearance" of Foo.[485]

The December 8th New York *Times* ad for Foo's return performance, to take place the next day, included a bill setting out the rest of the performers who would be sharing the stage with the Foo troupe, including a team of "diving seals," "the guy who put tone in baritone", and one of the first appearances, half way through the bill, of a very young "May West." Ms. West, would, of course, become known to the world as the legendary risqué film icon Mae West. (Chee Toy the mimic would find much to study in West's style.) A movie called *The Speed Demon* would also be included.

The Hammerstein's version of the Foo troupe also featured a "Chinese orchestra", once more differentiating it from your standard magic show, but perhaps not Foo's evolving sense of a form of Chinese variety show. The plan was for Foo and his Chinese orchestra to give "free concerts" the first day of their engagement on the balcony outside Hammerstein's from 1–2:00 p.m. and then from 7–8 p.m.[486]

"Next Monday afternoon, Dec. 9, the first appearance in this country in 14 years of Ching Ling Foo will positively begin at Hammerstein's Victoria."

Hammerstein's Victoria Theater and Roof Garden located at the corner of Seventh Avenue and 42nd Street, bordering what is now Times Square. (1899–1915)

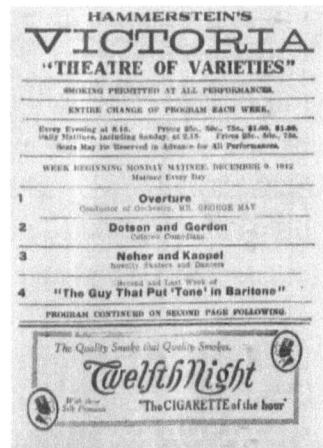

Excerpts from Hammerstein's Victoria theater playbill for December 9th, 1912 (enhanced and edited.). Apart from the always-numerous ads for beauty treatments, alcohol, and cigarettes to be found in the playbills, ads for new technologies also featured. Among these disruptive technologies of the times being promoted a "general news ticker" from the Stock Quotation Telegraph company, which promised to keep you up on the day's news in the most modern way: delivered on ticker tape straight to your home. The slogan of the company that manufactured the General News Ticker? "The up-to-date apartment has it. Has yours?" Within the pages of the playbill there was also, fittingly, an ad for a "cure" for alcoholism, drug use, or just plain nervous exhaustion. Hammerstein's knew its target audience.

Today's Celebration of Chinese Talent Very Different from How Things Were "When Father Was a Boy"

Opening night came and went and Foo and his troupe got a rave review for their performance at the Hammerstein's Victoria from a New York *Tribune* critic who, tellingly, remarks how the celebration of the Foo troupe's talent differed from the experience so many Chinese had when "father was a boy." In the midst of his review, he reminisces, "Out in California, in the days before China became a republic, the unregenerate boy gangs of the district used to have a derogatory jingle that was applied to all natives of the Oriental empire. It began, 'Ching, chong, Chinese,' and ended with that frightful threat to, in those days, the amputation of the Celestial's queue." The reviewer, looking back at this time, then remarked in the context of the respect and adulation Foo—and indeed, his troupe—now commanded, "How times have changed."[487]

December 12, 1912: Opening Night Reviews— "Ching Ling Foo is At His Old Tricks and New Ones, and They're Great!"

The reviewer went on to describe the troupe's performances as "positively uncanny." As regards Foo's production magic, he said he must revert to the "stock phrase of those who do not know what else to say." It could "only be seen to be appreciated."[488]

Charles Darnton continued the pile-on of superlatives the Foo troupe was receiving from the New York press. Writing in the sadly no longer extant New York *Evening World*, accompanied by wonderful illustrations by groundbreaking Mexican artist Marius de Zayas, Darnton's deft prose let his readers know that "Ching Ling Foo is up to his old tricks as well as several new ones." Darnton continued with an effusive overview of "this really wonderful" Chinese conjurer's latest "gorgeously staged and unusually clever act."

Above to the left Marius de Zayas illustration for New York *Tribune* article and, to the right, another illustration of Foo by de Zayas. Marius de Zayas was a talented Mexican illustrator and artist working in New York who ended up, on a visit to Europe, doing the first major interview with Picasso for North American audiences.

Darnton began by wisely noting the contrast between the "brilliant hangings" and Foo's "richly dressed fellow artists,-for artists they are" and the "dull blue figure of 'China's greatest magician.'" He then, perhaps still in the heady glow of post-performance, added, "no one would dispute the programme if it called him 'the world's greatest magician.'"

As to Foo himself, Darnton noted the "big of frame" Foo "doesn't look a bit like a wizard." Sometimes he moved "solemnly", although he also could "occasionally" be seen "chuckling" at "a little trick he appears to regard as childishly simple." As Foo began the production part of his performance—what Darnton described as the "real work"—Foo took "what seems as savage delight, growling and barking and showing his teeth" in his work. His production of a "huge" bowl of water left Darnton speechless. But, he said, Foo's "most astonishing feat" had not yet been displayed. It took place "after he has discarded his long loose robe and the rug." Foo, with the sleeves of his thin silk shirt rolled up and a small cloth the size of a handkerchief on his shoulder, ran across the stage, flipped into a somersault, and comes up with a large bowl of water in his hands. "He has come head-over-heels to the edge of the footlights without spilling a single drop." (Adding to the wonder would be the fact Foo at this time would have been around 58 years old.)

Darnton concluded "It's rabbits to doughnuts this wise old sorcerer knows more about 'magic' than is contained in any book with a Mephistophelian cover in black-and-red."

The other performers of the Foo troupe also received high praise and were not, as Darnton notes, on the stage merely to "shine in his reflected glory." "Yu Erh", this tour's juggler of heavy porcelain Chinese vases, repeatedly tossed the heavy pots into the sky and caught them on his forehead. "Resplendent" in baggy trousers of gold, Darnton observed, Yu Erh did his heavy work as "easily as you would make a salad."

These juggling feats were followed by "Miss Ching Chee Yun", who "spins plates with both hands while resting comfortably on her elbows with her feet about her neck." A "chubby tot whose name might be Ching Chee Chit also spins plates with almost equal skill."

"Dainty Chee Toy" was described as "exquisite ... She must be the prettiest Chinese girl in the world." Chee Toy sang "a ragtime ditty in English ... charmingly."

In addition, the Foo troupe included a "strong hair" act whose acrobats hung from straps and their hair as they swung from the flies and did somersaults across the stage. Darnton, given the performance was taking place in the second week of December, made a seasonal observation that "they would make a great hit on your Christmas tree." Another acrobatic team "performs strange stunts" on the Chinese horizontal bar.[489]

All this enthusiastic praise from a jaded New York reviewer at a time when Chinese-themed acts were commonplace says something about the quality of the Foo troupe, its key players, and the nature of its act.

Variety magazine noted the rapturous response the Foo troupe was receiving in New York and judges the Moosers, in bringing Foo back to America after touring half the known world, had not made a mistake. The magazine went over Foo's now 27-minute act, rightly observing the show is far from just Foo.

December 13th, 1912: "Ching Ling Foo is All Right for American Vaudeville. He is Different, and Vaudeville Needs Something Different"

In the wake of this early success, *Variety* prophetically judged that the troupe's second American tour would be a great triumph. As to precisely why, the industry magazine explains, "Ching Ling Foo is all right for American vaudeville. He is different, and vaudeville needs something different." They also recognized the overwhelming public interest in the act and the great opportunities it provided for promotion work, and concluded the Foo troupe was good enough to "make good on all the boosting."[490]

"Many of the Mandarin Coats, Embroideries, and Decorations furnished *The Yellow Jacket* supplied by us." In the wake of Foo's and other Chinese themed entertainment's popularity, Mandarin coats and other Chinese clothing became a bit of a fad. The company that supplied the theaters with Chinese costumes developed a profitable sideline selling Chinese clothing directly to the public.

Chinese Students Studying in America Applaud Foo's Success; Yale Students Arrange Dinner

In a demonstration of the pride Foo's burgeoning success instilled in both American Chinese and Chinese students studying in America, the publication *The Chinese Students Monthly* wrote of its members making pilgrimages to Hammerstein's Victoria Theater, the "greatest

The 15-cent-per-copy February 1913 edition of *The Chinese Students' Monthly*, shown here in enhanced and modified form.

vaudeville theater in New York," to see the Foo show. The journal's editors noted that while Foo was in New Haven, he hosted a well-attended dinner for Chinese students studying at Yale which was much enjoyed by all. Chinese students in Boston were now reportedly awaiting his arrival in their fair city and looking forward to a similar gathering.[491]

These sorts of high-level encounters between Foo and Chinese embassy officials in the U.S., top Chinese American businessmen, and Chinese students at elite U.S. colleges starkly demonstrate that Foo was no typical vaudeville act. In fact, it was a function of his inherent charisma and gravitas that he was held in great esteem by both the Chinese community and the general American audience.

A Chinese Marriage

Always looking to keep the Foo troupe in the papers, the news was spread that there would be a marriage among the members of the Foo troupe: An acrobat would marry a contortionist, who was Foo's niece. The public was also told the young lady was a "rare" younger "small foot" woman, given the foot binding custom was now illegal in China. The report also noted Foo's niece, a 17-year-old "Miss Ching," was on the successful side of the recent Xin Hai rebellion that brought down the Qing Dynasty and launched the new

Chinese Republic. During the upheaval, it was reported, Foo's niece volunteered as a Red Cross nurse and did service in Nanking (now known as Nanjing).[492] No mention was made of the documentary Foo made of the Wuchang Uprising that contributed to these historic events, and there was no indication Foo had incorporated any film displays into his U.S. tour.

The Chinese couple's engagement notice appeared in the New York *Times*. Interestingly, the announcement of the engagement came the same day as the famous conductor John Philip Sousa's daughter Helen's marriage announcement. Sousa—one of the major stars of his era—and Foo had been linked for about a decade as the two major subjects of the Great Lafayette's enormously popular mimic act.[493]

December 20, 1912: The Stars Begin to Align for the Clash with the United Booking Office

An appointment notice in *Variety* announcing George Mooser would be taking a management role in Oliver Morosco's New York theater business noted Mooser's work in China with Foo and other acts. Mooser's bringing Foo back to the U.S. was listed as one of his premier achievements.[494] Mooser's new position with the Morosco theater group further aligned the spheres for the upcoming clash with E.F. Albee, the B.F. Keith's circuit, and the United Booking Office (UBO).

Once More, Foo Donates His Time and Talents to Charity: Christmas Dinners and Toys for the Poor

As Christmas approached, the New York *Times* reported Ching Ling Foo had gotten into the Christmas spirit, as he would be among the "all-star volunteer cast" participating in the city's annual charity gala, to be held at the Hippodrome to raise money for Christmas dinners and toys for New York's poor. The goal was to provide for 10,000 New York families.[495] Other newspaper coverage noted Foo's charitable instincts also extended to his home country as the magician, being "something of a patriot," contributed some 100,000 Chinese taels—in today's dollars, well over US $2 million—to China's new Republican government.[496]

December 24, 1912: The Chinese Marriage Ceremony Goes Over Well—Mostly

Ching Chee Kwai, niece of Ching Ling Foo, as promised, married Foo troupe acrobat Chee You on stage the last night of the Foo's engagement at Hammerstein's Victoria Theater. The New York *Times* reported the audience was treated to a view of traditional Chinese marriage rites.[497] While the promotion went over well in most circles, there was a definitively unseasonal review of the events recorded by one critic in the December 27th edition of *Variety*.

The jaded journalist covering the wedding ceremony and associated banquet for *Variety* wrote in desultory fashion, "the newspaper men were invited to write it up and a few did … Ching and his party, also the *Yellow Jacket* company, sat around a long table and looked funny … A couple of pictures were taken to entice the dailies into a second flash for the stunt, built only for press agent purposes because it would make a good story, which it is because there has been no Chinese stage wedding here this long time. A neat little program was given out by Mr. Simon. After watching the mob gorge itself with the phony chicken and seeing Ching do some 'fine work' on the table with little feats of palming, Mike went over to Rector's for something to eat." Clearly, even in relatively cosmopolitan New York, not everyone was brimming with enthusiasm for all the Foo troupe had to offer.[498]

In the same December 27th edition of *Variety*, another piece examining the Foo act acknowledged the huge crowds the troupe was drawing, and that Hammerstein's was packed with people squeezed into the standing-room-only areas to see Foo. *Variety* also noted the act had been "slightly restructured to its benefit", in that the pace of the show had been accelerated. It also appeared that some acrobats of the Foo troupe, who had previously worn what the author described as "hideous makeups", had now "happily" abandoned that practice. Another big change from the Foo's performance noted from his previous U.S. tour of 1898 to 1900 was that in his current act, Foo did all his old tricks just as mysteriously, but now he did them "without the big flowing robes." The critic also conceded the children in the act were big favorites, and overall, the act was very popular and was deemed, with all the changes made since the act premiered, "a drawing card."[499]

Industry observers also recorded themselves as a bit surprised that Foo and his managers negotiated a contract with Hammerstein's that included a percentage of the theater gate receipts during their engagement.[500]

1913 January: No "Rag" for China

As the Foo act moved from success to success during its now-celebrated New York run, Chee Toy continued to attract particular attention. She was now singing the popular ragtime songs "Mississippi" and "Hitchy Koo" as part of her performance at Hammerstein's. Reporters eager to get her opinion on this emerging popular art form asked her for her view of ragtime and whether it would be a hit in China. Chee Toy, ever honest and direct, replied ragtime music would not succeed in China because first, the language issue, and second "very different tastes in melody."[501]

Hitchy-Koo (Music: Lewis F. Muir; Lyrics: L. Wolf Gilbert)

Oh, every evening hear him sing
It's the cutest little thing
With the cutest little swing
Hitchy-koo, Hitchy-koo.

Oh, simply meant for kings and queens,
Don't you ask me what it means
I just love that Hitchy-koo,
Hitchy-koo, Hitchy-koo.

Say he does it just like no-one could
When he does it say he does it good

Oh, every evening hear him sing
It's the cutest little thing
With the cutest little swing
Hitchy-koo, Hitchy-koo, Hitchy-koo....

January 10, 2013: Post-Hammerstein's and into the World of "Wildcatting"—the Moosers and the Foo Troupe's Battle with the UBO

By January 10th, 1913, the Ching Ling Foo troupe was now onto its fifth very profitable week at Hammerstein's Theater. At the same time. the UBO, under Albee's direction was actively increasing its stranglehold over the 'big time' vaudeville booking system. Foo and his management, who would soon require new engagements after finishing their run at Hammerstein's, would be in direct and now open conflict with the powerful and increasingly feared UBO.[502]

Some nascent criticism of the UBO quasi-monopoly, however, was beginning to emerge. A few industry insiders publicly accused the UBO of using their power to force acts, if they wanted to work UBO affiliated theaters, to accept almost 50% less than they would normally make. In addition, they claimed the UBO controlled many of the agencies who "represent" the talent, thus ensuring the performers' representatives did not protest or otherwise get in the way of UBO's profit-making ventures.[503] Essentially, by this point of their evolution, the UBO had arranged things so that it now handled all bookings within its theater membership (which comprised almost all the major high-end vaudeville theaters on the East Coast), determined the prices of those acts, and took a 5% cut of the performer's earnings. Not a bad business model.

These criticisms of the UBO emerged at the same time news of just how Albee and the UBO attempted to strongarm the Mooser Brothers and Foo when they first arrived in America to begin his second U.S. tour.

According to George Mooser, when he finally received permission from the U.S. Bureau of Emigration for Foo to tour the country in late 1912, he examined offers from theater managers to book Foo and accepted the aforementioned 52-week commitment from Oscar Hammerstein for an engagement at Hammerstein's Victoria Theater and Roof Garden in New York.

However, after Foo had arrived in California and was heading by rail to New York, Mooser learned Oscar's son William Hammerstein had taken over the management of the Victoria Theater. William openly questioned his father's judgement in engaging an expensive act like the Foo troupe for the Victoria Theater for so long. Mooser, upon arriving in New York and installing the Foo troupe in their hotels, now realized they might not get the full 52 weeks with Hammerstein's.

Looking to ameliorate his predicament and deferring to the advice of American friends, the Moosers faced the reality that they might just have to deal with Albee and the UBO if they wanted to successfully tour the U.S. Reluctantly, Mooser decided to meet with them to see what they might have to offer.[504]

True to form, Albee was blunt when he met with Mooser in mid-November 1912. The veteran entertainment executive, who had worked with P.T. Barnum and emerged out of America's early dime-store museums with his partner B.F. Keith, warned Mooser if Foo went forward with the engagement at Hammerstein's, which was arranged outside the UBO's control, they would ensure whenever the Foo act finished at Hammerstein's it would never get another booking anywhere in the country.

Albee then offered Mooser an out. He proposed to give the Foo troupe a test run at Keith's Colonial theater, and if things worked out and Albee approved of the performances, he would then give Mooser a contract for 50 weeks on the UBO circuit. Mooser, already feeling the pressure of his existing investment in the Foo troupe, decided to provide Albee and some UBO representatives with a sneak preview of the Foo act, with the goal of setting up a 50-week contract and not having any further worries about booking the troupe in the U.S. for almost a year.

Mooser showed up at the Colonial theater the next day with the Foo troupe in order to provide a demonstration of the act before a small audience comprised of Albee, some UBO executives, and some theatrical managers. As the sneak preview got underway, both Foo and Mooser began to realize it was a setup. Albee was demanding the troupe perform its acts before the invited audience as rapidly as possible, absent backdrops and with no music. The clear goal was to present the Foo act in as unattractive manner as possible.

A visibly angry Foo broke first. Addressing Albee in no uncertain terms, Foo reportedly stated that "he had never done an audition for an engagement in his life and would not start now." He also added, quite rightly, that, given their history, Albee needed no introduction to the nature of the Foo troupe's performance and that if Albee didn't like it, "he knew what he could do." Apparently, Foo's outburst required no translation.

Mooser and Foo then ordered everyone back to their hotels. Albee contacted Mooser the next day and unsurprisingly informed him that the collective minds of the UBO assessed the Foo troupe as not good enough for 'big time' vaudeville, and certainly not worth $700 a week. This was even less than Foo had made back in 1899. Nor would one of the managers represented at the performance, who represented over 100 theaters, think of engaging the troupe.

The Machiavellian Albee then suggested that he, being a charitable man, would, if the Moosers transferred the Foo troupe to his management, get the act booked and throw a little profit the Moosers' way.

As the Moosers knew and firmly believed in the Foo act to be one of the best in vaudeville, they, with Foo's hearty agreement, decided to defy Albee and take their chances. They would stick with the Hammerstein's engagement, and when it ended, rely on their skills at 'wildcatting'—representing themselves to find engagements and precariously jumping from gig to gig, relying on theaters or entertainment ventures unconnected to or willing to stand up to the UBO.

Thus began an unprecedented almost three-year stint for the Foo troupe of seeking to patch together a run of 'big time' vaudeville engagements without the support and approval of the near-monopoly UBO.

These developments also shed some light on the nature of those earlier letters from Foo to Albee, which were published at the time of the Boxer upheaval just after Foo had finished his triumphal last American tour. In the context of the later conflict, it seemed one goal

Albee had in ensuring those letters regarding Foo's fate were published so widely was not so much to inform the public of the fate of the almost universally-beloved Foo troupe, but rather to make clear that the Chinese conjurer, if he returned to America, was still under contract to Albee. With Foo's return to America under Mooser management, and with a successful booking at Hammerstein's already under their belt, clearly Albee's and Keith's plan to maintain control of the Foo troupe had failed—and they were angry.

January 1913: Connecticut Based S.Z. Poli Defies the UBO and Takes a Chance on Foo

Fortunately for Foo and the Mooser brothers, the Foo troupe's soon-to-be-completed engagement at Hammerstein's theater was wildly successful. Given this success, an ambitious theater owner in Connecticut who both recognized the potential of the Foo troupe and was not afraid to anger Albee and the UBO booked the Foo troupe for a two-week engagement at his theaters.

The risk-taking theater manager was S.Z. Poli, the owner/manager of Poli's Connecticut theaters. Poli took the considerable gamble of signing the Foo troupe to a $2,500-a-week contract to appear at his theaters in New Haven and Bridgeport.

By this point, Foo and the Moosers' challenge to the UBO monopoly had caught the attention of an entertainment community already beginning to chafe under the heavy-handed management of the UBO. The magic journal *The Sphinx*, in its February 1913 edition, published a note on the conflict and admiringly remarked of the "Mooser boys" that they "have nerve and you can't bluff them."[505]

Further steeling the Foo side's nerves in their battle with the UBO was the wide dissemination of additional details of the Hammerstein's Theater's tremendous success during the Foo troupe's run. Hammerstein's, during the Foo engagement, was almost continuously at capacity and doing 14 shows a week. This was seen as a "remarkable" turnaround for the theater, which had been struggling before the Foo troupe arrived. William Hammerstein was now receiving plaudits for bringing the Foo troupe in, since it was the Foo troupe that was given the lion's share of the credit for the theater's newfound profitability. Absorbing all this in Connecticut, Manager Poli found many reasons to reject increasing pressure by the UBO to break his engagement of the Foo troupe or face the consequences.[506]

Meanwhile, as they finished out their engagement at Hammerstein's, the Foo troupe continued to receive plaudits. Foo and Chee Toy were once more singled out for special attention. *Variety* acknowledged the special charisma the two performers wielded, stating Hammerstein's would make money if it just had Foo and Chee Toy to draw the crowds. The magician's daughter was described as making "a splendid individual hit for herself, singing American popular songs." This week she treated the Victoria Theater audience to "Row, Row, Row" and "Hitchy Koo."

Variety concluded, "From the way Ching and his troupe of Chinese entertainers are received the Chinese magician could run on indefinitely at 'the Corner.'" "The Corner" was the nickname for Hammerstein's Theater, and its audience was known as legendarily tough to please.[507]

Row, Row, Row (Music: James Monaco; Lyrics: William Jerome)

Young Johnny Jones he had a cute little boat	She would tell him when
And all the girlies he would take for a float	They'd fool around and fool around
He had girlies on the shore	And then they'd kiss again
Sweet little peaches by the score	And then he'd row, row, row
But master Johnny was a wis'un, you know	A little further he would go, oh, oh, oh
His steady girl was Flo	Then he'd drop both his oars
And every Sunday afternoon	Take a few more encores
She'd jump in his boat	And then he'd row, row, row
And they would spoon	
	(Repeat chorus)
And then he'd row, row, row	A little further he would go, oh, oh, oh,
Way up the river he would row, row, row	Then we'll drop both our oars
A hug he'd give her	Take a round of applause,
Then he'd kiss her now and then	And then we'll go, go, go

What is the Secret of Foo's Success?

In the midst of Foo's second run of unprecedented success and popularity in the U.S. the magicians' journal *The Sphinx* asked the important question: How can a magician like Foo make up to $2,500 a week despite the fact people generally have a pretty good idea how his tricks are done?

The analysis of the magazine's correspondent, Kobb, who had seen Foo perform several times in New York, was both simple and complex.

In Kobb's conclusion that Foo was "some" showman can be found much meaning. Kobb noted Foo had an unusual talent for misdirection. Foo could hold your interest even while he "stalls again and again." Furthermore, Kobb assessed all the Chinese magician's productions illusions as "jewels"—particularly the finale of his act, when Foo stripped down and did his somersault, resulting in the production of a large bowl of water containing goldfish. Huge applause always echoed through the New York theater—this in spite of the fact, as Kobb wisely notes, that the audience had a good idea of how the trick was done.

By way of explanation of the conundrum, Kobb presented the overheard conversation of two gentlemen sitting behind him at a Foo performance. The first, in assessing Foo's finale, said "He had the bowl under his clothes." The other audience member replied, "Yes, but how in the world does he do it?" Kobb than doubled down on his Foo as "some" showman point, explaining, "the attraction in magic does not depend entirely upon its mystery."[508] Clearly, technique, charisma and showmanship were also key, and Foo had all of those in spades.

CHAPTER THIRTEEN

FOO THE "WILDCATTER" TAKES ON THE UNITED BOOKING OFFICE (UBO) MONOPOLY AND HEADLINES THE LEGENDARY ZIEGFELD FOLLIES

January 20, 1913: Foo the Wildcat Moves on from Hammerstein's to Connecticut

By January 11th, 1913, Manager Poli had not only rejected the UBO's demands to think twice about engaging the Foo troupe, he was also making a publicity point out of the fact the Poli theaters were paying the troupe a record $2,500 a week to appear—this in the face of the UBO's original demands the troupe not be paid more than $700 per week.

Poli's Theater promoters, building up Foo's scheduled arrival in Connecticut for January 20th, described the Foo troupe—levering off their record-breaking success at Hammerstein's—as the "greatest act in vaudeville today" and the "Eighth Wonder of the World." UBO executives were not pleased.[509]

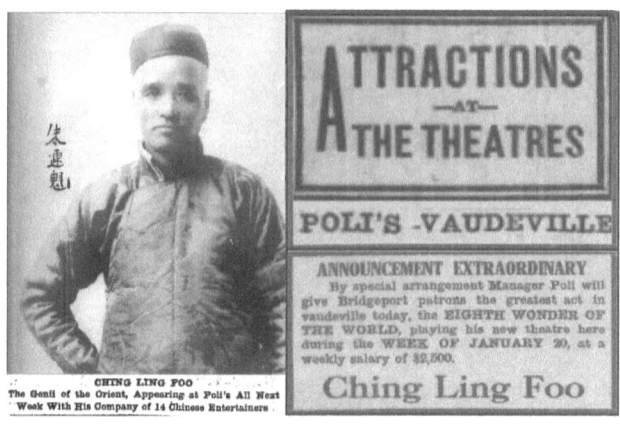

A jaunty-looking "Genii of the Orient."

The Foo Troupe Travels with Its Own Cooks and Chinese Foodstuffs

The Foo troupe, now safely ensconced in Connecticut and preparing for their Connecticut debut, had turned part of the top floor of the Stratfield Hotel in Bridgeport into a "special kitchen and dining room." The special kitchen and dining room had been set up in the suite adjoining Foo's own. Foo's cooks were reported to carry with them "a big stock of preserves and other Chinese delicacies." Keeping with a standard promotional technique, and one they seem to enjoy, Foo was going to be offering Chinese luncheons to be served to friends and journalists during the coming week.[510]

Even the Foo troupe's culinary habits were front page news.

In the Face of UBO Threats, Poli Adds a Second Week to Foo's Engagement

S.Z. Poli, in the midst of promoting the first performance of the Foo troupe at his Poli's Theater January 20th, revealed not only was he not bowing to UBO demands not to engage Foo; he was, in the face of record-breaking advance ticket sales, booking the magician for an additional week. In spite of this showmanship, Poli, in private, tried to down play the conflict he was having with the UBO. He asked Albee and others why his theaters should be treated differently than Hammerstein's, given they both were UBO-affiliated. Poli argued if Hammerstein could have the Foo troupe at his theater, UBO should not be too upset when Poli engages them for his Connecticut theaters.[511]

Poli then addressed the key performer salary issue and acknowledged the salary paid to Foo by his theater is "out of all proportion to what I have been accustomed to paying." But then, like a true showman, he countered, that there are times when taking a risk is justified, and Foo's popularity told him this is one such case. Poli was also providing Foo a percentage of the box office earned during his engagement at Poli's theaters.

Foo's act, with its magician, contortionists, singers, Chinese and Western music, acrobats, and a "small foot woman", was described as a "variety show within a variety show."[512] Poli's gamble on Foo was looking wiser and wiser, as by mid-January, reports already indicated that advance tickets sales at Poli's continued to be going very well.[513]

Bridgeport papers described Foo as the "brightest star" in the "vaudeville firmament" and breathlessly noted that he and his company of 14 were going to be in the city for a one-week headline engagement, while the Poli's in New Haven would host the troupe as headliners the following week. Poli's signing the Foo troupe to these engagements was described as "a coup." Vaudeville being vaudeville, the troupe would share the bill with "Morris' Baboons ... the last word in Simian intellect."[514]

"Ask the Man Who Owns One": Ching Ling Foo Drives a Packard—A Foo Celebrity Endorsement

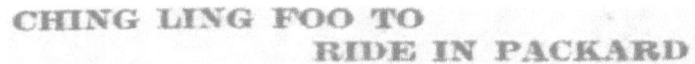

In Connecticut, Foo and his troupe engaged in early-form celebrity endorsements. They leased several Packard cars from John Weber, the local Packard dealer, for touring and sightseeing while in Connecticut, and that transaction was highlighted in the local papers. Stories were published publicizing these transactions and noting sightseeing was something the curious Foo and his group were said to do at each of their tour stops. The articles explain that Foo, "a thorough student", was keen to understand any place he is performing in and get out and see the sights, and the Packard was his favorite vehicle.[515]

"Ask the man who owns one." An advertisement, enhanced and modified to fit this page, for a 1913 Packard, the car Foo and members of his troupe would have been driving around Bridgeport in early 1913.

> As demonstrated, Foo, throughout his career, would engage in celebrity endorsements or have his name used without his permission to promote a product. One interesting example of this trading on Foo's fame came in the 1920s and 1930s, close to twenty years after he last left America. The ads for waterworks utilities turned on Foo's understood expertise in making "fountains of water" spout from anywhere. The phrase "understood expertise" is used in this context, because the production of fountains of water

from unexpected locations was, according to many, an illusion introduced by Japanese magicians. Foo seems to have adopted this illusion later in his career after sharing the stage with numerous Japanese magic troupes, and given Foo's status as *the* Asian magician, even this illusion was attributed to him—as so many other tricks, such as "Foo Cones", etc. were.

Ads of this nature appeared in ads placed across the country in the 1920s and 1930s. (Enhanced, reconstructed version of ad.[516])

"S.Z. Poli, in the Guise of Prince Charming, Makes a Big Offer"

Using a pair of 18-year-old Foo performer Miss Cho Kwai Gee's slippers, the Poli Theater offered the now-standard Foo troupe "Cinderella" shoe contest promotion. Accordingly, ads went out announcing "Mr. Poli wants to ascertain if anyone else in the world can wear the shoes and still live to tell about it." The shoe was described as measuring two inches from toe to heel and was worn daily. Poli offered "$100 to any Bridgeport woman who can fit the shoes on her and wear them to the theatre."[517]

January 21, 1913: "A Celestial Symphony of Merriment and Jollity"

When the time finally came for the Foo troupe to hit the Bridgeport stage, they were a tremendous success. The applause, at times, was "deafening." Chee Toy's singing was given the nod as one of the best things in the act. Acrobats, plate spinners and contortionists were wildly cheered. Critics deemed it "a Celestial symphony of merriment and jollity" and, once again, the difficult-to-mimic "joyous" nature of a Foo troupe performance was recognized. The supporting acts included Wilbur Sweatman, "the man who makes the clarinet talk." His ragtime version of "When the Midnight Choo Choo Leaves for Alabama" was a big hit.[518]

It seemed Mr. Poli's big gamble had indeed paid off. His engagement of the Foo troupe had been a tremendous artistic and commercial success. Capacity audiences were the rule and hundreds were turned away.

The Foo act at Poli's Theater broke the vaudeville box office record for Bridgeport, Connecticut. Some 3,680 (276 over capacity) paying guests attended the Foo troupe's first Saturday matinee. It bears repeating: A vaudeville theater in Connecticut those days held almost 4,000 people. This provides an indication of just how large these regular vaudeville audiences in even smaller cities across the U.S. were.

In the Connecticut coverage, the beloved Foo was again described as a millionaire and theater owner in China.[519]

The Foo Troupe Socialize with Local Media, Stimulating Interesting Analysis

Foo's wise courting of the local Connecticut media was evident in the positive reportage that stemmed from a "special séance" for the local reporters provided at the Stratfield Hotel's sun parlor the previous night. One resulting, mostly good-natured review provided a long litany of how the Chinese do so many things seemingly in the opposite fashion to the way things are done in the West.

The reporter noted that in China, women wore pants. Men wore long, braided hair. Chinese writing ran up and down instead of left to right, "as chirography does in the land of the free and the home of the brave." He concluded that Chinese villains are never punished in plays but are left to be dealt with by fate. "In America, we must see our villains punished—at least on stage."

At this private gathering, the Chinese men sang songs in a few Chinese dialects. It was assessed as "good music" but required "some getting used to." Chee Toy, dressed in pants, also sang in both English and Chinese and "presented a charming and unique figure to Ching's assembled guests." Foo, for his part, performed dazzling close-up magic while "absolutely surrounded" until he had almost no room to work in. The reporter of this piece's conclusion? "The Orient has the Occident lashed to the mast when it comes to the wizard game."

Finally, the reporter struck a rather poignant note in assessing that this sort of evening of amiable cultural exchange would be increasingly rare, as the U.S. government "is rigidly excluding Chinese actors" and the Foo troupe was here only "by virtue of a fortuitous interpretation of the immigration rules, which may never be repeated."[520]

As their engagement moved into its second week, the Foo troupe's run in Connecticut continued to break records. The audiences adored the whole troupe, Foo first and foremost but also Chee Toy, the "Chinese prima donna", a close second in their affections; and the crowd had secondary favorites, including China's premier strong man, the child performers, and the "really funny Chinese comedian."[521]

"A Few Kind Words for the Chinese" and the Nub of the Current China Question

Inspired by the reports emanating from the private show provided by the Foo troupe just a day earlier, The *Bridgeport Times and Evening*

Farmer, on January 23rd, published an interesting commentary entitled "A Few Kind Words for the Chinese."

In this piece, the author praised Chinese women for their use of pants, which are deemed far more practical than dresses. In fact, the author, who one suspects to be a woman, claimed the "wiser sort of woman" in the U.S. and the U.K. wanted to wear them as well. As to the fact Chinese drama did not often see the villain punished, the author said this should not be seen as a knock on the Chinese, but rather a mature reflection of reality. With regard to the listed cultural divergences, the writer opined that Foo "doubtless feels the same kindly contempt for the Occident and its ways that the Occident has for the flowery kingdom and its ancient customs."

The author then sought to encapsulate and get down to the core of what she saw as the nub of the current, much-discussed "China Question"—whether Chinese should be allowed to emigrate to the U.S., and whether they could assimilate to U.S. culture. She neatly summarized what she believes to be the true motivating factors driving those arguing the "no" side of this debate and seeking to keep Chinese out of the U.S. "The Chinese are too old-fashioned. They have practiced too long the virtue of thrift. They have devoted themselves too arduously to labor. This is why we have to keep them out of the country. They work so many hours and live on so little that no American could compete with them for jobs."[522]

A Private Tour of Barnum and Bailey's Winter Quarters

While in Connecticut, Foo and his troupe, during an off day, were taken by Sam McCracken, the general manager of Barnum & Bailey's Circus, for a private tour of Barnum & Bailey's winter quarters in that state. The troupe was also treated to private shows of the various acts. Foo and his performers greatly enjoyed the outing; in particular, the children in the troupe delighted in seeing the animal act rehearsals. The outing proved wonderful publicity for both entities.[523]

Foo Joins the Follies

After Connecticut, Mooser, still working around the UBO edict for related 'big time' vaudeville theaters not to engage the Foo troupe, had arranged for the troupe to be presented as a special "extraordinary feature" of the legendary Ziegfeld Follies, whose 1912 show was then touring America.

During its golden era from 1907 to 1927, the Ziegfeld Follies occupied a particular spot in U.S. popular culture. Inspired by the *Folies Bergère* of Paris, the Follies were, essentially, a hugely popular variety show that combined vaudeville and burlesque, providing eager audiences music, comedy, dancing and a constant supply of beautiful, elaborately dressed young women. These women were known as the Ziegfeld Girls, and they staged elaborately costumed living tableaus, often acting as living framing devices for the top-line performers who took center stage.

The Follies, with its high-concept choreographed music and dance numbers, was in many ways, the predecessor of today's Broadway musical spectaculars, and for its 1912–1913 season, Ching Ling Foo would be its headliner.

By 1913 the Ziegfeld Girls were already iconic figures in American entertainment.

After packing up in Bridgeport, the Foo troupe traveled to Boston on January 27th to catch up with the Ziegfeld show, which was performing at Boston's Colonial Theatre.[524,525]

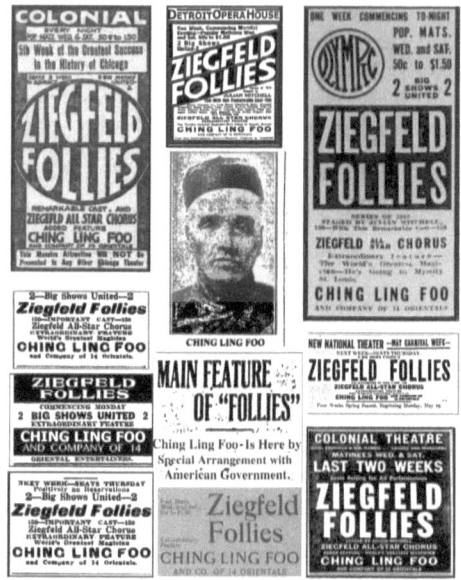

A sample of advertisements promoting the Foo troupe's appearance with the Ziegfeld Follies.

January 27, 1912, Boston: Headlining Follies Doesn't Prevent Cross-Cultural Conflict

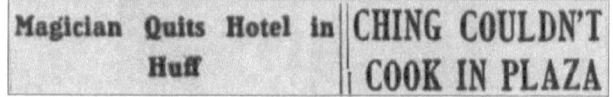

Despite this unprecedented degree of public adulation and success for a Chinese figure, there were limits to how much Foo would be accommodated outside the theater. In one well-noted, at the time instance, the Foo troupe, upon arriving in Boston, took its rooms in the newly built, luxurious Boston Copley-Plaza. While checking into the luxury hotel, it was made clear that the Foo troupe would not be allowed, as had been its practice to this point, to use one of their hotel rooms to prepare the Chinese fare its happiness and health was so dependent on. When the troupe insisted this was what it needed to do given its dietary preferences, and that other hotels had allowed it this courtesy, it was somewhat haughtily suggested the troupe was welcome to change hotels.

According to the Boston news coverage of the time, Foo was ultimately and superiorly "directed to Chinatown" if he wished to do such things.[526] This local reportage echoed a bit of the racial triumph that characterized newspaper coverage of acclaimed songwriter James Thornton's previously discussed alleged interruption of Foo's performance at Keith's Boston theater back in 1899. In the end, the Foo troupe changed hotels.

AN ACCOMPANYING MANIA FOR PEKINESE, CHOW, AND "CHING LING FOO" AND "CHEE TOY" DOGS

About the same time the mania for all things Ching Ling Foo and Chee Toy was cresting, a parallel mania for Chinese dogs occurred in the U.S. and the U.K. Both Pekinese and Chows became favored breeds and demanded extraordinary prices. During this period one type of dog became known as a "Ching Ling Foo" dog. A Boston report from a dog show of the time notes a "Ching Ling Foo dog" shown by a Mrs. Holland

> won Best in Show.[527,528] Mentions of "Chee Toy" dogs also became common in this period, referring to a type of "Chinese poodle", likely a Pekinese. It should be remembered that when Chee Toy arrived in San Francisco, news reports described her "garbed in a richly embroidered Oriental costume ... with her Chinese poodle ... ready to walk down the gangplank of the *Nile*".[529]

February 1913: The Foo Troupe and the Ziegfeld Follies' 1912–1913 Season

The Ziegfeld show that the Foo troupe would be joining toured across the country and consisted of two acts and 13 elaborate scenes utilizing over 150 entertainers.[530] Ticket prices ranged from 50 cents to a dollar and a half. The whole show lasted from 8:00 p.m. to midnight.

What the Ziegfeld Show Looked Like

A typical Follies show of the 1912–1913 season opened to a venue packed to overflowing, from the topmost seats to just in front of the orchestra.[531]

When the curtains went up, "immense billboards" were revealed on stage, creating a New York city street scene.

The manager of the Follies, Leon Errol, an Australian, then walked to the edge of the stage and announced that he and Mr. Ziegfeld have had great difficulties locating acts for the show and wonder if the audience might have suggestions. This was a cue for the Follies performers seeded amongst the audience to start the action.

A man arose from "row F" and suggested to Errol an old-time song and dance routine, which he then began to demonstrate. His performance was soon cut off by a young, gum-chewing vendor marching along the seats, who declared the man's performance "Rotten!" The boy quickly explained to Errol that he could sing far better than anyone currently engaged in the Follies, and after jumping on stage, began the demonstration of his talent, which consisted of yodeling.

Then, a "Frenchman," or at least the Follies' impression of one, interrupted the boy's yodeling by loudly suggesting what the show was really lacking was a little French opera. This request was quickly and vigorously derided by a bruiser in a second-story box seat who leapt down from his box onto the Frenchman and began a scuffle. This show-within-the-audience kept the crowd laughing and twisting their necks to see from what part of the crowd the next incident would spring.[532]

After this intro, the proper show as set out in the program began. It commenced with a "utterly absurd" comedy sketch starring the best-selling Black recording artist and comedian, Bert Williams. Williams, who was also the first Black American to take a lead role on the Broadway stage, played a cab driver in New York saddled with Nicodemus, a worn-out former racehorse. Williams got into an argument with "a very illuminated young alcohol burner" from whom he hoped to cop a huge fare. After much bickering, it was agreed to let the poor old horse ride in the cab while the men pull it. Audiences were left with "aching sides and in tears of laughter", and the sketch proved a strong seasonal favorite.

To the right, the legendary Bert Williams in a promotional photo, and to the left, Williams, Leon Errol, and Nicodemus the horse, in the "utterly absurd" opening act of the 1912–1913 Follies. Williams earned $1,000 a week as one of the top stars of the Follies.

The Williams comedy sketch was followed by an "Atlantic City Boardwalk Revue", which provided the audience the opportunity to be scandalized by a review of the latest risqué bathing costumes. As to this portion of the show, one reviewer noted, "proper pulchritude is paramount and drapery a consideration that is extensively ignored."[533]

Up next, a well-known song and dance duo sang the hit "You're a Great Big Blue-Eyed Baby" to the delight of the crowd.

You're a Great Big Blue-Eyed Baby (A. Seymour Brown, 1913)

Oh, honey, since I first met you,
I know why I have been so blue;
And I know that love is true,
You can plainly see such a change in me.
My arms are aching to enfold you,
Close to my heart I want to hold you,
But there's something that I haven't told you,
I just can't help loving you!

I only sleep to dream of you
And all the little things you do;
Every day brings something new
And you've grown to be all the world to me.
You'd never know how it would grieve me
If you should ever go and leave me;

Hold me close and say that you believe me,
Each breath of life, dear, is you!

For you're a great big blue-eyed baby!
You're the sweetest thing I know!
And, dearie, oh, oh, oh, oh,
I just like to betcha,
If you linger long, I'll getcha!
You're a great big blue-eyed baby!
I want to pet you like a child of three,
But there is one thing I want understood,
When you're around me,
I just can't be good!
I want to hug and kiss you like your mama would
Her great big blue-eyed baby!

Another crowd favorite of the 1912–1913 Ziegfeld Follies was the madcap Busby Berkley, before he perfected his *métier*-style dance sequence, wherein the audience saw the world as a whole gone mad, for the latest dance craze, "the Broadway Glide." The curtains opened to a huge tableau of a crowded, modern city street, employing the entire cast of over 100 performers playing every possible type of pedestrian, from messenger boy, office girl, society doyenne, and banker to neighborhood policemen and their favorite criminals. Once the music started, even "the infant in the perambulator" was doing the irresistible "Broadway Glide."

A few intermediate acts later, what many considered "the really beautiful part of the program" followed: the "Palace of Beauty." The famous Ziegfeld girls, led by a harlequin and an Ethiopian beauty, paraded on stage costumed as legendary beauties throughout history. Venus, Marguerite, the Duchess of Devonshire, Venus, Madame Pompadour, Cleopatra, Scheherazade, Recamier, Queen Louise of Prussia, Carmen, Joan of Arc, and Salome all appeared. These women arrived, moved into the light, struck a few poses, and retreated to the back of the stage. In the crowd-pleasing finale to the segment, the beauty of them all emerged when Ethel Amorita Kelley arrived to, as one Baltimore critic described it, "claim her own as the Twentieth Century Girl against the background of a modern boulevard."[534]

Foo Appears in the Finale

The 1912–1913 Follies closed with a "stupendous" circus scene, including two big choruses, that emerged with a "glorious blaze of superb coloring and jeweled gleam." It was in this final act that the handsomely costumed Foo troupe, the "wonder of wonders" of the Follies, was introduced in front of a curtain of crimson velvet and satin, wrought in gold figures. While capable of providing a show that lasted up to two and a half hours, the Foo troupe closed the Follies with a 30-minute version of their act.

Yu Erh started things off by juggling his heavy Chinese porcelain pots to the delight of the audience. He also took the lead in much of the comedy that interspersed the Foo troupe performance. Erh was described as a real Chinese clown, "with grotesquely painted face and a squeaky voice."

Then four Chinese acrobats performed gymnastics. Soon Fuh Sung and Soon Wo Kwai's work on the Chinese horizontal bar was assessed as something for which there is "no duplicate on any stage in the world." Once more, the men's service as policemen in the Boxer uprising in Tianjin was emphasized.

Chee Toy took the stage next and she was introduced as the first "Chinese prima donna that has ever appeared in America." She then sang her American songs in a "sweet wee voice that just suited her personality." The audience loved it. Her rendition of "Row, Row, Row" was a favorite, as were "On the Mississippi" and "Waiting for the Robert E. Lee."[535,536] Even though the audience knew she would be singing popular American songs, a reviewer notes "there is an audible shock when the American melodies and words come tripping so easily and prettily through those rosy Chinese lips."

Chinese music was also played, and there were the usual plate spinning marvels.[537]

The Follies and the Foo troupe act closed with Foo's production magic. His slightly modified production tricks for the Follies now included a production wherein Foo made not one, but two Chinese toddlers appear. For the finale, Foo performed what was now called his "Noo Du Moiau", or "Neptune's Pets", illusion. In this, Foo divested himself of almost all of his clothing except a tight-fitting shirt and pants, patted his body top to bottom to show nothing was under even this small amount of clothing, then ran from one end of the stage to the other, stopping to flip in midair, and came out of his somersault holding a large bowl of water containing live goldfish. All of this was done in close proximity to the audience and after he had turned around several times.[538] Impressed reviewers noted that for this trick, Foo wears only a "waistcoat which reaches the waistline, this making absurd the theory that the golden globe is concealed in the folds of his coat."

February 28, 1913, Baltimore: More Successful "Small Feet" Promotion Efforts

While in Baltimore in February, the Ziegfeld advance men and publicity team continued to earn their keep by generating splendid news coverage out of one of the Foo troupe's need for winter shoes.

Snow and sleet had caused Ching Chee Yuen, the Foo troupe's "small feet" performer, to seek out American shoes more suited to the winter weather. Her rather "absorbent" native shoes had become unusable. Yuen, with reporters in tow, ended up at a Baltimore shoe store, and two hours later the solution was found. Yuen was fitted with shoes that were normally worn by six-month-old American infants.

Somewhat surprisingly, after covering the fun of the hunt for the shoes, the article continued with a rather thoughtful examination of the foot-binding tradition and noted that currently, very few young women were having their feet bound, and that Yuan's case makes her a rarity even among her generation. In the new China, it was reported that binding of feet is now a capital offense.[539]

1913 March: Foo at the Follies Assessment and Reviews: Does Foo Act Fit?

The critical response to the Foo troupe-led Follies was generally uniform in assessing that the best parts of the show were Foo's remarkable illusions, Bert Williams' comedy sketch at the start of the Follies, and the parade of beauties through history.

Reviewers were also seemingly united in not quite being sure if the Foo troupe act in style and tone actually fit with the Follies and should not be treated as "something of a whole different order", given the general focus of the Follies' entertainment on "fresh daring" and features aimed to titillate, shock and "shoo the Puritan out of the house." After all, the Ziegfeld motto—"be not ashamed of anything but of being ashamed"—hardly fit the Foo troupe.[540,541]

Regardless of any inconsistencies in style, however, the addition of the Foo troupe was judged to "materially improve" the Ziegfeld Follies show and present sufficient entertainment for an evening in itself.[542] According to sources speaking to *Variety*, the Foo troupe was earning $1,800 a week with the Follies while Bert Williams, deemed by many the funniest man in vaudeville, ranked second in earnings, taking in $1,000 a week.[543] The Foo troupe salary seemed justified in that the Foo-led Follies was a success and tremendously profitable. According to *Variety*, with the Foo troupe on the bill, the show was regularly playing to full houses and bringing in $17,000 a week.[544] Much of the credit for these results were said to rest with the Foo troupe.

Both this contribution to the profitability of the Follies and the stylistic and tonal differences of the two entertainments was acknowledged in Detroit when ads for the show presented the Follies and the Foo troupe as "two big shows." Foo was not just on the bill as part of the Follies; the troupe was presented as a whole other act accompanying the show.

But not everyone was raving about the Follies and the Foo troupe. One rather disgruntled, contrarian St. Louis reviewer opined that the whole Follies show was too long by half and that the Foo act was not necessarily so great. He did allow, however, that Chee Toy, "a mischievous little Chinese girl," and her singing of American songs was the best part of the show.

March 1913: Fuming UBO Promotes Its Chinese Magic Champion, Rush Ling Toy

Still incensed at Ching Ling Foo and the Mooser Brothers for initiating a serious breach in their capacity to control both the performers and theaters of 'big time' vaudeville, the UBO brought Rush Ling Toy into the fray. Albee had the Chinese conjurer play Union Square in March of 1913. As noted earlier, Toy basically had the same act and accoutrements as Foo, and Albee hoped he might be able to replace Foo in UBO venues across the country.

Initial test results with audiences had been relatively encouraging, and trade magazine *Variety* remarked Toy had the serious bonus, from Albee's perspective, of being much cheaper than Foo.[545]

> In early April 1913, President Woodrow Wilson of the U.S. planned to recognize the government of the newly formed Republic of China on April 8th when the first duly elected Chinese congress of the republic met. (1913 04 01 *Honolulu Star Bulletin* P.1)

March-April: Foo, the Star of the Follies

While touring with the Follies, much of Foo's success with his magic was accredited to his ability to misdirect using not his words or hands, but his large, deep eyes, which were described as moving like "an Atlantic coast lighthouse beacon."[546] "They dart from side to side—a flash of somber brown, then a flash of white. The eyelids half cover them, but they are not dreamy. It is his long glance that confuses you, as you do your best to see what he is doing or about to do. He smiles and his face lights up. His eyes speak for him. They seem to say 'now watch closely'. You wait for his eyes to guide you, but they misguide you and after the trick is done you will ask, 'Why did I look at those eyes all the time?'"[547-551]

Further, during the Follies tour, Foo was presented as having a "dual personality." He was very serious off the stage, but while performing had "a wonderful smile" and "nothing seems to bother him." Again and again, reviewers felt compelled to reference Foo's "wonderful" smile—yet another tribute to the great charisma Foo seems to have exuded.

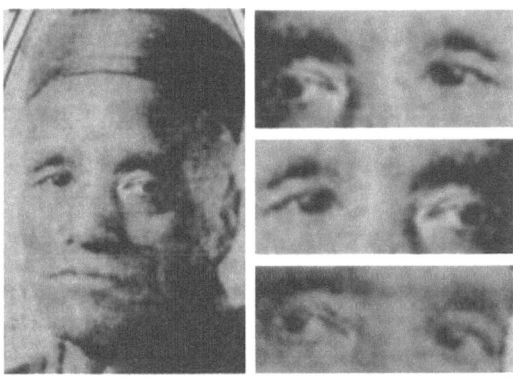

"Why did I look at those eyes all the time?"

Fools Audience by Misdirecting Gaze: Has Wonderful Smile on Stage, but IS Serious off It

"One of the Finest Types of Northern Chinese"

Throughout Foo's run with the Follies, the Ziegfeld advance machine, to which Foo's narrative was prisoner, inevitably described him as a descendant of Confucius, a mandarin, and a man of noble blood and breeding—"one of the finest types of Northern Chinese", a description that had followed him since before he arrived in Omaha. In addition, this exploited once again the North/South split that was sometimes presented with Foo's publicity and the common insistence that any non-whites performing on the U.S. stage ideally sprang from the nobility of their country of origin. Once more, one gets the sense the American audience, children of an ambitious young country on the rise, saw itself as, if not exactly royalty, at least the equivalent of "foreign" royalty. A pleasant proposition, to be sure and one that would endure.

This positioning of Foo as a mandarin and Chinese nobility was as an important part of the "booming" of the Foo troupe act as the illusion that Chung Ling Soo was Chinese to his. But more informed observers of Foo up close recognized the signs that the original Chinese conjurer, as rich and successful as a performer and businessman he might have been, was in the Chinese hierarchy solidly middle class.

Foo, for example, obviously had much more respect and understanding than his rival Chung Ling Soo of Chinese cultural mores. Foo, in his dress (when he wore dragon motifs) ensured he wore such designs only with three claws, the sign of the Chinese middle class. Four claws would signify a member of the nobility. Five claws signified a member of the royal family.

The Narrative on Foo's Appearance Remains Central in the Promotional Material

In the various Follies-generated promotional materials produced to boom Foo, much is made of what made Foo unique from a visual standpoint. As per earlier profiles on Foo, the focus was on his imposing size, his handsome profile, his smile, and the gracefulness of his movements. He was often described as being as agile as a ballet dancer, and reviewers rightly openly wondered at the ability of a 58-year-old man to race across the stage, leap into the air, and turn a somersault with as much ease as the young acrobats in his troupe.

CHINESE IMPACT ON FASHION

This prominent ad below from the Chicago *Tribune* displayed the impact Chinese style cues were having on clothing fashions at the time of Foo's second tour. (Ad image elements were reconfigured to fit space.)

"French Model ... Chinese Influence ... Not the exaggerated fad of the moment!"[552]

Interestingly, local papers simultaneous with the Foo troupe's success were running ads for stores selling "the latest models in suits and gowns just over from Paris," including "three of the latest French models, which show the Chinese influence". Items included a wrap "cut on the lines of a mandarin coat" and "adorable short jacket wraps, impossible to describe in detail but showing the influence of the Chinese." Purchasers were assured that this clothing was "not the exaggerated fad of the moment, but the conservative, smart things sought by women of taste."[553]

March 1913: Meanwhile, Over in England, Chung Ling Soo Carries On

March of 1913 found Chung Ling Soo, who was still proud to be a member of the China Reform Association and was contemplating staying in England after retirement, playing the Exeter Hippodrome. Europe's Original Chinese Conjurer's promotional material then focused on how superior Soo was to his many imitators. As noted earlier, Soo continued to evolve away from simple imitations of Foo's work and had constructed and developed a remarkable repertoire of top-flight illusions.

In his latest elaborate illusion, the "Willow Pattern Plate", Soo transformed Suee Seen into a full-grown orange tree in full view of his audience. He also did a levitation trick with Suee Sueen. Soo's most startling trick may have been his "Living Target" illusion. As discussed earlier, the illusion, along with its promotional poster, were notoriously copied by Hugarde after Soo's 1909 Australian tour. In this illusion, Soo fired an arrow, to which a cord had been attached, from a rifle at Suee Sueen. The arrow with attached cord passed through Seen and into the bull's eye of the target before which she was standing. Soo also performed his "Magic Cauldron" and "Dream of Great Wealth" illusions.

In the latter, "a lady's trinket is placed on a stand which is poured into a casket, a spirit lamp is lit underneath, and upon the casket being removed, streams of silver coins fall from it, then £5 notes, then a £1,000 note. This is suspended in mid-air, and instantly changes into an immense golden sovereign, which bursts into a star, and from which emerges a Chinese lady pouring forth golden sovereigns from a horn of plenty."[554]

In some versions of this wealth illusion, clouds of £5 notes floated from the stage over the heads of the audience, where they were clutched at by eager hands. Upon examination, the theatergoer would discover these £5 notes were not what they seemed and often contained advertisements for local business. In one instance, when Soo was playing in Belfast, they were headed "Royal Irish Distillery, Belfast" and went on to warn the reader against "many spurious imitations of Dunville's Old Irish Whiskey." No "spurious imitations" for Soo.[555–557]

April 1913, St. Louis: "A Chinese Magician Who Looks Like a Statesman"

In Chicago, the local media—who in previous years littered accounts of Chinese Americans with what they believed was comic pidgin English—must have startled a good portion of their readership with a series of laudatory articles concerning the dignified Foo. One article, headlined "A Chinese Magician Who Looks Like a Statesman", was accompanied by a striking photo of the square-jawed Foo that proved the point. Foo truly had a head worthy of a Roman coin. We had come a long way from the New Orleans reporter's assessment back during Foo's first U.S. tour that the Chinese magician was a "tall, ungainly individual" and "about as awkward and ugly-looking a Chinese person as could be found in all the oriental empire." It was a minority opinion then, and by 1913, clearly thoroughly overtaken by an entirely different narrative.

During his Follies engagement, Foo's profile was even positively compared with that of Sitting Bull, who was considered to have a classically noble countenance. In fact, a photographer of the famous Indian hero claimed Foo more closely resembled Sitting Bull than any individual he had ever studied. According to the noted portraitist, the two had high protruding foreheads with strong chins and exceedingly angular noses. According to the photographer, this resemblance even extended to the wrinkles in Foo's face and his complexion. After this exhaustive assessment of Foo's countenance, the reporter concluded "a psychologist would say the that these features denote great emotion, intellect, and a wonderful ability to misdirect attention."[558–560]

In addition, in keeping with the dignified tone of the piece, the author shared Foo's apparent serious dramatic ambitions with his audience. The Chicago critic noted that before he retired, Foo wanted to produce "a Chinese drama, founded upon a new idea, on the English stage."[561]

"A Chinese Magician Who Looks Like a Statesman." Foo truly had a head worthy of a Roman coin.

Foo's reported aspirations in this direction thus align both with Chee Toy's declared preference for classical music and George Mooser's earlier stated desire to work with Foo in developing such a play.

April 25, 1913, Detroit: Foo Prompts a Discussion of the "Exclusion Laws"

Amongst this more serious coverage, the Foo troupe once again inspired a discussion of the China Question and what was sometimes described in the popular press as "the queer clause" in U.S. immigration laws "which bars Chinese" and the "special arrangements" that had to be made with the government to have Foo and his company tour the country.[562] Reviewers noted that because of these laws, this may well have been audiences' last chance to see Foo before he returned to China to retire.[563]

Exclusion Laws Bar Chinese Actors From Appearing in America Unless Specially Sanctioned

Many Americans otherwise unaware of the "queer clause" in U.S. immigration law" which barred Chinese learned of it in the context of discussions stimulated by the success and popularity of the Foo troupe.

Foo continued his practice of contributing his services to charity when he took the time from the Chicago portion of his Ziegfeld tour to participate in a benefit to raise money for victims of the historic 1913 Indiana and Ohio floods. Other leading theatrical lights in Chicago participating in the benefits included, George M. Cohan, Bert Williams, and leading players of *The Yellow Jacket*, since the play continued to follow the Foo troupe tour.[564]

April 30, 1913, Detroit: Would Chee Toy Marry an American Man? "No." But Not for the Reason One Might Think

During the Follies' Detroit engagement, a reporter good-naturedly asked Chee Toy, given all the attention she was getting in the U.S., whether she would marry an American (and one can assume the reporter in question and the vast bulk of the reading public, by "American", presumed they were talking about a white man). Her immediate response caused a bit of a kerfuffle. "The little lady promptly and emphatically answered, 'No!'" Then, realizing she seemed to have hurt some feelings with the promptness and vehemence of her reply, she attempted to right the situation by explaining her position on this matter. She said, "'You see, I am married already. I think American gentlemen are very nice,' "and attentive to their ladies." But she felt as husbands they might be "lazy" because they were not willing to invest the time required to cultivate and care for the long rich queue she found so attractive in Chinese men."[565]

Interestingly, soon after the fall of the Qing Dynasty, Chinese men were no longer required to wear queues, but many did not abandon the practice till the last Emperor of China, Puyi, removed his queue in 1922. Foo stopped wearing a queue well before this time but continued to wear a false queue as part of his stage costume.

> A piece of news on Ching Ling Foo was circulated throughout North America via the wire services informing the public that Foo owned a chain of theaters back home.[566]

May 1913, Pittsburgh: Chee Toy, "Chinese Girl with the Follies," Aims for Higher Things

A very long, thoughtful interview, yet still very much of its time, conducted by prominent female journalist Gertrude Gordon, with the emerging star of the Foo show Chee Toy was prominently featured on the second page of the May 7th edition of the Pittsburgh *Press*.

"Little Chee Toy, Chinese girl with the 'Follies,' playing at the Nixon Theater this week, is dear and cunning, cute and piquant—well, for 20 precious minutes I have delved into my 'Book of Synonyms' trying to find something new, something which could adequately describe this enchanting bit of Chinese womanhood without impoverishing the English language. She looked like a little doll yesterday afternoon in her hotel when I went to interview her."

"'Interview her!' One might as well try to interview a bright-eyed little bird. One can only watch her and listen to her and enjoy her absolute uniqueness. About a dozen other girls were in the hotel parlor, singing and playing the piano. Chee Toy, in black silk trousers and coat, was watching them, laughing with them in their fun like a child would be, although she was not quite of their party. Quaint like a picture she stood when greeting me with her lively eyes shining, her marvelous plait of glossy, thick, silky hair swinging from her tiny head. She speaks English fluently, so although her manager was present, he was not needed as interpreter."

"She loves the stage; she loves the girls she meets, loves all American people—in fact, she likes the songs she sings in the show, but she likes classical music better. Her ambition is to be a prima donna with a whole Chinese troupe. She is not interested in woman suffrage as she is pure-blood Manchu and so is not particularly in favor of the present Republican form of government in China. She is aged 20 and has been married for three years."

"'My husband now is going to school on Long Island,' she said proudly, 'and when he is through there, he will go to Yale or Harvard. Here is his picture,' and from her purse she took two snapshots of a fine-looking young Chinese boy. 'He is just as old as I am,' she said." Chee Toy then sang "Because I Love You" and accompanied herself on piano. "Her voice is clear, rather metallic, true, and her enunciation is distinct."

"'I should like very much to have a whole Chinese company,' she said eagerly, when talking of her ambition. 'I like to travel around this America and I would like to sing fine, good music, not ragtime like I sing now. But this show is so hurry-up, no one who comes to see it wants classical music. They must have ragtime or they are not pleased.' With which opinion I heartily coincided. Imagine a Ziegfeld Follies audience listening to 'classical' music!"

"Ching Ling Foo, Chee Toy's father, is the magician with the show. He is worth about $1,000,000, but like his daughter, likes the show life and to travel. Chee Toy herself has about $200,000 of the most exquisite jewelry, the greater portion diamonds. In her ears yesterday she wore enormous diamond earrings. On her wrists were two bracelets, both actually solid gold. They bend like paper but are almost unbelievably heavy. On her third finger, on the left hand, she wore her wedding ring. It is like a signet, only it bears her husband's name carved on it instead of her own initials. She also wore a ring with her father's family name carved on it."

"Turquoise, diamond and pearl rings weighed down the tiny fingers of her other hand. While we were talking, she proudly showed me a letter from her husband with her name written in correct if awkward English characters, as well as in the Chinese words. She is a wonderfully little person, easily walking under a medium-sized person's arm. Her hands and feet are like babies', so neat and small are they. She is a student, too, studying all the time she is on tour, so she can equal her husband in his knowledge. In all, it was a very entertaining half-hour I spent with Chee Toy."[567]

May 1913: Follies Enters its Last Week; People Still Asking, 'Does the Foo Act Fit with the Follies?'

The Ziegfeld Follies entered its last week in Washington, where it would finish its season at the National Theater just three blocks from the White House. It was quite possible Woodrow Wilson took in the show or some portion of it at some point. Flo Ziegfeld had decided to end the Washington leg of the tour on May 17th.[568]

After all this discussion of the natural dignity of Foo and even Chee Toy, it was not surprising to see a recurring theme in the reviews of the Follies of 1912–1913 regarding the question of whether the Foo troupe was really a fit with Ziegfeld's style of entertainment.

During their stop in St. Louis the week of April 20th, for example, some of the more high-minded news outlets noted the Foo portion of the Follies as a "big hit" with the local audience and praised its work as "a performance of the first magnitude in its own distinctive class." Bert Williams, "the colored comedian", was also mentioned as "undeniably the bright particular star" of the Follies portion of the entertainment. They then, however, rapidly moved on to the question of whether the Follies, whose core business remained "presenting scantily dressed young women" often admittedly "spectacularly", along with very amusing but sometimes coarse comedy skits, really belonged at a high-class playhouse like the St. Louis Olympic Theater. The message was that while the Foo troupe was a fit, the coarser Follies were a questionable call. The reviewer then no doubt increased the show's box office by referencing the "especial recklessness" of the show's Atlantic City Boardwalk scene featuring a "half-dozen or more bathing girls."[569]

Once Foo was finished with Ziegfeld, there were potential plans to send him out West as the head of a vaudeville show. Foo had not played widely in the West. Under the contract made with the Mooser Brothers, Ziegfeld still had Foo for another four weeks, so it was under their management it would be handled.[570]

UBO Not Through with Foo, Someone Asks Albee: "Are You a Crook?"

The challenges to the UBO monopoly over 'big time' vaudeville that Foo and the Mooser brothers played a key role in initiating earlier that year were just beginning, and they continued to stir resistance and controversy. How rough and tumble the entertainment business was in those days is revealed by the news that a marquee above Dowling's Saloon, which sat directly opposite the windows of Albee's sixth-floor New York Putnam Building offices, was leased to proclaim in large lit letters "Are You a Crook?"

Further complicating matters, George Mooser, Foo's manager, was now also an advisor to John Cort, the man leading the revolt against the UBO, which *Variety* described in print in April 1913 as "a venomous monopolistic demon supported on wind and existing on graft" and which exercised "scandalous abuses of power" and "leads all the hogging monopolies." No confusion about where *Variety* stood on this issue.

George Mooser was well-placed to advise Cort in this battle, given it was UBO that warned and threatened the Foo troupe that if they dared to demand or accept more money for their act than they and E.F. Albee deemed appropriate, the Foo act would simply not be able to find work in any theater in America. But as we have seen, Foo and the Mooser Brothers rejected these demands, and in spectacular fashion. They thumbed their nose at Albee and UBO's threats to boycott their act by breaking every attendance record at Poli's Connecticut theaters, essentially signaling the beginning of the end of the UBO's vise-like control of both the performers and theaters of 'big time' vaudeville.

Variety, in April of 1913, noted the fact Ching Ling Foo had not been "idle a week" since defying UBO's threats and was now making over three times the weekly rate the UBO demanded he accept. Furthermore, in some cases, Foo was getting a percentage of the theater gate. The Chinese conjurer did all this while ensuring the theaters who paid him these great sums were profiting enormously, thus making it very difficult for the UBO to keep the old regime in place.[571]

CHAPTER FOURTEEN

MAY 1913—POST-FOLLIES, FOO CONTINUES WILD SUCCESS, OVERCOMES MORE UBO SHENANIGANS, DISRUPTS VAUDEVILLE'S 'SMALL TIME'/'BIG TIME' CONTINUUM

May 1913: Where To for Foo After the Follies?

The Foo troupe was having great success with the 1912–1913 Follies, but the Ziegfeld tour would be ending soon. Just where the Foo troupe would go next was up in the air, and given the environment, the subject of much speculation and keen negotiations.

One plan posited was for the Foo troupe to head up a revised version of the Follies that would tour the West Coast. Another rumor had Will Collins, a well-known London theatrical manager, claiming he had signed Ching Ling Foo for an upcoming ten-week engagement in London.[572]

By mid-May, theatrical production heavyweights Klaw and Erlanger were reported to have Ching Ling Foo under contract.

Engagements would need to be finalized quickly, as Foo's current engagement with the Follies ended the next week in Washington, where the Ziegfeld show will close its season.[573]

Foo Troupe Finishes with Follies Despite UBO Efforts; Hired for Proctor's 5th Avenue New York Theater Anniversary Celebration

As the Foo troupe finished up their engagement with the Ziegfeld Follies, E.F. Albee and the UBO were not about to forget about the quarrel with Foo and his management. Reportedly, there were attempts to scuttle the Foo troupe's booking to headline Proctor's 5th Avenue Theater in New York, but in the end, Foo was signed for $2,000 a week. Proctor's had hired the Foo troupe as part of an anniversary celebration. The group would likely move on to Hammerstein's after that engagement.[574,575]

During the Proctor's engagement, the Foo troupe would share the bill with Bill Welch, the Hebrew comedian, and "Uno, the Canine Paradox."[576–578]

Foo's Contractual Woes Continue

Given E.F. Albee had sworn Foo would never work again in the U.S. after incurring the UBO's wrath earlier this year, heads spun when Keith's, which was controlled by E.F. Albee, the general manager of the UBO, who also ran Keith's theaters across the country, dramatically offered an engagement for the Foo troupe to appear at Keith's Orpheum Theatre, Brooklyn, for $2,000 a week. The engagement would start June 2nd, after they completed their run at Proctor's 5th Avenue Theater.

A simultaneous report also noted George Mooser had written a pantomime called *The Viceroy's Concubine* in which Foo would play the principal role. Elements of Foo's magical act were to be worked into the play. This report claimed that Foo was "a noted actor" in China in his earlier days. This was the first time a claim of this nature had been made re: Foo's past. In addition, the report ominously noted that Klaw and Erlanger still had Foo under contract for the considerable future and may have wanted to send him out on a road show, hitting small time vaudeville theaters in which he would be expected to do up to three sets a day.

Close on the heels of this news, Foo and his management's relationship with Klaw and Erlanger began to break down. Foo had never agreed to do three sets a day, and three sets a day was a hallmark of the 'small time' vaudeville theaters and circuit. As a result, Foo's managers, the Mooser Brothers, reportedly wanted to break the contract they negotiated and take Foo to tour in England, then bring the troupe back the next fall to tour under a new booking system to be set up by Mooser business partner John Cort. The financials of the Klaw and Erlanger deal appear to have been a term of 46 weeks at $1,450 per week, of which Foo received $800. Klaw and Erlanger had sub-contracted Foo's services for $2,000 a week to other vaudeville theater managers after inking the deal.

The reason for the fallout with Klaw and Erlanger did appear to be the issue of the number of sets Foo will be required to play. Apparently, Klaw and Erlanger signed for Foo to appear in a theater in Baltimore that required acts to perform three times a day. In breaking the agreement with Klaw and Erlanger, the Foo team claimed there was an oral agreement that Foo would only be asked to perform twice a day at most. Klaw and Erlanger, which had placed Foo with the Ziegfeld Follies earlier in the year, declared Foo's refusal to accept the engagement in Baltimore a breach of contract.[579]

An engagement at Hammerstein's awaited Foo in July, and other theaters had also booked the act. It was reported that various actors unhappy with the Moosers' business practices had approached Foo about changing his management team, but Foo replied he was satisfied with his representation and "too old to be bothered."[580,581]

Meanwhile, the Klaw and Erlanger lawsuit dragged on. Despite the clear contract terms, George Mooser claimed Klaw and Erlanger ceased to employ the Foo troupe as of May 31st, 1912 but Mooser was unable to find other work for the troupe because the Klaw and Erlanger contract was, according to its terms, still in force. Mooser thus sued Klaw and Erlanger for money owing to Foo for the unexpired portion of the contract.[582]

June 23, 1913, Brooklyn: Foo Troupe Plays Brighton Beach, Hobnobs with Houdini

Ultimately, the Foo troupe ended up engaged at Brooklyn's Brighton Beach Music Hall, opening June 23rd. The ongoing conflict between the Mooser Brothers and Albee and the UBO continued to negatively impact engagement opportunities for Foo, including what would have been the fence-mending engagement Albee offered at Keith's Brooklyn Orpheum Theater. However, regarding that offer, one cannot know how serious or desirable it really may have been. Albee had the habit of making offers that would be rescinded at a moment's notice or that contained hidden risks, and given their past history, it would be understandable if the Moosers were cautious.

The Foo troupe playing Brighton consisted of 14 performers and lasted 45 minutes. The promotional material noted that all the performers were selected for their skill in various specialties and came from the "leading theaters of Canton, Hong Kong and Yeddo." Once more, Chee Toy was noted as singing "American songs in her own quaint, celestial style."[583] While playing Brighton Beach, the Foos took a week of holidays and were visited by their good friend Harry Houdini and the man who played the Chinese conjurer Okito—who was based on Foo—Theo Bamberg.

"The Best Magician to Ever Come Down the Pike"

Cartoon (enhanced) from June 1913 Brooklyn *Daily Eagle*. Chee Toy declares, "My father says he is the best magician that ever came down the pike. My father always speaks the truth."

FOO AND THE "ALLEGED" CHINESE FOOD: CHOP SUEY

In a July 1st edition of the Brooklyn *Daily Eagle*, Foo explained the origin of the "chop suey" dish served in restaurants throughout New York and across the country.

"'Not saying it is not tasty, just not really a Chinese dish … Thousands of your countrymen eat what they call chop suey,' he said, 'and gloat over the belief that they know what good Chinese food is when they taste it. My countrymen rent a little room, hang a few Chinese lanterns—of American make—buy a supply of chopsticks, invent a menu, burn a few punks, and then the army of chop suey eaters invades the place and, over their

> unmanageable chopsticks, talk of their wide acquaintance with Chinese dishes.'"
>
> "'Now, I have been fooling the public for more than 40 years, but I've never foisted so rare a joke upon people with would-be Oriental palates. Believe me, chop suey never saw China and China never heard of chop suey until American tourists called for it in the public restaurants of my country. After that there grew a demand for it but only from Americans.'"
>
> "'I wouldn't eat a chopstick full of the stuff—not because it is not clean and wholesome but because it is a big joke and I refuse to eat jokes.'"[584]
>
> In response to Foo's statement regarding America's beloved "chop suey", The Brooklyn *Daily Eagle* published an article written by a *Dramatic Review* editor declaring that if neither Ching Ling Foo nor the Chinese will claim "our humble chop suey," then America would! "It shall not wander waif-like o'er the face of the earth. As long as American hearts beat for freedom and human liberty, we shall offer a refuge to the homeless and oppressed of all nations, and chop suey shall find a resting place in the land of the free and the stomach of the brave."[585]

July 1913, Brooklyn: Foo Troupe Still a Hit; Introduces the "Xun" Chinese Musical Instrument to Western Audiences

While Foo was performing at the Brighton Beach Music Hall, he introduced a type of Chinese "mouth-pipe organ", which the Brooklyn audience found quite perplexing. "The most unusual melody of all was that furnished by a Chinese piper in the company of Ching Ling Foo when he essayed 'When the Midnight Choo Choo Leaves for Alabama.'" "The instrument was built like a beehive and was capable of giving any automobile horn a four-mile handicap on tonal penetration." The reviewer appeared to be referring to a xun, the ancient

Chinese musical instrument in use for over 7,000 years. It did indeed, in some ways, resemble a beehive.⁵⁸⁶

A traditional Chinese xun musical instrument, similar to what is called an ocarina in the West. "The instrument was built like a beehive and was capable of giving any automobile horn a four-mile handicap on tonal penetration."

Chee Toy made a much more favorable impression in her rendition of American ragtime. Several young Chinese children in the act were "in the parlance of a young Brooklyn maiden who attended the show, 'just too cute for anything.'" One child in the show, who appeared not over six years old, spun plates like an expert.

The troupe's acrobats elicited especial interest, "It would be of particular interest to amateur athletes to watch Soon Wo Kwai, the Chinese strongman of the troupe, perform on the horizontal bar. They would see some tricks that have never been taught in an American gymnasium." Foo's magic, meanwhile, as always, kept everyone "goggle-eyed with amazement."

Foo's current tour of the U.S. was presented as his last, after which he would tour the principal cities of Europe and then retire to China, where he would "enjoy life with his large fortune." Despite the evident skills of his troupe, Foo remained "the real magnet" for the crowds and his "remarkable ability to mystify his audiences."⁵⁸⁷

Chee Toy Continues to "Win All Hearts"

A piece in the Brooklyn *Times Union* noted Chee Toy sang "American" songs "so prettily she wins all hearts." Chee Toy was said to be "a little over four feet tall, but she is a demure married woman of twenty … the company were well received and the performance as a whole was voted the best of its kind." This last plaudit was telling. By rating the Foo troupe the "best of its kind", the author acknowledged the plethora of similar Chinese acts available and the superiority of the Foo troupe. Joe Welch, the "Hebrew entertainer", was part of the bill. He "received a warm welcome" and told "new and old stories in Hebrew dialect and sang parodies in a manner that pleased."[588]

July 5th, 1913: Indications of Things to Come—the Legendary Lillian Sits "In Front"

Lillian Russell, the "grand dame" of American theater, comes to see the Foo troupe.

"Don't Deprive the Children" of a Ching Ling Foo Performance

Brooklyn's Brighton Beach Music Hall published a Foo ad in the Brooklyn *Daily Eagle* scolding parents "Don't Deprive the Children" and encouraging them to take the family to see the Foo show. The ad promised you would see Foo pick "dry sand out of water." Foo's uninterrupted success continued as the Brighton Beach Music Hall with Foo as a "topliner" almost set a weekly attendance record.[589]

> **Don't Deprive**
> The children, nor, for that matter, yourself, of the opportunity of seeing the Great Chinese Magician, Ching Ling Foo, pick dry sand out of water. A good seat at the matinees for a quarter, and in the evenings for "Half a Dollar." So don't let the price keep you away.
>
> **BRIGHTON BEACH MUSIC HALL**

July 7, 1913: After Brooklyn's Brighton Beach, Foo Troupe Back to Hammerstein's New York Roof Garden Theater

Starting July 7th, the Foo troupe would be back with Hammerstein's as the chief attraction at Hammerstein's New York Theater and Roof Garden. Among the other acts at Hammerstein's featured under Foo were "Don, the Talking Dog," Ben Welch, Sophie Tucker, "female diving models", and an act featuring "The Dance of the Siren."[590,591]

July 25, 1913: What the Hammerstein's Roof Show Looked Like

The show consisted of 16 separate acts and it was a long one. The show's scheduled start was 8 o'clock and it wrapped up around 11:30 p.m. Most people were not seated before nine, so the acts before that time mostly passed without notice. According to reviews, "Juggling Wilbur" appeared nervous and left the stage less than a triumph. A female violinist followed, and she did well, given the early hour. She was followed by a moderately successful dance team, then the "Cadets of Gascogne", a singing group that made itself heard. They were followed by a simian act entitled "Prince Florio" that included a bit on bicycles that proved popular.

Another singing trio did well and was followed by a blind pianist who received strong applause. A "posing" act entitled "The Three Types" went on too long, and songstress Juliette Dika's act was primarily of interest to the audience for her wardrobe changes. Another dance duo followed, with an act entitled "The Dance of Fortune", wherein the woman played a fickle lady who presided over the wheel of fortune while her male partner played the part of a ruined gambler under her spell. A projected "stereopticon" image reading "Beware!" was projected regularly during the performance, reinforcing the act's purported moral lesson, which was reportedly conveyed through an energetic effort by the dancers, who wore "as few clothes as possible." There was an intermission, and the next act was a female impersonator. This was followed by the "Techow's Cats" animal act, and then "Dainty Marie", followed by "Borden and Hayden." Then came Ching Ling Foo.

Despite poor acoustics, especially if someone was speaking, the Foo troupe recorded another successful run at Hammerstein's Roof Garden Theater. Reviewers noted Foo, was "unquestionably the star of the bill. He seemed to be the one audiences were waiting for", and received "emphatic spontaneous applause."[592]

July 13, 1913: "Hear About the Magician's Dinner? 'Twas Some Tricky Affair"

On July 13th, 1913, the New York *World* published a long piece by Hazen Conklin with a wonderful full half-page illustration on the dinner Ching Ling Foo organized for Harry Houdini before he sailed for Europe. It was striking that the man who was among Foo's best Western friends would also be close to his great rival William Robinson, a.k.a. Chung Ling Soo. Be that as it may, Foo and Houdini were good friends, and Foo arranged the going-away dinner for the escape artist.

The dinner was held at midnight in Foo's suite at the Bellevue Hotel. Attendees included Foo, the host; Houdini, the guest of honor; Howard Thurston, premier illusionist; Theo Bamberg also known as the "Chinese" magician "Okito"; and Francis Werner, the President of the Society of American Magicians (S.A.M.). The guest

"The Magicians' Dinner".

list was filled out by other performers at work in New York and their spouses and friends. Of these non-professional magicians, it was observed "they all kept their hands in their pockets and suffered no harm."

Each of the magicians brought some tricks to perform. Foo handled chef duties in the kitchen; Foo's son Yee Dee, Chee Toy, and Yee Dee's wife handled the master of ceremony duties. This was the first instance where Chee Toy being married to Foo's son Chee Yee Dee was revealed to the public.

While they awaited dinner, each magician did a favored trick. Bamberg worked with sleight of hand tricks involving silver cocktail shakers, Thurston did tricks with dollar bills from the audience and returned them, Houdini worked marvels with cards, and then Foo appeared with the night's meal and announced his trick. That night, it was eat with chopsticks or go hungry.

Conklin went on to describe the erstwhile masters of prestidigitation's efforts to master their chopsticks to a reworking of what then would have been a well-known poem: "The Charge of the Light Brigade." In his version, the magicians became the "Eats Brigade" and their fate was similar to the brave but doomed soldiers who inspired the poem. "Noodles to the right of them, suey to the left of them, shark fins in front of them."

The next intercultural moment occurred when Thurston, gave a speech to let Foo know how welcome he was in America, with Chee Toy designated as translator. Reportedly, Thurston barely got out a short sentence indicating Foo was welcome and already a house-hold name in America when Chee Toy, according to Conklin, was off to the "translation races." "Fully six minutes then passed before Chee Toy had fleshed out these few sentences in worthy Chinese." Leon Mooser, who had some knowledge of Chinese, then explained that Chee Toy had merely extended his felicitations not just to Foo, but properly, all of his ancestors as far back as could be reckoned. This seemed to be an exaggeration of something that may have happened, or just a comic bit the author thought would work; regardless, it was a well-meaning and amusing write up of what must have been a fascinating dinner.[593]

Unfortunately, after setting off for Europe as planned, Houdini had to return immediately on the same steamer after learning en route to Europe that his mother had died.[594]

July 18, 1913: "Near All-Time Receipts Record!" Foo's Hammerstein Roof Garden Engagement Another Success! Foo Troupe Held Over!

Foo's engagement at Hammerstein's proved the best box office week of summer for the venue and amounted to a near-all-time receipts record. The Foo troupe's engagement was held over for another week. The show at Hammerstein's even included an act on the bill that did a travesty of Foo's magic act. Of the Foo troupe and its outstanding history of setting box office records, *Variety*, in a slight comedown from its early assessments of the revised Foo troupe act, said, "Any show that can draw such crowds is great. The box office is the answer, and it says something this week for Ching."[595]

WHAT AMERICA'S GREATEST SHOWMAN THINKS

New York City, July 21, 1913.

Messrs. GEO. and LEON MOOSER
Longacre Building, New York.

Gentlemen:—

I wish to extend my congratulations in you having Ching Ling Foo and his company, as I consider it one of the best feature acts I have ever played at Hammerstein's Victoria Theatre and Roof Garden.

Ching Ling Foo has proven himself such, artistically and at the box office.

(Signed) WILLIAM HAMMERSTEIN.

A full half page ad from the July 25th, 1913 issue of *Variety* in which William Hammerstein congratulates Ching Ling Foo and company as "one of the best feature acts I have ever played ... artistically and at the box office."

July 24, 1913: Chee Toy Organizes a Manhattan Rooftop Dinner at Midnight Attended by Valeksa Suratt, an Original 'Vamp' and "Empress of Fashions"

In some of the troupe's rare off time, Chee Toy arranged a special Chinese supper given at midnight on July 24th for members of the new Ziegfeld Follies company. The dinner would be held on the roof of Hammerstein's New York Theater. Invitations had been issued to "all the prominent theater people in town." The dinner provided yet another example of the mixing of cultures vaudeville encouraged and the social prominence of both Foo and Chee Toy.[596,597]

The dinner on the New York Theater roof was attended by about 50 invited guests.

They were mostly prominent theater and show business people, as well as former colleagues from the Follies. One notable attendee was Valeska Suratt. Foo reportedly met Miss Suratt when the Foo troupe was touring South Africa nine years prior.

Midnight seemed an apt time to invite the ever-exotic Ms. Suratt for dinner. Valeska Suratt was yet another influential female character Chee Toy would meet. Also known as the "Empress of Fashions," Suratt was named by *Vogue* as the best-dressed woman on the stage. She was famous for her "vamp" character (a term tellingly derived

VALESKA SURATT

Valeska Surratt, famous for her "vamp" character and notorious dance innovations, would not be out of place in today's music industry.

from "vampire") and her notorious "Apache Dance," which was like the tango, only more so.[598]

Meanwhile, in an early indication of where their careers were going and how the entertainment industry was evolving, in one of their many ventures at this time, the Mooser Brothers began work with the Lubin Company of Philadelphia to set up one of the first organized systems for import and exhibition of films in China. The Moosers believed the Chinese audience would happily pay up to 50 cents for admission to a moving picture show. Leon Mooser was to head to China in late August to further arrangements.[599]

The Popularity of Chinese Ragtime and the "Yellow Peril"

As Chee Toy grew in fame for her renditions of American ragtime, a Chinese quartet, comprised of four Chinese-American university students from San Francisco, following in her footsteps and calling itself the "Ching Hwa Four", singing both American and "Chinese" ragtime, appeared on stage to good reviews.[600] This rise of "Chinese" ragtime on the stage in New York prompted a good-natured column from a local daily in which current calls to beware the "Yellow Peril" in a current playlet were conflated with the rising popularity of Chee Toy and the Ching Hwa Four.

The author notes that despite the warnings, "we have made no effort to resist it. How could we, when it comes trotting along to ragtime?"[601] Of Chee Toy, it was noted she was a scene-stealer of the highest order, with "enough personality for a second Maude Adams", and who sang ragtime with just "the touch of an accent and with a thoroughly Parisian shrug of the shoulder." The author noted other signs of the imminent invasion, such as the installation of a "Chinese Wishing Tree" on the Hammerstein's roof.

Another humorous take on all the Chinese acts appearing on stage came from San Francisco. This report did an excellent job of tying the phenomenon to Harte's "Heathen Chinee" poem, with an interesting twist. In a report on the latest Chinese entertainment to take the stage, in this case a Chinese 40-piece band, a reviewer observed, "The 'yellow peril' seems to be threatening the stage, but as yet there has been no howl that 'cheap Chinese labor' is ruining the profession."[602]

If that was not enough, in the midst of all these Chinese intrusions into fields previously not considered their provenance, the Foo troupe hosted yet another of their coveted Chinese banquets, where the guests of honor were the "Chinese Baseball Nine." The "Nine" were a Honolulu-based "crack team of American Chinese ... barnstorming" across the U.S. playing top college and semi-professional teams—and winning much more than they lost. The team made money by receiving an appearance fee and taking a percentage of the gate.[603]

July 27, 1913: Foo Troupe Shares Bill with Animation Innovator Winsor McCay

The July 27th, 1913 ad for Hammerstein's Victoria Theatre and Roof Garden had Foo as the headliner but, importantly, included visionary Winsor McCay as one of the closing acts. McCay was the creator of *Little Nemo*

Winsor McCay's *Little Nemo* Sunday comic, his Gertie the Dinosaur character, and McCay himself working at his desk. McCay was a renowned illustrator/artist and animation pioneer.

in Slumberland, the most popular Sunday comic of its time and a masterpiece of Art Nouveau artwork. He was also a visonary animation pioneer.

McCay's vaudeville act included interaction with his animation products, which were projected on large screens strategically placed upon the stage. In one version of his act, McCay would roll a ball to one of his favorite characters, Gertie the Dinosaur. The friendly Brontosaurus would then gamely kick the ball back. McCay would end his act by riding off stage on the back of Gertie.

McCay's vaudeville work would soon be prohibited by his employer, William Randolph Hearst, who wanted the talented McCay to focus more on the work he did for Hearst Publications, including illustrating Hearst's thundering editorials.[604]

July 28, 1913: Foo Troupe Enters Fourth Week Heading Bill at Hammerstein's

By July 28th, 1913, the Foo troupe's run at Hammerstein's Theater was into its fourth week. That evening's performances almost got rained out when a heavy storm threatened to flood the roof. Entertainment for the lighter-than-usual audience began with Chester and Jones, a "conventional" singing and dancing act. They were followed by the "Lilliputian" Charlie Rossow, who sang a song and then "impersonated bandmasters past and present." Unfortunately for Charlie, his early position on the bill resulted in a not fully attentive audience. Charlie was followed by a juggling troupe billed as "The Five Mowatts". Only four showed up, but their high-speed act that involved juggling multiple objects and tossing them between the jugglers elicited the first enthusiastic response from the audience.

The Five Mowatts were followed by "the best comedy cycle act in vaudeville", comprised of three cyclists—Mosher, Hayes, and Mosher. The lead comedian-cyclist took several dangerous falls, and a reviewer noted that while "hard work seems to be a pleasure for these boys ... the talking should be dropped." The cyclists were followed by the composer Ernest Ball and the pretty Maude Lambert. Lambert sang while Ball accompanied her on the piano. There was a change of costume for each new number, and this atypical act for Hammerstein's roof nonetheless "put over a good-sized hit."

The posing act titled "Auburn, Blonde, and Brunette" came next, and in their third week on the roof, offered basically the same poses and scenes they had earlier in their run. The climatic fountain scene at the end of their act resulted in three encores. The best performers on the bill were now starting to appear, and the audience was ever more alert and appreciative. Elizabeth Murray, a "classy singing comedienne", demonstrated she was an "artist alone in her class", singing four songs. Then the largely visual spectacular "The Dance of Fortune", held over from the previous week, as noted, told the tale of one man's relationship with Lady Luck, took the stage and received much applause. "The Dance of Fortune" closed the first half of the evening show.

After a brief intermission, the Lilliputian Rossow troupe, of which the earlier-seen Charlie was a member, did their act, which included a burlesque boxing match. The Rossows were "real good performers." After the Rossows, a piano and singing combination, Wille Weaton and Mike Bernard, successfully performed some of Irving Berlin's newest hits. "Dainty Marie" followed.

A Winsor McCay Performance

The aforementioned Winsor McCay, who at that time was still allowed by Hearst to spend "half his time in vaudeville and the other half at newspaper cartooning", then offered "a very novel" performance wherein he combined live action with animations, including one involving a mosquito and the second McCay's popular Sunday comic strip character Little Nemo projected on a large screen behind him. A *Billboard* magazine critic, reviewing the show, described the Little Nemo animation as "a work of art" which would not surprise anyone familiar with the exceptionally gifted McCay's work on what was at that time the most popular Sunday comic strip in America at a time when digging into the Sunday comics pages each weekend was a much-anticipated event for readers of all ages.

The Foo troupe, in their last week at Hammerstein's, took the stage after McCay, closing the show, and kept an appreciative audience glued to their seats until the theater's 11 p.m. final curtain.[605]

Chee Toy: "A Lesson in Repression and Personality … Still the Most Appealing Vaudeville Figure on the Metropolitan Variety Stage"

No small part of the Foo troupe's current appeal could now be attributed to Chee Toy. Under a headline reading "Little Chee Toy Still Fascinates", one of the leading theatrical journals of the day described Chee Toy as "still the most appealing vaudeville figure on the metropolitan variety stage. The tiny Chinese maiden has that rare quality of magnetic personality—the ability to reach out across the footlights and make spectators her friends. It is a delight to watch the way Chee Toy 'puts her songs over' and the delicate use she makes of her hands. She is a lesson in repression and personality. Dynamic methods aren't necessary in vaudeville, despite the general belief."[606]

August 1913, Philadelphia: Foo Performing on the 'Small Time' Marcus Loew Circuit; "Changes the Complexion" of Vaudeville

Their engagement in New York finished, the Foo troupe, still wildcatting, was booked with the Marcus Loew circuit at the Philadelphia Metropolitan Opera House, to open August 11th. The Loew's theater chain was known as a 'small time' vaudeville circuit; the term was generally applied to theaters with smaller seating capacity, a lesser quality of entertainment, lower ticket prices, and a requirement the acts performed three sets per day. Therefore, Loew's engagement of Foo, currently the biggest act in vaudeville, was seen as part of an effort by Loew's to shake the 'small time' label. Foo would also play the Loew's Circuit theaters in Boston.[607]

Foo's weekly salary for the engagement is not known, but his arrangement with the Mooser's guaranteed him at least $800, and the Philadelphia show cost was projected to be well over $2,000 a week, with Foo getting a substantial portion of that. The engagement of Foo by the Loew's circuit was seen as revolutionary. As was observed by the respected industry magazine *The Stage*, "Heretofore, there had been a salary limit, owing to the price of admission at all the Loew theaters being so small. But since they have acquired several houses with huge seating capacity, it looks as if the limit is repealed for the time being. Ching's engagement was a big surprise for several reasons, the two principal ones being the salary which he is paid and the act being booked for two performances daily." Prior to Foo, the policy of the Loew theaters was for all talent to perform three shows a day. "But not for Foo. He is doing two."

Soon, 'small time' vaudeville, given Foo's success at Loew's, was now observed to be "out for all the big headliners they can lay their hands on." The business at Loew's Philadelphia Opera House during Foo's run had been "tremendous." The theater's take of around $1,250 daily, when most seats were priced between 10 and 30 cents with the most expensive being 50 cents, was seen as "something phenomenal."[608]

In a promotional development, Foo's tricks and illusions, in the fashion of the times, were now sporting exotic names including "The Mysterious Glass Bowl" and "The Tiger Lily." In his latest tour, he was once more demonstrating his expertise with the physics-defying spinning top known as the Diabolo.[609]

August 1913, Philadelphia: The Foo Troupe Show in Philadelphia

Fond memories of the hit Foo made in Philadelphia more than a decade ago were played out in the local papers under headlines like "Foo Makes Smashing Hit." Foo and his troupe of 14 performers were seen as one of the best shows Philadelphia audiences had seen for a long time. "Every box and available seat was occupied."[610]

As per the standard format, the Chinese troupe was presented to the audience, then the act began. The act involved several scene changes. During these scene changes, Yu Erh, Foo's comedic assistant, filled in the wait times with his remarkable juggling of heavy Chinese pots.

The show began with three gymnasts: one on a horizontal bar, the other two hanging from straps that would have been the Chinese equivalent of Western gymnastics rings. The men's acrobatic performance received strong applause. Foo then delivered his production act, producing plate after plate of food while his assistant provided comedic assistance. Chee Toy was next, and she reportedly "ragged to the perfection that is the heart's desire of all modern lovers of synocpatia." At some points, "a quartet of Chinese girls helped her in a chorus." There was a final scene change. The children in the act displayed their considerable skills, and Foo then returned for his now standard finale, performing a running somersault across the stage with the production of a large bowl full of water brimming with live goldfish upon landing.

Additional to the Foo act at the Philadelphia Metropolitan were "Love and Haight," two female impersonators performing a singing and dancing act, as well as other acts, and the inevitable and increasingly performance-time-consuming moving pictures.

FOO IN POPULAR CULTURE

An innovative Philadelphia milliner hoping to ride on some of the Ching Ling Foo mania gripping the city christened one of his new men's hats designs the "Wizard" and published a prominent ad featuring a photo of the hat, whose own magic trick was maintaining its shape however it was bent. It was available in brown, green and "drabs."[611]

"A regular Ching Ling Foo of a hat" with its own secret abilities. A 1913 ad makes references to Foo.

August 15, 1913: UBO Makes Another Engagement Offer, Then John Cort Counters

Variety reported the Foo troupe would likely play a Boston club for just two dates and be paid what they would normally receive for a week, and then have almost a whole week off before performing again.

Eyebrows were raised upon reading this report, as the Boston club had links to the UBO. The scheduled two dates were for August 19th and 21st. The plan would be for the troupe to open at Loew's Boston Orpheum on August 25th. The Boston engagement would be followed by a return to New York, likely to work for the UBO-connected Keith's circuit at a rate much higher than the Foo troupe received at Loew's.

However, as of the publication date of the report, these engagements were just plans being floated that had been picked up by the press. At this time, the Foo troupe was well-positioned to negotiate attractive engagements, as their experience and success in the 'small time' theaters such as Loew's and others had venues across the country offering the troupe up to $1,400 a week.[612] In this context, a potential warming of relations with Albee and the UBO based on mutual interests was not unthinkable.

However, in a sign the Foo troupe's engagement future was still up for grabs, just days later, after the UBO version of Foo's potential future was published, another competing tour path for them was publicized. This path for the upcoming season had the added credibility of being put forward by John Cort, an opponent of the UBO, who was currently working with the Moosers. Cort, the major 'legitimate theater' promoter of the time, revealed his plans to launch a country-wide vaudeville tour headlined by three of vaudeville's biggest current stars: Lillian Russell, Ching Ling Foo, and William Farnum. The combined salaries of just these three acts would cost Cort at least $6,500 a week.[613] For good reasons, this project quickly became known as "John Cort's Big Gamble."

August 22, 1913: A Record-Breaking Druggist's Convention and More UBO Shenanigans

The Cort tour, however, would not begin until October 1913, and the Foo troupe needed to book engagements to bridge the gap, all while dealing with a UBO organization now even more inclined to, to the extent they could, cause Foo and the Moosers grief. In the midst of what was a chaotic booking scene, the Foo troupe took on the lucrative two-day engagement in Boston which was on offer earlier. The engagement was to provide the entertainment at the 1913 annual international convention of the United Drug Company. The event involved some 3,200 owner-operators of the rapidly expanding Rexall Drug Store chain and their spouses.

Joining Foo in entertaining the druggists was their old companion from the Ziegfeld Follies, pioneering Black entertainer Bert Williams. The banquet at which they would perform was said to be the largest banquet ever held. Newspaper coverage noted there were "more than 50 women druggists at the convention" and that among the druggists were also 49 who were mayors of their home cities and 43 who were legislators in their home states.[614]

More UBO "Double-Crossing": "Foo Made Subject of Underhanded Dealing"

Even the druggist's convention, it appeared, served as a battlefield for the ongoing Foo-troupe-and-UBO war. Not long after the Foo troupe completed the engagement, theatrical trade magazines revealed the machinations the aspiring booking monopoly undertook to try and derail the lucrative engagement. With a blaring headline "Foo Made Subject of Underhanded Dealing," the then-pugnacious trade magazine *Variety* wove a complicated tale indicating that the UBO attempted to mislead the United Drug Company, which had engaged Foo for the dates of August 19th and 21st by—unbeknownst to Foo or the Moosers—informing the company that the magician could not perform at those times in Boston. This move was memorably described by *Variety* as the UBO extending "its very much stained, double-crossing dagger into the commercial world."

Puzzled, the Boston manager of the event then wired George Mooser regarding these shenanigans, and Mooser replied that the

UBO was providing misinformation and that Foo would indeed make the performance as agreed.[615] At this point, it seemed clear that if the Moosers and the Foo troupe would not agree to engagements and schedules set by the UBO, this sort of interference could be expected.

August 23, 1913, Boston: Foo Troupe at Loew's St. James Theater "Largest Audience Ever"

The latest UBO impediments out of the way, the Foo troupe, now numbering 14 performers, signed on for an engagement at Loew's in Boston beginning in late August. The Boston promotion materials emphasized the opportunity to see five Chinese women on stage. Apart from Chee Toy, there was Miss Ching Chee Yun, a plate spinner, and Miss Cho Kwai, a "girl acrobat."[616]

In Boston, the Foo troupe brought out "the largest audience ever" at Loew's St. James Theatre. Chee Toy was a big favorite, as was Yu Erh with his comedic juggling, while the troupe's acrobats "brought down the house."[617]

September 1913, New York: Foo Troupe Triumphs While Rush Ling Toy Struggles

By September 1913, the Foo troupe was back in New York at Loew's Seventh Avenue Theater, one of the Loew's 'small time' vaudeville venues looking to move up. Meanwhile, Rush Ling Toy, who continued to be used as a Foo stalking horse by the UBO to see if they replace Foo with a more pliable cheaper version, was headlining a UBO theater in the Bronx. Once more, the matchup went in Foo's favor. Loew's Seventh Avenue Theater continued to turn business away, while the Bronx theater, and most every other New York theater not featuring Foo, suffered at the box office.[618]

The results of this latest head-to-head featuring Foo and Rush led *Variety* to suggest UBO's Rush Ling Toy experiment was "not being attended with altogether fruitful results."

Fascinatingly, Rush himself was not too keen on his own act. The modest magician was reportedly not too eager to headline in the bigger houses because he knew his act was not good enough.

Rush, trying to meet the standard he felt required, had invested $2,800 of his own money in his act and wanted to add six Chinese musicians to the performance. For all this, he just wanted UBO to increase his salary by $100 a week, which is what he would have got if he was playing the 'small time' theaters. UBO, true to form, refused even this minor request from a performer who was bending over backwards to cooperate. As a result, indicating troubles to come, Rush refused to take the booking at a UBO Bushwick theater that was doled out to him.[619]

September 16, 1913, New York: Foo Troupe Continues Success at Shubert Theater

Meanwhile, going into mid-September, Foo, still at Loew's Seventh Avenue, continued to demonstrate the wisdom of the Moosers' decision to allow 'small time' vaudeville houses to pay for and feature Foo as a headliner.[620,621] The experiment of placing Foo with 'small time' theaters, but allowing the troupe to perform just twice a day, was a resounding success. After Loew's, the Foo troupe, whose quality "surpasses all other bills seen at this theater", moved on to play to capacity crowds at the Shubert Theater. Interestingly, they listed Foo as being 92 years old.[622]

As for the crowds at the Shubert Theater, the "novelty of the performance was not lost on spectators." Chee Toy's singing "called forth innumerable encores." Reviewers noted "It was a well satisfied audience that started homeward at 11:10 o'clock."[623]

September 19, 1913: A Rightly Fed-Up Rush Ling Toy Breaks with UBO

Rush Ling Toy, who was now headlining the Keith circuit theaters controlled by UBO, had decided to refuse to compete with Foo if not paid the same salary as the other Chinese magician. UBO, true to its miserly reputation, had still not given Rush the additional $100 a week he had asked for after augmenting his own act out of his own pocket. Furthermore, Rush refused to take a booking for Albany on September 29th that would have put him in direct opposition to Foo, who would be playing there as part of Cort's upcoming three big stars tour.

Things got worse for the aspiring monopoly. Pushed to the breaking point, Rush Ling Toy declared he had washed his hands of the UBO and said he would now work for anybody who would hire him whatever theater circuit they belonged to, whoever they were associated with, whether they were moving picture joints in Poughkeepsie or New York opera houses. All they had to do was pay him the salary he was asking. The UBO looked to have once more overplayed its hand.[624]

CHAPTER FIFTEEN

OCTOBER 1913—FOO TOURS WITH LEGENDARY DIVA AND "DICTATOR OF FASHION" LILLIAN RUSSELL'S "ALL STAR FEATURE FESTIVAL"

John Cort's Three-Star "Big Gamble" Tour Hits the Road

What had come to be known as the "John Cort Feature Festival" readied for its initial show at the Wilkes Barre Grand Opera House on October 2nd. The show would have approximately 40 entertainers. The plan was for the show to tour through to the Pacific, playing a specially selected list of towns and cities on the way.

Headlining the three-star show was Lillian Russell, the Oprah Winfrey or Gwyneth Paltrow of her time. She was being promoted just above Foo and Farnum on the bill. The legendary Russell was "still heralded as the queen of beauty and the greatest exponent of youth and health the world has ever known ... the most beautiful woman of professional renown." For the tour, she would introduce a new form of color motion pictures "in which is depicted her daily routine in the propagation of health and personal charms." After singing, she concluded her act with "a most elaborate display of the London and Paris fashion gowns she collected this past summer."

Meanwhile, William Farnum, "the handsomest man on the American stage", would appear as Virginius in *The Tragedy of Virginius*, with the assistance of six other actors surrounded by "the most magnificent scenic and costume detail ever given an American tragedian, ancient or modern." Cort planned to have Farnum star in his whole own production the following year.

Then, the usual Foo promotional material was given, with the added news that this would be the Foo troupe's first performance outside the big Eastern cities. Notably, Chee Toy was listed for the first time as a separate act from the Foo troupe. She was described as Foo's "lovely" daughter and the "Anna Held" of China.

Not without reason, this "John Cort Festival" was described as consisting of features of "widely contrasting" genres and styles that would "provide an evening's entertainment of great variety", and as the costliest entertainment production ever put forth in America.[625]

LILLIAN RUSSELL RIDES IN A ZEPPELIN: GOOD FOR PEACE AND THE COMPLEXION!

Lillian Russell, who had been touring Europe prior to the big Cort tour, made the news back in the U.S. after she took in a bird's eye tour of Berlin from a zeppelin airship. Russell described the experience as "wonderful." She added she "flew faster than a bird" and echoed the views of the popular 1912 play *Under Many Flags* as she saw this fast-advancing technology as a deterrent to war. "When the dirigible balloon is perfected there will be no more wars." Being Lillian Russell, she concluded on a cosmetic note, advising her many followers that as regards zeppelin trips, "the wonderful air should be good for one's complexion." Upon hearing of this, an unkind newspaper in the U.S. replied "Maybe a woman her age would be willing to try anything."[626]

September 21, 1913: Philadelphia — Chee Revealed as Foo's Daughter-In-Law and Married to Foo's Son Yee Dee

This was at least the second time it was clearly revealed in a major media outlet that Chee Toy was, in fact, Foo's daughter-in-law and married to Yee Dee, Foo's son. Chee Toy had been with the Foo troupe since she was only four years old, which would have been the time just before their first American tour.

Yee Dee was described as "a graduate of Columbia College and his father's confidant." Yee Dee "talks most of the time to his petite little wife in English." On tour, Chee Toy "manages the arrangements of her father-in-law's house (he carries his own chef and servants, and in every town he visits, takes a suite of apartments with a kitchen and carries all of his own food), so that she is a busy little body besides being a prima donna."[627] These latest revelations seemed primed to set the stage for a generational succession of the Foo troupe to Foo's son and daughter-in-law.

The Foo troupe was playing Nixon's Grand in Philadelphia, and reviewers noted that his act was and had been "widely copied." The competition over at B.F. Keith's Philadelphia Theater was headliner act "Eddie Foy and the Seven Little Foys", an iconic family vaudeville act.[628]

Excitement Regarding the Upcoming All-Star John Cort Tour Now Christened "Lillian Russell's Big Feature Festival" Continues to Build

"The Lillian Russell All-Star Feature Festival", as the Cort tour had now been christened, was touted as "the most expensive theatrical venture yet financed in America by any individual producer or capitalist." John Cort, the "capitalist" in question, was acclaimed for offering to the American public this "light entertainment" which was "at once refined, humorous, artistic, instantly clever and of the best offered" anywhere in the world.[629,630]

"Lillian Russell All-Star Feature Festival": What the Promoters Have to Say

The description of the main features of the tour provided by the tour's promoters is worth producing in full.

"An Epochal Adventure in the History of the American Stage."

"Lillian Russell—perennial beauty, paragon of health, mistress of song, comedienne, dictator of styles and fashion, and authority in hygiene—heads the bill which Mr. Cort is sending through the United States as the final and supreme effort to give the Anglo-Saxon public of this continent what is best and most beautiful, most inspiriting and most gratifying, and uplifting entertainment. Contrasts serious, magical, grotesque, musical, humorous are furnished with incessant rapidity and with a fine notion of the desire of inured theatergoers. William Farnum, the idol of many seasons of the legitimate drama; Ching Ling Foo, the indescribable and wholly unaccountable magician in feats of magic that begin where Herrmann left off; Ward and Curran, Fields and Lewis, Rose and Arthur Boylan, Margueritte Furrell, Chee Toy, and an assemblage of talented men and women of surpassing physical beauty combine to make this Feature Festival an epochal adventure in the history of the American stage.

"Mr. Cort has equipped, staged, and invested this production in the most elaborate and complete manner that is possible to daring faith in his public and to the purchasing power of money. The production, with its great company of artists, mechanicians, musicians, valets, maids, and supernumeraries, travels in a deluxe train on a special schedule, thus assuring promptness, completeness, and that freshness in physical presentation which characterizes the appearance of Lillian Russell's All-Star Feature Festival, an 'absolute production' in each of the principal cities of the United States and Canada where it will be offered.

"Miss Russell will now show the fashion-loving people of this country the newest, the most ingenious, and the most beautiful examples of the sartorial art of Europe's foremost modistes, milliners, and jewelers. She comes at the head of a great company in which special talent, eccentric modernity, music, laughter, and capital acting are comprised. To this she adds the fine wholesome stimulating message of health, sustained beauty, mirth, merriment, and long life to the women and men of her own country."

The "epochal adventure" was scheduled to begin October 1st at the Harmanus Bleecker Hall in Albany.

September 28, 1913, Philadelphia: "As a Vaudeville Feature for any Kind of Time, Ching Ling Foo and his Company Stands Right out in Front."

Meanwhile, the Foo troupe was successfully completing its last engagement in Philadelphia at the Grand Nixon Theater before the "All-Star" tour began. Chee Toy again seemed most popular. The Foo troupe did "tremendous business" and was held over for a second week at the Nixon. The emerging theater trade bible, *Variety*, declared, "As a vaudeville feature for any kind of time, Ching Ling Foo and his company stands right out in front."[631,632]

Rush Ling Toy Having Fled, the UBO Comes Up with Houan Yuan

In late September 1913, the Rush Ling Toy saga took another turn. Rush's defection from the UBO had left their East Coast theaters without a "Foo"-style Chinese magician. To remedy this problem, UBO reached into its bag and produced one "Houan Yuan", who was now playing Union Square. Initial reviews were not promising. It appeared doing a successful Chinese magic variety act was not as easy as some might have thought.[633]

> While all this was unfolding, Louise W. Hill, a Black woman, lost her discrimination lawsuit against a Rochester vaudeville house that would only provide her seating in a segregated area of its theater.[634]

A Week Before "Lillian Russell's Big Feature Festival" Kicks Off, First Ads, Placed Promotion Begun

Foo was, of course, positioned as one of the top three stars on the bill, but in a surprise, Chee Toy was given a large billing separate from Foo. She was billed as a "Musical Marvel of Four Continents."

"Lillian Russell's Big Feature Festival." An ad for the show, a portrait of Lillian, and a sample of her popular advice column that was published across the U.S.

Accompanying articles emphasized the private luxury trains being provided for the stars for their trans-continental tour. In Albany, where the tour would open, it was put thusly by the Ithaca *Cornell Daily Sun*, "In order to obviate the horrors of the average provincial hotel," all the performers "will live for 25 weeks in a private Pullman train surrounded by every comfort that can be devised and supplied by a solicitous management."[635]

Altoona, Pennsylvania was one of the planned early stops for the tour. In promoting the upcoming engagement, the Altoona *Times* marveled that the Russell festival would, on their "whirlwind tour of the United States", be traveling via eight Pullman cars plus three private luxury ones. "This unique coterie of players is traveling in fashion becoming royalty." The plan was to go to coast while stopping one or two nights in the small towns and playing longer engagements in the cities.[636]

October 1, 1913, Albany: Russell's Big Feature Festival Opens; Free-Rider Rush Ling Toy Sneaks Into Town First

Lillian Russell's Big Feature Festival kicked off in Albany at the Harmanus Bleecker Hall on Monday, October 1st and business was far from booming. The main concern was there were too many competing acts in Albany at the time, and some of the acts competed directly with Cort's offering.

These acts had even been in Albany the previous week, siphoning off potential business for the Cort show before they arrived. In the end, all of the acts at the various theaters suffered. In particular, it seemed the Ching Ling Foo act had been targeted by the decision of the competing Albany Grand Theater to run Rush Ling Toy at the top of their bill, while the papers built up the arrival of Ching Ling Foo the next week. In this manner, the Albany theater positioned itself as a free rider on all the promotion being given the opposing theater's Chinese magician.

October 2, 1913 In Harrisburg, Pennsylvania: Cort Show Boomers Promote Foo as Chinese Royalty, Then "God of Mystery"

The day after Albany, the troupe was in Harrisburg, Pennsylvania. The Harrisburg *Patriot* reveals "Ching is of royal blood and possesses a title equal to that of Mikado." Furthermore, the public was informed Foo "is appearing under an imperial permit issued to John Cort." One wonders if the "imperial" permit was issued by the Mooser Brothers.[637]

Not sure if just seeing plain old royalty would do it for the locals, the Cort publicity machine decided to promote Ching Ling Foo to "god." So we learned from the Wilkes-Barre *Record*, in whose town (at the Grand Opera House) Foo would appear that day, that Foo, apart from breaking vaudeville box office records, was, in his home country, "a noted statesman and philosopher as well as a performer." In fact, the newspaper continued, "in China, India, and Africa he is looked upon as a god of mystery, his wonderful gifts given him by the spirit world." No doubt this went a long way towards explaining why Foo's salary, along with Miss Russell's, were the major elements of the tour's financial package, making it "the most expensive present-day theatre amusement on tour in the United States."[638]

Having Lost Rush Ling Toy, UBO Now Loses Houang Yuen

While Foo was promoted to godhood in Pennsylvania, the Rush Ling Toy story took yet another twist. "Houang Yuen", who was brought into replace Rush in the UBO's Keith's theaters after Rush's defection, was revealed to be Theo Bamberg, a Foo acquaintance captured earlier in a photo along with Houdini visiting Foo in Brighton Beach, who otherwise performed as Okito, the Chinese magician with the Japanese name. To further complicate matters, W.J. Nixon, another magician, emerged and claimed Foo's friend, Theo Bamberg's, act was a "rank copy" of *his* act and that Bamberg was under an agreement stretching back to 1909 "not to appear in Chinese or similar character without my consent." Theo Bamberg, having been revealed as the man behind "Houang Yuen" and threatened with legal action, the Houan Yuen act was no more. UBO was once more without a "Chinese magician" to compete with Foo.[639] In the midst of all this "legal action", no one asked why Foo had not sued everyone.

October 5, 1913: What "Lillian Russell's Big Feature Festival" Looked Like

The show involved more than 50 performers. The first half had various dance and other acts, concluding with William Farnum and company performing scenes from *Virginius*. Early reports said the "mad scenes" excerpted from the play gave the audience "the shivers." Miss Russell opened the second half of the show with "Kinemacolor pictures of her daily pursuits; a lecture on health, and two songs, 'Island of Roses and Dreams,' and 'Come Down, My Evening Star.'" A minor scandal had attached itself to Russell's program before it began, as there was a segment of her act labeled as a depiction of Ms. Russell "disrobing", which temporarily excited the newspapers. However, it was soon addressed. Ms. Russell would simply disrobe from her outer garments to model new ones.

Next came a comedy bit, "Misery of a Hansom Cab", which was much appreciated as, according to reviews, no comedy had been seen in the show yet. The Foo troupe closed the show. *Variety's* assessment was that by adding a bit more comedy in the first half of the act, "Lillian Russell's Big Feature Festival gave promise of being one of the biggest attractions ever put together."

In Fort Wayne, Indiana, a local paper writing on the excitement-generating tour noted that Ching Ling Foo traveled with two Chinese cooks, three women servants, and an interpreter. Chee Toy was described as "a recognized professional beauty" and the only one of Foo troupe that spoke fluent English.[640]

Furthermore, papers in Colorado noted that Foo's private luxury rail car had an "oriental interior," which "is as rich as that of the most aesthetic of millionaires."[641]

Troubles in Tour Land: Russell's Big Feature Festival May Not Have Legs

Bookings and engagements in vaudeville could be pretty fluid, given the preeminence of investing wisely and ensuring your show was a winner and cutting your losses when you found it was not. John Cort, in assessing the cost and performance of his three-star tour which had barely begun its tour, had already decided to do some tinkering.

The company was doing a series of one-nighters, moving quickly through a lot of small cities and large towns. The results had not been encouraging. The stop in Schenectady proved their greatest success, and that only brought in $1,000 from both shows. Harrisburg's total for two shows was only a $500 gross. To address these issues, Cort had directed the tour to do more one-nighters, and consideration was being given to the Foo troupe being taken off the bill to reduce costs.

This latter option had caused some discussion in theater circles, as the Foo troupe portion of the act was generally acknowledged to be probably a better act to serve as the top of the bill if the goal was drawing big crowds. The reported problem with this promotion strategy was that the current top of the bill, noted diva Lillian Russell, had a non-cancellation clause in her contract and she would not appear on a bill where she was not at the top.[642]

As far as Ching Ling Foo went, it was acknowledged, if he was carved off the tour many managers would be eager to speak with the Moosers about engaging him.

Chee Toy as the Tour's Merrymaking "Mysterious Peacemaker"

The tour's advance men, perhaps sensing some unease among the cast, positioned Chee Toy in news releases as the "life and soul of the big company" and "a mysterious peacemaker as well as a merrymaker." If it was Lillian Russell they were attempting to placate, they misstepped when they added "Little Miss Chee Toy and her noble father travel in a special private Pullman car even more gorgeous than the private car of Lillian Russell herself."

The full description of Chee Toy provided in the Zanesville *Times Recorder* is produced in full below.

"Miss Chee Toy, the little Chinese maiden of Lillian Russell's company—one of John Cort's big theatric attractions at the Schultz opera house matinee and night today—is the mascot of the organization she is so happily associated with. The audience enthuse over her art and beauty, and her fellow players appreciate those attributes too, but their great joy over Chee Toy is their genuine love of the little woman's wonderful good nature, tenderness and merrymaking. She is the very life and soul of the big company, and every member adores her. Everybody and everything are sources of pleasant wonder to her on tour and during the working hours behind the scenes, and her life at all times is that of a happy bird. She is a mysterious peacemaker as well as a merrymaker, and no matter what the quarrel may be or between whom it may be raging, her mere appearance on the scene of the argument is the signal for the restoration of peace and quiet. Chee Toy always speaks of the gods and is as gentle and beautiful as the tenderest mortals can picture. So much of her social side. As a professional, she is equally charming. She plays angelic melodies on the piano, sings with a heavenly voice, and her general stage presence evolves a personal magnetism that softens and soothes every heart in the audience."[643]

October 12, 2013: San Antonio—Big Feature Festival Tour Tensions & Troubles Escalate

Tensions seemed to be building as, by the time the tour reached San Antonio, Texas. Lillian Russell—who technically was supposed to be headlining John Cort's Feature Festival—was reported by one mean-spirited scribbler to be "decidedly annoyed" that "all along the line the newspaper critics boldly and unfeelingly announce that 'Ching Ling Foo is the star of the Lillian Russell Festival,' now on tour."[644,645]

John Cort's worries over the performance of the tour were no doubt exacerbated by the fact it was indeed "the most financially extravagant theatre amusement on tour the present season ... the single salary of any one of the three main features of the attraction—Lillian Russell, William Farnum and Ching Ling Foo—actually equaling the cost of an ordinary first-class dramatic company." The show was scheduled to arrive in Sandusky, Ohio the next day, October 14th.[646]

NOT ALL ROSY FOR ROAD SHOWS; TWO OF THEM MEETING BAD LUCK

Jealousy Among Stars Is Said to Affect Two of the Four Troupes.

The multi-star touring vehicles Cort and Mooser had devised were a new phenomenon and considered the "chief novelty of the season." Four troupes featuring multiple stars were on the road as of October. Unfortunately for Cort, the Lillian Russell Feature Festival was one of two of these tours having difficulties. Internal dissensions were blamed in both cases for difficulties with the two wayward shows.

Echoing earlier rumors and adding to the fire, syndicated theater columnist Jan Drummond reported "that Ching Ling Foo, the Chinese wonderworker, is proving more popular than the star herself, in the Lillian Russell show is given as the reason why the troupe has not been going well."

The other multi-star tour in trouble was the Polaire-Hoffman-Richardson conglomeration, which was reportedly suffering from a "three-cornered strife" among the three women headlined. Drummond noted, "What particular grievances Gertrude and the Lady Constance are cherishing has not been made known, but Madame Polaire has come to the conclusion that she is the only dyed-in-the-wool artiste in the company."[647]

A Contrarian View on Foo

In a review published in their "On the Stage" column, the Harrisburg *Patriot* joined the minority that felt Foo's skills as a conjurer did not exceed those displayed by American-born illusionists. The reviewer noted "I have known a number of abler practitioners of the black art" and lists the original Herrmann and Kellar among them. Regardless, once more, Foo was the standard by which all other magicians were now measured, and one suspects this latest review, after Foo had already left town, was intended to promote another magician's act.[648]

Lilian Russell Explains How to Live Until 100

After the beating Miss Russell had been taking in the press during her current tour, the kind words of Indiana's New Castle *Morning Star* regarding her performance in their fine town must have been a balm. "Miss Russell is still of youthful appearance and seems destined to dazzle the theatergoer for some time to come." She sang a few songs.

She also gave a lecture on how to live to 100. Her films showed her beauty regime, including exercise. She was well received.[649]

The Lillian Russell Feature Festival Meets a Premature End

The earlier rumblings proved prescient. Less than three weeks into John Cort's "big gamble", "the most financially extravagant theatre amusement on tour for the present season" came to an end. As per earlier rumblings, Russell's tour would continue, but without the Foo troupe. The Russell tour would be criticized after Foo left of short-changing audiences, since the whole Foo act was only replaced by the single act of Bert Melrose.[650]

LILLIAN RUSSELL, PRESIDENTIAL IMMIGRATION POLICY CONSULTANT

Lillian Russell, who had spent a lifetime advocating for woman's suffrage, in 1922 undertook a fact-finding tour for President Warren Harding to Europe to report on issues surrounding increased immigration into the U.S. Russell's report, which argued for restricting immigration of southern and eastern Europeans and banning immigration of Asians, had a large impact on the crafting of the Immigration Act of 1924. She would die due to complications from injuries incurred while travelling back from Europe in 1922. There is no record of what, if any, impact touring with the Foo troupe had with her positions on immigration.

CHAPTER SIXTEEN

NOVEMBER 1913–JANUARY 1914— ANOTHER TOUR, ANOTHER DIVA; FOO TOURS WITH AVANT-GARDE ENTERTAINER GERTRUDE HOFFMAN, "THE WOMAN WHO DARES"

A New Touring Team: Dancing Star Gertrude Hoffman, Fleeing "Petty Jealousies and Enlarged Temperaments", Joins with Foo to Begin Anew

The Foo troupe settled on their next gig quickly. As of the 3rd of November, Ching Ling Foo would be paired with Gertrude Hoffman, the avant-garde dancer and variety show star, for a tour that would begin in the Southern United States. Hoffman and Foo would give the whole show, George Mooser had taken a share of the Hoffman-Ching troupe, and Leon Mooser managed the troupe. Hoffman's show ran about an hour.[651]

Miss Hoffman, who would be joining Foo on tour, had been one of three female stars on another three-star tour that had recently broken down. According to its management, the breakdown was due to "petty jealousies and the enlarged temperaments" of its three stars. The "exhausted" organizer, Morris Guest, claimed no stage "was large enough for these three divas to be on it in a single evening." The three tour stars—Hoffman; Mademoiselle Polaire, the French actress "who prides herself on being the ugliest woman on stage"; and Lady Constance Richardson, the "titled English classic dancer"—could not get along "on the billboards, the special train, or in the theaters."[652,653]

The three-star tour did quite well at the box office, but while the tour packed the houses, it made little money because of the cost of the three stars; thus, there was little motivation to try and keep the tour together in the face of mounting interpersonal strife.

Around the same time the three divas tour was unraveling, keen-eyed theater types observed Lillian Russell's increasing discomfort regarding touring with Foo. The Chinese magician was increasingly being acknowledged as the star and most popular part of the act. In the words of one critic, "Audiences forgot about Miss Russell, her marvelously retained beauty and acting. They couldn't see anything but the wonderful tricks of the wizard of the Orient and his wonderworkers."

Inevitably, Russell complained to Cort, and Cort, who had limited room to maneuver given the nature of Russell's contract, addressed the situation by allowing Foo to shift to the Hoffman tour.[654]

Foo Joins Gertrude Hoffman in Delaware: "Beautiful Vivacious Brunettes, Stunning Statuesque Blondes, and Inspiring Titian-Haired Beauties"

The ads for the Hoffman Foo show promised "Beautiful Vivacious Brunettes, Stunning Statuesque Blondes, and Inspiring Titian-Haired Beauties", all of whom were selected in an open competition by Miss Hoffman and "12 famous American artists", none of whom were named. Hoffman proclaimed she went about choosing chorus girls with "no experience" and "real youth" in New York before touring, as these beauties needed "no artificial aids."[655]

The Hoffman act required four special baggage cars to carry all the scenery and backdrop setups used in the 12 different scenes of her performance. Some of the act's more noteworthy scenes included "an express station in a New York subway, the tent of Sheik Shariar in the desert, Mme. Cavalieri's beauty parlor, a true Leon Baskts interior, the exterior of the Moulin Rouge in Paris, a Japanese Garden, the exterior of a Scotch cottage, a pavilion of Trouville, and many others." Not for nothing was Miss Hoffman referred to as "the world's most original dancer." During the progress of the revue, "Miss Hoffman gives impersonations of Eddie Foy, George M. Cohan, Anna Held, Harry Lauder, Eva Tanguay, Ethel Barrymore, Isadora Duncan, Mme. Ida Rubinstein, and a dozen other famous players."[656] Her entire performance was staged by Miss Hoffman herself and included "all the latest dance crazes." Promoters of the tour claimed Foo would appear in no other company this season.[657]

Hoffman toured in her luxury private railway car "The Mayflower", which was reputed to be the most beautiful and luxurious private rail

"Vivacious Brunettes, Statuesque Blondes, Titian-Haired Beauties ..."

car in the world. The train was touted as an attraction worth seeing even in and of itself. In fact, Miss Hoffman's private car was formerly used by "presidents of the United States when making trips and is more sumptuous than any other private car ever built."[658] The advance men claimed the new Hoffman Foo tour, which would be on the road for about two months, was the only tour that required three official interpreters. Chinese, French, and Arabic were the languages reportedly required to manage the show. Many of Hoffman's performers were French or Russian. The Arabs in the show were mainly from Morocco and acted as acrobats and dancers.[659]

While sharing top billing with Hoffman and presented as a headliner, Ching Ling Foo was listed second on the bill. Before Foo joined Hoffman, another act was added to the tour: Leo Nino, a 'trick' violinist.[660]

Hoffman-Foo Tour Kicks Off in Wilmington, Delaware and Way Through the South

The Hoffman-Foo show kicked off in Wilmington, Delaware. Once again, the local media did not care about the agreed order of the billing. It was the Foo troupe that generated the most interest and remained on the top of the media's bill as far as coverage and excitement was concerned.

A major piece in the Wilmington *News Journal* featured a large picture of the Foo troupe and a headline that read "Ching Ling Foo, Great Chinese Illusionist, and Company of 14 Orientals, with Gertrude Hoffman's Big Revue at the Playhouse Next Monday Night."

The Hoffman-Foo tour brought in approximately $2,000 at the box office for one show in Delaware before moving on.[661–663]

November 6, 1913, Charlotte, North Carolina: Talk of Foo's Retirement

In the latest promotions, Foo was described as almost 70 years old. Reportedly, he would retire after this tour and return to China to manage his many business ventures. "Since he first came to this country he has had many imitators, but none have quite been able to do his tricks." The lineup for Foo's illusions had not changed. Favorite tricks of the Southern audiences served in this tour included Foo's standard production tricks and his finale, wherein he "starts a somersault empty handed and winds it up with a glass vessel of water brimming with goldfish."664

Foo Was a Mandarin Who Avoided Being Beheaded in the New Chinese Republic By Purchasing His Liberty for $200,000

Foo was once more reported to have a chain of movie theaters in China. The North Carolina public was informed Foo was a mandarin, and that the title of mandarin ranked with the English "Sir." In addition, keeping an eye on the news, the advance men managed by the Moosers added, somewhat ill-informedly, that since China became a "Republic", most of the mandarins had been beheaded. They informed the readers that Foo only survived by buying his liberty for $200,000. Wisely, Foo said he would return to China when things were more settled to take care of his many businesses. It was noted Foo and his company were here under bond to leave the country at the expiration of a certain time, and thus their stay in America was limited.665

November 20, 1913, Hot Springs, Arkansas: Chee Toy, After Tour, Will Study in Paris

In November 1913 in Arkansas, Chee Toy was described as "dainty as a piece of fine porcelain and undoubtedly the prettiest girl that ever came from China." Similar to the plans set out for her by Hammerstein when she first arrived at the start of this second tour, Chee Toy informed her fans that once she finished her American tour, she was going to Paris to study and hoped someday to "establish opera of the Occidental sort in China."666

The Jefferson Theater had a seating capacity of around 1,500.

November 21, 1913, Birmingham, Alabama

The troupe played the Jefferson Theater in Birmingham, Alabama on November 21, 1913.[667] The Jefferson was typical of the types of theaters the Hoffman-Foo tour played in travels across the U.S. The Jefferson had a combined seating capacity of almost 1,500 seats, including 600 on the lower floor, 400 in the balcony, 400 in the gallery, and 32 in boxes.

November 23, 1913, Lexington, Kentucky: Foo on the Difference Between Western and Chinese Magic— "No One Can Buy My Fingers"—and His Theatrical Aspirations

After a one-night stop in Knoxville, Tennessee on November 22nd, the Foo troupe was at the Ben Ali Theater in Lexington, Kentucky. While being interviewed to promote the tour's engagement at the Ben Ali, Foo discussed the difference between most Western and Chinese magic. Foo claimed the Chinese magician was just happy to work with this hands and fingers, while the Western magician tended to like complicated apparatus, trap doors, and things. Foo concluded his discussion by claiming "you can buy any trick of the European in the store but no one can buy my fingers."

As far as his career as a magician began, he repeated the tale of the bedridden boy who amused himself with dry dates and found a career. He also mentioned his early years as a much sought-after "sand diviner", the accumulation of his first fortune, and his years spent as a traveling magician crisscrossing Asia.[668]

Foo Reveals His Theatrical Aspirations: "A True Chinese Play After Modern Methods in His Own Country"

While in Kentucky, Foo also once more expanded upon his theatrical ambitions with the press and claimed that he only decided to tour America in the first instance in 1898 so that he could "study firsthand American methods of play producing in order to apply them to the theaters that he owns in China." His current goal was to produce "a true Chinese play after the modern methods in his own country." Foo's newfound focus on this subject may well be an element introduced by the Moosers to promote their next project. Foo and the Moosers had long planned a Chinese play in the American style, with Foo as the lead.[669]

In a sign of Chee Toy's growing popularity, some advertisements for the November 25th, 1913 show in Lexington, Kentucky promoted Chee Toy, "The Charming Little Oriental Comedian", not only as a separate act, but with her name actually in larger type than that of Foo.

"Miss Chee Toy" is given separate billing.

November 25, 1913, Evansville, Indiana: Well's Bijou Guarantees "The Most Daring Costumes Ever Seen on Any Stage"

The Hoffman tour was quite the whistle stop tour and it ran through a remarkable array of smaller cities and towns. After November 26th, 1913, they stopped long enough to do an afternoon and evening show at Well's Bijou in Evansville, Indiana. The show's boomers guaranteed "the most daring costumes ever seen on any stage." Clearly, they were not referring to the Foo troupe.

November 27, 1913, Hot Springs, Arkansas: Audience Likes Foo Strongman, Learns it Runs in the Family

In Arkansas, some rare attention was conferred on Foo troupe Chinese "strongman" Soo Foh Sung, who did his performances on the Chinese horizontal bar. We learn Soo's great-great-grandfather was a strong man, and his great-grandfather was a strongman, and his grandfather and his father before him. The family's great-great-grandfather switched to acrobatics when he learned that was where his skills lay instead of acting, and happily, there was more money in it than being an actor. He did not train but merely practiced new tricks every morning, ate sparingly of chicken and rice, and meditated. Not surprisingly, Soo was training his sons to follow the family tradition.[670–672]

The Arkansas press also marveled over the capacity of Chee Toy to sing with no "discernible" accent. "Miss Chee Toy, who has a pleasing voice, sings American ragtime and other songs in English; and wonder of wonders for a native Chinese, no pidgin English or acent is discernible."[673]

> While Foo "wildcatted" through the South with Hoffman, more competitors emerged. At New York's Palace Theater, Bryant Cheebert's Manchurian Troupe of Acrobats were appearing mid-November. The group did a lot of

> acrobatics, but the eye-catcher in the performance was when two of the performers were lifted into the flies via a pulley attached to their queues as a third performer performed acrobatics by swinging from them. This was seen as the most interesting part of the act. The rest was standard acrobatics but, according to critics, the Chinese nature of the performers meant that it would attract some interest.[674]

December 2, 1913: Baton Rouge, Louisiana—Foo Troupe's Eating Habits on the Road Attract Attention

Before the troupe arrived in Baton Rouge, Louisiana, details were shared with the local media regarding the Chinese troupe's eating habits while on the road. It was disclosed that Lung Ng Yung of Foo's troupe not only did acrobatics hanging from the strap, he also was responsible for a good deal of meal preparation for the Chinese performers. Lung's culinary skills were apparently much appreciated, and despite having two official cooks with the tour, he took over the Pullman kitchen car and made meals for the Chinese at least once a day. Sometimes when they dined at a hotel, he worked from the hotel's kitchen. It was acknowledged, however, that the Chinese do eat and like "American" food. But they prefer their own and "need it at least once a day."[675]

December 8, 1919, Baton Rouge: As Tour Triumphs Throughout the South, Once Again, Media Chafes Against Foo Troupe's Second Billing

The problems that derailed the Foo troupe while touring with the fair Lillian recurred as reviewers in Baton Rouge declared it should be Foo and his troupe that receive top billing given that it was the "marvelous" Foo "and not Miss Hoffman" who delighted the large standing room capacity crowd at the Baton Rouge's Elk's Theatre. According to the Baton Rouge critic, Miss Hoffman "was a disappointment" and "did not come up to what the advance notices had led everyone to expect."[676]

December 5, 1913, Greenville, Missouri: Hoffman Gets More Appreciation

Hoffman got more appreciation in Greenville, where the local papers described her as "graceful", "lithe in form", and supported by both elaborate scenery and "a number of attractive girls who skipped over the stage in diaphanous gowns."[677]

December 7, 1913, Galveston, Texas: Arabian Ballet Scene "with Real Arabs as Dancers" Captures Audience's Imagination

The show passed through Galveston on December 7th and Hoffman's Arabian ballet scene, "with real Arabs as dancers", captured the local public's imagination. The tired bit about the Chinese cast names sounding like something you would order in a Chinese restaurant was repeated.[678]

December 8, 1913, New Orleans, Louisiana: Chinese Meal for Press to Be Had in Hoffman's Private Car

As part of the promotion for their New Orleans engagement, Foo was overseeing another promotional Chinese dinner for the top newspapermen and theater critics of New Orleans, to be held in Gertrude Hoffman's private railway car, "the Mayflower." The meal began at the stroke of midnight. Foo promised "rare dishes for uninitiated palates."[679]

December 15, 1913, San Antonio, Texas: Foo's Charisma and Presentation Skills Receive Warm Welcome in Texas; Hoffman Explains Why She Doesn't Give Interviews

Foo's charisma worked its magic in Texas. The Chinese conjurer was described as "a very large man with a quiet humorous way of going about his work that catches the fancy of audiences at once."680 Hoffman's act was promoted as having "twenty-five of the prettiest girls you could find in New York."

While in Texas, Hoffman explained why she had never provided any interviews to the press. She said she has never been interviewed because she just wants to dance and entertain. In Texas, she responded to interview requests with a simple statement.

"What does it matter what I think about suffrage or the hobble skirt if I can please the people by dancing or give them amusement by my efforts at impersonation? Shouldn't that be enough?"681

The Hoffman tour arrived in Texas just in time for the Great Flood of 1913, resulting from heavy rains causing rivers to overflow their banks and devastating the region. Disruptions caused "by water over main line" resulted in the cancellation of their first show in San Antonio.682

December 1913, 12 Waco, Texas

The show in Waco went forward on schedule and local reviewers once more found Foo had "a quiet humorous way" of going about his work that the audience loved.683

December 20, 1913, Fort Worth, Texas: "Motion, Motion, Motion; from the Start to Finish the Revue is a Whirl"

December 20th, 1913, the Hoffman and Foo tour hit Fort Worth, Texas, and Fort Worth *Star Telegram* critic Gordon K. Shearer could not have been happier. "It is a thing of dazzling lights, giddiness, and noise that catches you in a whirl like an old grad, gathered in by a crowd of celebrating students." He described the show, which "follows no accepted rules" as "more than original" and "almost weird."

The Fort Worth performance time seemed evenly split between Hoffman and Foo. Hoffman's portrait of the famous dancer Isadora Duncan in "Blue Danube" and a New York subway sequence were, according to Shearer, her best. Hoffman's act also included portrayals of Anna Held, Bessie McCoy, a burlesque beauty parlor sequence, a mermaid sequence entitled "Swim with Me", and a "Geisha Girl" scene.

As for Foo, Shearer's effusive praise found Foo's "wonderworkers" displayed skills that "will make even a two-dollar" audience keep up "a thunderous applause swelling into a greater volume with each new lightening feat."

Chee Toy wore "diamonds galore", while Foo's "inexplicable" act "outdoes the feats that made Herrmann and Keller famous, and the oriental mysticism added to them enhances the effect."

Other featured performers included Leo Nino, a talented violinist whose act, according to Shearer, was "as novel as the rest of the show." Nino "literally makes his violin talk, and ends by imitating a cow and a calf on a loosened D string."[684]

A bedazzled Shearer concluded, "Motion, motion, motion; from the start to finish, the revue is a whirl. One moment its tumblers are tossing about the stage like they were spun by a cyclone, next a classic dance of flashing limbs and draperies, then oriental writhing, tango, trotting, and dip. A burlesque one moment, a classic the next, and part of the time a circus, the revue refuses to be put in any classification. How an orchestra can help a show is ably demonstrated."[685]

December 20, 1913, Tulsa, Oklahoma: Hoffman "Stencils on" Her Stockings

Hoffman and the Foo troupe were in Tulsa, Oklahoma performing at the Grand Theater on December 24th. A report from the

Tulsa *Morning Daily* revealed that Miss Hoffman "stencils" on her attention-grabbing and much-remarked-upon stockings that were featured in her publicity photos before each performance, with the assistance of an aide who works with "a saucer of black watercolor and gets out the brush and cut stencils."[686]

December 21, 1913, Oklahoma City, Oklahoma

It's noteworthy that just three days before the Hoffman-Foo show arrived in town, "the Lillian Russell Feature Festival" had passed through Oklahoma City.

December 25 Kansas City, Kansas

Christmas Day, 1913, the Hoffman and Foo tour did a special show at Convention Hall in Kansas City, Kansas.[687]

"Company of 100—Mostly Girls."

December 30, 1913, Indianapolis, Indiana: "A Whole Lot Better Than Most of the Things We Have Been Forced to Put Up with This Season"

In Indianapolis, of the Hoffman show, it was written, "The girls were pretty too, and if they didn't catch cold It is because of the superior heating facilities of the Murat and not through any assistance rendered by the costumer."[688]

Care was taken to describe Miss Hoffman taking the stage for an Arab kidnap scene amidst "a clashing of cymbals and the blaring of brass", after which "she writhed and twisted and gyrated until the young man, supposedly her captor, went into an ecstasy." Then, after "a bit of Arab acrobatics", Hoffman was quickly back on stage doing her imitations, including Isadora Duncan. This was followed by Hoffman's "Blue Danube" ballet. Overall, the reviewer was quite positive, praising Hoffman's revue as "a whole lot better than most of the things we have been forced to put up with this season." So spoke Indianapolis.

At this point in the tour, the Foo troupe apparently did the first half of the show. Chee Toy and Foo, of course, were huge hits. The first act in the revue was Leo Nino, the trick violinist. Nino opened the bill just before Foo came out.

January 1, 1914, Columbus, Ohio

"America's most versatile artist," Gertrude Hoffman, and the Foo troupe appeared at the Southern Theatre in Columbus, Ohio. Two new dances, "Zobeides' Dream" and "Blue Danube", were introduced.[689]

LONG TACK SAM

In January 1914, more competing Chinese entertainment troupes and magicians continued to emerge. Even Foo's own manager, George Mooser, was now representing the "Pekinese Troupe", which was apparently owned by Long Tack Sam.[690]

Long Tack Sam would have a very long and successful career in stage magic, with an act that was very similar to Foo's act. At one point, he even had a small Chinese girl, obviously inspired by Chee Toy, who sang English songs in his troupe. Sam and/or his promoters even mirrored the vaudeville lore story of James Thornton's alleged 1899 onstage confrontation with Foo, dealt with towards the end of Chapter 5 of this book. In Sam's telling, the on-stage insult denigrating the magician as a mere "laundryman" was riposted by the pugnacious Sam with "an upper-cut" and the offending Fitzgibbon being carried off the stage to "roars" of approval.[691] It seems back in vaudeville's heyday if you saw a good story you tweaked it a bit and put yourself in the middle of it. Long Tack Sam would emerge as one of handful of accomplished Chinese magicians with the potential to rival Foo's success.[692] Years later, speaking of his "struggles and triumphs as a magician", Long Tack Sam would say he worked for Foo as a boy and when he asked for a raise Foo fired him and said he would be a bum.[693-695]

Long Tack Sam Ads: "Greater Than Ching Ling Foo";[696] "Bigger and more pretentious than ever before!" (1955, *Variety* Long Tack Sam poster. Long Tack Sam took out a full page in *Variety* to promote himself as "The Master Showman Who Out-Chings Ching Ling Foo."

January 11, 1914, Pittsburgh, Pennsylvania: "Ching Ling Foo is a Philosopher ... Like All His Countrymen is Exceedingly Secretive"

Under the headline "Ching Ling Foo Is a Philosopher", it is noted that Foo, who was playing at the Alvin Theater in Pittsburgh, had "a singular personality and, like all his countrymen, is exceedingly secretive." He is also "very devout ... saying prayers and burning incense at regular intervals." According to this piece, which was likely sourced from one of the Moosers or their advance men, "Last of all in the social scale in China are the actors. Beggars come before them, then barbers, and last actors."

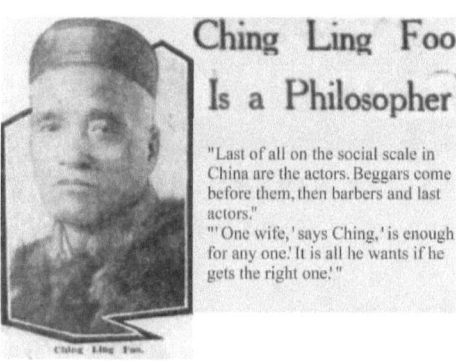

"Ching Ling Foo is a philosopher."

Foo apparently also had thoughts on the modern American woman, who he greatly admired in this telling. "The American women are pretty: pretty nice, pretty polite and pretty funny." He further supposedly added "women who run about a great deal learn something." Finally, he opined, "when a woman has her head set on something, it is no use for a man to oppose her … one wife,' says Ching, 'is enough for anyone.' It is all he wants if he gets the right one.'"[697]

January 18, 1914, Cleveland, Ohio: "Frolicsome and Fascinating"

The Hoffman-Foo tour hit the Cleveland Colonial Theater the weekend of January 26th and was advertised as "positively the most expensive organization on tour." Hoffman's revue was described as consisting of "100 mostly frolicsome and fascinating girls." The revue followed a one-week engagement at the Colonial of *The Whip*, the "World's Best Melodrama."[698]

January 19, 1914, Buffalo, New York: Foo Has a "Quiet Humorous Way of Going About his Work That Catches the Fancy of his Audience at Once"

The Hoffman and Foo revue appeared in Buffalo, New York at the Teck Theater. The Buffalo *Evening News* struck a now-familiar note about Foo, describing him as "a very large man with a quiet humorous way of going about his work that catches the fancy of his audience at once" and "stands alone in his class of magical work." They also rightly observed that "since he first came to this country, he has many imitators" but "none" provided a performance quite like Foo's—and his troupe was composed of "artists almost as wonderful as he." The paper went on to remind the readers that Foo was getting older and this would likely be his last tour, as he was "anxious to settle down and look after his affairs in China." Foo's trick, where he pulled handfuls of dry flour out of a bowl filled with water, was given particular attention. Overall, the Buffalo reviewers found Hoffman's act ranged from "fair" to "good", while the Foo troupe act was consistently "wonderful" and "kept the spectators interested every minute the curtain was up." The Hoffman-Foo revue would be in Buffalo for five nights.[699,700]

January 25, 1914: Foo Leaving Hoffman Tour

Announcements appeared indicating Foo would be leaving the Hoffman tour at the beginning of February and touring on his own. The Foo troupe was scheduled to appear at the Shubert Theater in Rochester in early February.[701]

Variety reported from Cleveland that this would be the last week of the Hoffman show and the Foo troupe would soon be taking up offers from vaudeville. As for Ms. Hoffman, she was under contract to Comstock & Gest, and they had not renewed her contract. The combined Hoffman-Foo bill apparently made good money while moving through the South in one-night shows, but profitability fell when the tour hit the large cities and engagements lasting a week. Leon Mooser, who was directing the show, had already left, and another manager closer to Miss Hoffman had been put in charge. She, too, would be moving to vaudeville engagements.[702]

In early February, news began to come out that the "temperamental" Ms. Hoffman's clashes with tour management, likely including Mooser, led to the cancellation of the Hoffman tour.[703,704]

January 27, 1914: Even in Last Week of Tour, Foo Continues to Attract More Attention Than Hoffman

The Hoffman-Foo ensemble played its last week at the Cleveland Colonial Theater. As was the case with the Lillian Russell tour, the Foo troupe always seemed to attract the most attention.

Yet Another Take on How Foo Became a Magician: An Early Pleasure Trip to the U.S. Inspired Him

This Cleveland *Plain-Dealer* sifted through the details of "wise old owl" Foo's early career as a sand diviner, capable of reading, past, present, and future. The newspaper, in a new take on Foo's early development, reported his kit for this career included "a board and a bag of sand." They reported that Foo became a tremendous success at sand divining and earned large sums, and he had clients among the most famous Chinese. According to this version of events, later, while on a pleasure trip through the U.S., he noted that magicians led good lives and decided to follow their example.[705]

Chee Toy, in Cleveland, Relates the Story of How Bound Feet Began

In late January, Chee Toy was featured in an interview with a paper in Cleveland, wherein she related the tale of how the now-banned practice of foot binding came to be in China. Chee Toy explained, in the tragic story, that the process was originated by an emperor who sought to render a prized but stubborn wife unable to flee. Her feet were then bound, and her hobbled walk was said to resemble the swaying of lotus and lily flowers swaying in the wind, so it became known as the "lily-walk." The practice soon spread throughout China.[706]

"Little Miss Chee Toy, the 'Chinese Prima Donna' with Ching Ling Foo and company, who are featured in Gertrude Hoffman's show at the Colonial Theater this week, told a pretty little story last night (through an interpreter) concerning the bound feet of the women of China ...' There is poetry even in this legend,' she said, 'for all poetry has some pain in it, it seems to me. Seven hundred years ago, Chao Whang was the august ruler of the Chinese. He had a beautiful little wife, who was perfect in his eyes, excepting she had what you call wanderlust. The emperor's wife would slip away from the grounds of the palace and cause him much pain and sadness. He sent for his wise men and asked them for some means of curing this roving disposition, and as they could suggest nothing, he ordered her feet bound. Near his palace window was a pond on which were pond lilies and lotus flowers, and when he first saw her hobbling along, he said that he was reminded of the swaying of these flowers in the wind.'

'It was new beauty in his eyes, and he even called it the lily-walk. And even in those far-off times, people were just as much interested in fashions as they are today, and the court was supposed to establish the newest fads. So quickly, without an imperial edict, aspiring mothers ordered the feet of their daughters bound so they would be more beautiful in the sight of men. Such things change very slowly, and even today, the lily-walk is considered the most graceful for the Chinese lady.'"[707] The Foos would also note that despite this romanticized history, foot binding in "modern" China was now a capital offense.

CHAPTER SEVENTEEN

JANUARY 1914–OCTOBER 1914— MORE CONTRACTUAL TROUBLES AND DIFFICULT BOOKINGS FORCE FOO TO EUROPE, AND UNKNOWINGLY, STRAIGHT INTO WORLD WAR I

In February 1914, Foo and Hoffman Split: Foo Troupe Plays Rochester, New York

Now no longer touring with Hoffman, the Foo troupe, still navigating UBO efforts to freeze them out of related theaters, are as per the Mooser Brothers' plan, playing smaller vaudeville markets for the same big-time salary. Foo and his troupe played the Schubert Theater in Rochester the week of February 2nd, 1914.[708,709]

In Rochester, the Foo troupe was described as the "biggest attraction in present day vaudeville", and Foo "the world's greatest magician ... his company comprises fifteen Chinese performers—men women, boys and girls, and their feats in magic, plate spinning, singing, dancing, acrobatic and Risley work is said to be a whole show in itself." As far as audience appreciation went, Chee Toy was as popular

"An International Question of Great Moment." Also playing in Rochester in February at the "morally perfect" Temple Theatre was Nina Morris in "The Most Sensational Dramatic Playlet Ever Produced on Any Stage", *The Yellow Peril*. "An International Question of Great Moment."

as Foo and ranked with him in applause. (A Risley act is one where the performer lies on his back and balances something like a chair with their feet.)[710]

Foo, "Yellow Peril" or no, was, according to industry experts, still bringing in the crowds and thus demonstrating he was worth his salary, and conversely, that small time vaudeville could afford to engage big time headliners. Chee Toy's profile continued to grow, and her popularity was noted as rivaling that of Foo.[711]

Yee Dee Plays His Father's Comic Assistant

The public got some additional insight into the role Yee Dee played in the act as Foo's comic assistant when the troupe played Rochester. Yee Dee was reportedly presented to the audience as a "puzzled young Chinese" standing at Foo's elbow, earnestly endeavoring to discover how Foo did his tricks. He exaggeratedly and comically peered around the cloth and behind Foo to see what he could find without success. Foo, meanwhile, shook the cloth to show nothing was behind it as he good-naturedly indulged the curious youth. Foo's last production in the act was a small Chinese boy.

For the reviewers, Chee Toy, who as we have learned was Yee Dee's wife, remained Foo's most interesting associate. She swayed gracefully as she sang and, depending on which city the review was coming from, she did so without any, or with only the slightest, "oriental accent." There was a small child doing gymnastics and the young contortionist who did the ever-popular act with the fake dummy head between his legs—as always, a favorite. A young Chinese boy and girl also danced the tango.[712]

Chee Toy's enduring popularity with women and children led to the creation of an afternoon "special" wherein women and children would have an opportunity to meet Chee Toy on stage, accompanied by "the clever Chinese children" performing with the troupe. Attendees would receive a free souvenir photo of Chee Toy. The troupe was performing twice a day in Rochester at both 2:15 in the afternoon and 8:15 in the evening.[713]

February 20, 1914: Back in New York; Film Continues to Encroach on Live Performance

The Foo troupe was back in New York by mid-February. They would be at New York's Hamilton Theater for a week starting February 17th. The theater lobby was wrapped in Chinese regalia, including streamers and flags, to promote the upcoming engagement. Incense was also burning in the lobby.

Demonstrating the evolving nature of the entertainment business, the Foo troupe would be sharing the bill at the Hamilton with "two film features" and no other live acts. Theater managers were slowly coming to the conclusion that films, not vaudeville, appeared to be the way of the future. Foo clearly saw the writing on the wall when he invested in his own chain of movie theaters in China.[714]

The encroachment of film into the live performance space was a phenomenon stretching over many lower-priced vaudeville theaters across the country. Many of these theaters were turning towards a focus on showing feature films at their houses at the cost of engaging live vaudeville acts. Pricing was apparently the only thing that was keeping vaudeville in the game. The distribution system for feature films was still quite fragmented, and film distribution companies were being accused of price-gouging while the gouging is good. They were reportedly asking $500 to $700 a week for showing a film, and small-time theater managers were saying this was too high.[715]

March–April 1914: More UBO, Foo, Mooser Mix-Ups and Contretemps

CHING PLAYING FOR U.B.O.

In March 1914, another possible thaw in the Foo troupe-versus-UBO standoff appeared to be in the offing when Albee made yet another offer to the Foo troupe. Negotiations were undertaken to see if Foo could be engaged to play the UBO-related Poli Theater circuit after being engaged through the UBO. Speculation was that the deal was set up to end a lawsuit Foo and Mooser had against Klaw and Erlanger, who had Foo under contract. If Foo did do a deal with UBO as a quid pro quo, the Moosers would have to withdraw the lawsuit against Klaw and Erlanger.

This all occurred as the Foo troupe were taking a few "rest" weeks in New York and George Mooser was considering offers to play 20 weeks in London and England on the Oswald Stoll circuit.[716]

Most importantly, Albee and the UBO were making this offer at a time they knew the Foo troupe's contract with the Mooser Brothers had expired.[717] Clearly, Albee and the UBO would like to have separated the Foo troupe from the Mooser Brothers' pugnacious management style. By the end of March the negotiations were complete the England tour was put on hold, and the Foo troupe is booked to appear in Keith's houses and other theaters associated with the UBO.

About this time, the respected British industry journal *The Stage*, through their American correspondent, took a direct shot at the UBO for their treatment of the Foo troupe in reporting news of this grudging reconciliation. "It seems a pity that this well-known act has been 'wildcatting' around the country playing here there and everywhere", and dealing with all kinds of "hard sledding", simply because it "got in bad" with the UBO quasi-monopoly.[718]

Clearly, most of the entertainment world had been pulling for Foo in his struggle with the UBO, and recognized the great lengths the extremely popular act had to go to be able to perform before the crowds that so much wanted to see them.

March 23, 1914, Scranton, Pennsylvania: Foo Promotional Materials Begin to Acknowledge Copycats

As a result of the new engagement with the UBO, Foo ended up playing a week at the Scranton Poli's Theater, a UBO-affiliated venue that had first employed Foo at the commencement of his hostilities with Albee. Poli's employed a special ad involving a dragon motif to publicize Foo's engagement.[719]

Foo ad by Scobie in the style employed by Poli in 1913.

During the Poli's engagement, promotional material for Foo shows on the East Coast finally began to acknowledge the damage to the value of the act that had been done by Foo's myriad imitators of wildly varying skill levels.

The new promotional material admitted Foo's tricks were similar to those the imitators produced, but held out the claim—which did have some credence—that none of these competitors could do them like Foo. The promotional material added that this was why Foo, in the face of this army of imitators, had still "broken box office records across the country" and "in practically every city he has established a new house record." Foo, described as "the Greatest of All Headliners", was reported as going for the princely sum of $2,500 a week.[720]

This view of the Foo troupe as impervious to the impact of copycats won out in Scranton. Performing in the small Pennsylvanian city, the Foo troupe continued to draw crowds and plaudits. Foo was described as working "rapidly and smoothly" and presenting a program that was altogether new. The capacity audiences that greeted Foo were "wildly enthusiastic" and the local papers reported "Ching can pack the theater for a month and win as much enthusiasm on the last day as he did last night."[721] So, despite all the competitive pressure, Foo continued to be described as a "box office magnet" and "well worth" his $2,500 a week.

In fact, one Scranton reviewer acidly added, "judging him by some $2,000 stars in vaudeville, he is worth twice as much."[722,723]

March 30, 1914, Springfield, Massachusetts: Foo Troupe Beyond Mere Performing Tricks, "On Outer Fringe of Art"

By March 30th, 1914, the Foo troupe—now numbering 14—is continuing its stint on "Poli time" and is heading the bill at Poli's Palace in Springfield, Massachusetts. Also on the bill are Marie Lo and Company in "Porcelain, a Study of Posings."[724] A review of the show praised Foo and Yee Dee's work as Foo's comic assistant. The reviewer noted Foo "produces enormous objects" with "a bonhomie as attractive as his skill", while describing Yee Dee as "a Chinese comedian with American methods."

Another Massachusetts reviewer marveled over the rare ability to charm an audience that he exhibited so readily, and remarked how many of his competitors came nowhere near his talent in this area. Chee Toy was also singled out for praise as singing "American ragtime and popular songs with all the sophistication and skill of a Broadway favorite, and no Broadway favorite could have wished for a more enthusiastic audience."

Reviewing the full Foo act, the enthusiastic reviewer noted, "One feels that such juggling has gone beyond mere performing tricks and is on the outer fringe of being an art."[725]

Captain Charles F. Gammon, Lecturer and Writer on Chinese Topics, Joins the Act

In a fascinating early 1914 addition to the Ching Ling Foo act, Captain Charles F. Gammon, lecturer and writer on Chinese topics, was added to the show. Gammon supposedly went through the Boxer Uprising and consulted with the Japanese in their war with Russia. He reportedly was appointed an advisor to the Chinese government under the administration of Li Hung Chang, and spoke fluent Chinese. Gammon essentially lectured on this experience as part of the act.

With regard to Gammon's Chinese language skills, the Springfield critics noted that with Chee Toy, his Chinese language skills would be unnecessary, as her English was excellent and no "idiom escapes her," including the comic and "overworked" line "'I should worry.'"[726] The addition of Gammon into the act also seemed to align with Foo's vision of gradually evolving the troupe act so it could serve more of an educating function with regard to life in China. In this context, it is important to remember the thousands of feet of film Foo had shot of daily life in China and his intent to introduce it into his shows.

While we know Foo integrated his film of the Wuchang Uprising into his act in China after the late 1911 event, there are no indications the documentary he made of that uprising, or the other films he took of life in China, were displayed to audiences during his second tour of the US. Time constraints in the length of acts in continuous vaudeville and audience tastes likely played a role in this. In many instances, the entire Foo act, with some 14 performers, had to be complete in 30 minutes or less.

No doubt Wu Ting Fang and others would have supported efforts to further educate the American audience on China through film, but screening of Foo's China footage for American vaudeville audiences appears not to have occurred.

April 4, 1914, Buffalo, New York: Foo Shares the Stage with Mutt and Jeff Creator Who Invented the Modern "Comic Strip"

The plaudits for Foo and Chee Toy continued in Buffalo, where the young diva was described as "a dainty maiden" whose "singing has been greeted with storms of applause everywhere she has been seen." Meanwhile, Foo was a "wonderful Chinese" and "peer of the world's greatest magicians … in his native Chinese robes, he is a picture, and his skill is always puzzling and sensational. The act is gorgeously mounted with magnificent stage settings."[727]

As they did in New York, in Buffalo, while performing at Shea's Theater, the Foo troupe shared the bill with a famous illustrator. In this instance, it was with trailblazing cartoonist Bud Fisher, creator of the enormously popular *Mutt & Jeff* comic strip. Fisher shared the bill with the Foo troupe as a "special extra attraction."[728] In a nod to the enormous popularity nationally distributed Sunday comics had at that time, Fisher's inclusion was a major boost to the bill and was recognized as such by reviewers. "Mr. Fisher and his pen children are household words throughout the length and breadth of the land. He has an attractive offering and draws his well-known characters to the delight of his admirers."[729] As Winsor McCay was an acknowledged pioneer in animation, Bud Fisher was essentially

"Special Extra Attraction ... America's Foremost Cartoonist, Creator of *Mutt & Jeff* ... Master of Chinese Magic and Dainty Chee Toy Coming".

acknowledged as the inventor of the comic "strip" format, where more than one panel is employed to tell the story. Fisher's vaudeville act consisted of drawing his hugely popular Mutt and Jeff characters on stage on oversized panels to the delight of their many fans in the audience. Mutt and Jeff, the first ever successful comic strip, was published for over 75 years, from 1907 to 1983. Fisher's wife, Pauline Welch, a well-known singer, also performed on the bill, as did Lo Lotte, "the skating bear."

On April 7th, 1914, when the whole show was reviewed, critics found it "a tossup whether Bud Fisher, creator of the inimitable *Mutt & Jeff*, his charming wife Pauline Welch, or Ching Ling Foo, world-renowned Chinese magician ... receive the most applause." Of Fisher, they added "Bud never says a word he doesn't have to, for his unrivaled sketches talk for themselves."[730]

A competing act in another Buffalo theater was the "great" Polish wrestler "Zbyszko." Zbyszko's promotions included a "substantial money prize" offered to any who could "stay on the mat with him" for a specified time. The promotion promised Zbyszko "will meet all comers."[731]

April 20, 1914, Detroit, Michigan: Detroit Chapter of the Society of American Magicians has a Dinner to Honor Foo

The Foo troupe played Detroit the week of April 20, 1914 at the Temple Theatre, and the Detroit Society of American Magicians (S.A.M.) hosted a dinner on April 23rd for Foo. Yee Dee was reported to have acted as Foo's interpreter. Foo's English was described as something he did not use "smoothly."

The Foo troupe replaced the famous Fannie Brice at the Detroit Temple Theater; she was headlining there the previous week.[732] Foo's path would cross with Fannie Brice again less than a year later when a company, riding Foo's notoriety, created a "good luck ring" engraved with the Chinese characters (彩 好) which roughly translated as "good luck", all while using Ching Ling Foo's name in the ad. The ring, which was supposedly endorsed by Fannie Brice, was advertised in newspapers across the U.S.

The Foo troupe's performance at the Detroit Temple included several comedic elements that caught the attention of reviewers. "Imagine if you can, a pretty little Chinese girl proclaiming, 'I Love the Cows and the Chickens But This is the Life!' in true Broadway fashion; conjure up a vision of the tiniest little Oriental you ever saw doing the tango with another of the race but slightly larger, then fill in the background of deft plate-spinners sword jugglers and magicians, and dream that interspersed between snatches of the purest Chinese language you hear such phrases as 'Ich gebibble,' 'nobody home,' 'go to it,' etc. ad lib, and you have a picture of the act presented

"Send No Money! ... the Chinese Good Luck Ring is the fad of the hour in fashionable New York and Chicago ... Millions sold in the cities." Foo and Brice's path would cross again in the promotion of a mail order "lucky ring" widely advertised over many years across the country. The Ching Ling Foo ring allegedly brought Fanny Brice "$2,000 in 48 hours." Two Chinese characters on ring read left to right 好彩 "hao cai" meaning "good luck". There is no indication of whether Foo or Brice received any payment for these endorsements, and one suspects they did not. Over 50 years later, Barbara Streisand would star in a film rendering of the iconic Brice's life entitled *Funny Girl*.

by Ching Ling Foo and his troupe of Chinese actors in the Temple this week."[733]

In the Face of Escalating Booking Struggles, the Foo Troupe Abandons the U.S. for Europe

As noted earlier, when the Moosers brought Foo back to the U.S. in late 1912, E.F. Albee, head of the UBO, tried to exercise his organization's control of Foo with regard to bookings and salary. Neither Foo nor the Moosers would have any of it. At the end of a tempestuous meeting, George Mooser began arranging 'independent' bookings outside the UBO's network. A full season went by, and rarely did the UBO miss the chance to try and undermine Foo's situation by either seeking to intimidate theaters into not hiring him or placing cheaper, less skilled copycat Foo acts in the markets Foo was playing in to draw away business and damage Foo's cachet. But towards the end of the season, having so evidently failed to put a significant crimp in Foo's sails, the UBO turned around and hired Foo for a run at the Scranton Poli Theater. But this apparent olive branch did not end the troubles.

When Mooser called upon Albee at the UBO offices in April 1914 to see what other bookings might be available for Foo, things went south soon. According to *Variety*, as tensions and voices rose, "Albee asked Mooser if he knew to whom he was speaking. Mooser reported he didn't give a tinker's oath who he was. Albee mentioned Mooser was talking to him in his own (Albee's) office. Mooser replied "the place wasn't so particular." The discussion quickly further degenerated into a full-scale shouting match and mutual recriminations. George Mooser once more told Albee what he thought of him, the UBO, and the Keith's circuit, and Albee told him what Foo's future was with any of those organizations or any circuit or theater group they held influence with. Thus ended the interview.[734]

The venerable magic periodical *The Sphinx* also covered the altercation and reported that Foo had once more "quarreled with his managers" and rejected UBO control of his bookings.[735] What was interesting here is that it was not clear whether *The Sphinx* was referring to Foo quarreling with the UBO or the Moosers. It was also rumored at the time that Foo was getting a bit fed up with the Mooser Brothers' taste for constant conflict, as well. In fact, as noted, several theater managers had already reached out to Foo including Albee, suggesting to him that his career would go much more smoothly if he rid himself of the Moosers as his managers. Foo, near retirement and the end of his second U.S. tour, reportedly once more responded he was "too old" to contemplate changing managers at this late date in his career.

As a result of the ongoing animosity with the powerful UBO, George Mooser wisely decided to reexamine some offers for engagements outside the country, the result being that Mooser beat a strategic temporary retreat from the American market and was soon, as earlier rumors had indicated, booking engagements for the Foo troupe in Scotland, England, and Germany, where Mooser had several good contacts and the UBO little influence. The Foo troupe was scheduled to leave the U.S. in mid-May.

June 5, 1914, New York: Foo and Kellar Guests of Honor at June 1914 S.A.M. Annual Dinner

Before heading to Europe, Foo was a guest of honor along with Harry Kellar at the June 5th, 1914, annual banquet of the Society of American Magicians (S.A.M.).

The annual S.A.M. dinner had 150 guests; the menu was grapefruit, celery, olives, filet of sole, tartar sauce, Julienne potatoes, mignonette of Lamb Massena, roast duckling, applesauce, mashed potatoes, green peas, salad, vanilla ice cream, assorted cakes, and coffee. Various 'party favors' were passed around, including a "neat little telephone trick" from the owner of the Philadelphia Magic Shop and an "exploding cigarette box" from the S.S. Adams Company.[736]

After five magicians performed some work for the crowd, Chee Toy assisted in providing the night's entertainment, singing "They're On their Way to Mexico" and other tunes. In the *Conjuring Record* report, Chee Toy was identified as the wife of Mr. Ching Ling Foo Jr. (Yee Dee).

Material from the June 5th, 1914 Society of American Magicians festivities, including a photograph of some of the attendees with Chee Toy standing beside the Foos' good friend Harry Kellar and Foo seated with Yee Dee standing behind them.

The Legendary Guy Jarett Remembers Meeting Foo

More evidence of Foo's strong camaraderie with the U.S. magician's fraternity came from a fascinating incident from about this time

Yee Dee, Chee Toy, and Foo in another photo from around the period of the S.A.M. annual dinner.

recounted by noted magician and illusion craftsman Guy Jarrett. In his classic 1936 book *Magic and Stagecraft*, Garrett related the story of a good-natured gathering of professional magicians with Foo at Martinka's thusly.

"Once at the shop, Ching Ling Foo asked me for a glass ball that was laying in the show case. It was about an inch and a quarter in diameter. While everyone watched, he did a lot of good palming. He pretended to place the ball in his mouth, bulge his cheek, push in the bulge, swallow, and take the ball from under his jacket. He then reversed the move. Sometimes, he actually put the ball into his mouth to hide it. He would often laugh with his mouth wide open, the ball being in his hand.

"Of course, everyone was whispering that it was very good palming, letting each other know that they knew where the ball was at any time. But in one of the moves, the ball got lost and Foo could not find it. He questioned one or two of us while laughing, his mouth empty, but did not call attention to it. He then discovered the ball in the air, coaxed it to the end of his finger in pantomime, and asked me if I could see it. Of course, I said that I could, and he laughed hard, his mouth wide open, and pointed to the others, for they couldn't see the ball. He closed his hand around the imaginary ball, put it under his jacket and motioned upwards. A bulge appeared in his cheek. He held his hand below his mouth and deliberately spat the ball out.

"I howled with laughter; Ching laughed and was highly pleased. He knew that I had instantly 'got it' and appreciated it. The other guys just stood there, bewildered.

You see, all the passes and moves were just to string you along, to clean you up in the end with the real trick. The old bird swallowed the ball and retched it up when he wanted it."[737]

Another Take on 1905's World Championship of Chinese Magic

Prior to the Foo troupe's return to England, an interesting spin was put on Foo's historic contest with Soo in some early coverage of Foo's return to Britain. In this telling, the challenge for the event came from Soo, and the late Empress of China "sent for the Court magician Ching Ling Foo from Foo Chow and ordered him to come to England and take up the challenge." As for the outcome, the Moosers (for no doubt they were the source of this material) allowed that "owing to a misunderstanding, the actual contest did not take place." Such was the official version of the famous contest the Foo troupe management was putting out. In addition, Foo's team shared that since his time in England, Foo had been touring "Mongolia and North and South America" under George and Leon Mooser's management.[738]

1914 June 24: First News of the Foo Troupe's European Tour First Stop Glasgow

In late June, the Foo troupe sails on the soon to be ill-fated Lusitania and arrives in Glasgow, Scotland. On July 6, 1914, they begin a week's engagement at the Moss Hall Theater. Foo received thirty percent of the gross receipts of each theatre he performed at in Glasgow and the deal holds for the provincial theaters he will play in the three additional weeks the Foo troupe will tour the British provinces prior to his arrival in London for an August 10th engagement.

George Mooser also arranged European engagements for Foo once he had completed his bookings in England. Charles Gammon, the military and China expert, was acting as Mooser's representative for the Foo act in Europe.[739] Given the historic events that will soon unfurl on the continent this would turn out to be a far more fortuitous move by Mooser than he could imagine.

The week of July 6th, 1914, the Foo troupe was in Scotland performing at the Glasgow Empire Theatre. Other acts on the bill with Foo in London included "A.D. Robbins, the cycle tamer" and "Lonzo Cox, the scissors silhouette artiste"—acts that would clearly not survive vaudeville's passing.[740]

As it was summertime, given the heat, matinees were discontinued and shows were given twice nightly at 6:45 and 9:00 p.m.[741–743]

Foo was written up by the *Scottish Referee*'s "Stageland" theater columnist as part of his "crisp gossip from the halls." He described Foo as the "Court Magician to the late Empress of China", who provided "a performance that simply bewilders." As for others in the troupe, he found "Miss Chee Toy sings American ditties in a pleasing manner." Also on the bill: A.D. Robbins, "the cycle-tamer", was described as excelling in "trick riding." Robins' act included assistants riding "bucking" bikes and other novelty bicycles.[744]

July 28, 1914, Birmingham: "Mirth and Mystery"—Harry Weldon and the Foo Troupe

In July of 1914, an ad for the Foo troupe performance at the Empire Theater in Birmingham, England included, along with Foo and Chee Toy, two of the Foo troupe performers whose names were otherwise seldom included on the bills. Liu Chin Tang was presented as the Diabolo expert and Li Lea Tseng was the "Wizard of the Whirling Spears."[745] The troupe's competition in Birmingham included the play *A White Slave Victim* at the Alexandria Theater.[746]

Due to strong box office returns, Foo's engagement at the Birmingham Empire was extended, and by the end of July Foo was still performing in Birmingham and sharing a bill with Harry Weldon as the two combined to provide "Mirth and Mystery" at the Empire.[747,748]

Weldon was hugely popular in Britain. His specialties were comic monologues and songs.

The Foo troupe also shared the bill with the "Australian McLeans," a dance team from down under who "danced in ecentric and whirlwind fashion."

> World War I officially began this day.[749]

July 31ˢᵗ, 1914, Stratford: Foo Pays Tribute to the Bard, as Did Soo

Foo and Yee Dee's signatures in the Shakespeare's birthplace visitor's book in Stratford, England. (See the two highlighted signatures in the top image.) They visited the site on July 31ˢᵗ, 1914. Underneath their signatures are images of the signature left ten years earlier on October 5ᵗʰ, 1904 by Chung Ling Soo.

On July 31ˢᵗ, 1914, Ching Ling Foo and his son Yee Dee visited Stratford, England and signed Shakespeare's birthplace's visitor's book. Some ten years earlier, on October 5th, 1904, Chung Ling Soo had also visited Stratford and also signed the visitor's book. Soo, however, not surprisingly, did a much poorer job with his Chinese characters.[750]

August–September 1914: Foo, Antwerp, and the Fog of War

It is unclear from the records where the Foo troupe went in August of 1914. No doubt the confusion caused by the start of World War I disrupted many touring plans. What we do know is that they did, seemingly ill-advisedly, travel to the European continent after the war had begun to tour, and by September 1914 found themselves "marooned" in the Belgian city of Antwerp just as the war's rapid progression led the Germans to threaten to bombard the fortress city. The aerial bombardment of Antwerp began September 23rd, 1914. Over a million Belgian refugees would flee to the Netherlands by the time Antwerp fell to the Germans on October 10th, 1914.[751]

To the left, Themistokles von Eckenbrecher's September 1914 painting of the dirigible bombing of Antwerp, September 28th, 1914. To the right, elements from the playbill for the Shubert 1912–1913 production *Under Many Flags*. The terrible death-dealing weapon envisaged in the Shubert production less than two years earlier did indeed come into existence, and instead of leading to a "Treaty of Universal Peace", as was envisaged in the pacifist spectacular that so delighted Chee Toy, was instead rapidly deployed for war.

By some reports, the Foo troupe was trapped in the besieged city for over two weeks. According to others, the Foo troupe's European manager, Tim O'Donnell, who was nearby in France during this period, managed to make his way to Antwerp and "smuggled his charges out along with the other refugees", fleeing the city just ahead of the bombing.

There is no record of what role Gammon, the military specialist, played, but if he was still connected with the troupe, he would have surely proved an asset during this period.

Once rescued, Foo, along with the ten other members of his troupe, made it back to England and prudently cut short their European tour. At the first opportunity, the troupe sailed back to America from Liverpool, the plan being to complete their tour across America, then return to China.[752]

Due to booking complications caused by the war, the Foo troupe ended up leaving England in October on a ship full of 'war brides' headed for Canada. Once landed in Canada, they headed to New York. Finally back in New York on October 25th, the Foo troupe was once more bonded into the U.S. and ready to tour.[753,754]

Boxers, Wuchang Uprising, and World War I; no strangers to tumult was the Foo troupe.

CHAPTER EIGHTEEN

NOVEMBER 1914–MARCH 1915— NEW YORK TO CALIFORNIA; FOO RETURNS FOR A TRIUMPHANT AMERICAN FAREWELL

The Foo troupe took about two weeks to recover from their European adventure, and their initial return engagement at Hammerstein's was fixed at two weeks beginning November 9th.

Wire service pieces appeared across America in early November heralding the return of Ching Ling Foo, Chee Toy, and Foo's son Yee Dee to America, and explaining that the war prevented them from

> **CHING LING FOO RETURNS**
> Ching Ling Foo and his troupe of Orientals have returned to this country for some more of the American coin.

How some saw Foo's return to America. News of Foo's return was published across the country.

appearing in vaudeville in Europe. On the positive side, Chee Toy did learn "It's A Long Way to Tipperary" while touring the U.K.[755]

November 21, 1914, New York: Foo Troupe Once More a Great Success at Hammerstein's; Chee Toy Stops the Show

The Hammerstein's show began by screening films from *Pathé Weekly*, followed by "Pepino, the accordionist," who was followed by the comedians "Loretti and Antonetti" and then female impersonator "Stuart the Male Patti", who did "three numbers wearing three costumes, the last two entirely Parisian, that would make a hit at any 'drag.'" The Foo troupe was described as "the first solid hit of the bill."

The reviewers noted that there were some welcome "new" elements in the Foo act, including the "whirling spear" and Chee Toy's new songs. In fact, Chee Toy was such a hit singing "Burgundy" and "Tipperary" that she reportedly "stopped the show" and had to perform several rigorously demanded encores before the Foo troupe could continue with its act.

After the Foo troupe performance, the audience saw the "Three Keatons" and "Toots Paka and her company of Hawaiians in 'The Queen of Fire.'"

"The Queen of Fire" was presented as "a pantomimic story adapted from a native legend", but reviewers had a hard time discerning what the story was, and to them, even along with the two special sets and backdrop used by the act, the turn was essentially the same act Toots had offered earlier in the season. "The Queen of Fire" was not well received by the crowds."[756] Toots Paka was actually a Broadway actress who was married to Hawaiian musician and band leader July Paka.

Reports circulated that Foo was heading to China in two weeks to raise a new troupe of 40 performers for the Chinese Village to be featured at the upcoming San Francisco Fair.[757]

HAN PING CHIEN

One of the latest Chinese magicians chasing Foo's success was Han Ping Chien; sometimes promoted as "the only rival of Ching Ling Foo". Originally from China and arriving in the U.S. via London, Keith's newest potential Foo substitute was said to have some good tricks. The act involved five performers and was originally billed as the "The Pekin Mysteries." After arriving in the U.S. and starting their tour, the billing for the act was altered to feature Han Ping Chien. Han was promoted as a younger version of Foo, "animated and always smiling." His signature move was to tap a ringing brass plate with a stick after every trick. However, Han's feature illusion, "the insertion and removal of several short sticks into and from his nose", was judged as potentially not very well-suited to an American audience.[758] The Pekin Mysteries stage settings were declared "massive and beautiful"[759], yet their success and welcome came nowhere near the reception accorded to the Foo troupe. This demonstrated yet again that the mere technical magic and acrobatic "stunts" were not the key element of the Foo troupe's appeal, which went beyond being a mere "race" act.

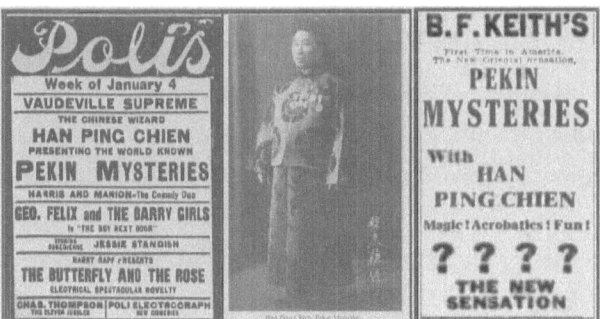

"The Chinese Wizard", the bemedaled Han Ping Chien, was promoted by Keith's as "the only rival of Ching Ling Foo". Han was very talented and presented his "Pekin Mysteries", a show that attempted but did not quite succeed in capturing the appeal of the Foo troupe. Nonetheless, the Pekin Mysteries, if not as beloved as the Foo troupe, did tour the U.S. for a significant amount of time, headlined occasionally, and had solid successes.

December 9, 1914, Pittsburgh: Another Version of Foo's Past and Passions; Foo Tells his Real Name

In Pittsburgh, towards the end of Foo's final tour of America, Foo granted yet one more interview, providing yet one more version of his past and his passions that once more adhered to the early-established pattern when it came to Foo's past of mixing fact with "advance man" fiction.

The author began by noting Foo's age as 61 and that his real name was "Chee Ling Que", which was correct on both counts. He also got correct that Yee Dee was Foo's son and Chee Toy was now Yee Dee's wife. Yee Dee was described as "the stout, jolly" fellow "that assists in the trickery." Foo also had a daughter married to a military official living in China. The children were all born in Tianjin. With regard to Foo's wife, she was back in Beijing taking care of the family's vast business enterprises. It was also put forward once again that Foo's father died when he was young, and his family was from the agricultural merchant upper-middle class. So far, so good.

The interview tread some new ground in the description of Foo's early adulthood. In this latest version, Foo's mother wanted her son to enter the family business, but magic had already taken a hold of him. Having traveled widely through China in his youth, Foo was, as an adventurous young man, now disinclined to settle down to "prosaic" business affairs. In this telling, Foo "became a gambler, a card expert who hired himself out to play games for amusement of those who were able to pay for them." In this manner, Foo gradually learned the prestidigitation skills honed by these gamblers and other conjuring skills.

"Little by little he gained proficiency in the arts of magic and was persuaded to return to Peking, his birthplace and the imperial capital of China, to perform there."

This turned out to be a mixed blessing. as the engagement as the Emperor's magician involved no payment but mainly his keep, a small stipend, and fabulously wealthy gifts that could not be sold. Only

28 years old at the time, Foo sought his escape from this gilded cage through "the cunning of his magic" and "simply disappeared."

After escaping the palace, Foo traveled to America to perform at the Omaha Exhibition in 1898 and his fame in America began. Upon his return to China, due to his great triumph, he was pardoned by the Dowager Empress, and in 1912 returned to America with a revised troupe with which he was enjoying his current success.

The interview also reasserted the more credible claims that Foo had a chain of shops in China in addition to a chain of motion picture theaters. Interestingly, the article noted these theaters were "built of bricks and stone, according to the best method of foreign theater construction" with a capacity of almost 2,000. The report added that general admission to these cinemas was about 30 cents in American money and rising upward to a dollar for seats in a private box.[760]

December 11, 1914: Foo Will Play Orpheum Circuit Out on the West Coast Prior to Return to China

In mid-December of 1914, the Foo troupe's future became clearer when *Variety* revealed Foo's farewell tour would run through the Orpheum circuit of theaters through the Midwest and out to San Francisco. Once the engagement with the Orpheum theaters was completed, Foo would return to China to retire.[761]

December 24, 1914, Chicago: Ashton Stevens of the Chicago Examiner *Provides Another Classic Review—"Spellbound"*

By December 20, 1914, Foo and his troupe were performing at Chicago's Palace Music Hall, where they shared the bill with a very youthful version of the legendary Marx Brothers.[762]

Despite being in the third year of their second U.S. tour and surrounded by imitators of every type claiming to replicate their act, the

Foo troupe miraculously continued to generate strong box office and enthusiastic reviews.

In this latest case, it was Ashton Stevens of the Chicago *Examiner*, at the time widely regarded as "the dean of American drama critics," who was entranced by the troupe. Stevens wrote, "It was the first-time Mr. Foo and I had met across the footlights and I was greatly spellbound. Doubtless many of our readers know precisely how Mr. Foo produces from his sublimated handkerchief and tight skirt these many gallons of water in open porcelain and crystal bowls, but I am not so wise." Stevens further noted Foo appeared "in an atmosphere of Oriental extravagance" and for Stevens, Foo's "untortured magic" was the "brilliant best" of the show.

According to Stevens, Foo "appears to work in a fourth dimension that is beyond the ken of the fourth estate." However, after all this praise to Foo, Stevens, who had grown up in San Francisco near that city's Chinatown, confessed his biggest surprise from the performance was "the modern ragtime singing of Chee Toy." She was "irrefragably" Chinese. Yet when Stevens "closed his eyes and listened to her wan soprano, I could have sworn she was a Caucasian debutante in the cabaret."[763] Stevens was not all praise for the act, however; the Foo troupe's sceneries were ranked only "so-so."[764]

While performing in the Orpheum Palace in Chicago, the Foo troupe shared the bill with a young version of the Marx Brothers. They performed together for the entire week.

December 27-January 19, 1914–1915: St. Louis, Memphis, and New Orleans

After leaving Chicago, the Foo troupe played very successful one-week engagements in St. Louis, Missouri, and Memphis, Tennessee, before opening for a week's engagement at the New Orleans Orpheum starting January 11th, 1915. In Memphis, the S.R.O. (standing room only) sign was displayed at one performance.[765–767]

Advertisements for the Chicago 1914 shows that would have featured Foo along with the Marx Brothers, as well as a photo of the legendary Marx Brothers as they would have appeared around the time; they shared the stage with the Foo troupe in Chicago. Managed by their mother Minnie, they performed a combination of music and comedy that gradually began to focus on their evident comedic skills.

New Orleans critics claimed the magic and juggling feats performed by the troupe "are not only puzzling and dazzling, but also so truly marvelous that critics have exclaimed that productions of this character have surpassed even the dreams, not counting the expectations, of the amusement world."

Once more, Chee Toy was promoted as "one of the most captivating characters on the stage today." Her rendition of "It's a Long Way to Tipperary" was reportedly "especially effective."

Foo continued to share the bill with Grace La Rue, "the American prima donna", whose vast wardrobe always appealed to the ladies in the audience.[768] The bill also included a comedy called *The Circus Girls* that included songs and dances and a "clever travesty on telepathy."

The bill would close with a regular feature of the New Orleans Orpheum's shows, "the Orpheum Travel Weekly." The week the Foo troupe was performing, the Travel Weekly was a film of Venice's carnival, promoted as "one of the few rivals" of New Orleans' own Mardi Gras.[769,770]

January 10, 1915, New Orleans: "Foo to Return Home Soon … Going Back to Aid in the Advent of Enlightenment in the Realm of Cathay"

After describing Foo as the "Martin Beck of China" because he owned a chain of theaters in China and was "wealthy enough to retire", a New Orleans journalist noted once more, in the only recognition we had seen of Foo's activities with regard to China's new order, "It has only been a few years since he donated 100,000 taels to the war chest of China, for Ching Ling Foo believes in the new order of things. Now that he has converted enough American gold into these taels he is going back to aid in the advent of enlightenment in the realm of Cathay."[771]

By mid-January 1915, the Foo troupe had played more than two weeks in New Orleans and continued to play to large audiences.[772]

January 24, 1915: "Bewildered By Chinese Magic" — Foo Troupe Plays San Francisco, California

On January 24th, 1915, the Foo troupe arrived in San Francisco, center of Chinese life in early 20th-century America to play the Orpheum.[773]

Under a headline reading "Bewildered by Chinese Magic", a San Francisco reviewer marveled over Foo using only his "heavily brocaded with figures of Chinese dragons and other celestial gamebirds" silk cloth to "make bulky objects appear where a second earlier there was nothing." But he found Chee Toy's singing even more miraculous, claiming even Foo was "outstripped as a miracle maker" by his "pretty and dainty daughter."

"Bewildered by Chinese Magic."

He then made a powerful analogy for the Chinese capacity for assimilation into American life when he described Chee Toy, "with her light orange complexion and her glossy black hair" as she "trips out on the stage and by trilling a few notes", transforming "the broad Pacific into a babbling little brook over which one may step in a second from the Cliff House to the Shanghai water front" through her mastery of American popular culture. "The sundry thousands of miles between San Francisco and China shrink to inches when Miss Chee Toy, arrayed in her gorgeous Oriental blouse and black trousers sings 'When You Wore a Yellow Tulip and I wore a Big Red Rose.'"[774]

"Miss Chee Toy Not Only Sings Pleasingly. She Wins the Audience with a Personal Charm of a Rare Quality."

In this performance, Chee Toy responded to cries for an encore with a version of "Tipperary" done in an American Irish dialect "injected with just a pinch of Irish comedy into the last line." The reviewer concluded, "Miss Chee Toy not only sings pleasingly. She wins the audience with a personal charm of a rare quality."

All this from a San Francisco critic who would have seen more than his share of Chinese acts and who would have little patience with the race-novelty acts featuring Chinese which might have gone over in the smaller markets in the East. Switching back to the subject of Foo's illusions, he judged them "startling" and singled out Yee Dee's work as Foo's comic assistant, who provided "dry humorous comment" infused with a deep knowledge of "American slang."

The Foo troupe's warm reception in San Francisco caught the attention of the magician's periodical *The Conjuring Record*; its editors noted the "enthusiastic ovation" that greeted Foo's performance at the Orpheum.[775]

ALSO ON THE SAN FRANCISCO ORPHEUM UNDERCARD: "CURSE YOU JACK DALTON!" AND OTHERS

Also on the bill with Foo were two men who looked remarkably alike and a pretty girl who did a pantomime "of headliner quality" entitled "The Broken Mirror." In addition, there was Jack E. Gardner, who advertised himself as "head of a large company", but whose act consisted of him interacting with characters flashed on a film screen positioned behind him. In his piece called "Curse You Jack Dalton!", Gardner engaged with a large company on celluloid.

A professional heckler of poor films before it became a cornerstone of inexpensive late night television, Gardner, to much comic effect, took on and engaged the characters of an old-time melodrama, "quarrels with the villain, scolds the heroine … and gloats over the discomfiture of the villainess."[776]

January 31, 1915, San Francisco: Amidst the Raves, a Somewhat Off-putting Interview

Amidst all the positive reviews the Foo troupe was receiving, almost as a reminder of the vexed environment Chinese people in general experienced living in California at that time and the divided views attached to the ever-present "China Question," an article appeared on Yee Dee and Chee Toy, no doubt designed to be knowing and humorous, that came off as something quite different.

Some West Coast reporters being, they believed, more knowledgeable about the Chinese than people in other parts of the country seemed, in some cases at least, almost more eager to embrace negative stereotypes regarding the Chinese. Indeed, in this case, a reporter for the San Francisco *Chronicle*, no doubt believing he was projecting the worldly air of a man accustomed to dealing with the Chinese, came off to a modern reader as considerably more hostile, dismissive, and condescending than reporters in other parts of the country, or even more cosmopolitan reporters in his own city.

This presumption of knowledge of the Chinese he held was deceptive, because while he may have a bit more experience of a perfunctory, shallow nature than those in the East as regards the Chinese—say, occasionally passing through Chinatown or reading the local paper's sensational stories of "highbinders"—that limited interaction had clearly not engendered any great knowledge.

As a result, one of the few interviews featuring Yee Dee and Chee Toy that discussed their relationship was marred by more than a little xenophobia and presumption. That is not to say, however, that Yee Dee and Chee Toy were not up for the bargain of being misinterpreted and misrepresented in order to achieve the Foo troupe's promotional goals.

Here, then, a sampling from that January 31st, 1915 interview.

"'We marry by love each other,' explained Mr. Yee Chu, putting his Chinese heel on another illusion ... Mrs. Yee Chu nodded demurely.

ORIENTAL WAYS

It was none of your 'impudent off-hand nods,' either, but proud and independent and American. It did not appear to have come from the Yellow Sea, but from Western waters and the land of the free and home of the brave. She beamed proudly upon her spouse and then straightaway fell to fearing. She said it might interfere with their vaudeville popularity if the fact of their matrimonial alliance was divulged, and Mr. Yee Chu hastened to advise me that the public's interest in Chee Toy would languish the instant it knew she wasn't Ching Ling Foo's daughter of the blood, but only his daughter-in-law. One mustn't be married, it seems, in vaudeville even though like Chee Toy and Ching Ling Foo's husky son, they married 'by love each other, not Chinese fashion.'"

Of course, the counter to this narrative was that Chee Toy had already revealed she was a married woman almost two years ago, only a few months into the second Foo troupe tour of the U.S. Indeed, there was major coverage of the relationship between Yee Dee and Chee Toy during both their New York and Pittsburgh engagements. That said, in the 1900s, news in one newspaper was not easily accessible after it was published, so the impact of news in one region on knowledge in another could be limited.

The reporter also revealed himself to be a bit of a scamp when he revealed in his perhaps not too serious piece that he agreed not to publicize their nuptials. "Of course, I agreed not to say a word about it, for who would deny pretty Chee Toy any request, and in this case, for once, I might be gallantly false and never be found out?" The reporter here presented the two as being incapable of reading an English newspaper or having reviews of their show read to them. A weak proposition indeed.

Chee Toy told the reporter that in her opinion, it would take "about 80 years or maybe 100 for the example she has set matrimonially to become popular in China." Yee Dee posited it might take even longer than that. The reporter noted that when Yee Dee spoke, Chee Toy "closed her carmined lips and sat a diminutive little heap, mostly ears and approving nods." The reporter also briefly delved into the Chinese regional animosities between north and south Chinese by means of explanation as to why he could report Foo's frustration as a proud northern Chinese having to work with what was essentially a Cantonese or southern Chinese stage name. All this was a result of the fact Foo's fame blew up while he was in the south of China, and once the fame arrived, the name had to stay. In the reporter's words, once the magician became famous with the name Foo, "the damage was done" and the name Foo "became synonymous at once with stunts that Aladdin's wicked 'uncle' could not do."

Where some relevant and credible information did come out of the interview was where Chee Toy noted that her mother died some 20 years ago, and while her foster mother was caring for her, she caught Foo's attention, and the original conjurer adopted her as a very tiny toddler of perhaps not yet two years old, and from an early age, she trained in music with the troupe. These circumstances, of course, pointed to a much more traditional path for Yee Dee and Chee Toy's marriage.

Worst Thing About Touring for Yee Dee and Chee Toy is Finding a Decent Chinese Meal

The couple noted the worst thing about touring was the difficulty in finding a good Chinese meal, and for that reason were happy the final leg of their tour had taken them to San Francisco, which abounded in good Chinese restaurants. Lastly, they noted, they looked forward to retiring back to northern China, where they would have a little shop where, according to the reporter, "the money they have saved will insure a life in luxury in a commercial environment where a dollar and a half is loaded on a cart and moved with reverent deliberation."⁷⁷⁷

As always, the interviews with the Foo troupe mixed fact and fiction with the goal of entertaining the audience, always a few paces ahead of truly informing them.

Foo's San Francisco Orpheum Show in Its Second Week

Foo's Orpheum show, in its second week, opened with Rae Eleanor Ball, a violinist, followed by the dancers Mr. and Mrs. Douglas Crane. A short satiric play, *Woman Proposes*, demonstrating how women control the courtship and marriage process, follows. A big star on the bill was Jeanne Jomelli, a famous prima donna who sang classical and popular arias in Italian and English. She was reputedly a dramatic soprano of tremendous volume and power. Over their shared passion for classical music, Chee Toy and Jomelli would become "great friends." Jomelli reportedly taught Chee Toy "a part of 'The Jewel Song' from *Faust*', and Chee Toy shared with Jomelli that one of her goals was to "carry home with her to China one of the newer and better brands of phonograph" to better enjoy her collection of classical recordings.⁷⁷⁸

Also included were Maryon Vadie's troupe of ballet and interpretive dancers, and Milt Collins, the German dialect comedian, who delivered a humorous political speech. The show closed with the Foo troupe, featuring Foo and Chee Toy. The "bewitching" Chee Toy was considered to sing "American songs better than many a Broadway winner."⁷⁷⁹

Overall, the show appeared more cosmopolitan and demanding on a general audience than most entertainments being presented today.

February 6, 1915: Chee Toy Raises Money for the Child Labor Convention

Towards the end of their San Francisco engagement, "fascinating" Chee Toy, somewhat fittingly, participated in an afternoon fundraiser at the Palace Hotel to raise money for "bringing the Child Labor Convention and exhibit to San Francisco." Also participating in the event were "winsome Peggy O'Neil"—Peg o' My Heart from the Cort Theater—and Mr. and Mrs. Douglas Crane, the dancers.[780]

February 6, 1915, Oakland, California: "To Be Even Conceived This Remarkable Offering Must Be Seen"

The Foo troupe, at the Oakland Orpheum, was promoted as "one of the most remarkable acts ever seen in local vaudeville." Diabolo manipulation by Liu Chin Tang opened the Oakland act, and Li Loa Tseng, "wizard of the whirling spears" followed him. Chee Toy was described as "a winsome Oriental miss" who "sings English songs and sings them well." The show moved from music to acrobatics and acrobatics to magic "with startling rapidity." The reviewer closed "To be even conceived the remarkable offering must be seen."

Also on the bill at Oakland was Maryon Vadie's dance troupe, offering "classical dances", and Kate Elinore, a female comedienne working with Sam Williams "whose laugh making abilities are only matched by the dimensions of the lady herself." This comedy duo was followed by "The Aerial Costas", consisting of one man and three girls who performed on the horizontal bars and rings. The show closed with Orpheum motion pictures and an amateur night competition.[781-783]

February 13, 1915, Sacramento, California: Chee Toy Sings Her Way "Into the Hearts of the Audience"; Her "Enunciation of English Words ... is Clearer and More Perfect Than That of Many American Singers"

In Sacramento, Chee Toy was once again, with Foo, the hit of the show. She even inspired a rhyme: "Petite of figure, pathetic of face, donning the mannerisms of the American singer with becoming grace." Reviewers reported that in her first appearance at the Sacramento Orpheum, "the Chinese Prima Donna" made an "instantaneous hit."

Chee Toy was front and center in this Sacramento *Bee* illustration. Unfortunately, the illustrator, Arthur Buel, seemed not quite up to the task of capturing Chee Toy's appearance. In fact, it appears Buel was capable of producing just one profile. (Images from original cartoon were reconfigured to fit space available.)

She had "a sweet and flexible voice of greater volume than one would be led to believe from such a miniature maiden." Contrary to the report from the San Francisco reporter this reporter adjudges her mastery of English elocution as a thing to "elicit wonder." "Her enunciation of English words ... is clearer and more perfect than that of many American singers." The reviewers also marvel at her ability "to get into close touch with her audience."

Even in Sacramento, the Foo troupe had another Chinese variety show-style competitor in tow. The "Imperial Tai Pien Troupe", consisting of "ten genuine Chinese magicians, jugglers, and acrobats" formerly with Barnum & Bailey's circus, and whose act included acrobatics done while being suspended from their hair, was playing an engagement at the Sacramento Pantages.[784–787]

February 13, 1915, San Jose, California: "A Sensation in San Francisco ... Best Known Celestial in the Occident" and the Contemporary of an Emerging Charlie Chaplin

In San Jose, at the Victory Theater, the Foo act was promoted by reports of the "sensation" the troupe created in San Francisco.

Kate Elinore was on the bill with them, as was Else Rueger on the cello and a trained dog called Toque, who performed "daring stunts", including "a double somersault in mid-air over the head of seven men covering a distance of 30 feet." In addition, exclusive Orpheum motion pictures were shown.[788,789]

By February 15th, the fast-moving Foo troupe was at the Orpheum Clunie Theater in Sacramento.[790]

By February 17th, 1915, the troupe was playing a number of days at the Yosemite Orpheum. Foo was rightly touted in this California city as "the best-known Celestial in the Occident."

However, the hit of the Yosemite Orpheum bill was once again Chee Toy. "The pretty little Celestial maiden" sang "When You Wore a Tulip and I Wore a Big Red Rose" and "Tipperary."

Chee Toy's "pleasing voice and piquant grace" "took her audience by storm and she was called back from the wings many times." The rest of the troupe was also well-appreciated, as were the elaborate stage settings featuring many Chinese-embroidered hangings. Also on the bill was classical cellist Elsa Rueger, who apparently had "the willpower to refrain from responding to the applause with popular music."[791]

Chinese Prima Donna Hit of Orpheum Bill

In an indication of the evolving entertainment market and the impending doom of vaudeville, the troupe's chief competition in the town came from two separate films in two separate theaters featuring the emerging film star "Charles Chaplin." Chaplin, not yet know by the name he would become most famous, is still billed as "Charles", not the more informal "Charlie Chaplin."

As vaudeville star Foo departed the stage, film star Charlie Chaplin emerged. To the right, Chaplin in the film *His New Job*.

In Stockton, Mr. Chaplin featured in two films, *Tillie's Punctured Romance*, wherein he plays a supporting role and is promoted as "the World's Greatest Funny Man", and *His New Job*, which stars Chaplin and was promoted as "a scream".

In an almost contemporaneous intercultural exchange Chaplin's popularity would extend over to China. Where 桌別麟 (Zhuo Bie Lin), as he was known in China, would become a very popular film star and his little tramp character a favorite with Chinese audiences for decades to come.

Chaplin's film *Sunnyside* brought in both Chinese and foreign audiences when it played Shanghai in 1919. Above is an enhanced version of one of the film's advertisements, which appeared in Chinese magazines of the time.

February 22, 1915, Los Angeles, California: Foo Troupe Sophistication, Choice of Hotels Outside Chinatown Discombobulates Some

In late February, the Foo troupe was playing the Los Angeles Orpheum, and interest was taken in the fact they would not be staying in Chinatown. The fact that the troupe's advance man was finding them accommodation "downtown" in the better hotels caused a bit of a stir.[792]

Unlike in San Francisco, some reviews for the act in Los Angeles, while positive, betrayed an unease among some that Chinese could present a sophisticated entertainment. Foo was praised for his "marvelous magic" turn that must be seen to be appreciated. But the reaction to Chee Toy, who did not present a quite standard Chinese act, was more complicated. In one case, a reviewer claimed she "is quite the most fascinating little prima donna we have seen in a long time" and added "her efforts to appear sophisticated in her singing and dancing numbers are delicious."

Being presented with Chinese who crossed easily between Chinese and Western performance styles in an act that is simultaneously dignified, comic, entertaining, and sophisticated clearly somewhat discombobulated the reviewer.[793]

The fact the Foo troupe also held their own when sharing the Orpheum stage on February 22nd, 1915 with the prima donna of the New York Metropolitan Opera Company, soprano Jeanne Jomelli, as

The Foo troupe and classical opera, comfortably on the same bill.

"joint headliners" in a special show celebrating George Washington's birthday—and the fact Jomelli publicly voiced her great respect for Chee Toy's singing ability—must have provided the reviewer even more pause for thought.[794]

"The Clever Josher" Yee Dee and His Wife Chee Toy Make the Los Angeles Times Gossip Column; Yee Dee Active in the Film Business

While in Los Angeles, members of the Foo troupe appearing at Los Angeles Orpheum were treated as bona fide celebrities and made it into a Los Angeles *Times* gossip column. In an interesting note that revealed how the burgeoning film business was drawing talent out of vaudeville, a gossip item was published regarding Yee Dee's work in the film distribution business. A piece referring to Yee Dee stated, "Yee D. Chu, the clever 'josher' who is 'honorably fat,' is the husband of the dear little singer, Chee Toy, who is winning everybody's heart with her delightful quaintness and fascinating orientalism. Mr. Chu owns a motion-picture house in Pekin, and he has purchased several feature films for his house produced by local motion-picture concerns."

The gossip item ended with a reference to Ching Ling Foo, the "magician at the Orpheum", who was "72 years old and growing cunninger in his trade every day."[795]

Another gossip item focused on Yee Dee and Chee Toy appearing about a week later claimed that Yee Dee, Chee Toy's husband and assistant to Foo on stage, was "a mandarin in his own country." This statement appeared with some other questionable assertions under the headline "Maybe So!" Chee Toy, meanwhile, was described as Yee Dee's wife and a "delicious little prima donna."[796]

As they were in San Francisco, the other big market city of California, the Foo troupe was a hit in Los Angeles. The act was held over as headliners for another week at the Los Angeles Orpheum.[797] An impressed reviewer in the Long Beach *Telegram and Daily News* noted what, in an ideal world, would be the unremarkable news that "Foo has demonstrated that the Chinese have a sense of humor, as well as artistic ability." Old tropes die hard. He also concluded, as far as "magicianship" went, Foo had "shown 'em all."[798]

The first week of March was the Foo troupe's last week at the Los Angeles Orpheum.[799]

A TESTAMENT TO AMERICA'S TROUBLED HISTORY OF RACE RELATIONS

The same week the Foo troupe triumphed in its headliner role at the Orpheum, D.W. Griffith's film *The Clansman*, soon to be rebranded *Birth of a Nation*, was breaking box office records at the Los Angeles Auditorium Theater. Hugely controversial, even in its time, but wildly successful, *Birth of a Nation* unfortunately simultaneously introduced countless new film techniques and marketing innovations along with a racist depiction of American Blacks and glorification of the Ku Klux Klan (KKK) that in no small manner inspired the resurgence of the Klan shortly after the film's very successful run.

"Now Breaking the World's Motion Picture Record": *The Clansman*, the 1915 film rebranded as *Birth of a Nation*, as advertised in the March 1915 Los Angeles *Express*.[800]

March 7: Foo's Los Angeles Apartment Hub for Celebrity Gatherings

Foo had his own cook living in his own apartment beside his, in an apartment complex favored by touring celebrities. During their time in Los Angeles, the Foo troupe organized many of their famous midnight Chinese supper parties, to which the city's celebrities and denizens of "Incandescent Alley" (the theater neighborhood) reportedly flocked.[801]

End of the Tour: A Holiday with Harry and High Praise; Foo the Equal of the Dean of American Magic Harry Kellar

With their tour of the U.S. complete, the Foo troupe fittingly enjoyed their last days in the United States in the company of Foo's great friend, the Dean of American Magic, Harry Kellar, who was now, according to magic insiders, in happy retirement "enjoying his big house in California."

The magazine of the Society of American Magicians (S.A.M.) took special note of the strong, longstanding friendship that existed between Kellar and Foo. "Harry Kellar, supreme as a magician, the first in standing of his race, has found a companion in the mystic means and a mental adjunct in breadth of thought and study in Mr. Ching Ling Foo, the Chinese magician, now at the Orpheum." The magazine describes Foo as the Chinese "counterpart" to "Dean of American Magic" Kellar.

The magazine reported that Foo would stay a week or two as Kellar's guest at the magician's "beautiful" Southern California home, and during their holiday prior to returning to China, Foo and his family would be guided "through the mazes of Southern California's beauty via" Kellar's "big motor car."[802] Everything Kellar had was big.

Harry Kellar's "big house in California", pictured in the early 1920s. This is where Foo and family would stay as guests of the Dean of American Magic prior to their return to China. Kellar's "big car", in which the happy group toured the Golden State, can be seen in the driveway.

Foo, Yee Dee, and Chee Toy would spend a full two weeks holidaying with Kellar in California, from about mid-March 1915 until their departure for China on March 27th.

Kellar on Foo: "He is a master ... His Art is Finished and Perfect, and Besides He is a Prince of a Fellow."

The affable Kellar, who with his air of amiable Midwestern hucksterism was often claimed to have served as L. Frank Baum's inspiration for the Wizard of Oz, did indeed take Foo, Chee Toy, and Yee Dee on a driving tour of his beloved state.[803] The travelers stopped at a upscale restaurant inn in Riverside, California. After their visit, the inn's proprietor contacted, the local newspaper to report that Foo, Yee Dee, and Chee Toy took in and much appreciated the inn's prize collection of antique Chinese porcelain. In the report, the proud innkeeper noted Chee Toy was "a master of the English tongue."

As part of his contribution to the article, Kellar informed a reporter following up on the story that he and Foo first met in China during Kellar's tours of Asia in the late 1870s–1880s and became

"He is a master ... his art is finished and perfect, and besides he is a prince of a fellow." Kellar and Foo, friends and masters of the black arts; two of Martinka's "great men".

"firm friends." Kellar said of his fellow conjurer, "He is a master ... his art is finished and perfect, and besides he is a prince of a fellow." These words of praise echoed Kellar's later words provided to the S.A.M. when he was contacted by that organization to speak on Foo's legacy as the Chinese sorcerer prepared to leave the country for the last time.

A Going Away Gift: Kellar Gives Foo Talking Tea Kettle Fluent in Chinese

Kellar's assessment of Foo was characteristically generous and accurate. "Foo is at the head of his profession and is a gentleman who graces any company." Kellar reminisced about a gift Foo had presented him two years earlier, a "priceless" ancient jade buckle for a mandarin belt which Kellar still treasured. For Foo's departure, Kellar provided Foo with a gift of equal value: Kellar's famous "Talking Tea Kettle"—fully capable now, after a few tweaks by Kellar, of speaking Chinese.

THE TORTURED HISTORY OF THE TALKING TEA KETTLE ILLUSION

Ghosts that Talk —by Radio

An Exposé of Some of the "Spiritualistic Phenomena" Perpetrated by Fraudulent Mediums for Getting Money from Their Credulous Followers

By HOUDINI

MAGICIANS have used the radio telephone in their performances for several years—long before radio was generally known to the public. I am not at all surprised that the radio is being used by fraudulent mediums to convince their patrons that they are in direct communication with the dead.

THE SECRET OF THE KETTLE
The receiving coil hidden in false sides collects the energy sent out from a transmitting coil that may be several yards away, and this energy is converted into sound by the telephone receiver in the spout.

"The Talking Tea Kettle" exposed. Houdini may have been focused on exposing fraudulent spiritualists but his revelation angered fellow magicians

The "talking tea kettle" was the type of clever technology-based stage illusion that would have appealed to Kellar. The kettle supposedly allowed communications with the deceased. Questions would be asked, and the spout was pressed against one's ear to hear the ghost's replies. The illusion was developed by noted Omaha, Nebraska-based magician and illusion technician P.J. Abbott in 1907. Made of papier-mâché, the device was essentially an early radio transmitter/'walkie-talkie' with conduction coils and a microphone hidden in the tea kettle, while a confederate nearby in another room would listen to the questions via his radio set and reply through his microphone. Houdini caused a bit of a scandal among the magic community when, in the October edition of *Popular Radio*, he authored an article titled "Ghosts That Talk By Radio" that exposed the science behind the popular illusion.[804] While Houdini's stated intent was to expose fraudulent spiritualists who were defrauding the credulous, who came to them for solace regarding deceased loved ones. Magicians who used the illusion as part of their stage act, and Abbott, who developed the illusion, were incensed. The informal magicians' code of never revealing a magician's secret to a non-magician

> had been violated. The repercussions were serious. Magicians called for Houdini to resign as President of S.A.M., and a special meeting of the organization was called. In the end, Houdini escaped serious censure by explaining it was the magazine's editor and not he that had explained the trick, and introducing a formal code of conduct for magicians that set out their responsibility not to reveal tricks of fellow magicians and how to deal with this issue in the context of fraudulent mediums. As for Foo's kettle, reports were that it was, along with so many of the other illusions he had purchased in the U.S., destroyed in the 1916 fire that destroyed his home.

With the holiday complete, Foo, Yee Dee, and Chee Toy boarded the ship that would return them to China. As evidence of their friendship, almost immediately upon their return, Yee Dee and Chee Toy sent Kellar a letter stating "they had the time of their life" while his guests in California, and they, if not Foo, were considering a return. Foo had Yee Dee and Chee Toy send along with their letter a special Chinese mandarin coat for his old friend, which Kellar described as "a thing of beauty."[805,806]

It seemed fitting, if no less sad, that Leon Mooser, longtime manager along with his brother George of Foo's theatrical career, would pass away in San Francisco, where he was acting as general manager for Olive Morosco, just a few short months after the Foo troupe left America for the last time.[807] Mooser's death may also explain why Foo never appeared at the San Francisco Panama-Pacific International Exhibition running from February 1915 until December 1915, as earlier planned.[808]

CHAPTER NINETEEN
1916—FOO EASES INTO SEMI-RETIREMENT IN SHANGHAI

After their triumphal second U.S. tour that spanned over two years and a brief European detour, Foo and his troupe returned to Shanghai. Back in China, Foo's focus moved from stage performances to his wider business interests, including film theaters and a travelling circus.

A business card from one of his many businesses—in this case, Tianjin's Colon Cinema, which was located at 93 Rue Du Baron Gros Tien Tsin (Tianjin), which would have been in the French-controlled portion of that city.

Chee Toy Performs Separately, Then the Troupe Gets Together for a Series of War-Related Charity Gigs

Chee Toy, however, continued to take to the stage as a solo act. For the week of April 22, 1916, the young singer played Shanghai's Victoria Theater. The last time she had performed at the Victoria Theater was in 1910. The Shanghai audience was reportedly much impressed with how her talents had developed since they had last seen her.[809]

Then, only a month later, the whole Foo troupe was cajoled back on the stage to perform in a charity event celebrating "Empire Day" at the old Shanghai Lyceum on Museum Road. The Overseas Club (Shanghai branch) was raising money for Charing Cross Hospital in London as part of British Shanghai's support for the war effort. The program noted that this would be Foo's "first appearance since his sensational tour of the United States." Chee Toy's appearance was announced in a separate billing as the "the Prima Donna of the Celestial Land." A little over a week later, in June of 1916, Foo performed at yet another war benefit at the Old Lyceum.

At this point, Foo was splitting his time between Tianjin and Shanghai, as he was still running his theater in Tianjin after his return

The May 1916 playbill recording the participation of the Foo troupe and Chee Toy ("the Prima Donna of the Celestial Land") in a Shanghai Empire Day celebration raising money for the war effort.

to China. Dr. Richard Rowe and his wife, "Mystic Mora", performed at Foo's Tianjin theater during this period in 1916. According to Rowe, Foo and the couple spent time together after the performances, and Foo even showed them the talking tea kettle Kellar had presented Foo on his departure from the U.S. Foo apparently was taken with Mystic Mora's technical skills, which he ranked higher than those of her husband, and he taught her several illusions.[810]

1916 June: When Magic Failed—A Terrible Fire

When Magic Failed

In June of 1916, fate proved it was not yet finished with the old conjurer when a fire lay waste to his treasure-laden Shanghai mansion and estate.

Shortly before three in the afternoon on Friday June 22nd, 1916, flames raced through Foo's Shanghai home. Despite a hard-fought two-hour battle involving the entire Shanghai fire brigade and the resources of two nearby corner hydrants, once morning came, little was left of the once-grand home and its contents. By the time the fire department had contained the blaze, its flames had also claimed a tiger Foo kept on the property, as well as an unfortunate monkey.

Learning of the still-trapped animals, members of the Shanghai fire brigade had made a courageous effort under the cover of streams of water to mount a rescue. Sadly, however, the heat was too great, and they were forced back.[811] Also tragically lost in the fire were thousands of feet of film depicting life in China Foo had used in his act, including his historic and prized *Wuhan Uprising* documentary.

The losses did not end there. The grand home encompassed storage areas where some of Foo's voluminous stage materials, backdrops, equipment, and illusions, including those recently purchased in America and specially made for him, were stored. These too were lost to the fire.[812]

The financial impact of these losses would have been all the greater for Foo given that he had just lost his Hankow theater, in what is now known as Wuhan, in yet another fire shortly before this latest calamity struck his Shanghai home. Estimates of his losses from the two fires were calculated to be well over US $200,000, which would be approximately $4,400,000 in today's dollars.[813]

In covering the fire, there were the inevitable for the time insensitive jokes in the media asking why Foo had not used his occult skills with water production tricks to counter the fire or make the poor tiger "disappear."[814]

A collection of letters between the magician Edwin A. Dearn and J.B. Findlay included a note by Dearn that he "was present at the fire in which Foo lost most of his show."[815] This clearly appeared to be a reference to the June 1916 fire. Dearn, who would have been just 24 years old at the time, had been pursuing his passion for magic since arriving in Shanghai two years earlier, and became acquainted with Foo. Dearn also became an ardent collector of magic memorabilia, and his collection, which included Foo memorabilia, was covered by a Shanghai magazine called *The Town Traveler* in their June 1926 edition.

A photo of Foo that survived the fire beside a photo taken of Dearn in Shanghai in 1926 "reading to his favorite death's head."

CHAPTER TWENTY

1917–1922—SOO MAKES AN ANTI-CLIMATIC WWI ERA VISIT TO SHANGHAI; SOO, THEN FOO, PASS AWAY

One Last Puzzle: Did Chung Ling Soo Make it to Shanghai During WWI?

In England, the war and its austerity environment had made it increasingly difficult for the Soo act to operate profitably. As a result, yet another world tour was planned. Soo was scheduled to depart England in January 1917 on an ambitious world tour that was planned to last five years. Included in the scheduled stops were India, China, Japan, Burma, the Straits Settlements, the Malay States, Australia, South Africa, South America, Mexico, the United States, and Canada.[816]

By early summer of 1917, Soo was well into his tour and performing in India. Reports coming from Bombay from other touring artists indicated Soo had run into some difficulties with promoters in India, but had them sorted out. From India, the troupe moved on to Singapore and then Hong Kong where they arrived May 4th.[817] After two middling weeks in Hong Kong Soo appears to have cancelled his last planned weekend of shows in Hong Kong and headed for

Shanghai all while working on arrangements to move on to the still not confirmed Australia and New Zealand portions of his tour.[818–820]

So. While it does appear Chung Ling Soo did indeed perform in Shanghai in 1917, unfortunately, in the fog, austerity, and melancholy of a world war, it seems the whole affair, much like the earlier portions of Soo's ill-fated world tour, was somewhat muted and anticlimactic. Soo's appearance on Foo's home territory and the potential for an epic rematch appear to have generated nowhere near the excitement one might have hoped.

According to contemporaneous reports, Soo could not even procure a Shanghai theater venue with a stage large enough for his special effects and equipment-heavy act. An entertainment raising money for the Red Cross and the war effort was occupying the Shanghai Lyceum, which would have been the ideal venue. Soo thus had to make do with the entertainment spaces available. As a result, the not-so-original, Chinese conjurer was forced to present his act on the relatively cramped confines of Shanghai's Victoria Theater.[821]

Shanghai's Victoria Theater, located on Hai Ning Road. Twelve years after their legendary confrontation in London, an ailing Chung Ling Soo gave an anticlimactic performance in this theater, whose stage was too small for his act, before a relatively indifferent public and a seemingly absent or uninterested Foo.

Meanwhile, Ching Ling Foo, from all indications, was either out of town attending to his many businesses, indisposed from encroaching illness brought on by recent misfortunes, or, 12 years on, simply supremely indifferent to the presence of his old foe on his home territory.

Thus, in a distracted environment focused on the war and domestic issues, the opportunity for a reprise of perhaps the most famous magicians' duel in world history was lost.

In the end, Soo's Shanghai performance attracted little attention, and according to the London trade journal *The Stage*, "did not do as well as expected."

On top of all this, while in China, Soo reportedly suffered from a gastrointestinal illness picked up in India, the effects of which no doubt impacted his Shanghai performance and would soon force him, less than a year in, to cancel his world tour altogether.[822]

A letter written by the aforementioned Edwin Dearn to a correspondent in London looking back at that period from the vantage point of 1971 indicated that, according to Dearn's recollection, Soo was indeed in Shanghai during this period and played the Victoria into mid-June. Dearn, in his correspondence, also recounts his memories that Soo's Shanghai turn was not seen as a success.[823] Interestingly, in this letter, Dearn also recounts that during his Shanghai performance, Soo was heckled for posing as a genuine Chinese. conjurer. However, by that point in his career, Soo (William Robinson) had been careful to stay a step ahead of his doubters by publicly professing to be half-Scottish and half-Chinese and being very careful in the manner he courted and gained the favor of local Chinese communities in his performance areas. (In the latter part of his career Soo even had promotional posters made up celebrating his newly discovered multi-ethnic heritage.)

Even more intriguingly, in this 1971 letter Dearn also reported that Soo, while in Shanghai, had issued some sort of challenge to Foo that had been ignored. According to the letter, Foo's lack of response to the challenge was due to the fact Foo could not "read or write" his own language. Another claim that given current information does not bear much scrutiny. First, one imagines if this public challenge had indeed been issued in Shanghai, there would be some record. However, an examination of available sources show none. Second, the rationale Dearn relates as to why Foo did not respond to Soo's challenge—that Foo could not read or write his own language and therefore did not see the notices given other information available—strains credulity. In fact, these claims sound very much like something a peevish Soo—who, during the run-up to their 1905 London challenge, incensed the Original Chinese Conjurer by referring to him as "low caste" and a mere "street corner juggler"—could have come up with while smarting from his dismal Shanghai gate receipts and still struggling with the gastrointestinal difficulties that would soon derail his world tour.

The fact the anecdote reflected poorly on Foo would likely have only increased its appeal to Dearn, who was a very close friend of Long Tak Sam. Sam, as noted earlier, like Soo, had his own complicated relationship with Foo and struggled mightily throughout his career to emerge from the Original Chinese Conjurer's shadow. Dearn, for his part, rarely missed an opportunity to declare his Sam's superiority over Foo.[824]

These indications of Soo's ongoing antipathy towards Foo raise the question of just what William Robinson really thought of Foo, the man he spent so much of his adult life mimicking. Clearly, we can never definitively know. However, as James Steinmeyer, leading illusionist and author of *The Glorious Deception*—the definitive biography of William Robinson/Chung Ling Soo—has noted, Robinson while clearly a product of his ethnocentric time thought well enough of Foo's act and his artistry to make Foo the template for his career. So surely, there was a grudging respect, but also, no doubt, an ego-driven desire to exceed and be acknowledged to have exceeded his inspiration. Something perhaps analogous to the "anxiety of influence" the critic Harold Bloom so aptly described as influencing the relationship between great writers and the literary giants who went before them.

FOO, PICASSO, AND *PARADE*

May 18th, 1917: The production of Sergei Diaghilev's ballet *Parade* premiered. The entertainment was a febrile collaboration combining the skills of Picasso, Jean Cocteau, and Erik Satie. The work was created for Diaghilev's ground-breaking Paris-based ballet company, Ballets Russes. It envisaged a small troupe of performers working outside the entrance to

To the right, Picasso's design for the Chinese conjurer's costume for the Ballet Russe's production of *Parade* in 1917. To the left, a photograph of the actual costume betraying the wear and discoloration of age. In 2017, the hundredth anniversary of the ballet, a retrospective featuring Picasso's artwork and designs for the production was curated by London's Victoria and Albert Museum. The Chinese conjurer outfit only survived because the last dancer to play the part, recognizing the historical significance of the costume, hid it away in a carefully buried trunk in his native Poland at the start of World War II. It was retrieved after the war had ended.[825]

a travelling circus seeking to lure those willing to pay into the tents behind them to see the actual show. Highly controversial due to its avant-garde design elements, the ballet featured a Chinese magician as a principal performer. The conjurer's costume, as were the sets and other costumes, was designed by Picasso. At the time, Picasso was in his cubist phase.

The Chinese magician was first played by Leonide Massine, who had just taken over from Vaslav Nijinsky as principal dancer for the famed dance troupe.

> Matthew Solomon, writing on the ballet, noted the inclusion of the Chinese conjurer in the piece as evidence of the enduring "aesthetic allure" of the Chinese magician to the Western imagination. Solomon also saw the Chinese magician archetype as an example of "trans-cultural impersonation" that was so popular in the earlier part of the 20th century. Solomon noted "the Chinese conjurer's move from middlebrow to highbrow culture via the modernist makeover of *Parade* was but one of the figures many historical displacements and relocations."[826]
>
> Foo, as the original, archetypical Chinese conjurer in the modern Western mind, must take much of the credit for this enduring allure.

Foo Seriously Ill; Chee Toy & Husband Called to His Side

Only six months after Soo passed through Shanghai in January of 1918, Foo was seriously ill, and his son Yee Dee and daughter-in-law Chee Toy were called to his side.[827] This illness may explain, in part, why Foo was nowhere to be seen during Chung Ling Soo's early 1918 visit to Shanghai. With regard to Foo's health, it could not have been positively affected by the recent loss of his home and Wuhan theater to fires and the related devastating financial losses.[828]

Fated to be always linked in something, akin to the quantum physics concept of interaction at a distance, Foo's reported deathly illness occurred around the same time Chung Ling Soo, a.k.a. William Robinson, was tragically killed on stage during a performance in London.

March 1918: Chung Ling Soo Dies on Stage in London; Killed When "Defying the Boxers Illusion" Goes Horribly Wrong

On the evening of March 24th, 1918, at the Wood Green Empire Theater in London, Chung Ling Soo was killed when something went terribly wrong during a performance of his "Defying the Boxers" illusion.

For over 100 years, magicians had been doing variants of the bullet-catching trick. Many of these illusions involved modifying muzzle-loading rifles. Forensic examinations of Soo's rifles performed during the inquest that followed his death confirmed Soo had also modified his rifles to perform the illusion.

The actual rifle barrels were never intended to fire. Instead, Soo had modified the tube used to hold the rifle's ramrod which was attached to the underside of the barrel to secretly hold a second charge that could be harmlessly fired. This second charge in the ramrod tube would, when the rifle's trigger was pulled, ignite, explode and emit a flash. Any observer in the audience would assume the rifle had fired. In truth, the gunpowder pushed down the actual rifle barrel never ignited, and the bullet that pressed in against the charge never left the barrel. After the fake firing of the barrel, Soo, who had, with the assistance of a confederate, palmed the bullets that the audience marked, stood at the other end of the stage and "caught" the bullets in his specially designed porcelain Chinese plate. That, at least, is how things were supposed to work prior to the night of March 24th.

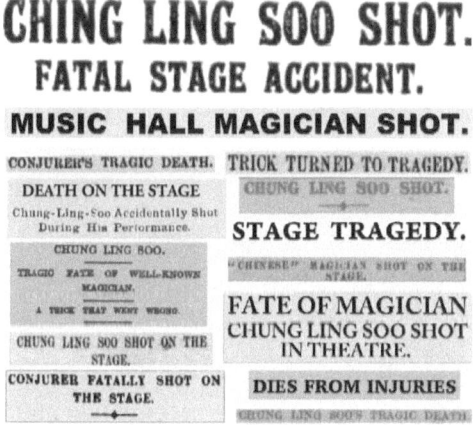

Samples of March 25th, 1918 headlines relating the news of Chung Ling Soo's death. (In some cases, text has been enhanced.)

Tragically, on that day in 1918, over a decade of use caused one of the rifles to develop cracks in it that allowed a trail of gun powder to gradually create a link between the powder that would be fired as part of the flash coming out of the ramrod tube and the powder packed into the actual rifle barrel to fool the audience. As a result, that night, Soo, instead of merely pretending to catch the bullets in the porcelain plate he held before his chest, received a mortal wound.

Upon being struck by the bullet, the normally mute Chung Ling Soo shouted in perfect English, "Something's gone wrong; close the curtain!" Robinson, bleeding profusely from his chest with his companion Dot at his side, collapsed to the stage floor. The curtains were closed. "God Save the King" played, and a confused and anxious crowd was escorted from the theater.

Soo was taken to the hospital but died the next day. Newspapers first reported the illusion gone wrong and the death of the famous "Chinese" magician to a shocked world. Then, just as quickly, they followed up with the even more astounding news, for the English general public, that the deceased was not a Chinese magician, but rather an American illusionist named William Robinson.

The coroner's examination that followed would involve one of the first forensic examinations of a rifle in a death inquiry, and would rule William Robinson's passing, despite many suspicions, a "death by misadventure."

At the time of his death, Robinson, performing as Chung Ling Soo, was one of the most popular and highest paid performers in England, having performed several times before King George and earning the equivalent of $1,500 per week, including a percentage of the gate receipts when he played "the provinces."[829–832]

Foo's faulty rifle would be auctioned in Cleveland in 1976, along with some other rare magic memorabilia.[833] Seemingly inevitably, in a report on the auction, Soo's faulty rifle was mistakenly referred to in the report as Ching Ling Foo's rifle. The rifle now reportedly holds a place of honor in David Copperfield's private Las Vegas magic museum.

Foo and Soo Confused Even in Death

Even in death, Ching Ling Foo and Chung Ling Soo were confused. Soo's death was initially reported in American papers as Foo's death. The smaller local papers, like those of Duluth, Minnesota, were not even aware of Chung Ling Soo and automatically assumed the report of Soo's death referred to Foo.[834]

Some of Foo's copycat competitors in the U.S. even leapt at the apparent opportunity to bury Foo and assume his mantle as America's premier Chinese magician. In July 1918, the opportunistic Ah Ling Foo, while playing Pittsburgh's Sheridan Square Theatre, identified himself as Ching Ling Foo's son, and proclaimed he was ready to take the place of his "father."[835]

Even in Australia there was confusion. The confusion on that continent, however, had an additional layer due to the Australian magician Hugarde's earlier turn as "Ching Ling Foo" during an Australian tour that followed his very meta appropriation of Soo's act and Foo's name after Soo had toured Australia in 1909.

Addressing that tangle in a June 1918 letter to the editor of Australia's *Western Champion* newspaper, one F.E. Matthews added some confusion of his own when he rightly informed the paper's audience that Hugarde, who had performed as Ching Ling Foo in Australia, was alive and well and touring, but then dropped the ball when he referred to the magician who had died in England as the very much still in the world Ching Ling Foo, not Chung Ling Soo.[836]

That Ching Ling Foo was not, in fact, dead became clearer to his many fans in the U.S. and other Western countries in late 1920, when ambitious Midwestern American entertainment manager Charles Hugo returned from China and made it clear that despite a notice

CHINESE MAGICIAN REPORTED DEAD PLANS A COMEBACK.

published in *Billboard* magazine and many rumors to the contrary, Ching Ling Foo, the father of all Chinese magicians and the "famous grand old man of China," was not dead.

Hugo, who had been in China during the fall of 1920 and met with Foo, shared that the "misinformation" about him was spread by rival troupes seeking to usurp the legend's place in the hearts of American theatergoers. This may well be true, but a large portion of the error was also based on the already-discussed confusion created by reporting on his rival Chung Ling Soo's death that repeatedly entangled the two.

While in China, Hugo had made a special trip from Shanghai to Hangzhou to verify the rumor of Foo's passing and meet up with Foo, still in the land of the living. Hugo had learned earlier in Shanghai that Foo, at that time, was the owner of one of China's largest circuses and had been touring Central and Northern China. Hugo said he found Foo in Hangzhou in the best of health and "as supple and mystifying as ever." Foo's illusions were the focal point of the circus, and like a good promoter, Hugo noted that many of Foo's tricks were "new and startling feats" that would be "a sensation in America."

At that time, Foo reportedly had the only trained elephant in China, and it was proving a great attraction.

In the Chinese interior, the audiences for Foo's circus were overwhelmingly Chinese, and Hugo said Foo's circus was doing terrific business. The Chinese conjurer did complain, however, to the American promoter that the practice at that time in the unrulier parts of China for men dressed in military attire to be allowed free of charge into entertainments cut considerably into his profits when he toured those areas.

Hugo further informed *Billboard* readers that upon learning of his alleged demise, Foo was "very much vexed" and had "authorized Mr. Hugo to try and arrange a tour for him." Foo, according to the promoter, communicated his "very highest regard for America."[837]

Interestingly, prior to his talk with Hugo, Foo had been under the impression that Harry Kellar had recently died, as that was the news in China, and Foo was delighted to learn his dear old friend was still among the living.

Hugo stayed as a guest of the Foo family for three days in Hangzhou. At the end of that period, Foo and Chee Toy traveled with him to Shanghai to see him off when Hugo sailed back to America. Hugo's attempts to arrange a third U.S. tour for Foo gathered additional steam a few months later, when the February 1921 edition of *The Magazine of Magic* repeated the news that Ching Ling Foo was, contrary to recent reports, "very much in the land of the living" and that "he is coming back and will show up the imitators who no doubt started the false rumor in hopes of trading on the name of the grand old man of China."

Sadly, however, like so many other plans to have Foo tour America, despite Hugo's best efforts, this final Foo tour never materialized.[838,839]

Foo's Film Legacy Continued: Mentored and Inspired Legendary Special Effects Pioneer Jerome Ash

Fittingly, given the tangled relationship between magicians of the late 1800s and early 1900s and the development of the nascent film industry—including Foo's own early recognition of the significance of the medium demonstrated in his investments in the film business and pioneering work in documentary film—almost last on the list of the legion of significant individuals, entertainers or otherwise, who claimed Foo left an indelible mark on them (either as an inspiration or mentor or some combination of the two) was Jerome Ash. At some point between Foo's second tour of America beginning in December 1912 and his death in 1922, the old conjurer's path crossed with this former child magician eager to learn. This interaction would provide Foo the opportunity to have one last significant, if indirect, impact on

American popular culture and the ever-encroaching, expanding, and ultimately lethal for vaudeville, new medium of film.

According to Ash, as a young magician, he came to Foo eager to learn more about magic. However, while Ash learned much about illusions in his time with Foo, he would ultimately most effectively put this knowledge to work not in a career as a stage magician as he had originally hoped; rather, he would adapt to changing times and technologies by becoming a legendary pioneer of the new field of film special effects, wisely recognizing the future lay with film.

Ash would become known to many as the "father" of special effects and be lauded by no less than George Lucas, the founder of Industrial Light and Magic, and others for his seminal effects work in such groundbreaking entertainments as the hugely popular *Flash Gordon* serials of 1936 and 1939's *Buck Rogers*, which served as inspiration for the phenomenon of today's *Star Wars* films and others like them.[840–843]

So it was that in Ash's heyday in the 1930s, while touring the country promoting his latest films, he would fondly relate during interviews working for Foo and watching from backstage as the Chinese magician made "elephants vanish" and "fountains rise" from the heads of stage hands, all while "operating in full view of the audience." Ash told the pressmen covering his latest films that "after that, turning human faces into clay masks and making movie actors walk on beams of light with a whole studio of technical staff to help him build the illusion was pretty much a vacation."[844]

Ash had spent two years in Asia in his youth studying the techniques of Asian magicians, and said it was during his time as an offstage man working with the Chinese conjurer on his illusions that he honed his skill with the "optical novelties" that later would become his specialty.[845–847]

Ash's time spent in Asia and his reference to Foo working with an elephant hint that the young magician's time working with Foo could have taken place after Foo had returned to China after his second

Reconfigured images from the *Flash Gordon* movie serial of 1936.

U.S. tour and was, as Hugo reported, touring with his own circus that included what for China was the rarity of an elephant.

Chefalo Tells a Tale of Foo and Additional Financial Woe

The last information on Foo's final years in the post-World War I era were contained in a note from the magician Chefalo. In a 1948 interview in *The Sphinx*, Chefalo recalled meeting Foo after World War I in Shanghai. He estimated the Chinese conjurer would have been at least 70 years of age. Chefalo was passing through China on a world tour and learned that the elderly Foo had "lost a large part of his fortune in a bad investment in a zoological garden."[848] What Chefalo was likely referring to there was not a "zoological garden", but rather what the Chinese called an "entertainment garden" similar to Shanghai's Chang Su-Ho Gardens or Zhang Gardens, which the Mooser Brothers had invested in.

These Chinese gardens typically had free spaces open to the public but also cafés, restaurants, and theaters which people would pay to access. The Chang Su-Ho Garden investment had given the Mooser Brothers many difficulties, and a Chinese boycott of foreign-owned businesses in 1905 forced them to sell their share in the entity.[849] It is not clear whether Foo had shared in that investment, or retained his share when the Moosers were forced to relinquish their share. There is a reasonable possibility that Foo's bad investment in a "zoological garden" may have been an investment he had made in Chang Su-Ho Gardens or another entertainment garden.

These financial setbacks, combined with the relatively difficult environment for touring theater and circus groups in what was known as the "Warlord" era in China hinted at by Foo in his earlier conversations with Hugo, may well have been the motivating forces leading Foo to contemplate, with Hugo's assistance, yet another U.S. tour. However, Foo as noted above, would not have a third tour.

Foo is Dead

Not long after these last reported contacts with Foo, reports began to emerge from China that this time, the great wizard had finally truly left this mortal veil. In late 1921, Wang Voong Ung, a Chinese magician based in Washington D.C. who had performed before President Woodrow Wilson and Sun Yat-Sen, returned from a visit to China "emphatically" claiming Ching Ling Foo, this time, was definitively dead.[850] Additional reliable reports of the Chinese conjurer's death would accumulate over the next months, and the year 1922 would eventually become solidified as the year of the grand old man's death.[851]

Shortly after Foo's death, in the April 1923 edition of the *M.U.M.* publication of the Society of American Magicians, Houdini, who was president of the society at the time, wrote of an upscale Chinese-themed restaurant and café located in San Francisco, incongruously named the Aladdin Café and run by Hattie and Minnie Mooser. These were the younger sisters of Leon and George Mooser. Houdini noted that since the brothers managed Foo for several years,

Photo of the interior of the Aladdin Studio, and to the right, an ad for the café touting Houdini's patronage from the San Francisco *Chronicle* in 1923.

after Foo had passed, the Moosers came into possession of a lot of the shawls, robes, drapery, and other materials Foo had used to decorate the stage during his act. Houdini then informed readers Hattie and Minnie were currently using those materials as central features of the very successful Aladdin Studio's décor. He also noted the elegant venue served as the unofficial headquarters for the S.A.M. in San Francisco, and that on special occasions drinks were served from the large bowl Foo produced as the finale of his production illusions, which was kept in a place of honor at the Aladdin. Houdini noted the venue, which was also a favorite of the theater crowd, was a fitting and respectful resting place for this Foo memorabilia.[852]

EPILOGUE: THE RICH LEGACY OF THE ORIGINAL CHINESE CONJURER

Among stage magic's greatest proponents, the period capped by the death of Soo and the retirements and subsequent deaths of Kellar and Foo seemed to finally bring down the curtain on what was the Golden Age of stage magic. No less an authority than Francis Martinka, the founder and owner of New York's legendary Martinka's Magic Shop—supplier of illusions from off-the-shelf ten-cent tricks to the most elaborate and costly bespoke first-class stage illusions—felt both in his business ledger and his bones that America's long love affair with stage magic had finally come to an end. Thus, in 1918, he prophetically proclaimed, "The great days of magic are gone … the art has declined … the great men have grown rich and retired or they have died."[853]

Foo, described as a "super magician" in Houdini's 1920 classic *Miracle Mongers and Their Methods*, and whose performances were praised by more than one critic as "on the outer fringe of being an art"[854], was of course numbered among Martinka's "great men." The effortlessly engaging Foo will always have, among conjurors and those that follow their craft, a place on the Mount Rushmore of great Golden Age stage magicians.

Beyond Foo's remarkable technical skills in up-close and stage magic, it was the uniquely charismatic Chinese magician's ability to enthrall and transfer to an audience a bit of the joy that he and his troupe seemed to radiate during a performance that elevated him above the endless parade of imitators, destined for country circuses and dime-store museums, that repeatedly sought but failed to replicate his magic. The core elements of Foo's major illusions may well, early on in his career, have been available for purchase through the mail. However, the personal magnetism, bonhomie, and presentation skills that kept people coming back over and over again to see a man perform illusions whose inner workings had already been repeatedly revealed to them were decidedly not.

As a perceptive correspondent for *The Sphinx* so wisely noted when assessing Foo's success, "the attraction in magic does not depend entirely on its mystery."[855]

Foo's legacy, however, extended far beyond his mastery of the presentation of occult illusions. Beyond his remarkable achievements in stage magic, but absolutely intertwined with them, were the magician's pioneering work in sound recording, documentary film, and the people-to-people diplomacy through which he succeeded in introducing, at a vital time, "a different picture" of the Chinese to the American public.

It was in this last area, even more than in producing the historically impactful *Wuchang Uprising* documentary, that the magician may have had his greatest impact. Foo and his talented troupe, over a period of almost 20 years, through the joyful and dignified presentation of their sheer talent in the era of the China Exclusion Act and under the long shadow of the "Heathen Chinee", managed to present to an America awash in very hostile representations of the Chinese a very "different picture", and those looking for 30 minutes or more of good entertainment and improved relations between the two peoples were all the better for it.

Dwight Taylor, noted American playwright, screenwriter, and child of vaudeville veterans, wrote in 1965, "I can recall to this day the tremendous fanfare that accompanied the arrival of Ching Ling Foo, the great Chinese magician, to this country; and how we hustled down to the theatre as fast as we could to get close to the footlights to see every single thing that was going on. And how Ching Ling Foo, this dignified and very tall Chinese, in his magnificently embroidered robes, suddenly turned a somersault, and came up with a large bowl of live goldfish in his outstretched hand, and a kindly and amused smile on his face which made me feel good all over. In fact, it still makes me feel good."[856]

As fitting an epitaph as any for the one and only "Original Chinese Conjurer."

March 1929 cover of *The Linking Ring*, publication of the International Brotherhood of Magicians, commemorating Foo's career. (Image courtesy of the International Brotherhood of Magicians at www.magician.org)

APPENDIX A

ILLUSTRATIONS

P. vii: Jean-Baptiste Perroneau. "*Magicien Chinois*," pencil drawing, 1738–1745. Metropolitan Museum of Art, New York, NY.

P. 5: Photo of pre-Omaha part of Ching Ling Foo's career, displaying the Chinese conjuror with one of his bowls from his signature production illusion.

P. 5: French poster promoting a performance of an early contemporary of Foo, who Houdini claimed was the Hungarian conjurer David Gueter.

P. 9: Interior sketch of the "Old" Shanghai Lyceum, a regular venue for the Foo troupe.

P. 9: Photo of the Shanghai Lyceum today.

P. 14: Omaha World's Fair poster.

P. 14: Photo of the Omaha World's Fair artificial lagoon.

P. 15: Treasury Secretary Lyman gage and Chinese-American businessman Hip Lung.

P. 17: Photos of the China Pavilion of the 1898 Omaha World's Fair.

P. 18: Photos of tickets to the Chinese Village and Chinese Theatre.

P. 20: Reproduction of the cover of M.P. Shiel's *The Yellow Danger*.

P. 20: Hermann Knackfuss. "*Völker Europas, Wahrt Eure Heiligsten Güter*," lithograph, 1895. German National Museum, Nuremberg.

P. 22: Newspaper headlines and photos of the Foo troupe. Images copyright Drowsy Emperor Ltd, not to be reproduced without permission.

P. 24: Roentgen and "Chiquita" exhibits at the Omaha World's Fair, courtesy Trans-Mississippi and International Exposition Digital Archive, University of Nebraska-Lincoln.

P. 27: Artist's recreation of poster promoting Foo's decapitation illusion. Illustration by Scobie; copyright Drowsy Emperor Ltd., not to be reproduced without permission.

P. 30: Portrait of Chinese minister Wu Ting Fang and illustration of Minister Wu from *Harper's Weekly*, 1900.

P. 34: Advertisement for Foo's Omaha "Grand Farewell Performance", Omaha *World-Herald*, November 14th, 1898, p. 5.

P. 37: Theatrical listings including Foo troupe at the Star Theater, Chicago *Daily News*, December 12th, 1898, p. 2.

P. 37: Hopkins Theater chain advertisement for the Foo troupe, Chicago *Daily News*, December 27th, 1898, p. 2.

P. 39: "CHINESE MAGICIAN'S TROUBLES"

P. 41: "Explains Foo's Tricks" newspaper article, Omaha *World-Herald*, January 22nd, 1899, p. 20.

P. 45: Fountain Theater advertisement, Cincinnati *Post*, February 18th, 1899, p. 2.

P. 46: Isadora Duncan newspaper listing, Chicago *Inter Ocean*, March 2nd, 1899, p. 12.

P. 48: Headlines around Foo's deportation. Image copyright Drowsy Emperor Ltd., not to be reproduced without permission.

P. 49: Headlines concerning Foo's deportation and 'recall' by the emperor. New York *Times*, April 2nd, 1899, p. 1.

P. 50: Keith's advertisement.

P. 55: Courtroom sketch of Foo deportation proceedings. Chicago *Daily News*, April 7th, 1899, p. 2.

P. 55: Judge Christian C. Kohlsaat & attorney Adolph Marks.

P. 56: Foo deportation trial headlines.

P. 56: Additional Foo deportation trial headlines.

P. 57: Chinese Exclusion Act "shot full of holes". Omaha *World-Herald*, April 30th, 1899, p. 4.

P. 59: Keith's Union Square Theatre playbills. *Music Hall and Theatre Review*, London, England, May 12th, 1899, p. 7. (Original playbills courtesy of the Houghton Library, Harvard University.)

P. 61: T. Dart Walker, "The Visit of the Ambassador of China", pen & ink, September 12th, 1896. Library of Congress, Washington, D.C.

P. 61: Richard F. Outcault, *Yellow Kid* cartoon on Li Hung Chang's visit to America, 1896.

P. 62: Boston *Globe* advertisements for Foo and Keller. Boston *Globe*, May 28th, 1899, p. 19.

P. 64: Advertisement for Martinka's Magic Shop.

P. 65: Chinatown headlines.

P. 66: Headlines from Foo's visit to Providence, RI.

P. 66: Headlines from Foo's interview with Mildred Irving.

P. 66: Headlines from Foo's visit to Boston.

P. 66: Letter from Foo to Boston child.

P. 77: Photographs of Cissy Loftus.

P. 78: Exposé of Foo's bowl trick. St. Louis *Post-Dispatch*, June 18, 1899, p. 37. Image property of Drowsy Emperor Ltd., not to be reproduced without permission.

P. 83: Keith's advertisement from 1899 featuring Chee Tai.

P. 84: "Cinderella" promotional feature, Philadelphia, 1899.

P. 85: Keith's New York theater ad featuring Foo & the Great Lafayette, New York *Tribune*, September 3rd, 1899. Enhanced image, copyright Drowsy Emperor Ltd., not to be reproduced without permission.

P. 89: Ads for *A Night in Chinatown* and *King of the Opium Ring*, Washington *Evening Star*, October 13th, 1900, p. 20, and Wilkes-Barre *Sunday News*, November 12th, 1899, p. 3.

P. 90: Illustrated pamphlet version of Harte's "The Heathen Chinee". Image copyright Drowsy Emperor Ltd., not to be reproduced without permission.

P. 92: Review of Foo performance at Shen's Garden Theatre, with excerpt from "The Heathen Chinee". Buffalo *Review*, February 13th, 1900, p. 5.

P. 93: Replica of flag presented to Foo by Empress of China.

P. 94: Foo's thousand-dollar challenge. New York *Tribune*, August 20th, 1899, p. 12.

P. 95: Keith's advertisements of Foo's "high-caste" troupe. *Sun* and New York *Press*, October 29th, 1899, p. 13.

P. 101: Keith's Boston theatre promotional material. Boston *Globe*, June 4th, 1899, p. 19.

P. 101: Thornton promotional advertisement, Boston *Globe*, June 4th, 1899, p. 19; Thornton's New York *Times* obituary.

P. 110: Harry Houdini poster.

P. 112: Diabolo and Marcel Meunier. Image copyright Drowsy Emperor Ltd., not to be reproduced without permission.

P. 114: Headline regarding "Mme. Ching Ling Foo".

P. 115: The Riggs Hotel in Washington, D.C.

P. 122: Foo troupe coverage in Brooklyn newspapers. Brooklyn *Times Union*, January 28th, 1900, p. 13; Brooklyn *Citizen*, January 28th, 1900, p. 10; Brooklyn *Times Union*, January 30th, 1900, p. 7.

P. 123: The Great Lafayette's Ching Ling Foo "travesty". *Music Hall and Theatre Review*, London, February 22nd, 1901, p. 128.

P. 124: Sheet music for the "Ching Ling Foo Rag March and Two-Step".

P. 125: Foo troupe's engagement in Brooklyn; male impersonator Zelma Rawlston. Brooklyn *Daily Eagle*, January 28th, 1900, p. 24.

P. 129: Elsie Janis and "How Salaries Have Leapt". Image copyright Drowsy Emperor Ltd., not to be reproduced without permission.

P. 133: Empire Theatre advertisement for Foo troupe performance. Oberlin *Review*, Oberlin, OH, March 8th, 1900, p. 23.

P. 141: Promotion for Foo's New York Bijou engagement. New York *Daily Tribune*, April 8th, 1900, p. 13.

P. 142: Ads for competing Foos—live and on screen—in New York.

P. 143: Advertisement for Foo short film and promotional photo for Corbett/Jeffries championship bout. Maitland *Daily Mercury*, Maitland, Australia, December 6th, 1900, p. 1.

P. 147: Chung Ling Soo and Suee Suan.

P. 148: Listing for Houdini at the Richmond Bijou.

P. 154: U.S. headlines concerning the Boxer Rebellion. Image copyright Drowsy Emperor Ltd., not to be reproduced without permission.

P. 155: The Philadelphia *Record* quotes "Heathen Chinee" on its front page. Philadelphia *Record*, July 26th, 1900, p. 1.

P. 156: Foo as stand-in for China in editorial cartoons. Image copyright Drowsy Emperor Ltd., not to be reproduced without permission.

P. 157: News headlines of Foo's fate following his return to China.

P. 161: More headlines concerning Foo in China.

P. 162: Advertisement for floor mats trading on Foo's reputation.

P. 164: Posters for Chung Ling Soo.

P. 165: News headline speculating about Foo's return to America. Image copyright Drowsy Emperor Ltd., not to be reproduced without permission.

P. 167: Soo appears in *Cosmopolitan*.

P. 172: Coney Island's Luna Park advertises its "new" Foo. Brooklyn *Times Union*, May 16th, 1903, p. 5.

P. 173: Soo's book of Chinese fairy tales and promotional review from *Quiz Magazine*, Sydney, Australia, 1903.

P. 174: Promotional shots of Soo from *The Tatler*, London, January 1st, 1904.

P. 183: Soo's cannon illusion. *The Bystander*, London, January 11th, 1905, p. 37.

P. 184: Soo's "Condemned to Death By the Boxers" illusion and circular promotional cards. Image copyright Drowsy Emperor Ltd., not to be reproduced without permission.

P. 185: "Rivals in Art of Magic" headline regarding the Foo challenge.

P. 187: The 1905 London version of the Foo troupe. *The Bystander*, London, January 11th, 1905, p. 37.

P. 190: London headlines touting Foo as the originator of Chinese magic.

P. 191: Headlines about the forthcoming "War of Rival Wizards". *Yorkshire Evening News*, Leeds, England, January 3rd, 1905, p. 2.

P. 198: The Hotel Provence in London's Leicester Square, where Foo hosted a Chinese dinner for guests.

P. 200: London headlines on the "invasion" of Chinese jugglers. London *Tatler*, February 15th, 1905, p. 264. Image copyright Drowsy Emperor Ltd., not to be reproduced without permission.

P. 201: Soo's colorful touring car.

P. 206: Soo revels in his 'victory'. Ads from the Bristol *Magpie*, Bristol, England, July 27th, 1905, p. 10; *Music Hall and Theatre Review*, London, January 13th, 1905, p. 5; and *Entr'acte*, London, January 14th, 1905, p. 5. Images copyright Drowsy Emperor Ltd., not to be reproduced without permission.

P. 209: John Northern Hillard defends Foo in the pages of *The Sphinx*. *The Sphinx*, Chicago, Vol. 4, Issue 1, March 15th, 1905, p. 2.

P. 211: The Foo troupe donates Chinese items to a museum during its Prague tour stop.

P. 212: Early advertisement for Soo's "The Robes of His Ancestors" exhibit.

P. 213: Artist's rendering by Scobie of "The Robes of His Ancestors" exhibit. Image copyright Drowsy Emperor Ltd., not to be reproduced without permission.

P. 216: Soo continues to boast of his victory over Foo. *Derbyshire Times*, Chesterfield, England, June 2, 1906, p. 7; Perth *West Australian*, October 6th, 1906, p. 1. Images copyright Drowsy Emperor Ltd., not to be reproduced without permission.

P. 217: Composite of images on Soo exposé of 1905. Image copyright Drowsy Emperor Ltd., not to be reproduced without permission.

P. 220: Soo introduces his "baby conjuror".

P. 221: Photos of the "Bamboo Flower", Nina Kametaro. *Genii*, Washington, D.C., Vol. 42 Issue 6, June 1978, p. 51. Image copyright Drowsy Emperor Ltd., not to be reproduced without permission.

P. 223: "Chinese Performers Barred" headline.

P. 234: "Foo to Return" headline.

P. 235: Program for Foo troupe show at the Theatre Royale.

P. 237: Fake Soo-style posters employed by Hugarde. Image copyright Drowsy Emperor Ltd., not to be reproduced without permission.

P. 237: Promotional materials for Hugarde's All Star Entertainers. Images copyright Drowsy Emperor Ltd., not to be reproduced without permission.

P. 240: Foo with Nicola in Tianjin.

P. 241: Chinese-language articles praising Foo. *Chinese Word Daily*, Hong Kong, June 16th, 1911, p. 3, and June 12th, 1911, p. 3.

P. 245: Still from Foo's war documentary *Wuchang Uprising*. Image courtesy the Shanghai Library.

P. 247: Foo honored in 2011 as one of the founders of Chinese documentary cinema.

P. 254: The new Foo troupe in America. *The Sphinx*, Chicago, Vol. 37, Issue 4, June 1938, cover.

P. 255: Headline on the quarantine of the *Nile* Liner. San Francisco *Call*, November 11th, 1912, p. 22.

P. 255: "Quarantine Annoys Chinese Songbird" headline.

P. 256: Collage of Chee Toy coverage. Image copyright Drowsy Emperor Ltd., not to be reproduced without permission.

P. 257: "Ching Ling Foo In" headline.

P. 259: Surety bond issued for Foo.

P. 260: Playbill for *Under Many Flags*. Image copyright Drowsy Emperor Ltd., not to be reproduced without permission.

P. 261: Promotional materials for *The Yellow Jacket*. Image copyright Drowsy Emperor Ltd., not to be reproduced without permission.

P. 262: "Mike McGraw" runs into a cast member from *The Yellow Jacket*. Image copyright Drowsy Emperor Ltd., not to be reproduced without permission.

P. 264: Notice of Foo's appearance at the Victoria theatre. New York *Clipper*, December 7th, 1912, p. 14.

P. 264: Hammerstein's Victoria Theatre and Roof Garden.

P. 265: More playbills for Foo at the Victoria Theatre. Courtesy of the Houghton Library, Harvard.

P. 267: Marcus de Zavas illustrations from Foo troupe review. Image copyright Drowsy Emperor Ltd., not to be reproduced without permission.

P. 269: Advertisement for Soy Kee & Co., suppliers of Chinese clothing.

P. 270: Issue of *Chinese Students' Monthly* featuring Foo. Image copyright Drowsy Emperor Ltd., not to be reproduced without permission.

P. 282: Promotional materials for Foo at Poli's Vaudeville Theatre. Bridgeport *Times and Evening Farmer*, Bridgeport, CT, January 11th, 1913, p. 5, and Bridgeport *Evening Farmer*, Bridgeport, CT, January 12th, 1913, p. 6. Image copyright Drowsy Emperor Ltd., not to be reproduced without permission.

P. 282: Headline on Foo's Chinese dining room. Bridgeport *Times and Evening Farmer*, Bridgeport, CT, January 17th, 1913, p. 1.

P. 283: "Ching Ling Foo to ride in Packard" headline.

P. 284: Modified Packard advertisement from 1913. Image copyright Drowsy Emperor Ltd., not to be reproduced without permission.

P. 285: Ching Ling Foo conjured in ad for the St. Joseph Water Company. Image copyright Drowsy Emperor Ltd., not to be reproduced without permission.

P. 289: Ziegfeld Follies poster. Image copyright Drowsy Emperor Ltd., not to be reproduced without permission.

P. 290: Composite of Foo promotional materials from the Ziegfeld Follies. St. Louis *Dispatch*, April 21st, 1913, p. 6; St. Louis *Globe Democrat*, April 20th, 1913, p. 37; Boston *Herald*, February 2nd, 1913, p. 33; *Daily Northwestern*, Evanston, IL, March 19th, 1913, p. 4; Chicago *Tribune*, March 30th, 1913, p. 17; Detroit *Times*, April 26th, 1913, p. 4; Washington *Evening Star*, May 4th,

1913, p. 27; Washington *Herald*, May 11th, 1913, p. 20. Image copyright Drowsy Emperor Ltd., not to be reproduced without permission.

P. 290: "Magician Quits Hotel in Huff" headline.

P. 291: The Chow and the Pekingese gain popularity during the Foo craze. Image copyright Drowsy Emperor Ltd., not to be reproduced without permission.

P. 293: Ziegfeld Follies stars Bert Williams and Leon Errol.

P. 299: The eyes of Ching Ling Foo. Image copyright Drowsy Emperor Ltd., not to be reproduced without permission.

P. 301: "French model … Chinese influence".

P. 304: "The Chinese magician who looks like a statesman". Image copyright Drowsy Emperor Ltd., not to be reproduced without permission.

P. 304: The "queer clause" of the Chinese Exclusion Act.

P. 315: Ching Ling Foo and his "clever company". Brooklyn *Citizen*, June 29th, 1913, p. 16. Image enhanced and remastered.

P. 317: A traditional Chinese xun. Brooklyn *Daily Eagle*, July 1st, 1913, p. 7, Image copyright Drowsy Emperor Ltd., not to be reproduced without permission.

P. 318: Lillian Russell attends a Foo troupe performance. Brooklyn *Citizen*, July 5th, 1913, p. 7.

P. 319: "Don't deprive the children." Brooklyn *Daily Eagle*, July 5th, 1913, p. 3.

P. 321: "The Magician's Dinner". New York *World*, July 13th, 1913, p. 2. Image enhanced.

P. 323: Hammerstein's extends its congratulations to Foo.

P. 324: Valeska Suratt.

P. 326: Pioneering cartoonist and animator Winsor McCay. Image copyright Drowsy Emperor Ltd., not to be reproduced without permission.

P. 331: More of Foo in popular culture: a Philadelphia millinery advertises a "wizard" of a hat.

P. 340: Advertisement for Lillian Russell's "Big Feature Festival". Altoona *Tribune*, September 26th, 1913, p. 12.

P. 342: Another "Big Feature Festival" ad and Lillian Russell's advice column.

P. 348: Headlines on ongoing tour troubles. Spokane *Daily Chronicle*, October 13th, 1913, p. 8.

P. 353: Hoffman's dancing girls. *Evening Post*, Charleston, SC, November 8th, 1913, p. 9; Greensboro *Record*, Greensboro, NC, November 7th, 1913,

p. 7; Charlotte *Evening Chronicle*, November 8th, 1913, p. 6. Image copyright Drowsy Emperor Ltd., not to be reproduced without permission.

P. 356: Jefferson Theatre in Birmingham, Alabama. Image copyright Drowsy Emperor Ltd., not to be reproduced without permission.

P. 357: Kentucky promotional materials for Hoffman show featuring Chee Toy. Lexington *Leader*, November 22nd, 1913, p. 2.; Lexington *Leander*, November 29th, 1913, p. 16.

P. 363: "Company of One Hundred—Mostly Girls". Kansas City *Star*, Kansas City, KS, December 13th, 1913, p. 3.

P. 365: Headlines for Foo rival Long Tack Sam. Image copyright Drowsy Emperor Ltd., not to be reproduced without permission.

P. 366: "Ching Long Foo is a Philosopher". Pittsburgh *Post-Gazette*, January 11th, 1914, p. 20. Image copyright Drowsy Emperor Ltd., not to be reproduced without permission.

P. 372: Nina Morris and *The Yellow Peril*.

P. 374: "Ching Playing for UBO".

P. 375: Foo ad by Scobie in the style employed by Poli in 1913. Image copyright Drowsy Emperor Ltd., not to be reproduced without permission.

P. 379: Foo on tour with *Mutt & Jeff* creator Bud Fisher. Buffalo *Courier*, April 7th, 1914, p. 8.

P. 381: "Chinese Good Luck Ring".

P. 383: Foo and others at the S.A.M. annual dinner. *M.U.M.*, New York, Volume 2, June 1914, p. 4.

P. 384: Another shot of Foo at the S.A.M. dinner. *The Conjuring Record*, Bronxville, NY, Volume 2, Issue 4, June 1914, p. 1.

P. 387: Foo and Soo both sign the guest book at Shakespeare's birthplace. Image copyright Drowsy Emperor Ltd., not to be reproduced without permission.

P. 388: Bombing of Antwerp contrasted with *Under Many Flags*.

P. 391: "Ching Ling Foo Returns". Tampa *Tribune*, November 22nd, 1914, p. 20.

P. 393: Promotional materials for another Foo-influenced conjuror, Han Ping Chien. Image copyright Drowsy Emperor Ltd., not to be reproduced without permission.

P. 397: Foo with the Marx Brothers. Image copyright Drowsy Emperor Ltd., not to be reproduced without permission. Chicago *Tribune*, December 23rd, 1914, p. 9.

P. 399: "Bewildered By Chinese Magic". Image copyright Drowsy Emperor Ltd., not to be reproduced without permission.

P. 402: "Oriental Ways". San Francisco *Chronicle*, January 31st, 1915, p. 17.

P. 406: Arthur Buel illustration of Foo in the Sacramento *Bee*. Sacramento *Bee*, February 15th, 1915, p. 14.

P. 407: "Chinese Prima Donna Hit of Orpheum Ball". Stockton *Evening Mail*, February 18th, 1915, p. 3.

P. 408: Foo fades, Chaplin rises. Stockton *Evening* Mail, February 16th, 1915, p. 6. Image copyright Drowsy Emperor Ltd., not to be reproduced without permission.

P. 408: Reproduction of Chinese-language poster for Charlie Chaplin's *Sunnyside*. Image copyright Drowsy Emperor Ltd., not to be reproduced without permission.

P. 409: Foo and opera at the Los Angeles Orpheum for Washington's Birthday Bill.

P. 411: Advertisement for D.W. Griffith's controversial silent film *Birth of a Nation*, a.k.a. *The Clansman*.

P. 413: Harry Kellar's "big house in California".

P. 414: Kellar & Foo.

P. 415: Houdini spills the secrets of the "talking tea kettle".

P. 417: Business card for Foo's cinema.

P. 418: Playbill for Foo troupe at Empire Day show. Image copyright Drowsy Emperor Ltd., not to be reproduced without permission.

P. 419: "When Magic Failed".

P. 420: Photograph of Foo & Edwin A. Dearn. Image copyright Drowsy Emperor Ltd., not to be reproduced without permission.

P. 422: Shanghai Victoria Theatre.

P. 425: Picasso's design for a Chinese conjuror's costume for *Parade*, and the actual costume.

P. 427: Headlines on the death of Chung Ling Soo. Image copyright Drowsy Emperor Ltd., not to be reproduced without permission.

P. 429: "Chinese Magician Reported Dead Plans a Comeback".

P. 433: *Flash Gordon* movie serial poster with special effects by Jerome Ash.

P. 435: Aladdin Studio and Tiffin Room.

P. 439: *Linking Ring* magazine cover from 1929 featuring Foo. *Linking Ring*, Eustis, FL, Vol. IX, 1929, cover.

APPENDIX B

END NOTES

Introduction

1. Dwight Taylor, *Variety*, June 1, 1965, p. 28. (In the quote, "this dignified and very tall Chinese" the term "Chinaman" was replaced with the term "Chinese".)

Chapter One

2. Sydney *Evening News*, March 10, 1905, p. 8.
3. Boston *Herald*, February 2, 1913, p. 30.
4. 中国纪录片研究中心 China Documentary Research Center, Beijing Communications University Weixin Post, November 29th, 2019.
5. 中国纪录片研究中心 China Documentary Research Center, Beijing Communications University Weixin Post, November 29th, 2019.
6. *The Sphinx*, Volume 18 Issue 7, September 1919, p. 9.
7. Ling Look, real name Dave Gueter, was a Hungarian who reportedly died in Hong Kong shortly after his brother, who was also part of the Royal Illusionists troupe, lost his life in Shanghai as a result of heart trauma arising from a bizarre bowling ball incident. Harry Houdini, *The Miracle Mongers and Their Methods* (New York: E.P. Dutton, 1920).
8. London *Evening News* and *Evening Mail*, December 29, 1904, p. 3.
9. Chicago *Inter Ocean*, April 7, 1899, p. 6.
10. *Stanyon's Magic*, Volume 1, Number 1, 1900, p. 6.
11. The North China *Herald*, May 9, 1890, p. 3.
12. The Straits *Times*, July 13, 1894, p. 2.
13. Singapore *Free Press*, February 1, 1897, p. 5.
14. Boston *Herald*, June 25, 1899, p. 14.

15 Washington (D.C.) *Evening Star*, January 10, 1900, p. 12.
16 North China *Herald*, "Ching Ling Foo Troupe", August 13, 1897, p. 22.
17 North China *Herald*, October 25, 1895, p. 19.

Chapter Two

18 Mark Kishlansky, Patrick Geary, and Patricia O'Brien, *Civilization in the West*, 7th Edition (New York: Pearson Education Inc., 2008).
19 Official Chinese participation was reportedly withheld as a mild protest of the 1882 U.S. Chinese Exclusion Act.
20 A second well-connected group—fronted by Wong Chin Foo, another prominent Chicago-based Chinese-American—was, as a consolation, granted a less significant concession located in another part of the fairgrounds, basically amounting to an exhibition of Chinese manufacturers. One of the things that tipped the scales towards the Mee Lee Wah group was that many of the Chinese-Americans involved in that bid had been involved in the Chinese Village that appeared at the Chicago fair.
21 The issuance of the special certificates allowing hundreds of Chinese to enter the U.S. for the purpose of participating in the Omaha Exhibition was a sensitive matter. Previous exhibitions, including the Chicago exhibition of 1893, had seen Chinese admitted for the purposes of these exhibitions not return to China and disappear into existing Chinese communities in the U.S. Critics of the Chinese entrepreneurs behind Chinese participation in the fairs claimed charging Chinese who had no intent of returning to China high fees to be brought to the U.S. under the useful guise of participating in the exhibitions was a very profitable sideline for those behind the Chinese villages. Some reports had the Mee Lee Wah Chinese Village Company getting approval to bring in over 500 Chinese, but this figure may have conflated the Mee Lee Wah Company quota with that of the other group granted a concession for a mercantile exhibition.
22 The Nebraska *Journal*, Omaha, May 7th, 1989, p. 5.
23 The Nebraska *Journal*, Omaha, September 12th, 1989, p. 5.
24 Ibid.
25 *Hiawatha World*, Brown County, KS, September 23rd, 1898, p. 2.
26 The *Tennessean*, Nashville, March 12, 1898, p. 8.
27 Glenwood *Opinion Tribune*, Glenwood, IA, June 2nd, 1898, p. 2.
28 The Nebraska *State Journal*, Lincoln, NE, July 23rd, 1898, p. 5.
29 The Nebraska *State Journal*, Lincoln, NE, August 21st, 1898, p. 15.
30 Richmond *Times*, Richmond, VA, March 11th, 1900, p. 12.

31 Chicago *Inter Ocean*, April 7th, 1899, p. 23.
32 The Nebraska *State Journal*, Lincoln, NE, August 21st, 1989, p. 15.
33 The Nebraska *State Journal*, Lincoln, NE, July 29th, 1898, p. 5.
34 It appears that not long after reports of his son's death, Foo, while still appearing at the Chinese Village and Chinese Theater, found time to travel to Philadelphia to try out his act at Keith's Theater. It would later be the Hopkins Theater chain, not Keith's, that would ultimately sign him on for his first post-Omaha exhibition tour (Philadelphia *Times*, August 2nd, 1898, p. 3). How this engagement occurred, or its outcome, remains a mystery, other than the record of its occurrence.
35 Interestingly, in one of the funeral reports, it was indicated that Chinese in the village were the target of racist taunts by "tough young men" who gathered on the Midway (Omaha *World Herald*, January 8th, 1898.)
36 Omaha *World Herald*, November 7th, 1898, p. 8.
37 Richmond *Times*, Richmond, VA, March 11th, 1900, p. 12.
38 Interestingly, less than a year after the Richmond interview, when William Robinson—who would become Foo's great rival Chung Ling Soo—conspired to duplicate Foo's act, Robinson would also use "interpreters" to translate his gibberish when he was interviewed by reporters, and pretended to speak Chinese. Robinson, while not a stutterer and obviously proficient in English, reportedly suffered from a nasal, uncommanding voice that had repeatedly proven, to Robinson's ongoing regret, unsuitable for engaging and holding an audience. For a detailed discussion of William Robinson's life and career, see Jim Steinmeyer's *Glorious Deception: The Double Life of William Robinson, a.k.a. Chung Ling Soo, The "Marvelous Chinese Conjurer"* (Boston: Da Capo Press, 2005).
39 Ottawa *Daily Republic*, Ottawa, KS, August 20th, 1898, p. 1.
40 Another popular anecdote from the exposition regarding Chinese-American interaction at the Fair focused on differing female fashions in the two countries. According to these accounts, some female fairgoers attending the Chinese Village's ethnographic exposition, while observing the small feet of many of the Chinese women, expressed both astonishment and commiseration. When they began a long discussion of how this brutality could occur only in a "heathen land", one of the Chinese women—apparently somewhat offended—rose up and addressed the American woman in perfect English, inquiring about the U.S. custom of lace-drawn corsets. (St. Joseph *Gazette-Herald*, St. Joseph, MO, August 10th, 1898, p. 4.)
41 Omaha *World-Herald*, October 2, 1898, p. 3.
42 Omaha *World-Herald*, October 12th, 1898, p. 12.

43 The Nebraska *State Journal*, Lincoln, NE, June 12th, 1898, p. 2.
44 The Nebraska *State Journal*, Lincoln, NE, June 19th, 1898, p. 6.
45 The Nebraska *State Journal*, Lincoln, NE, July 2nd, 1898, p. 5.
46 The Nebraska *State Journal*, Lincoln, NE, October 13th, 1898, p. 2.
47 Application of the China Exclusion Act to America's new Philippine territory would have made life very difficult for the Chinese, given the level of trade and cultural exchange between the two countries.
48 Omaha *Daily Bee*, November 7th, 1898, p. 5.
49 *The Sphinx*, Volume 8 Issue 2, April 1909, p. 9.
50 Christopher Stahl, *Outdoing Ching Ling Foo: Performing Magic on the Western Stage* (London: Palgrave MacMillan, 2016, Francesca Coppa, Lawrence Haas, and James Peck, eds.), pp. 151–174.
51 Omaha *Daily Bee*, November 17th, 1898, p. 5.
52 Omaha *World-Herald*, November 17th, 1898, p. 3.
53 By the time the Exposition was coming to an end, multiple news reports covering it praised Foo as "the best magician ever seen in the U.S.," Kenneth G. Alfers, "Triumph of the West: The Trans-Mississippi Exposition", *Nebraska History* Vol. 53 (1972): pp. 312–329.

Chapter Three

54 Omaha *Daily Bee*, November 17th, 1898, p. 5.
55 Brooklyn *Times Union*, July 1st, 1913, p. 4.
56 Lincoln *Journal Star*, Lincoln, NE, January 2nd, 1901, p. 8.
57 *The Billboard*, December 29th, 1900, p. 8.
58 New York *Dramatic Mirror*, June 3rd, 1899.
59 Chicago *Daily News*, December 19, 1898, p. 10.
60 Chicago *Tribune*, December 19th, 1898, p. 5.
61 New Orleans *Times Picayune*, January 26th, 1899, p. 11.
62 St. Louis *Republic*, January 15th, 1899, p. 3.
63 Ibid.
64 St. Louis *Dispatch*, January 9th, 1899, p. 7–8.
65 Omaha *World-Herald*, January 22nd, 1899, p. 20.
66 Omaha *Daily Bee*, January 1st, 1899, p. 1.
67 London *Observer*, January 22nd, 1905, p. 6.
68 New Orleans *Times Picayune*, January 26th, 1899, p. 11.
69 New Orleans *Times Picayune*, January 23rd, 1899, p. 3.
70 New Orleans *Times Picayune*, January 27th, 1899, p. 6.
71 New Orleans *Times Picayune*, January 23rd, 1899, p. 3.
72 Cincinnati *Post*, February 18th, 1899, p. 2.
73 Chicago *Inter Ocean*, March 14th, 1899, p. 3.

Chapter Four

74 New York *Times*, April 2nd, 1899, p. 1.
75 Arthur Frank Wertheim, *Vaudeville Wars: How the Keith-Albee and Orpheum Circuits Controlled the Big Time and Its Performers* (London: Palgrave MacMillan, 2006).
76 Boston *Globe*, June 18th, 1899, p. 18.
77 The Nebraska *State Journal*, Omaha, NE, March 12th, 1930, p. 1.
78 Philadelphia *Inquirer*, April 1st, 1899, p. 14.
79 Los Angeles, *Times*, December 29th, 1904, p. 6. Adolph Marks would end up defending Chinese magicians from deportation again in 1904, when four magicians performing at the St. Louis World's Fair were arrested on charges of violating the Chinese exclusion laws. They were released on bonds signed by Marks, who claimed the Chinese were all "of good families in Peking" and were granted permission to travel to the U.S. for the fair.
80 *Daily Iowa Capitol*, Des Moines, IA, April 5th, 1899, p. 4.
81 Chicago *Inter Ocean*, April 6th, 1899, p. 6.
82 Chicago *Daily News*, April 5th, 1899, p. 10.
83 Ibid.
84 Ibid.
85 Marion *Star*, Marion, OH, April 7th, 1899, p. 1.
86 Chicago *Inter Ocean*, April 7th, 1899, p. 6.
87 *The Salt Lake Tribune*, Salt Lake City, UT, April 7th, 1899, p. 3.
88 Chicago *Tribune*, April 2nd, 1899, p. 2.
89 Chicago *Inter* Ocean, April 5th, 1899, p. 6.
90 Chicago *Daily News*, April 7th, 1899, p. 2.
91 New York *Times*, April 26th, 1899, p. 8.
92 Krystn Moon has done extensive research into the issues surrounding Chinese migration into the U.S.; see "'On a Temporary Basis': Immigration and the American Entertainment Industry, 1880s–1930s," *Journal of American History* Vol. 99 (Bloomington, IN, 2012): pp. 775–776.
93 Stockton *Evening Mail*, Stockton, CA, April 27th, 1899, p. 2.
94 Omaha *World-Herald*, April 30th, 1899, p. 4.
95 Ibid.
96 The China Exclusion Act of 1882 was seen as necessary bynativist labor leaders of the time, who believed Chinese workers depressed wage levels, and xenophobes, who simply could not tolerate an increase in the non-white population of the U.S. These sentiments were particularly strong in California, where at one point during the Gold Rush era, Chinese men represented up to 25% of all working-age wage earners in the

state and where the state government had developed a small cottage industry of drafting discriminatory anti-Chinese laws. The resident Chinese were not allowed vote, and thus had precious little influence over the politicians being lobbied to enact these laws.

97   *The Era*, London, England, May 20th, 1899, p. 18.

Chapter Five

98   Boston *Globe*, June 18th, 1899, p. 18.
99   New York *Times*, May 2nd, 1899, p. 14.
100 New York *Times*, May 9th, 1899, p. 7.
101 The Pawtucket *Times*, May 13th, 1899, p. 8.
102 The Pawtucket *Times*, June 10th, 1899, p. 8.
103 Boston *Herald*, May 28th, 1899, p. 14.
104 Izola L. Forrester, *Dramatic* Magazine, May 899, pp. 25–28.
105 *The Phonoscope*, June 1899, p. 12.
106 *St. Andrew's University Berliner*, Berlin, NJ, July 21st, 2009, listing of recording dated October 10th, 1899, of recording by Foo of Chinese Song No. 17 from the *Wen Zhao Guan Peking Opera*.
107 *Mahatma*, Vol. 2, No. 12, June 1899, p. 6.
108 Ibid., p. 11.
109 The Pawtucket *Times*, June 8th, 1899, p. 7.
110 Ibid.
111 Boston *Sunday Globe*, June 11th, 1899, p. 26.
112 Boston *Herald*, June 11th, 1899, p. 14.
113 Ibid.
114 Ibid.
115 Ibid. (In this quote the term "Chinaman" has been replaced with the term "Chinese".)
116 The Pawtucket *Times*, June 13th, 1899, p. 10.
117 Ibid.
118 At the time, Britain's Lord Chesterfield was considered the arbiter of proper social conduct.
119 The Pawtucket *Times*, June 15th, 1899, p. 8.
120 Ibid., p. 6.
121 Boston *Globe*, June 17th, 1899, p. 8.
122 Boston *Herald*, June 17th, 1899, p. 17.
123 Boston *Globe*, June 18th, 1899, p. 18.
124 Boston *Sunday Post*, June 18th, 1899, p. 10.
125 Ibid.
126 Ibid.

127 Boston *Herald*, June 18th, 1899, p. 14.
128 Boston *Post*, June 18th, 1899, p. 11.
129 Boston *Globe*, June 20th, 1899, p. 2.
130 Boston *Herald*, June 24th, 1899, p. 6.
131 Ibid.
132 Ibid.
133 Ibid.
134 Boston *Traveler*, March 28th, 1951, p. 29.
135 Boston *Sunday Globe*, June 25th, 1899, p. 18.
136 Boston *Globe*, July 4th, 1899, p. 8.
137 Boston *Herald*, July 4th, 1899, p. 6.
138 Philadelphia *Times*, July 23rd, 1899, p. 28.
139 Knoxville *Journal and Tribune*, July 17th, 1899, p. 6.
140 Cambridge *Chronicle*, Boston, July 22nd, 1899, p. 9.
141 Philadelphia *Inquirer*, July 23rd, 1899, p. 8.
142 *Juniata Sentinel and Republican*, Mifflin Town, PA, August 2nd, 1899, p. 2.
143 Philadelphia *Times*, August 3rd, 1899, p. 9.
144 Philadelphia *Inquirer*, August 6th, 1899, p. 8.
145 Philadelphia *Inquirer*, July 25th, 1899, p. 7.
146 Philadelphia *Times*, August 13th, 1899, p. 18.
147 *Music Hall and Theatre Review*, London, July 28th, 1899, p. 10.
148 Philadelphia *Times*, July 30th, 1899, p. 30.
149 Philadelphia *Inquirer*, August 20th, 1899, p. 23.
150 Ibid.
151 New York *Times*, August 20th, 1899, p. 13.
152 New York *World*, September 12th, 1899, p. 5.
153 *Music Hall and Theatre Review*, London, August 25th, 1899, p. 11.
154 Washington *Times*, September 17th, 1899, p. 15.
155 Ibid.
156 Wilkes-Barre *Dollar Weekly*, September 23rd, 1899, p. 5.
157 New York *Sun*, September 3rd, 1899, p. 12.
158 Elmira *Star Gazette*, Elmira, NY, October 26th, 1899, p. 3.
159 Brooklyn *Daily Eagle*, January 28th, 1900, p. 24.
160 Buffalo *Commercial*, February 3rd, 1900, p. 5.
161 Harrisburg *Telegraph*, January 1st, 1900. p. 2.
162 Carlisle *Evening Herald*, Carlisle, PA, November 17th, 1899, p. 1.
163 Harte and Mark Twain, driven by the financial opportunities presented, actually ended up collaborating on a "China question" play with the alleged goal of providing an "illustration of the Chinese character" in 1876. The two popular humorists completed "Ah Sin" in 1876. The play, which

opened in 1877, attracted significant attention—not surprisingly, given the prominence of its authors—and mixed reviews. While the "serio-comic lecture" featuring Harte's most popular character proved popular, the theater critic of the New York *Sun* assessed the play as devoid of art and Ah Sin, the scheming centerpiece of the work, as "a caricature made up of two or three external oddities of manner" "who steals everything he can lay his hands on." Ah Sin was, of course, portrayed through yellowface. (New York *Sun*, August 5th, p. 3.

164 New York *Times*, August 27th, 1899, p. 16.
165 New York *World*, August 29th, 1899, p. 3.
166 New York *Sun*, August 20th, 1899, p. 20.
167 *Mahatma*, Vol. 3, No. 3, September 1899, p. 4.
168 *Variety*, New York, Marth 29th, 1918, p. 5.
169 *Mahatma*, Vol. 3, No. 3, September 1899, p. 7.
170 One wonders if the fact *Mahatma* profited from the advertisement of the devices that duplicated Foo's illusions in their pages and subsequent sales played a role in their editorial position on these issues.
171 Council Bluffs *Daily Nonpareil*, September 10th, 1899, p. 9.
172 The *Era*, London, September 23rd, 1899, p. 23.
173 Guy Jarrett, *Magic and Stagecraft* (Chicago: Magic, Inc., 1936).
174 London *Observer*, January 22nd, 1905, p. 6.
175 New York *Times*, September 24th, 1899, p. 18.
176 *Mahatma*, Vol. 3, No. 4, October 1899, p. 2.
177 *Music Hall and Theatre Review*, London, October 6th, 1899, p. 10.
178 Philadelphia *Times*, November 12th, 1899, p. 33.
179 *Neptune Ocean Grove Times*, Neptune Township, NJ, October 7th, 1899, p. 5.
180 *Mahatma*, Vol. 3, No. 5, November 1899, p. 3.
181 Ibid. (In this quote the term "Chinaman" has been replaced with the term "Chinese".)
182 Philadelphia *Times*, December 3rd, 1899, p. 6.
183 *Genii*, Vol. 3, Issue 1, September 1938, p. 20.
184 Philadelphia *Inquirer*, October 27th, 1938, p. 32.
185 New York *Times*, July 29th, 1938, p. 17.
186 New York *Times*, November 1st, 1899, p. 7.
187 Philadelphia *Inquirer*, November 12th, 1899, p. 30.
188 Philadelphia *Inquirer*, November 14th, 1899, p. 5.
189 Harrisburg *Telegraph*, November 16th, 1899, p. 3.
190 Philadelphia *Inquirer*, November 19th, 1899, p. 30.
191 *The Era*, London, November 18th, 1899, p. 20.
192 Philadelphia *Times*, November 19th, 1899, p. 30.
193 Philadelphia *Inquirer*, November 26th, 1899, p. 30.
194 Philadelphia *Inquirer*, December 3rd, 1899, p. 30.

195 Ibid.
196 The Pawtucket *Times*, December 12th, 1899, p. 8.
197 The Pawtucket *Times*, December 13th, 1899, p. 7. (In this quote the term "Chinaman" has been replaced with the term "Chinese".)
198 This would be in great contrast to what had been termed the "bachelor culture" of the working Chinese in San Francisco and other areas where the China Exclusion Act of 1882 and the earlier Page Act of 1875 had effectively prevented Chinese women from entering the U.S. and thus allowing Chinese men already in the country to form families.
199 The Pawtucket *Times*, December 13th, 1899, p. 7.
200 Boston *Globe*, January 7th, 1900, p. 14.
201 Boston *Globe*, January 9th, 1900, p. 2.
202 Boston *Herald*, January 21st, 1900, p. 14.
203 Washington *Times*, January 14th, 1900, p. 14.
204 Washington *Evening Star*, January 6th, 1900, p. 20.
205 Washington *Times*, January 16th, 1900, p. 7.
206 Washington *Post*, January 17th, 1900, p. 7.
207 Washington *Evening Star*, January 10th, 1900, p. 12.
208 Washington *Evening Star*, January 13th, 1900, p. 21.
209 Washington *Evening Star*, January 20th, 1900, p. 20.
210 Jefferson *Bee*, Jefferson, IA, February 1st, 1900, p. 1.
211 Washington *Evening Star*, January 20th, 1900, p. 20.
212 Washington *Times*, January 21st, 1900, p. 16.
213 Ibid.
214 Washington *Evening Star*, January 27th, 1900, p. 20.
215 Brooklyn *Daily Eagle*, January 21st, 1900, p. 24.
216 Brooklyn *Citizen*, January 30th, 1900, p. 10.
217 Buffalo *Inquirer*, January 22nd, 1900, p. 5.
218 Washington *Evening Star*, March 7th, 1900, p. 11.
219 Washington *Evening Star*, March 10th, 1900, p. 19.
220 Brooklyn *Daily Eagle*, January 23rd, 1900, p. 9.
221 Brooklyn *Daily Eagle*, January 30th, 1900, p. 9.
222 Brooklyn *Daily* Eagle, January 28th, 1900, p. 24.
223 Buffalo *Enquirer*, February 3rd, 1900, p. 5.

Chapter Six

224 Washington *Evening Star*, February 3rd, p. 22.
225 Washington *Evening Star*, February 24th, p. 22.
226 Chicago *Examiner*, December 20th, 1914, p. 16.
227 Washington *Post*, January 17th, 1900, p. 7.
228 Buffalo *Courier*, March 10th, 1918, p. 50.

229 Buffalo *Morning and Illustrated Express*, February 6th, 1900, p. 6.
230 Buffalo *Morning and* Illustrated *Illustrated Buffalo Express*, February 6th, 1900, p. 6.
231 Buffalo *Courier*, February 6th, 1900, p. 8.
232 Buffalo *Evening News*, February 6th, 1900 p. 12.
233 Buffalo *Evening News*, February 13th, 1900, p. 14.
234 Buffalo *Courier*, February 13th, 1900, p. 6.
235 Buffalo *Morning Express*, February 6th, 1900, p. 6.
236 Buffalo *Review*, February 13th, 1900, p. 5.
237 Buffalo *Commercial*, February 26th, 1900, p. 11.
238 Buffalo *Courier*, February 28th, 1900, p. 2.
239 *Saturday Night*, Toronto, March 31st, 1900, p. 6.
240 *Mahatma*, Vol. 3, No. 9, 1900, p. 7.
241 Toronto *Globe and Mail*, February 10th, 1900, p. 10.
242 *Music Hall and Theatre Review*, London, March 2nd, 1900, p. 10.
243 Cleveland *Leader*, February 15th, 1900, p. 7
244 Philadelphia *Inquirer*, March 4th, 1900, p. 27.
245 Cleveland *Plain-Dealer*, February 20th, 1900, p. 10.
246 Cleveland *Plain-Dealer*, February 22nd, 1900, p. 8.
247 Brisbane *Courier*, February 22nd, 1900, p. 2.
248 Richmond *Times*, March 4th, 1900, p. 11.
249 Richmond *Times*, March 6th, 1900, p. 3.
250 Ibid., p. 4.
251 Richmond *Times*, March 11th, 1900, p. 12.
252 Richmond *Times*, March 6th, 1900, p. 3.
253 Richmond *Times*, March 11th, 1900, p. 12.
254 Richmond *Dispatch*, March 11th, 1900, p. 8.
255 Ibid. (In this quote the term "Chinaman" has been replaced with the term "Chinese".)
256 Washington *Evening Star*, March 7th, 1900, p. 11.
257 Washington *Evening Star*, March 3rd, 1900, p. 19.
258 Washington *Evening Star*, March 13th, 1900, p. 10.
259 Baltimore *Sun*, March 17th. 1900, p. 7.
260 Baltimore *Sun*, March 20th, 1900, p. 7.
261 *Mahatma*, Vol. 3, No. 9, March 1900, p. 7.
262 *Mahatma*, Vol. 3, No. 10, April 1900, p. 3–4.
263 Ibid.
264 New York *Sun*, March 25th, 1900, p. 10.
265 New York *Times*, April 1st, 1900, p. 18.
266 *The Era*, London, April 21st, 1900, p. 9.
267 New York *Tribune*, April 8th, 1900, p. 12.

268 New York *Times*, April 14th, 1900, p. 14.
269 New York *Times*, April 9th, 1900, p. 5.
270 New York *Clipper*, April 14th, 1900, p. 168.
271 Maitland *Daily Mercury*, Maitland, Australia, December 6th, 1900, p. 1.
272 Boston *Globe*, September 30th, 1900, p. 23.

Chapter Seven

273 *Mahatma*, Vol. 3 No. 10, April 1900, p. 4.
274 *The Era*, London, March 31st, 1900, p. 18.
275 *Mahatma*, Vol. 3 No. 11, May 1900, p. 6.
276 Ibid.
277 *The Sporting News*, London, April 21st, 1900, p. 2.
278 *London North Mercury and Crouchend Observer*, August 18th, 1900, p. 5.
279 *Mahatma*, Vol. 4, No. 1, July 1900, p. 2.
280 Richmond *Times*, Richmond, VA, April 22nd, 1900, p. 17.
281 Brooklyn *Daily Eagle*, April 25th, 1900, p. 5.
282 Washington *Post*, April 29th, 1900, p. 26.
283 Philadelphia *Inquirer*, April 26th, 1900, p. 9.
284 Philadelphia *Inquirer*, April 29th, 1900, p. 9.
285 New Orleans *Daily Crescent*, April 20th, 1900, p. 2.
286 New York *Sun*, April 30th, 1900, p. 10.
287 *Music Hall and Theatre Review*, London, May 4th, 1900, p. 10.
288 Richmond *Dispatch*, May 9th, 1900, p. 1.
289 *Music Hall and Theatre Review*, London, May 11th, 1900, p. 10.
290 New York *Clipper*, May 12th, 1900, p. 243.
291 Boston *Globe*, May 15th, 1900, p. 2.
292 Washington *Post*, April 29th, 1900, p. 26.
293 *Echo de l'Ouest*, Minneapolis, MN, May 25th, 1900, p. 4.
294 Winnipeg *Free Press*, May 25th, 1900, p. 3.
295 London and China *Telegraph*, June 19th, 1900, p. 474.
296 Philadelphia *Times*, July 26th, 1900, p. 5.
297 Xu Mei Mei, "Knowledge Development: Cinema in China prior to WWI," doctoral dissertation, University of Bonn, February 17th, 2016, pp. 222–223.
298 Washington *Evening Star*, July 26th, 1900, p. 1.
299 *Daily Nonpareil*, Council Bluffs, IA, July 29th, 1900, p. 3.
300 New York *Tribune*, August 1st, 1900, p. 3.
301 The Pawtucket *Times*, August 10th, 1900, p. 8.
302 Philadelphia *Inquirer*, August 13th, 1900, p. 9.
303 Windsor *Review*, Windsor, MO, August 9th, 1900, p. 2.
304 *Music Hall and Theatre Review*, London, August 17th, 1900, p. 10.

305 London *North Mercury and Crouchend Observer*, August 11th, 1900, p. 3.
306 Philadelphia *Inquirer*, October 14th, 1900, p. 27.
307 *Mahatma*, Vol. 4, No. 7, January 1901, p. 452.
308 New York *Buffalo Enquirer*, March 11th, 1901, p. 3.
309 New York *Times*, February 22nd, 1901, p. 2.
310 Ibid.
311 Boston *Herald*, March 3rd, 1901, p. 17.
312 *Virginian Pilot*, Norfolk, VA, March 10th, 1901, p. 7.
313 *Virginian Pilot*, Norfolk, VA, April 12th, 1901, p. 11.
314 Washington *Evening Star*, March 16th, 1901, p. 23.
315 *Gazette de Charleroi*, Brussels, May 26th, 1901, p. 4.
316 Buffalo *Enquirer*, March 1st, 1902, p. 7.
317 *Stanyon's Magic*, London, Vol. 2, No. 6, March 1902, p. 6.
318 Ibid.
319 *The Chronicle*, Leigh, England, December 5th, 1902, p. 6.
320 It was an era before easily accessible databases, and what one said in one locale to a newspaper a few months ago could not easily be discerned by the public or even newspapermen. This encouraged carelessness with the constant reforming of the narratives.
321 *The Chronicle*, Leigh, England, December 5th, 1902, p. 6. (In this quote the term "Chinaman" has been replaced with the term "Chinese".)
322 "The Best Tricks of Famous Magicians", Ruth Everett, *The Cosmopolitan*, New York, December 1902, p. 146.

Chapter Eight

323 Shanghai *North China Herald*, December 31st, 1902, p. 16.
324 Shanghai *North China Herald*, January 7th, 1903, p. 20.
325 Minneapolis *Journal*, March 27th, 1903, p. 7.
326 Rochester *Democrat and Chronicle*, April 12th, 1903, p. 17.
327 *The Sphinx*, Chicago, Vol. 2, Issue #5, July 1903, p. 6.
328 *The Wasp*, San Francisco, August 22nd, 1903, p. 205.
329 *Quiz Magazine*, Sydney, Australia, 1903.
330 *The Stage*, London, September 24th, 1903, p. 7.
331 New York *Times*, March 20th, 1904, p. 12.
332 *The Sphinx*, Chicago, Vol. 3, Issue 2, April 1904, p. 23.
333 *Stanyon's Magic*, London, Vol. 4, No. 8, May 1905, p. 5.
334 *Music Hall and Theatre Review*, London, June 10th, 1904, p. 9.
335 Leeds and Yorkshire *Mercury*, September 13th, 1904, p. 8.
336 Birmingham *Daily Gazette*, Birmingham, England, September 27th, 1904, p. 9.

337   *Mahatma*, Vol. 8, No. 1, July 1904, pp. 6–7.
338   Sometime in 1904, George Mooser reportedly purchased a half-interest in Shanghai entertainment center Zhang Gardens. Zhang Gardens was one of the most important entertainment complexes in Shanghai at the time. Only one year later, in August 1905, he would be forced to sell this share in the Gardens when the Mooser Brothers' businesses were targeted as part of an anti-Western boycott. Xu Mei Mei, "Knowledge Development: Cinema in China prior to WWI," doctoral dissertation, University of Bonn, February 17th, 2016, pp. 222–223.

Chapter Nine

339   *St. James Gazette*, London, December 10th, 1904, p. 10.
340   *L'Illusionniste*, Paris, Vol. 2, 1904, p. 263.
341   *Lincolnshire Echo*, Lincoln, England, December 20th, 1904, p. 5.
342   *Mahatma*, Vol. 8, No. 8, February 1905, p. 4.
343   London *Daily News*, December 29th, 1904, p. 11.
344   London *Evening News and Evening Mail*, December 29th, 1904, p. 3.
345   *The Sphinx*, Chicago, Vol. 3, Issue 12, February 1905, p. 10.
346   San Diego *Union*, February 5th, 1905, p. 10.
347   *The Sphinx*, Chicago, Vol. 3, Issue 12, February 1905, p. 10.
348   Ibid.
349   London *Daily News*, December 29th, 1904, p. 11.
350   *The Sphinx*, Chicago, Vol. 3. Issue 2, February 1905, p. 10.
351   *The Standard*, London, December 29th, 1904, p. 4.
352   *Music Hall and Theatre Review*, London, December 30th, 1904, p. 9.
353   Ibid.
354   London *Evening Standard*, December 30th, 1904, p. 4.
355   Ibid.
356   Soo used to plant stories that while on his tours, he visited local Chinese communities who would honor him with dinners wherein he would "delight them with a speech in their native tongue." *Western Mail*, Cardiff, Wales, March 26th, 1918, p. 2.
357   *Yorkshire Evening News*, Leeds, England, January 3rd, 1905, p. 2.
358   *The Entr'acte*, London, January 7th, 1905, p. 4.
359   *The Scotsman*, January 3rd, 1905, p. 5.
360   London *Evening Standard*, January 3rd, 1905, p. 2.
361   *Music Hall and Theatre Review*, London, January 6th, 1905, p. 9.
362   London *Evening Mail*, January 7th, 1905, p. 5.
363   *The Entr'acte*, London, January 7th, 1905, p. 4.
364   Ibid.

365 London *Evening Star*, January 3rd, 1905, p. 2.
366 *Music Hall and Theatre Review*, London, January 6th, 1905, p. 6.
367 *Illustrated Sporting and Dramatic News*, London, January 7th, 1905, p. 40.
368 *North China Herald*, Shanghai, February 17th, 1905, p. 43.
369 *Stanyon's Magic*, London, Vol. 5, No. 6, March 1905, p. 6.
370 At this point, it almost goes without saying that Soo, along with Foo's act, also copied his promotional techniques, including the invitation of a select group of journalists for Chinese dinners. *The Stage*, London, January 5th, 1905, p. 17.
371 London *Daily News*, January 7th, 1905, p. 4.
372 *The Sphere*, London, February 11th, 1905, p. 18.
373 *Illustrated London News*, January 7th, 1905, p. 3.
374 *The Entr'acte*, London, January 7th, 1905, p. 4.
375 *Mahatma*, Vol. 8, No. 8, February 1905, p. 6.
376 London *Evening Mail*, January 7th, 1905, p. 5.
377 *Mahatma*, Vol. 8, No. 8, February 1905, p. 6.
378 Ibid.
379 The seemingly facetious suggestion put forward by some at the time that Foo had a conflicting urgent dental appointment seems an even less likely rationale.
380 New York *Clipper*, February 4th, 1905, p. 1,190.
381 The Walsall *Advertiser*, Walsall, England, November 11th, 1905, p. 10.
382 London *Observer*, January 22nd, 1905, p. 6.
383 *M.A.P. (Mostly About People)*, London, January 14th, 1905, p. 9.
384 *Mahatma*, Vol. 8, No. 8, February 1905, p. 6.
385 *Stanyon's Magic*, London, Vol. 5, No. 5, February 1905, p. 2.
386 *The Irish Independent*, January 10th, 1905, p. 5.
387 *The Sphinx*, Chicago, Vol. 4, Issue 1, March 15th, 1905, p. 2.
388 *Mahatma*, Vol. 8, No. 7, January 1905, p. 8.
389 *Music Hall and Theatre Review*, London, April 21st, 1905, p. 10.
390 New York *Clipper*, April 29th, 1905, p. 2.
391 Bristol *Magpie*, Bristol, England, July 27th, 1905, p. 10.
392 *The Musical Times*, London, November 11th, 1905, p. 1.
393 *North China Herald*, Shanghai, September 15th, 1905, p. 33.

Chapter Ten

394 Boston *Herald*, June 17th, 1906, p. 50.
395 Ibid.
396 Chicago *Inter Ocean*, July 15th, 1906, p. 18.
397 *Yorkshire Evening Post*, Leeds, England, May 26th, 1911, p. 5.

398 Hartlepool *Northern Daily Mail*, Hartlepool, England, February 9th, 1907, p. 1.
399 *East Anglian Daily News*, Ipswich, England, October 18th, 1909, p. 2.
400 *The Bystander*, London, June 3rd, 1908, p. 24.
401 Perth *Western Australian*, February 17th, 1909, p. 9.
402 Manchester *Courier*, January 18th, 1908, p. 6.
403 Sydney *Sunday Times*, April 2nd, 1907, p. 2.
404 Pittsburgh *Daily Post*, July 24th, 1907, p. 3.
405 *Billboard*, New York, December 8th, 1906, p. 12.
406 *Variety*, March 31st, 1906, p. 13.
407 Brooklyn *Standard Union*, March 19th, 1911, p. 9.
408 *Variety*, New York, February 16th, 1907, p. 10.
409 Ibid.
410 *Variety*, New York, October 11th, 1911, p. 21.
411 Brisbane *Telegraph*, December 23rd, 1907, p. 13.
412 *Ashburton Guardian*, Canterbury, New Zealand, February 8th, 1908, p. 2.
413 *North China Herald*, Shanghai, June 20th, 1908, p. 774.
414 Singapore *Straits Times*, August 6th, 1908, p. 7.
415 *Variety*, New York, June 11th, 1910, p. 16.
416 *Variety*, New York, December 10th, 1910, p. 133.
417 Owensboro *Messenger*, Owensboro, KY, November 19th, 1911, p. 8.
418 *Variety*, New York, November 21st, 1911, p. 9.
419 Mansfield *News-Journal*, Mansfield, OH, November 9th, 1907, p. 16.
420 *Conjurer's Monthly* Magazine, Washington, D.C., Vol. 2, Issue 4, December 1907, p. 20.
421 *Daily Independent*, Monessen, PA, January 21st, 1908, p. 1.
422 Rockford *Republic*, September 10th, 1908, p. 4.
423 The Sheboygan *Press*, September 21st, 1908, p. 5.
424 *Binghamton Press and Sun*, April 3rd, 1909, p. 4.
425 Lexington *Leader*, January 2nd, 1910, p. 26.
426 *The Sphinx*, Chicago, Vol. 8, Issue 11, January 15th, 1910, p. 11.
427 Portsmouth *Daily Times*, Portsmouth, OH, September 20th, 1910, p. 10.
428 *Conjurer's Monthly* Magazine, Washington, D.C., Vol. 2, Issue 4, December 1907, p. 20.
429 *Conjurer's Monthly* Magazine, Washington, D.C., Vol. 1, Issue 9, May 1907, p. 4.
430 *Music Hall and Theatre Review*, London, October 11th, 1907, p. 7.
431 *Conjurer's Monthly* Magazine, Washington, D.C., Vol. 2, Issue 12, August 1908, p. 14.
432 *North China Herald*, Shanghai, January 2nd, 1909, p. 52.
433 *The Sphinx*, Chicago, Vol. 8, No. 2, April 15th, 1909, p. 9.
434 Ibid.

435 The Hong King *Telegraph*, July 3rd, 1909, p. 4.
436 *Variety*, New York, July 17th, 1909, p. 11.
437 New York *Clipper*, August 2nd, 1909, p. 2.
438 New York *Clipper*, August 7th, 1909, p. 654.
439 *The Sphinx*, Chicago, Vol. 8, Issue 6, August 1909, p. 4.
440 *Edwards' Monthly* Magazine, Bridgeburg, Canada, Vol. 1, No. 8, September 1909, p. 4.
441 *North China Herald*, Shanghai, November 2nd, 1909, p. 52.
442 Cairns *Post*, Cairns, Australia, November 29th, 1909, p. 2.
443 *The Silence of Chung Ling Soo*, Todd Karr (Los Angeles: The Miracle Factory, Inc., 2001), p. 121.
444 *The Argus*, Melbourne, March 30th, 1939, p. 1.
445 San Francisco *Examiner*, May 24th, 1910, p. 20.
446 *Chinese Word Daily*, Hong Kong, June 12th, 1911, p. 3.
447 *Chinese Word Daily*, Hong Kong, June 16th, 1911, p. 3.
448 New York *Clipper*, October 28th, 1911, p. 3.

Chapter Eleven

449 *Routledge Handbook of Chinese Media*, Gary D. Rawnsley & Ming-Yeh T. Rawnsley, eds. (New York: Routledge, Taylor, and Francis Group, 2015)
450 Xu Mei Mei, "Knowledge Development: Cinema in China prior to WWI," doctoral dissertation, University of Bonn, February 17th, 2016, pp. 234.
451 *Oxford Handbook of Chinese Cinema*, Carlos Rojas & Eileen Chow, eds. (New York: Oxford University Press, 2003), p. 592.
452 Matthew David Johnson, "International and Wartime Origins of the Propaganda State: The Motion Picture in China, 1897–1955," dissertation, University of California at San Diego, 2008, p. 57.
453 *Oxford Handbook of Chinese Cinema*, Carlos Rojas & Eileen Chow, eds. (New York: Oxford University Press, 2003), p. 593.
454 Luo Xian Zhe, 摄于1911年的《武汉战争》. Beijing: China Academic Journal Electronic Publishing House, 1994–2015.
455 *Oxford Handbook of Chinese Cinema*, Carlos Rojas & Eileen Chow, eds. (New York: Oxford University Press, 2003), p. 592.

Chapter Twelve

456 *Variety*, February 3rd, 1912, p. 3.
457 Ibid.
458 Pittsburgh *Post-Gazette*, February 11th, 1912, p. 30.
459 New York *Clipper*, February 17th, 1912, p. 20.
460 London *Evening News*, July 20th, 1912, p. 7.

461   *The Herald*, Preston, England, March 30th, 1912, p. 11.
462   Ibid.
463   Brooklyn *Citizen*, August 25th, 1912, p. 7.
464   Washington *Post*, May 5th, 1912, p. 3.
465   Wilkes-Barre *Evening News*, September 3rd, 1912, p. 6.
466   *Variety*, New York, November 1st, 1912, p. 5.
467   *The Hawaiian Gazette*, Honolulu, November 5th, 1912, p. 8.
468   San Francisco *Call*, November 12th, 1912, p. 22.
469   San Francisco *Examiner*, November 12th, 1912, p. 6.
470   Ibid., p. 5.
471   San Francisco *Chronicle*, November 11th, 1912, p. 5.
472   Ibid.
473   Tacoma *Times*, November 21st, 1912, p. 3.
474   Sacramento *Star*, November 25th, 1912, p. 10.
475   San Francisco *Examiner*, November 12th, 1912, p. 6.
476   *Variety*, New York, November 22nd, 1912, p. 6.
477   *Bridgeport Times and Evening Farmer*, Bridgeport, CT, January 18th, 1913, p. 5.
478   *Variety*, New York, November 29th, 1912, p. 6.
479   Brooklyn *Standard Union*, December 2nd, 1912, p. 6.
480   Ken Bloom, *Routledge Guide to Broadway* (New York: Routledge, Taylor, & Francis Group, 2007), p. 121.
481   Springfield *Daily News*, Springfield, MA, December 4th, 1912, p. 9.
482   New York *Evening World*, February 1st, 1913, p. 8.
483   New York *Times*, December 23rd, 1912, p. 18.
484   San Francisco *Examiner*, December 19th, 1912, p. 24.
485   *Variety*, New York, December 6th, 1912, p. 38.
486   New York *Evening World*, December 9th, 1912, p. 14. (In this quote the term "Chinaman" has been replaced with the term "Chinese".)
487   New York *Tribune*, December 10th, 1912, p. 5.
488   Ibid.
489   New York *Evening World*, December 12th, 1912, p. 14.
490   *Variety*, New York, December 13th, 1912, p. 16.
491   *The Chinese Students Monthly*, New York, Vol. VIII, No. 4. February 10th, 1913, p. 281.
492   New York *Times*, December 16th, 1912, p. 13.
493   New York *Times*, December 18th, 1912, p. 15.
494   *Variety*, New York, December 20th, 1912, p. 6.
495   New York *Times*, December 21st, 1912, p. 13.
496   Sacramento *Bee*, December 28th, 1912, p. 22.
497   New York *Times*, December 24th, 1912, p. 9.
498   *Variety*, New York, December 27th, 1912, p. 7.

499 Ibid., p. 22.
500 *Variety*, New York, January 3rd, 1913, p. 20.
501 Ibid., p. 5.
502 *Variety*, New York, January 10th, 1913, p. 5.
503 *Day Book*, Chicago, February 3rd, 1917, p. 30.
504 *Variety*, New York, August 22nd, 1913, p. 7.
505 *The Sphinx*, Chicago, Vol. 11, Issue 12, February 1913, p. 4.
506 *Variety*, New York, January 10th, 1913, p. 11.
507 Ibid., p. 23.
508 *The Sphinx*, Chicago, Vol. 11, Issue 11, January 1913, p. 6.

Chapter Thirteen

509 Bridgeport *Times and Evening Farmer*, Bridgeport, CT, January 11th, 1913, p. 5.
510 Bridgeport *Times and Evening Farmer*, Bridgeport, CT, January 17th, 1913, p. 1.
511 *Variety*, New York, December 6th, 1914, p. 8.
512 Bridgeport *Times and Evening Farmer*, Bridgeport, CT, January 19th, 1913, p. 5.
513 *Variety*, New York, January 17th, 1913, p. 6.
514 Bridgeport *Evening Farmer*, Bridgeport, CT, January 18th, 1913, p. 2.
515 Bridgeport *Times and Evening Farmer*, January 20th, 1913, p. 3.
516 Fort Madison *Evening Democrat*, St. Joseph, MS, November 12th, 1931.
517 Bridgeport *Times and Evening Farmer*, January 21st, 1913, p. 7.
518 Ibid., p. 4.
519 Bridgeport *Times and Evening Farmer*, January 22nd, 1913, p. 4.
520 Ibid., p. 3.
521 Bridgeport *Times and Evening Farmer*, January 23rd, 1913, p. 4.
522 Ibid., p. 6.
523 Ibid., p. 1.
524 Boston *Herald*, January 26th, 1913, p. 30.
525 Boston *Herald*, January 25th, 1913, p. 12.
526 Boston *Post*, January 27th, 1913, p. 7.
527 Boston *Globe*, February 27th, 1913, p. 2.
528 Boston *Globe*, February 28th, 1913, p. 6.
529 San Francisco *Examiner*, November 12th, 1912, p. 6.
530 York *Gazette*, York, PA, February 22nd, 1913, p. 6.
531 Baltimore *Sun*, February 25th, 1913, p. 7.
532 Washington *Evening Star*, May 13th, 1913, p. 12.

533 Ibid.
534 Baltimore *Sun*, February 25th, 1913, p. 7.
535 Boston *Globe*, January 26th, 1913, p. 57.
536 Ibid., p. 54.
537 Boston *Globe*, February 16th, 1913, p. 50.
538 Boston *Globe*, February 28th, 1913, p. 4.
539 Baltimore *Sun*, February 28th, 1913, p. 9.
540 Chicago *Tribune*, March 2nd, 1913, p. 17.
541 Chicago *Inter Ocean*, March 4th, 1913, p. 6.
542 Boston *Globe*, February 2nd, 1913, p. 50.
543 *Variety*, New York, March 2nd, 1913, p. 2.
544 *Variety*, New York, March 14th, p. 11.
545 Ibid., p. 4.
546 Boston *Sunday Post*, January 26th, 1913, pp. 24 & 36.
547 Washington *Evening Star*, May 11th, 1913, p. 23.
548 *Variety*, New York, April 4th, 1913, p. 11.
549 Detroit *Times*, April 21st, 1913, p. 7.
550 St. Louis *Star and Time*, April 21st, 1913, p. 9.
551 Detroit *Free Press*, April 29th, 1913, p. 4.
552 Chicago *Tribune*, March 30th, 1913, p. 17.
553 Chicago *Examiner*, March 30th, 1913, p. 22.
554 Preston *Herald*, Preston, England, June 24, 1916, p. 6.
555 Belfast *News-Letter*, October 15th, 1955, p. 2.
556 *Devon and Exeter Gazette*, Plymouth, England, March 15th, 1913, p. 3.
557 *Devon and Exeter Gazette*, Plymouth, England, March 19th, 1913, p. 1.
558 St. Louis *Star and Times*, April 17th, 1913, p. 6.
559 Chicago *Tribune*, March 2nd, 1913, p. 17.
560 Chicago *Inter Ocean*, March 4th, 1913, p. 6.
561 Chicago *Tribune*, March 2nd, 1913, p. 24.
562 St. Louis *Star and Times*, April 15th, 1913, p. 6.
563 Detroit *Times*, April 25th, 1913, p. 4.
564 Chicago Examiner, March 29th, 1913, p. 4.
565 Detroit *Times*, April 30th, 1913, p. 4.
566 Jackson *Daily*, Jackson, MS, March 16th, 1913, p. 20.
567 Pittsburgh *Gazette*, May 7th, 1913, p. 2. Gertrude Gordon was a pioneering celebrity female journalist in Pittsburgh. Gordon was reportedly "fearless" and engaged in stunts like sitting in a cage full of lions and flying in the first balloons and planes for her stories. She interviewed most of the good and great who passed through Pittsburgh. There is a scholarship for female journalism students each year awarded in her name.

568 Washington *Post*, May 13th, 1913, p. 11.
569 Pittsburgh *Daily Post*, May 6th, 1913, p. 8.
570 *Variety*, New York, March 14th, 1913, p. 5.
571 *Variety*, New York, March 18th, 1913, p. 1.

Chapter Fourteen

572 *The Sphinx*, Chicago, Vol. 12, Issue 2, April 1913, p. 4.
573 *Variety*, New York, May 9th, 1913, p. 6.
574 *Irish American Weekly*, New York, May 17th, 1913, p. 10.
575 *Variety*, New York, May 16th, 1913, p. 7.
576 *Irish American Weekly*, New York, May 17th, 1913, p. 10.
577 New York *Times*, May 18th, 1913, p. 6.
578 *Variety*, New York, May 23rd, 1913, p. 5.
579 *Variety*, New York, June 6th, 1913, p. 7.
580 *Hamburger Anzeiger*, Hamburg, Germany, June 8th, 1913, p. 34.
581 *The Stage*, London, June 19th, 1913, p. 23.
582 New York *Times*, June 26th, 1913, p. 4.
583 Brooklyn *Citizen*, June 29th, 1913, p. 16.
584 Brooklyn *Daily Eagle*, July 1st, 1913, p. 7.
585 Brooklyn *Daily Eagle*, July 13th, 1913, p. 13.
586 Brooklyn *Daily Eagle*, July 1st, 1913, p. 7.
587 Brooklyn *Citizen*, July 1st, 1913, p. 3.
588 Brooklyn *Times Union*, July 1st, 1913, p. 4.
589 Cleveland *Leader*, July 6th, 1913, p. 27.
590 Ibid.
591 New York *Daily People*, July 6th, 1913, p. 2.
592 *Variety*, New York, July 11th, 1913, p. 20.
593 New York *World*, July 13th, 1913, p. 2.
594 *MUM*, New York, Vol. 2, July 1913, p. 2.
595 *Variety*, New York, July 18th, 1913, pp. 15 & 17.
596 Brooklyn *Daily Eagle*, July 24th, 1913, p. 21.
597 *Variety*, New York, July 25th, 1913, p. 20.
598 Suratt's fame would wane in the 1920s. When she was discovered living in a cheap hotel in the 1930s, the performer Fanny Hurst raised money for her. Unfortunately, upon receiving the funds, Suratt disappeared and later returned to the same cheap hotel after blowing the $2,000 on gambling. She died in 1960.
599 *Variety*, New York, July 25th, 1913, p. 8.
600 Buffalo *Sunday Morning News*, July 27th, 1913, p. 45.
601 New Orleans *Times Democrat*, July 27th, 1913, p. 18.

602 *Variety*, New York, July 12th, 1912, p. 6.
603 *The Sphinx*, Chicago, Vol. 12, Issue 6, August 1913, p. 4.
604 New York *Sun*, July 27th, 1913, p. 71.
605 *Billboard*, New York, August 9th, 1913, p. 10.
606 New York *Dramatic Mirror*, July 30th, 1913, p. 12.
607 *Variety*, New York, August 8th, 1913, p. 5.
608 *The Stage*, London, September 4th, 1913, p. 26.
609 Philadelphia *Inquirer*, August 10th, 1913, p. 37.
610 Philadelphia *Inquirer*, August 12th, 1913, p. 6.
611 Philadelphia *Inquirer*, August 22nd, 1913, p. 10.
612 *Variety*, New York, August 15th, 1913, p. 5.
613 Indianapolis *Star*, August 21st, 1912, p. 9.
614 Boston *Herald*, August 22nd, 1913, p. 3.
615 *Variety*, New York, August 22nd, 1913, p. 7.
616 Boston *Journal*, August 23rd, 1913, p. 5.
617 Boston *Globe*, August 26th, 1913, p. 4.
618 *Variety*, New York, September 5th, 1913, p. 3.
619 *Variety*, New York, September 12th, 1913, p. 6.
620 Ibid., p. 1.
621 Brooklyn *Daily Eagle*, September 14th, p. 15.
622 Brooklyn *Citizen*, September 16th, 1913, p. 7.
623 Brooklyn *Standard Union*, September 16th, 1913, p. 8.
624 *Variety*, New York, September 19th, 1913, p. 7.

Chapter Fifteen

625 Wilkes-Barre *Times Leader*, September 20th, 1913, p. 23.
626 Washington *Post*, September 1st, 1913, p. 5.
627 Philadelphia *Inquirer*, September 21st, 1913, p. 48.
628 Philadelphia *Inquirer*, September 23rd, 1913, p. 5.
629 Altoona *Tribune*, September 25th, 1913, p. 14.
630 Altoona *Tribune*, September 26th, 1913, p. 12.
631 *Variety*, New York, September 26th, 1913, p. 29.
632 Philadelphia *Inquirer*, September 28th, 1913, p. 28.
633 *Variety*, New York, September 26th, 1913, p. 3.
634 Ibid., p. 8.
635 *Cornell Daily Sun*, Ithaca, NY, September 27th, 1913, p. 7.
636 Altoona *Times*, September 30th, 1913, p. 9.
637 Harrisburg *Patriot*, October 2nd, 1913, p. 5.
638 Wilkes-Barre *Record*, October 2nd, 1913, p. 9.
639 *Variety*, New York, October 3rd, 1913, p. 6.

640 Fort Wayne *Journal Gazette*, October 5th, 1913, p. 16.
641 Colorado Springs *Gazette*, November 16th, 1913, p. 28.
642 *Variety*, New York, October 10th, 1913, p. 1.
643 Zanesville *Times Recorder*, Zanesville, OH, October 11th, 1913, p. 4.
644 Fort Wayne *Journal Gazette*, October 12th, 1913, p. 18.
645 San Antonio *Light*, October 12th, 1913, p. 40.
646 Sandusky *Register*, October 13th, 1913, p. 7.
647 Spokane *Daily Chronicle*, October 13th, 1913, p. 8.
648 Harrisburg *Patriot*, October 14th, 1913, p. 6.
649 New Castle *Morning Star*, New Castle, IN, October 16th, 1913, p. 2.
650 Little Rock *Arkansas Gazette*, December 11th, 1913, p. 4.

Chapter Sixteen

651 *Variety*, New York, October 17th, 1913, p. 10.
652 Trenton *Evening Times*, October 18th, 1913, p. 7.
653 Oakland *Tribune*, October 20th, 1913, p. 8.
654 Fort Worth *Telegram*, November 23rd, 1913, p. 43.
655 Galveston *Daily News*, December 12th, 1913, p. 4.
656 San Antonio *Light*, December 7th, 1913, p. 27.
657 San Antonio *Light*, December 14th, 1913, p. 42.
658 *State Times Advocate*, Baton Rouge, LA, December 4th, 1913, p. 8.
659 Winston-Salem *Journal*, November 11th, 1913, p. 16.
660 Wilmington *Morning News*, October 31st, 1913, p. 10.
661 Wilmington *Evening Journal*, October 31st, 1913, p. 9.
662 *Variety*, New York, October 31st, 1913, p. 6.
663 Wilmington *New Journal*, November 1st, 1913, p. 12.
664 Charlotte *News*, November 6th, 1913, p. 11.
665 Charlotte *Evening Chronicle*, November 10th, 1913, p. 7.
666 Hot Springs *New Era*, Hot Springs, AR, November 20th, 1913, p. 3.
667 Birmingham *News*, Birmingham, AL, November 17th, 1913, p. 2.
668 Louisville *Courier Journal*, November 23rd, 1913, p. 49.
669 Lexington *Leader*, November 19th, 1913, p. 3.
670 Pine Bluff *Daily Graphic*, November 27th, 1913, p. 2.
671 Hot Springs *New Era*, November 26th, 1913, p. 3.
672 Pine Bluff *Daily Graphic*, November 27th, 1913, p. 2.
673 *Daily Arkansas Gazette*, Little Rock, AR, November 30th, 1913, p. 17.
674 *Variety*, New York, November 28th, 1913, p. 16.
675 Baton Rouge *State Times Advocate*, December 2nd, 1913, p. 2.
676 Baton Rouge *State Times Advocate*, December 8th, 1913, p. 8.
677 Greenville *Daily Democrat*, Greenville, MS, December 5th, 1913, p. 4.
678 Galveston *Daily News*, December 7th, 1913, p. 22.

679 New Orleans *Times Picayune*, December 8th, 1913, p. 13.
680 San Antonio *Light*, November 23rd, 1913, p. 22.
681 San Antonio *Light*, December 15th, 1913, p. 6.
682 San Antonio *Light*, December 16th, 1913, p. 7.
683 Waco *Morning News*, December 18th, 1913, p. 6.
684 Fort Worth *Star Telegram*, December 20th, 1913, p. 8.
685 Ibid.
686 Tulsa *Morning/Daily World*, December 20th, 1913, p. 6.
687 Kansas City *Star*, Kansas City, KS, December 13th, 1913, p. 3.
688 Indianapolis *Star*, December 30, 1913, p. 15.
689 Granville *Times*, Granville, OH, January 1st, 1914, p. 4.
690 *Variety*, New York, January 2nd, 1914, p. 24.
691 Winona *Daily News*, October 11th, 1957, p. 6.
692 Ibid.
693 *M.U.M.*, New York, Vol. 42, July 1952, p. 35.
694 Fort Wayne *Journal Gazette*, January 24th, 1917, p. 10.
695 *The Chat*, Brooklyn, NY, December 5th, 1914, p. 5.
696 *Variety*, New York, December 26th, 1919, p. 42.
697 Pittsburgh *Post-Gazette*, January 11th, 1914, p. 20.
698 Cleveland *Plain-Dealer*, January 18th, 1914, p. 9.
699 Buffalo *Evening News*, January 19th, 1914, p. 7.
700 Buffalo *Commercial*, January 21st, 1914, p. 10.
701 Rochester *Democrat and Chronicle*, January 25th, 1914, p. 26.
702 *Variety*, New York, January 30th, 1914, p. 1.
703 Allentown *Democrat*, January 31st, 1914, p. 6.
704 Allentown *Morning Call*, February 2nd, 1914, p. 10.
705 Cleveland *Plain-Dealer*, January 29th, 1914, p. 6.
706 Cleveland *Plain-Dealer*, January 26th, 1914, p. 6.
707 Ibid.

Chapter Seventeen

708 Rochester *Democrat and Chronicle*, January 25th, 1914, p. 26.
709 Rochester *Catholic Journal*, January 30th, 1914, p. 4.
710 Rochester *Democrat and Chronicle*, February 1st, 1914, p. 23.
711 Ibid.
712 Rochester *Democrat and Chronicle*, February 3rd, 1914, p. 9.
713 Rochester *Democrat and Chronicle*, February 7th, 1914, p. 18.
714 *Variety*, New York, February 20th, 1914, p. 20.
715 *Variety*, New York, February 13th, 1914, p. 6.
716 *The Conjuring Record*, Bronxville, NY, Vol. 2, Issue 1, March 1914, p. 1.
717 *Variety*, New York, March 20th, 1914, p. 6.

718 *The Stage*, London, April 2nd, 1914, p. 23.
719 Scranton *Truth*, March 21st, 1914, p. 12.
720 Ibid.
721 Scranton *Republican*, March 24th, 1914, p. 13.
722 Scranton *Truth*, March 24th, 1914, p. 7.
723 Scranton *Republican*, March 24th, 1914, p. 13.
724 Springfield *Daily News*, Springfield, MA, March 30th, 1914, p. 12.
725 Springfield *Union*, Springfield, MA, March 31st, 1914, p. 17.
726 Springfield *Daily News*, Springfield, MA, March 31st, 1914, p. 2.
727 Buffalo *Commercial*, April 4th, 1914, p. 4.
728 Ibid.
729 Ibid.
730 Buffalo *Courier*, April 7th, 1914, p. 8.
731 Buffalo *Times*, April 5th, 1914, p. 32.
732 Detroit *Times*, April 14th, 1914, p. 3.
733 "Ich gebibble" or "Ish kabibble" meant, in derisive slang, "I should worry?" Or "What are you gonna do?" It came into fashion in 1913. Suspected to be derived from Yiddish *'nisht gefidlt.'* Detroit *Times*, April 21st, 1914, p. 4.
734 *Variety*, New York, May 1st, 1914, p. 18.
735 *The Sphinx*, Chicago, Volume 13, Issue 3, May 1914, p. 5.
736 *The Conjuring Record*, Bronxville, NY, Vol. 2, Issue 4, June 1914, p. 2.
737 Guy Jarrett, *Magic and Stagecraft* (Chicago: Magic, Inc., 1936)
738 *Lanarkshire Daily Record*, Glasgow, July 4th, 1914, p. 3.
739 *Variety*, New York, June 26th, 1914, p. 13.
740 Glasgow *Daily Record and Mail*, July 4th, 1914, p. 3.
741 *The Scottish Referee*, Glasgow, July 10th, 1914, p. 3.
742 *The Scottish Referee*, Glasgow, July 6th, 1914, p. 6.
743 *Daily Record*, Birmingham, England, July 7th, 1914, p. 6.
744 *The Scottish Referee*, Glasgow, July 10th, 1914, p. 4.
745 *Daily Record*, Birmingham, England, July 6th, 1914, p. 4.
746 Birmingham *Daily Post*, Birmingham, England, July 25th, 1914, p. 4.
747 Birmingham *Daily Gazette*, Birmingham, England, July 28th, 1914, p. 8.
748 Birmingham *Daily Post*, Birmingham, England, July 25th, 1914, p. 4.
749 Birmingham *Daily Gazette*, England, July 28th, 1914, p. 8.
750 Maosheng Hu, a postdoctoral scholar at the University of Birmingham's Shakespeare Institute, contributed this information to the shakespeare.org website.
751 *Variety*, New York, October 31st, 1914, p. 8.
752 *M.U.M.*, New York, Vol. 3, Issue 23, October 1914, p. 2.
753 *Variety*, New York, October 23rd, 1914, p. 10.
754 New York *Times*, October 26th, 1914, p. 4.

Chapter Eighteen

755 Akron *Evening Times*, November 6th, 1914, p. 7.
756 *Variety*, New York, November 21st, 1914, p. 21.
757 *Variety*, New York, December 4th, 1914, p. 7.
758 Ibid., p. 16.
759 Harrisburg *Courier*, December 6th, 1914, p. 7.
760 Pittsburgh *Post-Gazette*, December 9th, 1914, p. 4.
761 *Variety*, New York, December 11th, 1914, p. 9.
762 Chicago *Examiner*, December 24th, 1914, p. 7.
763 Chicago *Examiner*, December 22nd, 1914, p. 12.
764 *Variety*, New York, December 18th, 1914, p. 16.
765 St. Louis *Globe Democrat*, December 27th, 1914, p. 27.
766 St. Louis *Star and Times*, December 29th, 1914, p. 4.
767 *The Conjuring Record*, Bronxville, NY, Vol. 2, Issue 11, January 1915, p. 5.
768 New Orleans *Item*, January 13th, 1915, p. 14.
769 New Orleans *Item*, January 10th, 1915, p. 26.
770 St. Louis *Star and Times*, January 1st, 1915, p. 2.
771 New Orleans *Item*, January 10th, 1915, p. 5.
772 New Orleans *Item*, January 16th, 1915, p. 2.
773 San Francisco *Chronicle*, January 24th, 1915, p. 17.
774 San Francisco *Chronicle*, January 22nd, 1915, p. 5.
775 *The Conjuring Record*, Bronxville, NY, Vol. 2, Issue 12, February 1915, p. 2.
776 San Francisco *Examiner*, January 25th, 1915, p. 6.
777 San Francisco *Chronicle*, January 31st, 1915, p. 17.
778 Los Angeles *Times*, February 26th, 1915, p. 26.
779 San Francisco *Examiner*, February 1st, 1915, p. 5.
780 San Francisco *Chronicle*, February 6th, 1915, p. 7.
781 Oakland *Tribune*, February 8th, 1915, p. 7.
782 Oakland *Tribune*, February 4th, 1915, p. 6.
783 Berkeley *Daily Gazette*, February 6th, 1915, p. 3.
784 Berkeley *Daily Gazette*, February 13th, 1915, p. 3.
785 Sacramento *Bee*, February 10th, 1915, p. 12.
786 Sacramento *Bee*, February 15th, 1915, p. 14.
787 Ibid.
788 San Jose *Evening News*, February 18th, 1915, p. 3.
789 San Jose *Evening News*, February 13th, 1915, p. 8.
790 Sacramento *Star*, February 15th, 1915, p. 4.
791 Stockton *Evening Mail*, February 18th, 1915, p. 3.
792 Los Angeles *Times*, February 22nd, 1915, p. 18.
793 Los Angeles *Times*, February 23rd, 1915, p. 18.
794 Los Angeles *Evening Express*, February 22nd, 1915, p. 12.

795 Los Angeles *Times*, February 25th, 1915, p. 24.
796 Los Angeles *Times*, March 2nd, 1915, p. 24.
797 Los Angeles *Times*, February 25th, 1915, p. 16.
798 Long Beach *Telegram and Daily News*, February 27th, 1915, p. 12.
799 Los Angeles *Times*, March 4th, 1915, p. 20.
800 Los Angeles *Express*, March 3rd, 1915, p. 19.
801 Los Angeles *Times*, March 7th, 1915, p. 29.
802 *M.U.M.*, New York, Vol. 3, Issue 28, March 1915, p. 2.
803 Riverside *Independent Enterprise*, Riverside, CA, March 9th, 1915, p. 3.
804 *Popular Radio*, Los Angeles, October 1922, p. 100.
805 *The Magician Monthly*, London, Vol. 11, June 1915, p. 142.
806 *The Sphinx*, Chicago, Vol. 50, Issue 1, March 1951, p. 26.
807 New York *Evening World*, July 12th, 1915, p. 4.
808 *The Magic Wand*, London, Vol. 5, Issue 49, September 1914, p. 112.

Chapter Nineteen

809 *Billboard*, June 24th, 1916, p. 20.
810 *Magicana*, Hamilton, New Zealand, Vol. 565, December 15th, 1926, p. 118.
811 *North China Herald*, Shanghai, June 30th, 1916, p. 26.
812 Ibid.
813 *M.U.M.*, New York, Vol. 7, No. 55, October 1917, p. 10.
814 Sydney *Mirror*, March 10th, 1917, p. 12.
815 The J.B. Findlay Collection, Part II—Books and Periodicals on Conjuring and the Allied Arts, Sotheby's Auction House Lot #883, 1980.

Chapter Twenty

816 Nottingham *Evening Post*, April 22nd, 1916, p. 3.
817 *Deseret Evening News*, Salt Lake City, June 2nd, 1917, Hong Kong *Daily Press* Hong Kong, May 4th, 1917, p. 3.
818 *Port Adelaide News*, Adelaide, Australia, June 1st, 1917, p. 3.
819 *Auckland Star*, June 9th, 1917, p. 14.
820 Adelaide *Critic*, Adelaide, Australia, June 16th, 1917, p. 8., Hong Kong *Telegraph* Hong Kong, May 8th, 1917, p. 5, Hong Kong *Telegraph*, Hong Kong, May 18th, 1917, p. 1.
821 *The Stage*, London, August 30th, 1917, p. 4.
822 *M.U.M.*, New York, Vol. 7, No. 55, October 1917, p. 5.
823 Letter from Edwin Dearn to Jimmy Findlay, May 19th, 1971, private collection.
824 In all likelihood, this story, along with the claim Soo was heckled for not being an authentic Chinese, were well-received anecdotes Dearn may have

enjoyed sharing and massaging over the decades. Any suggestion Foo was illiterate flies in the face of multiple sources and the fact that, as noted earlier, Foo had a substantial magic library that he left to a very grateful Houdini. In addition, Foo's position in a major Chinese trading firm and his middle- to upper-middle-class background in a country where Chinese literacy expert Evelyn Rawski found even during the late Qing period literacy rates among all Chinese males was around 50%. Urban males such as Foo, particularly business professionals whose livelihood depended on the exchange of contracts and terms, had a literacy rate that was much higher.

825 *The Guardian*, London, March 29th, 2010, p. 3.
826 Matthew Solomon, "Disappearing Tricks: Silent Film, Chinese Magicians, and Film Theater", *Early Cinema and the National* (Bloomington, IN: Indiana University Press/John Libbey Publishing, 2016; Richard Abel, Giorgio Bertellini, and Rob King, eds.), pp. 248–257.
827 *M.U.M.*, New York, Vol. 7, Issue 58, January 1918, p. 10.
828 Ibid.
829 Aberdeen *Daily Journal*, Aberdeen, Scotland, March 29th, 1918, p. 4.
830 Leeds *Mercury*, March 29th, 1918, p. 4.
831 *Variety*, New York, March 29th, 1918, p. 5.
832 Sheffield *Independent*, April 5th, 1918, p. 3.
833 *Linking Ring*, Eustis, FL, Vol. 56, Issue 6, June 1976, p. 104.
834 Duluth *News-Tribune*, May 19th, 1918, p. 2.
835 Pittsburgh *Press*, July 25th, 1918, p. 4.
836 *The Western Champion*, Barcaldine, Australia, June 15th, 1918, p. 9.
837 *Billboard*, New York, December 18th, 1920, p. 26.
838 Seattle *Daily Times*, November 29th, 1938, p. 15.
839 *The Sphinx*, Chicago, Vol. 47, Issue 6, August 1948, p. 12.
840 Stamford *Daily Advocate*, Stamford, CT, February 10th, 1936, p. 4.
841 Seattle *Daily Times*, November 29th, 1938, p. 15.
842 Xenia *Evening Gazette*, Xenia, OH, April 14th, 1939, p. 1.
843 Apart from his camerawork in science fiction films, Ash's camera skills also played a key role in classic films such as *All Quiet on the Western Front*. Los Angeles *Times*, June 1st, 1953, p. 27.
844 Seattle *Daily Times*, November 29th, 1938, p. 15.
845 Ash's linkage to Ching Ling Foo was first widely revealed as part of the promotional campaign for the 1936 Universal Studios film *Flash Gordon*. Ash had been in charge of developing and supervising the film's revolutionary and still appreciated special effects. Ash also lent his talents to films like *Rocket Ship*, *Mars Attacks the World*, and *Legion of Lost Flyers*. In total, Ash worked on over 80 films as either a lead cameraman or cinematographer.

He also worked on less seminal but nonetheless enjoyable works as 1945's low-budget horror film *The Pillow of Death* Stamford *Daily Advocate*, Stamford, CT, February 10th, 1936, p. 4.

846 Seattle *Daily Times*, November 29th, 1938, p. 15.
847 Xenia *Evening Gazette*, Xenia, OH, April 14th, 1939, p. 1.
848 *The Sphinx*, Chicago, Vol. 47, Issue 6, August 1948, p. 12.
849 *North China Herald*, Shanghai, September 8th, 1905, p. 568.
850 *Billboard*, New York, July 30th, 1921, p. 44.
851 *The Sphinx*, Chicago, Vol. 23, Issue 9, November 1924, p. 21.
852 *M.U.M.*, New York, Vol. 12, Issue 10, April 1923, p. 4.

Epilogue

853 New York *Herald*, June 9th, 1918, p. 49.
854 Springfield *Union*, Springfield, MA, March 31st, 1914, p. 17.
855 *The Sphinx*, Chicago, Vol. 11, No. 11, January 1913, p. 6. (In the quote, "this dignified and very tall Chinese" the term "Chinaman" was replaced with the term "Chinese".)
856 *Variety*, New York, June 1st, 1965, p. 28.

www.ingramcontent.com/pod-product-compliance
Lightning Source LLC
Chambersburg PA
CBHW030314100526
44592CB00010B/429